the *DREAM*

and

the *TEXT*

SUNY Series in Dream Studies
Robert L. Van de Castle, editor

the *DREAM*

and

the *TEXT*

Essays on Literature and Language

edited by

Carol Schreier Rupprecht

State University of New York Press

Published by
State University of New York Press, Albany

For information, address State University of New York
Press, State University Plaza, Albany, N.Y., 12246

Production by Marilyn P. Semerad
Marketing by Fran Keneston

Library of Congress Cataloging- in- Publication Data

The Dream and the text : essays on literature and language / Carol
    Schreier Rupprecht, editor.
        p.   cm. — (SUNY Series in dream studies)
    Includes bibliographical references.
    ISBN 0-7914-1361-6 (hardcover). — ISBN 0-7914-1362-4 (pbk.)
    1. Dreams in literature.   2. Dreams.   I. Rupprecht, Carol
    Schreier, 1939-   .   II. Series.
    PN56.D75D74   1993
    809'.93353—dc20   92-4560
                                                              CIP

10 9 8 7 6 5 4 3 2 1

To Jody and Whitney, With Love

And in memory of the lost boys,
John Schreier 1952–1953
Peter Michael Schreier 1957–1959

CONTENTS

Part I Foregrounding Theory

Part II Historical, Political, Cultural, and Social Aspects

Part III *A Dreamer and a Text: Case Studies*

Part IV *Dreams in Texts*

Foreword: The Literarity of Dreams, the Dreaminess of Literature

Norman N. Holland

You are looking at a book on dreams and literature. Or should I say *in* literature? Or *of*? Or *about*? Or *for* literature? Whichever, you are about to consider one of the more paradoxical questions in literature-and-psychology, the relation of literature to dreams and vice versa.

I do not want to "introduce" these chapters by telling you how they interrelate in this book. Carol Schreier Rupprecht and Kelly Bulkley do that expertly in their opening chapter. I do want to pique your curiosity. I want to show you why this whole topic of dreams and literature is so curiously involved in perplexities. These chapters continually balance on an intellectual tightrope between the two extremes of dreams.

Dreams are a microcosm of all human experience in that they exist in two opposed modes. First, dreams are an experience. They simply happen to us. Something irrupts from somewhere, and we see visions and hear sounds. Second, as in my words "something" and "somewhere," dreams are an enigma to be explained.

When I was a boy, I used to make Möbius strips out of the bands that the laundry put around my father's shirts. I would form the band into a six-inch ring with a half twist in it. Then, if I cut down the center of the strip, around the ring, when the scissors reached the beginning of the cut, blip! the small band would suddenly become a twelve-inch ring with three half twists in it. There was always that peculiar moment just before it changed, when I could see it was a six-inch band, almost cut through, and I would know it was going to lurch into something altogether different, but I could never understand why. I still can't, and I still want to.

Dreams are like that. They start as experiences, but at a certain moment, they become something to be analyzed. It is not enough for us humans just to experience something. We feel we need to know why. We need to anchor our momentary experience in some system, larger or more long-lasting than our mere sensations or emotions. If we cannot, we are troubled. We humans suffer from a *libido sciendi* that is both our joy and our tribulation. A dream is thus not only an experience, complete in itself, but also a question. It asks us to answer it in ways yet unknown and perhaps unknowable.

When it comes to explaining dreams, we have, loosely, two approaches. I call them dream explaining and dream worshiping.

The two approaches began when the Greeks distinguished two kinds of dreams. Some came through the gates of ivory, and they were genuine messages from the gods. Others came through the gates of horn, and they meant nothing. They were—who knows what? They were something visual in sleep that could have been caused by, say, too much symposium.

I think the Greeks' distinction corresponds not to two kinds of dreams, but to two ways of thinking about dreams. Dream worshipers treat dreams as messages, if not from the gods, at least from something otherwise beyond our ken. Dream explainers want to compass the dream in rational explanation. (One could regard, I suppose, the dream worshipers as also explaining dreams, but *ir*rationally.)

Freud is the great dream explainer. Free association, he assures us, will lead us to an explanation for any dream. "The poets and philosophers before me discovered the unconscious. What I discovered was the scientific method by which the unconscious can be studied"[1] (Berman 1985). This is an important statement. It anchors Freud's claims in a quasi-experimental procedure. If followed, this free-association procedure will, Freud says, provide evidence of what any given dream means, and I believe he is right. You need actually to follow the procedure. You need to free associate to a dream in the presence of a witness. You need, in other words, to repeat the method Freud demonstrated over and over in *The Interpretation of Dreams*. If you do, you will be able to attest to the extraordinary, Aha! way the craziest mix of opaque details will yield a coherent meaning. As always, with psychoanalysis, one must actually test and experience its claims. By contrast, I think many of today's literary theorists uncritically parrot writings on symbolism and theory. This mere book-psychoanalysis leads, I think, nowhere.

When we follow Freud's procedure, we find, against resistance (further evidence in itself), coherence and meaning for our dreams.

The nonsensical dream expresses quite sensible thoughts about things that matter to us, even distress us. We may not choose to call the dream a wish-fulfillment, but it certainly does dramatize our most private wishes and fears.

In addition to Freud I would number Jung among the dream explainers and nowadays, a variety of experimental researchers who investigate sleep, dreams, and brain activity in general. These scientists, using methods of which Freud could not even have dreamed, have tried to nullify his explanation. I am thinking of Michael Gazzaniga, but more specifically of J. Allan Hobson and even more specifically of Ebenezer Scrooge, whom I take to be their prototype.

Scrooge tried to dismiss Marley's ghost as "an indigested bit of beef, a blot of mustard, a crumb of cheese, a fragment of an underdone potato." In the same way, Gazzaniga holds that "dreams represent the random collision of memories activated by chance during sleep." Then the interpreting left brain tries to make sense of them by producing the bizarre images of the dream (Gazzaniga 1988, 192–95). Hobson and McCarley give the same idea more detail. Like a locomotive come to rest in the station and whooshing the steam out of its cylinders, the brain, before its deepest sleep, fires off a skyrocket of cascading electrochemical impulses. It may be practicing adaptive strategies. It may be clearing its memory banks for further computing on the morrow. The point is, the activity is random. Then the mind—which may be just another part of that brain—tries to make sense of this barrage of signals. The brain-mind tries to assemble what are ultimately just dots on the retina into a coherent message. It fits stories and pictures to the random impulses to achieve a partial kind of sense. The dream is, so to speak, the best the brain can do (Hobson and McCarley 1977; Hobson 1988; Dolnick 1990).

What intrigues me about this account is that it does not really contradict Freud—provided we go back to fundamental Freud, free association. Even if Marley's ghost is a dream and even if Scrooge is right and the dream is caused by a crumb of cheese, Scrooge has still not explained why he dreamt of Jacob Marley on Christmas Eve. He has not exempted himself from the unconscious guilt that drives his nocturnal education.

When people such as Hobson say they are disproving Freud, what they disprove, typically, are Freud's over-enthusiastic remarks on symbolic interpretation, added to *The Interpretation of Dreams* after 1910. Despite these additions, Freud never abandoned his fundamental thesis, that the basic method of interpreting a dream is free association. Interpretation, in other words, depends on the dreamer, not some system of symbols. What Hobson and others describe and dis-prove as "Freudian" interpretations, aren't.

Let me quote a letter I received recently from a dear friend, now reluctantly retiring after a long, distinguished career as clinician-academic. "I finally applied for retirement by filing the appropriate papers with TIAA. Two nights after that I dreamed that I was applying for my clinical internship, an activity I completed in 1949 or 1950." There is no set symbolic meaning for applying for one's retirement annuity. What it means depends entirely on the dreamer's associations, which were quite obvious to my clinician friend. "It is a good thing," he dryly continues, "that dreams result from random electrical discharges from the brain and don't mean anything."

As my friend's comment makes clear, Gazzaniga and Hobson have missed the point. It may well be that the dream we experience comes from Gazzaniga's interpreter or Hobson's coherence-making brain. Nevertheless, Freud's free association still works. It still yields a meaning for the dream and the meaning, typically, is a wish or, more precisely, a combination of wish and fear. Surely it is more elegant, in a scientific sense, to assume that the meaning and the associations on which it depends have something to do with the electrical discharges than that they do not. It is probable, is it not, that my friend used even random electrical discharges to express a wish that he was not retiring, but starting all over.

It is a pity that almost all American psychology departments teach Freud or psychoanalysis in so hostile and unforgiving a way. (Freud and psychoanalysis are, by the way, not the same, although few outside professional psychoanalytic circles properly distinguish today's psychoanalysis from Freud's.) The result is a failure to see the parallels and the remarkable potentialities in combining psychoanalytic insights with experimental discoveries. In this instance, it is a failure to see that Freud's idea of free association would unravel the mind's making sense of random fireworks.

The problem comes about because Gazzaniga, Hobson and others like them think Freud posits a fixed, narrow repertory of themes and symbols. Not so. Freud does not *assume* this repertory. He *finds* it in hundreds of free associations to dreams. Nor is it so narrow if we rethink it in the phrase suggested by Charles Rycroft (1979), my favorite writer on dreams. The themes and symbols of dreams express our "biological destiny," like the fear of aging and death implicit in my friend's dream.

There is a different problem with Freud's free association, however. Freud often writes as though free association takes us back through the process by which the dream was made. The associations follow thematic clusterings that mirror the thematic clusterings that gave rise to the dream in the first place. Free association would be like tracking Ariadne's thread back, not to the entrance, but to the heart of the labyrinth, the navel of the dream. Freud calls it, "its point of contact with the unknown" (1900a, 111n).

Reader-response critics like me, however, have shown that, *whenever* people free associate to a poem or story or movie, they arrive at their characteristic wishes and fears, just as if they were associating to a dream (Holland 1975). Hence, when Freud's early patients associated to a dream and came up with wishes and fears, they may not have been revealing the origin or meaning of the dream, just their own characteristic wishes and fears.

Further, then, if all free associations lead to current wishes and fears, if I were to associate to, say, my friend's dream of applying for his clinical license, I would come up with Norm Holland's schemes and concerns, just as my friend came up with his. Curiously, then, it may not matter who dreams the dream. The dream will nevertheless evoke for each of us our personal cluster of fears and wishes. Maybe. Or maybe I go too far.

Explaining dreams leads to this super-individualism. At the opposite extreme are the dream worshipers. Impressed, I think, by the recurrence of particular symbols and themes in dreams (our biological destiny?), they regard the dream as an irruption from something beyond our ken. Even Freud, early Freud, regards the dream as having that navel that reaches down into the unknown.

Although it relies on the unknown, this mystical approach also tries to explain dreams. It anchors our momentary experience of the dream in something permanent and universal. It draws, however, not on impersonal forces of material causality, but something supernatural. Dreams tell us what we otherwise could not know. We peep through the bed curtains that box in our mortal four-poster, and we get a momentary glimpse of the hidden future, the past before we were born, or a present unknown to us. In short, we make supernatural connections beyond our ordinary paths in time and space. Dreams must be, then, messages from the gods or god.

Looked at another way, the dream worshiper is saying dreams need no explanation, because any explanation of that other realm of gods or god would be beside the point. It is not to be questioned. It is simply there. Irrational this may be, but it is close to our experience of dreams. They just happen to us. They are just there.

Jung gives us the most sophisticated version of this approach to dreams. Jung argues that if the body can hold traces of previous evolutionary stages, why not the mind? If alchemical symbols or gnostic emblems appear in our dreams, why are these not traces of a mind-evolution? In general, things like ancient Chinese emblems do appear in our dreams. (Yes, this happens, sort of.) Our dreams transcend our conscious knowledge of such things, and we know no method by which they could be transmitted to us. Then, Jung's argument goes, our dreams must be tapping into something not individual to the dreamer but biologically present in all humankind at all times and places from our Neanderthal origins on. There must be a kind of substratum of common human themes and symbols that is part of our collective humanity rather than our individuality. We are genetically programmed with them just as we are programmed for the ten-ness of our toes or our curiously shaped ears.

So the argument goes. A skeptic and materialist like me could counter by saying there is a more economical explanation. Each generation of humans recreates these themes and symbols because they are part of our experience. They describe our biological destiny. We have no need to posit a collective unconscious diachronically present—unless we wish to rescue religion from unbelievers like me. Is that the reason for the persistence of the dream-worshiping approach, a desire to rescue religion in our God-is-dead era? Perhaps.

In any case, I have turned the question around, from asking, Why dreams?, to asking, Where do dreams come from? Or, Who is the author of the dream?

Dream worshiping, taken far enough, says it is this collective unconscious, mystically present in each of us. More precisely, the dream is authored by some combination of the individual dreamer with that collective unconscious or spiritual dimension that the mystical approach posits. Who is the author of that collective realm? It must be the same as the author of any other part of the world, namely, whatever god or gods you happen to believe in. That's why mystical interpretation of the dream can claim to provide some clue to what those gods are about.

From a skeptic's point of view, however, there are no gods. The world beyond the dream is the product of natural, material laws. It has no author. The dream, then, does not come from any mystical realm. Its author is simply the dreamer himself. Interpretation of the dream can tell us nothing about the world, only about the dreamer. Maybe not even the dreamer. After all, free association, taken far enough, says that it doesn't matter who dreamt the dream. I can associate to anybody's dream as well as my own.

A brain scientist, rigorously following Scrooge's model, could go even further than that. There is no author of the world, and there is no author of the dream, either. It is just as much a product of natural, material, impersonal laws as a case of indigestion.

But the chapters that follow engage us in another, still more devious question. Who is the author of a dream in a literary text? That query rests on another, Who is the author of a literary text? In these postmodern times, to ask that question is to invoke the spirit of Michel Foucault. He is supposed to have said that there is no author. The author has disappeared. There is only discourse, systems of text and code, that permeate the authorial activity the way radio waves or neutrinos are shooting through our bodies all the time.

Foucault's own words are not so dramatic. In fact, he is rather commonsensical in his claims:

> These aspects of an individual which we designate as making him an author are only a projection, in more or less psychologizing terms, of the operations that we force texts to undergo, the connections that we make, the traits that we establish as pertinent, the continuities that we recognize, or the exclusions that we practice. (1977)

Foucault is simply saying we construct the author Shakespeare out of the way we read the plays. "The author is the principle of thrift in the proliferation of meaning."

Conversely, there is no way we can derive Shakespeare's plays from the historical Shakespeare, the young man who was born in 1564, married Ann Hathaway, begot three children, and so on. Those facts tell us nothing about his authorship. If, however, we infer his personality from the plays, we can conclude that the man who wrote them idealized father-son relationships, feared the influence of sexual women, and felt guilty about his own aggressive and vengeful impulses. Or we might conclude that this man admired kingly authority, men's domination of women, whites' domination of people of color, and otherwise accepted the conventional values of his time. Or we might conclude that he disliked bread, dogs, and garlic, and that he suffered from insomnia. We cannot say, however, that any facts of Shakespeare's life led to this or that feature of his plays. All we can say is that this or that feature of his plays may allow us to project some attribute onto the historical Shakespeare. We can then use that projection to understand other writings and the general phenomenon of his authorship. I would phrase it: the author, looked at from the point of view of the literary work, is always a construct.

There is nothing either radical or new about this statement. Foucault's position exactly parallels that taken by the New Critics when they eschewed Beardsley and Wimsatt's "intentional fallacy" of 1946. The historical author could not limit meaning; only interpretation could. Hence interpretation defines the author. Indeed Foucault himself regarded the position as commonplace. Authors had been disappearing constantly, he said, since 1898.

If this modernist and postmodernist position is right, if the author is someone we construct from the product of authorship, then what can we say about the authors of, respectively, the world, the text, and the dream?

We can start with Freud's scientific point of view. To such a materialist, the authors of the world, that is, the conventional god or gods, are surely constructs. Are authors of literature also? Freud himself did not think so. Rather, he was confident he could read from Hamlet's to Shakespeare's Oedipus complex. I think today, however, most psychoanalytic critics would agree with Foucault's statement on authors. And the dreamer? Here a psychoanalyst of any period would insist, I think, that the person making the dream and freely associating was the real person lying on the couch, and the analyst's interpretations affect that real person.

On the other hand, from the point of view of most modern cognitive and perceptual psychology, one can know that person, like anyone else, only through one's personal system of inferences and beliefs. We humans are, to one another, constructs. In that sense, the dreamer, the free associater, the psychoanalyst, and the author of the text are all real in a physical, historical sense, but we know them only as constructs. And they know themselves the same way. They can only think about themselves through personal systems of construction. They even *experience* the dream or the text or the world or themselves through these same systems. The scientific materialist thus has little trouble with the idea of the author as construct.

From a mystical or religious point of view, however, the idea that the author of the world is a construct must be distinctly unsatisfying. That is really an agnostic's position. As for the author of a text, I suppose a religious person would have no more trouble than Foucault in finding that the author of a text is a construct. But the author of the dream? We infer the dreamer from the free associations. Yes, that seems reasonable. But does that mean the dream just happened? That there was no dreamer? No, but if we say that the author of a dream is a construct, what room does that leave for the idea of a "real" substratum of collective unconscious? It must be a construct too. I think Foucault's author-as-construct poses problems for the mystical view of dreams and authorship.

What about the Scroogists? I assume they would follow Freud in treating "the author of the universe" as a construct with no physical existence. I assume, too, they would have no trouble in following Foucault with the idea that the literary author (in his capacity as author, not as historical human being) is also a construct. Has the dreamer also disappeared? Hardly. The Scroogists themselves would have to say that someone secretes the dream even if it is as automatic a process as secreting adrenaline. I suppose they would insist that one can infer nothing about the dreamer from the dream, since it expresses nothing but random brain sparkles. Or would they say (as a reader-response critic might) that the true dreamer of the dream is the one who interprets it, because the only meaning a dream has is what the interpreter gives it? Since the dream has no meaning by itself, it is the dream-interpreter who is the author of the dream. Maybe.

I should, though, return to the subject of this book, dreams in literature. What does it mean to say that the author of a dream in a literary text is a construct? If we grant that "the author" is a construct, who is the author of a dream in the novel the author-construct wrote? It is tempting to say the author of the novel is the author of the dream. But here we run up against Freud. His longest, most polished, and most convincing literary study is his analysis of Wilhelm Jensen's *Gradiva*. In it, he demonstrated that one could analyze dreams in a literary text like real dreams, by a combination of free associations, symbolism, and inference from the principle of wish-fulfillment. I think he proved his point in that essay.

The author of the literary dream, then, is for Freud the literary dreamer—the character. But the character is a creation of the author. Hence we have a layering of constructs. The author is our construct. The character who dreams is the author's construct. The dream dreamt is the construct of the character. The dream in a literary text is the construct of a construct of a construct.

However, at this point in the argument (or the obfuscation), the mystic pops up again. The dream in literature always reaches toward a substratum of meaningfulness. A literary text, because it is authored, always has a principle of coherence or meaning or, to be postmodern, anti-meaning. The dream, like everything else in the literary text, has to fit that principle.

Consider some Shakespearean dreams. Clarence's dream of his brother pulling him over the gunwales into the stormy sea tells of Richard's villainy although Clarence is not yet aware of it. Similarly

Hermia will dream of her lover's infidelity before she knows he has been unfaithful. Romeo's dream in Act V foreshadows Juliet's kissing his dead body two scenes later. In short, the literary dream takes us into the world of prophecy, foreknowledge, ghosts, and Nancy Reagan's astrologer.

The literary dream must always be paranormal, because that is the way literature itself is. Somebody made the story with more of a shape and a form than everyday life has. Somebody gave it a moral, a unity, and a rationality, or at least the skilled critic can show it is rational and analyzable. The world depicted in literature is pregnant with human purposes, even if its purpose is to show that there is no purpose. A dream, like everything else in a literary work, must share in that purposiveness. The dream in literature necessarily does more than ordinary nature allows. The dream in literature is thus always supernatural, because the literary dream always occurs in a world that does have an author. In that way, the dream in literature is not like the dream in life—at least to an atheist like me or Freud.

The dream in life, for Freud and the scientist, always admits a naturalistic explanation, but one that points inward, toward the psyche of the dreamer, not outward toward the "real" world. The literary dream, however, points toward the world around it, telling us more than a true dream can. At the same time, though, as Freud showed in his *Gradiva* study, the literary dream can be interpreted like a dream in life, as pointing only to the psyche of the dreamer. We are back to our root distinction. The *interpretation* of the literary dream differs from the prophetic, supernatural *experience* of the literary dream.

The mystics may be wrong about the real world, but they are right in finding an author for the literary world. So the mystics are correct about literary dreams, and it is Freud who is confused when he claims one can interpret imagined dreams like real dreams. One has to add the supernatural dimension.

Or is he? Freud proved that the literary dream is like a real dream. If so, then a real dream must include something of the supernatural, for the literary dream does. Except that the supernatural, that supposed purpose for the literary text or for the real world, is no more than our construct. . . .

I think I had best break off here. Theorizing is not my *métier*, as you may by now have surmised. I think at this point I am, simply, lost. I had best turn to some theoretical Park Ranger to lead me out of the dark wood in which I have entangled myself. You will find thirteen of them in the chapters that follow. I am not counting myself, because I cannot guide myself, since I am only a construct of myself to myself. . . .

In these chapters, you will find all these positions that I have been stumbling around and through. You will find the dream as experience and the dream as something to be explained. You will find dream worshipers and dream explainers. You will find those who cling to the dream as an experience that feels supernatural and supernaturally points to truths about the world-order. You will find those who agree that a dream feels supernatural, but who explain it in natural terms as pointing inward to the psyche of the dreamer. You will find some who think dreams in literature are like dreams in life, and you will find some who don't. You will find those who think dreams are unformed and so is the rest of experience. You will find those who think experience is unformed but dreams are formed. You will find those who think the interpretation is the dream and those who think dream and interpretation have little to do with one another. You will, in short, find questions galore and no final answers, but, if you like literary conundrums, you will also find all the fascinations of a hall of mirrors.

Notes

1. Psychoanalytic critics owe thanks to Jeffrey Berman for having located the source of this important statement, originally quoted in 1940, without attribution, by Lionel Trilling and endlessly re-quoted by subsequent psychoanalytic writers (Berman 1985, 304 n. 40).

References

Beardsley, Monroe, and W. K. Wimsatt, Jr. "The Intentional Fallacy." In *The Verbal Icon: Studies in the Meaning of Poetry*. Lexington: University Press of Kentucky, 1954.

Berman, Jeffrey. *The Talking Cure: Literary Representations of Psychoanalysis*. New York: New York University Press, 1985.

Dolnick, Edward. "What Dreams Are (really) Made Of." *Atlantic* 266.1 (1990): 41–61.

Foucault, Michel. "What is an Author?" *Language, Counter-memory, Practice: Selected Essays and Interviews*. Edited by Donald F. Bouchard. Ithaca: Cornell University Press, 1977. 113–38.

Freud, Sigmund. *The Standard Edition of the Complete Psychological Works*. Translated and edited by James Strachey. Assisted by Anna Freud, Alix Strachey, and Alan Tyson. 24 vols. London: The Hogarth Press and the Institute of Psycho-analysis, 1953–74.

Gazzaniga, Michael S. *Mind Matters: How Mind and Brain Interact to Create Our Conscious Lives*. Boston: Houghton Mifflin Co., 1988.

Hobson, J. Allan. *The Dreaming Brain*. New York: Basic Books, 1988.

Hobson, J. Allan, and Robert W. McCarley. "The Brain as a Dream State Generator: An Activation-Synthesis Hypothesis of the Dream Process." *American Journal of Psychiatry* 134.12 (1977): 1335–48.

Holland, Norman N. *5 Readers Reading*. New Haven: Yale University Press, 1975.

Rycroft, Charles. *The Innocence of Dreams*. New York: Pantheon, 1979.

ACKNOWLEDGEMENTS

Two essays in this volume have previously appeared in print. Norman N. Holland's "Hermia's Dream" was first published in *The Annual of Psychoanalysis* in 1977 and an earlier, shorter version of Kay Stockholder's essay appeared in *Dreaming: Journal of the Association for the Study of Dreams* in 1991 as "Dreaming of Death in *The Merchant of Venice*." Our appreciation goes to the Editors of the journals for their kind permission to republish these contributions.

We are grateful to photographer Eddy Van Der Veen and to Time-Life Books for permission to include reproductions of two photographs, of Delacroix's "Apollo Destroying Python" and Géricault's "Raft of Medusa," from the LIFE LIBRARY OF ART, *The World of Delacroix*, 1966, pp. 140 and 49 respectively.

Hearty thanks go to all my contributors for their cheerful forebearance, cooperation, and complete professionalism in the lengthy process of bringing this collection into print. I am especially grateful to Kelly Bulkley whose enthusiasm about the whole venture was as sustaining as his collaboration on Chapter 1 was inspiring, and to Norman N. Holland for his extraordinary "grace under pressure" in composing a Foreword for our volume with characteristic wit and energy despite the demands made upon him through his leadership in the literature-and-psychology field.

The dedication names principally those two beings who have since their birth lightened and enlivened all of my life and work, my daughter Jody and my son Whitney. Appreciation for support in this as in all my various endeavors goes to my husband, Richard P. (Peter) Suttmeier, to friends and mentors Jane White-Lewis, Victoria Vernon, and Jeffry Klugman, to Joan Montgomery Byles who came through on short notice at a crucial stage in the project, to members of the international Association for the Study of Dreams, and to a very special secretary who is the sine qua non of my professional life, Esther Delaney of Hamilton College.

All of us whose work appears in this volume offer further thanks to the two Readers. Their responses to our manuscript were knowledgeable, thoughtful, perceptive, and suggestive. They have made this a better book.

1. Reading Yourself to Sleep: Dreams in/and/as Texts

Carol Schreier Rupprecht and *Kelly Bulkley*

Reading yourself to sleep. The image is not one of anticipated reader response to this book. Rather it represents a set of relations unifying the fourteen individual contributions which comprise the book, a set of relations between wakefulness and sleep and the intermediate process of "rising" into the former and "falling" into the latter; between reality and dream and the intermediate stage of the imaginal we are accustomed to calling fiction; between the non-sense of "it was only a dream," the beyond-sense vision of "I have a dream," and the intermediate sense of "life is (just) a dream."

The opening image may figure a process personally known to many readers of this book but it is also a process familiar to many dreamers in literary texts. Tolstoy's Anna Karenina drowses over a novel, reading herself in and out of a reverie of liminal consciousness; Chaucer's narrator in *The Book of the Duchess* nods off over a romance narrative containing a dream and in the process has himself yet another dream within a text; Bronte's Lockwood, reading Catherine Earnshaw's diaries and the titles on the bindings of sermon pamphlets, drifts off into not one but two powerful nightmares.

"Reading yourself to sleep" can also be read as a provisional statement of the nature and practice of oneirocriticism, which is the core process of this book. "Oneirocriticism" is not a postmodern neologism but an ancient term and a similarly ancient practice undergoing a consciousness (or unconsciousness) raising in this turn-of-the-century period. The Greek word *oneiros*, of the many Greek terms for dream the one referring specifically to message dreams from the gods, has become the generic term for dreams of any kind. "Oneirocriticism" as the activity engaged in here can be described this way. It involves the use of critical methods from various fields of study to explore dreams, the use of critical insights from dreams to explore var-

1

ious kinds of texts, and the development of a dialogue among these explorations. Dreaming is thus both a subject/object of inquiry itself and a process by which inquiry proceeds. Double focusing on dream texts and literary texts highlights their differences, as well as their similarities, by foregrounding their shared aesthetic components: image, language, and narrative.

While many societies of the world have a rich oneirocritical history, in recent centuries, in the West at least, this richness has been reduced to polarized perspectives constrained within disciplinary boundaries: religion *or* psychology *or* history *or* literary criticism. Take only one component of a complex system, the dream represented within a literary text. There are those who have treated such dreams as nothing more than simple, transparent structuring devices. Dreams are read as framing mechanisms by which the author chooses to convey something that would lose its desired effectiveness if directly stated, simply represented, or incorporated into the main narrative stream. Once that function is served, however, the dream is essentially discarded. Then there are those who have treated dreams in literary works as psychological proof-texts, confirming the validity of a particular psychological theory. Here, too, the dream itself is dismissed once it serves its use.

The legitimacy of and necessity for mutually informing and balanced interdisciplinary approaches to dreams-and-literature to counter existing inadequacies have been persuasively argued by individual voices from a variety of schools: Shoshana Feldman and Meredith Skura[1] for the psychoanalytic tradition, for example. But foregrounding the dream and its content rather than instrumentally using dreams for other ends has not come readily. The chapters in this collection, however, separately and in their intertextual exchange, constitute an entirely transforming oneirocritical landscape. Certain developments in this century have opened the way for a return of respect for the multifarious implications of dreams, both "real" and "literary," in and of themselves. The contributors to this volume have come of age in the midst of these developments and the chapters that follow this one in our volume demonstrate the many ways in which the interdisciplinary study of dreams-and-literature is devising new strategies of inquiry which reflect these other changes in society.

First, there has been an erosion of Freud's hegemony as the supreme authority on the meaning of dreams and a similar revaluation of Jung's stature as an oneirologist. Individuals and organizations now aim to wrest dreams from the hands of the "experts" and place them back in the hands of the dreamers themselves. Second, neurophysiological studies of dream formation such as the "activation synthesis" hypothesis of Allan Hobson and Robert McCarley[2] have demonstrated the complex interplay between brain and mind in the creation of dreams. Such research has heuristic implications for an understanding of the way humans use images and narrative structures to render their experiences meaningful and coherent.

Third, virtually all fields in the human sciences have in recent decades undergone a philosophical transformation in the way they regard language, texts, meaning, and the process of interpretation. Language is no longer considered, even hypothetically, univocal and transparent; texts are seen as fluid, not fixed—as processes, not objects; meaning is not "there" in the text but depends on the particular questions that are asked of it; and "interpretation" involves an interaction between the world of the text and the world of the interpreter. In short, the natural scientific model has given way, or one may more accurately say returned, to a hermeneutic model. This shift has provoked new investigations in many fields: anthropology, theology, law, art, history, linguistics, psychology, and sociology.

Fourth, recent work by anthropologists such as Barbara Tedlock and Waud Kracke and sociologists such as Peter Berger has provided us with new understanding of the social construction of reality and the interdependent relationship between dreams and culture.[3] Such studies show the great extent to which the assumptions of a given culture shape the way dreams are experienced, reported, interpreted, and brought into relation with waking life. Their findings require a reexamination of dream theories that have insisted on the universality of dreaming processes, on the timelessness and the cross-cultural continuities of dream meaning and dream content (whether "manifest" or "latent"). At the same time that this social science research testifies to the somewhat determining effect on dreaming of the psychological, social, epistemological, and religious assumptions of a culture, it reveals the force of the reverse process: dreams also shape cultures. By critiquing current social conditions, envisioning new possibilities, motivating individual and collective action, and in myriad other ways, dreams have an impact that often changes the cultural paradigm in which they occur, an impact often ignored or obscured in Western culture.

In addition, oneirocriticism becomes an oneirolinguistics also whether we consider dreams as intrapsychic communication, metacommunication, or not communication at all. In the first place, though many dream theorists insist on the priority of visual over verbal phenomena in dreams, the dreaming brain is a notorious punster.

Wordplay, and in fact image-play of an analogous kind, is one of its salient characteristics in virtually all languages and cultures. Secondly, discourse about dreaming is impossible to conduct without dissolution of all traditional linguistics boundaries. Indeed, the impulse toward categorization and taxonomy that rears up in the dream theory texts of almost any age in almost any culture has been identified as a defense against the bewildering indeterminacy of dreams and of discourse about them.[4] Perhaps this indeterminacy explains why no volume like this has yet appeared in English and why until now no one has ventured to bring out a multidisciplinary array of writings on dreams.

We are transgressing linguistics boundaries as soon as we begin to talk about our own sleeping mentation as a "real" dream to distinguish it from a dream we call "fictitious" or "make-believe" because it is the sleeping mentation of an "unreal" person, that is, a person who is a character in a fictional narrative and who is, obviously and therefore, *not* like us who are, after all, *really* "real." That is, we live in "real" houses where we read (real? fictional?) books and we are not imaginary characters in the books we're reading. But we have already made a radical shift in perceptual labeling when we try to make such a distinction between dreams in life and dreams in literature because, prior to picking up the novel or poem or play, we had readily been using the unreality of sleep mentation (it was a dream and not real) to distinguish our dream people, events, and feelings from the "real" people. "real events," and "real feelings" of our waking life.

Reading yourself to sleep further suggests the transitionality of the waking/reading/sleeping/dreaming continuum and its intertextual bias. Is a character in a novel we read who later appears in our dream therefore a "fictitious" figure in a "real" dream who needs to be distinguished from those real people in our waking, non-reading life who also appear in our dreams? Is the Hamlet of my dreams more or less real than a consanguineous relative, say Aunt Betsey, who is having a conversation with Hamlet in my sleeping mentation? Don't we need levels of "day residue" to differentiate between dream content that clearly derives from novels or stage drama or film or painting or sculpture (or TV) from that content which derives from our families, our jobs, and other diurnal preoccupations that involve us on a cognitive level?[5]

The chapters which follow are grouped into four somewhat arbitrarily devised parts. Each of the parts is preceded by a brief statement of the section's focus. But we also offer in the next several pages some guidelines for the reader. First, these chapters are not simply about dreams and literary texts and the relation between them; they make important contributions to our knowledge about dreams themselves—their nature, function, meaning, and potential. The chapters should thus be of interest to all those involved in dream study whether they work from the imaginal perspective or not. Second, there are an amazing number of intratextual dialogues going on among the chapters. In this way, the collection is (surprise!) like a dream itself and can be read/interpreted as such. To collaborate in this dream-reading exercise we provide the following observations of our own.

There are several keen, and often amusing, reflections on oneiric issues in this collection. One is a classic essay on reading as a transactive process by Norman N. Holland reprinted here from its initial appearance in 1977. Reading a dream within a literary text, such as Hermia's dream in Shakespeare's *A Midsummer Night's Dream*, complicates this process, especially when we take account, as Holland does, of our subjective responses; when we withdraw the projections we have made onto the text and analyze "them" along with "it." Reading yourself to sleep and then dreaming about your "real" life and about the fabricated, invented life in the literary text may be the ultimate transactive process.

Also, following on an irrepressibly playful impulse that seems to strike everyone who writes on dreams in/and/as texts, Bert O. States extends this multiplicity of inference and reference even further. He reports a dream he has fabricated in "a hypothetical work of fiction" he has created just for the occasion of his essay. Then he turns himself into a reader of this fiction to demonstrate the multiple simultaneous negotiations the brain undergoes as it "reads" a narrative, with or without a dream in it. Holland also toys with the issue by citing an anecdote about Henri Matisse. Holland reports Matisse's reply to the charge by a viewer of one of his paintings that an arm of the woman in it was too long: "Madame, you are mistaken. That is not a woman, that is a picture."

Laurence M. Porter tackles the multivalenced complexity hinted at above in a somewhat different way, as does Jane White-Lewis. They juxtapose "real" dreams by "real" people—in Porter's case himself, in White-Lewis's case her clients in therapy—to literary representations of dreams. Porter then looks at a "real" author, Nerval, who turned his own dreams into fiction in the form of the most famous novel of French Romanticism, *Aurélia*. Suzi Naiburg treats a similar process in Henry James's career where an actual nightmare recorded by James becomes transformed into literary material. Naiburg also explores the further wrinkles of aesthetic complexity that arise because James's nightmare was stimulated by his boyhood experience among the paintings in the Louvre. Thus James is engaging in a dizzying intersemiotic translation.

As the collection unfolds, it begins to take on some of the qualities of the Chuang-Tse butterfly dream experience which various authors invoke. And States suggests an analogy between dream-and-text analysis and Douglas Hofstader's "strange loop" or "tangled hierarchy." If reality proves to be a social construct and the self a narrative construct, as some contemporary theories of criticism want to argue, then what are dreams and texts made of and how can a simultaneous discourse on both proceed? Readers may want to take on a "willing suspension of disbelief" as they work their way through the volume.

Other contributors concern themselves with dreaming in earlier genres and cultural systems: ancient Babylonian epic and the Hebrew Bible (Kelly Bulkley); dream commentary from the Talmud and Midrash (Ken Frieden); historical and poetic documents from early pre-Han China (John Brennan); medieval Spanish dream poetry (Harriet Goldberg); theoretical dream texts of Renaissance Italy (Carol Schreier Rupprecht); dreams in the drama of Elizabethan England (Kay Stockholder, Joseph Westlund) and of the Spanish Golden Age (Frederick A. de Armas); prophetic dreams in nineteenth-century Russian poetry and prose fiction (C. Nicholas Lee).

De Armas uses oneirics to redeem a text that has been called the least successful play of a second- or third-rate playwright. He is able to show not only the aesthetic value but also the historical interest of this drama that may have been the first Golden Age play on the discovery of America. Westlund demonstrates the way use of psychoanalyst Heinz Kohut's self psychology in approaching a dramatic character who dreams focuses the reader on the character's psychologically healthy sector rather than on his psychopathology. Westlund's method produces a deepened reading of a late romance by Shakespeare, *Cymbeline*, which complements the excellent Freudian analysis of the dream within the play by Meredith Skura.[6] White-Lewis fills in a major gap in dream theory by showing the neglect of nightmares, and especially of their symbolic value and teleological potential, in the psychologies of Freud, Jung, and their descendants. She then explores clinical and literary cases illustrating the important functions nightmares perform in lives and in texts.

Examining dreams in Chinese sources from the earliest dynasties to the Han era, Brennan discovers a major change in dream content. He is led by his readings to wonder if history shows that dream content, and by implication the patterns of the unconscious, changes even more radically than culture does, "beyond the predictable changes in material culture." Brennan reports that message dreams—communications from the gods—lose status and decrease in frequency of report in China from the Han period (206 BCE–220 CE) on. He notes that Dodds cites a similar shift in the oneiric tradition in Greek culture. These hypotheses parallel, though on a different cultural scene and different timetable, Rupprecht's view on the abandonment of beliefs in divinely originating prophetic dreams as a major marker of sixteenth-century Europe. These chapters also trace a relocation in the meanings and origins of dreams to within the mental state of the individual dreamer and away from dreaming as a process embedded in a "broader impersonal system of signification and causality" of which the dreamer is only an instrument.

Brennan also, like Bulkley and de Armas, addresses the role of dreams in political contexts, especially the effects of naively or deliberately misconstrued interpretations with serious political outcomes. All three writers mediate evidence from the texts of creative writers with evidence from actual governmental records.

Versions of the oneiric in realism and romanticism are treated by Lee and Porter, showing the contrast between the oneiric and the fantastic and the persistence in certain cultures of belief in prophetic dreams. Westlund treats the nexus of *psychological* realism and romance in late Shakespearean drama. And Goldberg shows how one poet in only four poems can create an oneiric range encompassing the aesthetic, the erotic, and the political. Read in the sequence offered, the chapters possess, like a series of dreams in one night, a deep-level lateral homology even though each one, except Holland's, was composed especially for *The Dream and the Text* with no knowledge about the other topics or contributors, and all the others, except Stockholder's, appear in print here for the first time.

In moving through this book, the reader will encounter an often-familiar populace but one that appears in many new guises. Freud, Jung, Tzvetan Todorov, Jacques Lacan, Heinz Kohut, Ernest Jones, Ernest Hartmann, David Foulkes and Medard Boss, J. Allan Hobson and Robert McCarley, Francis Crick and Graeme Mitchison. But such "authorities" on dreams are invoked only to be challenged, extended, modified, and re-visioned. The reader will find Shakespeare, Henry James, Emily Bronte, Tolstoy, Dostoevsky, Goethe, Poe, Nerval, and Calderon, but also Santillana, Claramonte, Tyutchev and Supervielle, but should refuse to take even this roll call at face value. There is no intention here to launch a new field of study, or to reinvigorate an old one, depending on your historical perspective, by producing an instant canon of privileged texts and commentators. For example, Frieden challenges the Freudian orthodoxy from within by unveiling Freud's perhaps deliberate disguise of his debt to Jewish predecessors in dream commentary. Also Bulkley asserts that the multivalency of every dream and text demands commensurately multivalent, hence multidisciplinary, readings.

We started with what we have known to stimulate ventures into the unknown. There is an acknowledged bias toward premodern texts as a result of the editor's training and scholarly interests. And there are acknowledged omissions of many other kinds which we invite readers to hasten to fill. What about gender? Is there a "common language of women's dreams" as the editor proposed several years ago?[7] Why does gender difference appear to be the one unvarying presupposition in dream theory across cultures and times as she observed in 1988?[8] What does oneirocriticism tell us about sex and power, and economics? Kay Stockholder makes some suggestions about these issues in her provocative work on incest in *The Merchant of Venice*. What is the role of race in the matrices of dreams and texts? Dreaming is a universal human phenomenon. How universal is dream content and meaning and function?

Incubation was a practice in the ancient Near East designed to facilitate the occurrence of "big" dreams, but it seems to have been neither practiced nor encouraged in Biblical and ancient Chinese cultures. What is to be made of this difference and of other information emerging from multidisciplinary dream studies? For example, nightmares outnumber positive or affectively neutral dreams by at least ten to one in the texts cited in this volume, texts from a variety of genres, time periods, and cultures. Why has so little theoretical attention been devoted to nightmares?

Is there a core of truth to mythological representations of sleep, dreams, and death as members of the same family? Despite Freud, the erotic—naked or disguised—makes a surprisingly minimal number of appearances in the dreams from the texts studied here while death occupies a much more significant position. Are erotic dreams less frequent in literature than in life? Or are these two categories of dream —eroticism and death—really one?

Such questioning reminds us that dreams are inherently dialogical. They involve dialogues between consciousness and the unconscious; between individual and culture; between past, present, and future. And fittingly this jointly authored chapter and this multiply authored text are dialogues about those dialogues. While the temptation with any collection is to read only a few of its pieces—those contiguous to one's own immediate interests or discipline—readers thus tempted will miss the crucial interplay of multiple perspectives offered here. They will miss the opportunity to read themselves awake to the potential of oneirocritical inquiry, to seek out dreams that appear in/and/as texts and to begin to read, and to write, about them.

Notes

1. See among their many writings Shoshana Felman's "To Open the Question," in *Literature and Psychoanalysis—The Question of Reading: Otherwise*, a special issue of *Yale French Studies*, nos. 55/56 (1977): 8–9 and Meredith Skura's book, *The Literary Use of the Psychoanalytic Process* (Yale University Press, 1973), and her many excellent articles. See n. 6. [See also chapter 11 by Joseph Westlund.] Prof. Skura had graciously consented to the reprint of one classic article, "Revisions and Rereadings in Dreams and Allegories," in this volume; unfortunately, however, limits of length, financial constraints, and the priority of printing new essays made it impossible to include her material. Readers are urged to consult this author as a fine resource on dreams-and-literature. Also see Carol Schreier Rupprecht, "Enlightening Shadows: Between Feminism and Archetypalism, Literature and Analysis", *C. G. Jung and the Humanities: A Hermeneutics of Culture* (Princeton: Princeton University Press, 1990), 279–93.

2. See J. Allan Hobson and Robert McCarley, "The Brain as a Dream State Generator: An Activation-Synthesis Hypothesis of the Dream Process," *American Journal of Psychiatry* 134. 12 (December 1977), 1335–48 as well as later articles by both and Hobson's recent *The Dreaming Brain*, (New York: Basic Books, 1988). See also Kelly Bulkley, "Interdisciplinary Dreaming: Hobson's Successes and Failures," *Dreaming*, I. 3 (1991) for critical assessment of his work.

3. See *Dreaming: Anthropological and Psychological Interpretations*, ed. Barbara Tedlock, (Cambridge and New York: Cambridge University Press, 1987) for essays by Tedlock, Kracke, and others. Also, Peter Berger, principally *The Sacred Canopy* and with Thomas Luckman, *The Social Construction of Reality: A Treatise in the Sociology of Knowledge*, New York: Doubleday, 1966).

4. An example would be David G. Hale's article on medieval poetry, "Dreams, Stress, and Interpretation in Chaucer and His Contemporaries," *Journal of the Rocky Mountain Medieval and Renaissance Association* 9 (1988) 47–61.

5. An Italian Renaissance dream text treated in chapter 6 of this volume indicates that this was a vexing issue in 1562. See Girolamo Cardano's

Somniorum Synesiorum, omnis generis insommnia explicantes, libri iiii (Basel: Henry Petrie, 1562).

6. See "Interpreting Posthumus' Dream from Above and Below: Families, Psychoanalysts, and Literary Critics," *Representing Shakespeare: New Psychoanalytic Essays*, eds. Murray M. Schwartz and Coppélia Kahn (Baltimore: Johns Hopkins University Press, 1980), 203–216.

7. Carol Schreier Rupprecht, "The Common Language of Women's Dreams: Colloquy of Mind and Body," *Feminist Archetypal Theory: Interdisciplinary Re-visions of Jungian Thought*, ed. Estella Lauter and Rupprecht (Knoxville: University of Tennessee Press, 1985), 187–219.

8. Address at the University of Virginia, Charlottesville in the annual conference of the Association for the Study of Dreams, later revised and printed as an article, "Our Unacknowledged Ancestors: Dream Theorists of Antiquity, the Middle Ages, and the Renaissance," *The Psychiatric Journal of the University of Ottawa* 15.2 (1990), 117–122.

PART I

Foregrounding Theory

The writing that constitutes this section is inventively theoretical, drawing on but also playing with earlier views of psychologists and literary critics. Using phenomenological theories of experience to take himself outside of disciplines conventionally used to analyze dreams, Bert O. States addresses a fundamental question that can arise around any experience of dreaming or any textual representation of a dream: what precisely makes a dream "bizarre"? He argues that bizarreness is not an inherent quality of dreaming but only appears as such from the waking perspective. He also claims that "real" and "literary" dreams, however different, are united in one important capacity: both function to enhance the correlational powers of the mind.

Laurence M. Porter daringly begins with one of his own dreams, a nightmare about mental illness. This leads him back into his personal past while simultaneously propelling him, as a scholar of European Romanticism, into linguistic, literary, and psychological probings of dreams in texts. He is thus led to conclude that "literary" dreams differ from "real" dreams in being, on the whole, more elaborated in the psychoanalytic sense.

Porter's method of moving along an inward and outward dynamic—dream as intrapsychic communication and dream as outward formal representation—hauntingly reminds us that one's own personal sleeping mentation affects, and is affected by, the dream material we work on in our professions. Jane White-Lewis's chapter reinforces this pattern of interaction. As a practicing clinical psychologist, White-Lewis starts from the position of real people—her clients in psychotherapy—who have reported "real" dreams. Focusing on nightmares, she moves deftly from her own experience through the writings of Freud, Ernest Jones, and especially Jung, showing how psychological theories can serve as beneficial "yeast" to literary criticism. Via this route White-Lewis arrives at a disclosure of new meanings in the nightmares of Raskolnikov in *Crime and Punishment* and Lockwood in *Wuthering Heights*.

2. Bizarreness in Dreams and Other Fictions

Bert O. States

The assumption that dreams are bizarre, or contain extraordinary images that are inconsistent with realities in the waking world, is perhaps the most universal point of agreement among people who study or think about dreams. My objective here is not to correct a mistake I think everybody has been making, but to worry the problem of bizarreness from a perspective that might bring dreams and waking fictions closer together as variations of a common operation in which bizarreness, so-called, is the *modus operandi*.

My leading question could be phrased: how is it that the bizarre becomes bizarre? My suggestion will be that bizarreness is best considered as a species-specific phenomenon that is somewhat like beauty in being in the eye of the beholder, or more specifically in what the eye is capable of beholding in specific psychic states. To define bizarreness as discrete monstrosity or, as Allan Hobson does, according to *Webster's New Collegiate Dictionary* ("strikingly out of the ordinary" [Hobson 1988, 259]) effectively ignores a fundamental point of dream bizarreness: that it is a bottom-to-top condition beginning in the composition of the image; monstrosities are simply extreme variations of the dream image's peculiar "normalcy." The dream is just as distorted when it is being "realistic" and sensible as it is when it is producing outrageous aberrations of nature. In other words, should a dream image suddenly break out into an impossibility—a double-headed man, a giant, a talking plant—that is simply one of the *probabilities* of dream transformation, like anger or fear suddenly breaking out of temperate human behavior.

The best way to approach the phenomenon might be to trace it to the preconditions of its appearance. We should begin, therefore, by noting the obvious: that, where dreams are concerned, we are attaching the words "bizarre" and "distorted" to a form of mental experience that strikes us as perfectly normal while we are having it. One might argue that reality is so obviously an objective fact and that dreaming is so palpably insubstantial and subjective that there is little doubt about which should serve as the standard of "normalcy," especially since waking reality is the place in which we do all of our measuring and theorizing. But I am always struck by the paradox posed by Chuang-Tse's famous butterfly dream and by a more recent variant of the same dilemma—let us call it the Two Body Problem—offered by the German phenomenologist Medard Boss:

> While waking observers see him fast asleep in bed in Zurich, the dreamer may feel that he is skiing, with consummate physical grace and pleasure, down an Alpine slope. The question now is, which body is the "real" one, the body that others see lying in bed, though the dreamer is unaware of it, or the body that the dreamer himself feels so intensely but that no waking observer can perceive? We are at a loss for an answer, probably because the question is inadequately formulated. We may discover that both bodies, the recumbent and the active one, belong equally to the bodyhood of the sleeper's existence. In any case, however, physicality has shown itself to be no criterion for distinguishing between the human waking and dreaming states. (Boss 1977, 197)

So too it is possible that we have inadequately formulated the question of the dream's bizarreness. If we proceed from the standpoint of "physicality" (what is possible in waking reality) we arrive at one view of the matter; if we proceed from the standpoint of consciousness (the reality one *thinks* one occupies) we arrive at another. The word *bizarre* itself carries the implication that the bizarre image could have been presented "realistically" had the system been working differently. And indeed, most dreams aren't noticeably bizarre at all, most of the time, but consist of fairly normal events and images.

Suddenly, however, a dream will produce one of these "bizarre intrusions" (Crick and Mitchison 1986, 231) that may be strong enough to awaken the dreamer or to provide a topic of conversation at breakfast. But somehow this division of dream images into normal and bizarre seems rather like a visitor's report from a foreign country that the people there behave in "strange" ways. Would we say that water becomes "bizarre" at 32° F or "unreal" at 212°? In order to understand the behavior of water properly we must consider what happens to "it" under a range of conditions—"it" being not simply the liquid that runs from our faucets but a certain chemical proportion of hydrogen to oxygen that also assumes the form of ice or steam, depending on temperature conditions. In short, steam and ice are not variant forms of water but, along with water, variant forms of H_2O.

H_2O is the genus; water, ice, and steam are the differentia. If we apply this principle to imaging behavior we would surely have to say that in distinguishing "bizarre" dream images from "normal" images we are treating differentia as genus, or at least implying that bizarre images are an aberrant form of normal image, deformed either by censorship at the preconscious level (Freud and most psychoanalytic theory), by chemical processes in the brain (Hobson and McCarley), by the brain's attempt to "trash" unwanted memory (Crick and Mitchison), or some other intentional or non-intentional influence (fever, drugs, psychosis, etc.).

Many researchers are well aware, as David Foulkes has said, that "characterizing images, or image sequences, or image contents as . . . 'bizarre' . . . almost inherently directs attention to [the dream's] affect on us, rather than to its own constituents." Indeed, Foulkes cites the need for further study of what bizarre features may "reveal about peculiarities in the processes by which the dream organiz[es] its mnemonic sources" (Foulkes 1985, 89, n. 34). Most of the literature, however, seems content to deal with bizarreness as something that is visually more or less in evidence and can be tabulated on a quantitative/qualitative scale. Hobson, for example, conceives of the brain in the dream state as somehow struggling to make sense of the bizarre things it produces as a consequence of random chemical bombardment. "How can a companion be a stranger?" he asks in connection with the "Customs Building" Dream. "He cannot. Therefore the dreamer corrects the situation by turning him into a known person" the assumption being, I gather, that the dreamer is somehow aware of the dream's "inconsistencies" and strives to change them into regularities. Or, he asks, why are there confusions in the dream? Might they not "reflect the undistorted efforts of the brain-mind to perform one of its most essential functions: to establish orientational stability." Above all, in the REM stage of sleep, the brain/mind suffers from "disorientation": that is, "external orientational cues are absent (because the dreamer is asleep and cut off from the world), and . . . his own brain compass is spinning (because the brain mechanisms serving memory, attention, and insight are disabled)" (Hobson 1988, 272–75).

What Hobson refers to as "disorientation" leads us to the phenomenon Allan Reichschaffen calls the dream's single-mindedness. To review briefly, single-mindedness is "the strong tendency for a single train of related thoughts and images to persist over extended periods without disruption or competition from other simultaneous thoughts and images." Waking consciousness consists of "at least two prevalent streams" of thought: voluntary mental productions and sense impressions, on one hand, and, on the other, "a reflective or evaluative stream which seemingly monitors the first and places it in some perspective." In the dream state, however, this second, "reflective stream of consciousness is drastically attenuated" i.e., we are (normally) unaware that we are dreaming. Reichschaffen expresses this idea still another way by saying that dreams "lack imagination"—meaning that the dream state, lacking "reflective awareness" (i.e., being single-minded), has no "capacity to conjure up images and thoughts which may occupy consciousness simultaneously or near simultaneously with another stream of thoughts and images." Although he acknowledges that in another sense dreams may be "considered among the most imaginative of human productions," they are nonimaginative in that the dreamer cannot, as a waking person can, dream of one thing ("sitting at my desk") while "simultaneously imagining a tennis court" (Reichschaffen 1978, 97–101).

While the general idea is plausible, this notion of imagination seems to me restrictive. For example, Arthur Koestler has used the same terminology, in reverse, to describe the difference between the mind in a routine state of waking thought, which he calls single-mindedness (or capable of thinking only on a single plane) and the mind in the creative state, or double-mindedness, which is a "transitory state of unstable equilibrium where the balance of both emotion and thought is disturbed" (might we say bizarre?) and the mind is capable of operating "on more than one plane" (Koestler 1969, 35–6). In short, where Hobson would find "disorientation" (disequilibrium) a somewhat crippling state, as regards clarity of thought and insight, Koestler would find it ("unstable equilibrium") the special province of creativity. For Koestler, imagination implies a metaphorical operation of thought, or what he refers to as "bisociation," the fundamental mental process of all scientific discovery or artistic production. And one of its strongest manifestations occurs in the dream state where *"we constantly bisociate in a passive way*—by drift, as it were; but we are, of course, unaware of it because the coherence of the logical matrices is weakened, and the codes which govern them are dormant" (p. 178).

Still, I think both Reichschaffen's and Koestler's meanings of single-mindedness are valid in their own contexts and indeed I should add that they are not talking about precisely the same processes of thought. However, I feel that Gordon Globus offers a useful critique of Reichschaffen's thesis in reminding us that we also fall into single-minded or non-reflective states in our waking life (Globus 1987,

80–84), and we also produce involuntary thought in this state. Perhaps we could put the case as follows: on one hand, the dream state is one of pure *imagination* (Koestler's double-mindedness or passive bisociation); on the other hand, paradoxically, while the dream state is driven by imagination, it *has no imagination* (in Reichschaffen's sense) with respect to its own productions. That is, it cannot, like the brain in the waking or the daydream states, willfully change its mind and follow a new course *unlike* the course it has set; nor can it keep two courses in mind simultaneously. In other words, the dreaming brain is capable of imagining *anything* but, having done so, it is stuck with what it imagines—it cannot imagine what it imagines (somewhat as consciousness cannot be conscious of itself). And this limitation bears centrally on Reichschaffen's conjecture that dream hallucinations may, after all, be "secondary to dream single-mindedness" rather than the other way around (Reichschaffen 1978, 101), as Hobson would apparently have it.

I doubt that we can so securely claim what the brain *can* and *can't* do in the dream state because there are so many different declensions of "mindedness" from lucid dreaming to hypnogogic imagery to the state of half-sleep where one seems to be a creature of one world as much as the other. But let us at least grant the point that there is this gross difference in capability between the waking and dreaming states and try to see where it may lead. Let us apply the idea to a practical example that will enable us to compare literary and dream experience and to arrive at some notion of what bizarreness actually involves in the way of mental processing. Here is a passage from a hypothetical work of fiction I have written for this occasion:

> It was perhaps the way she was sitting, or the familiar blue dress she wore, but as I looked at Sarah crying there on the sofa I was reminded of Aunt Julia sitting in her kitchen on the afternoon that Edgar was killed in the car accident. I can still hear Julia say, "The last thing Edgar said when he left the house was 'I won't be back!'"

I have composed this passage in the most straightforward style possible in order to see what sorts of mental transactions are involved in the reading of "normal" fiction. The most elementary thing to be said, perhaps, is that the passage virtually disappears as an object (words on paper) and reappears as an experience in the mind's eye. Or, as Georges Poulet puts it in his phenomenology of reading, it becomes a mental object "in close *rapport* with my own consciousness"; my consciousness "is modified in such a way that I no longer have the right, strictly speaking, to consider it as my *I*. I am on loan to another, and this other thinks, feels, suffers, and acts within me" (Poulet 1980,

42–45). And indeed something of this kind happens in the typical daydream and even more profoundly in the REM (Rapid Eye Movement) dream state: I perceive the dream world not in the "weak" way that I perceive a literary text, no matter how well it has been "internalized," but as a world I somehow inhabit which "thinks" itself in me, as Poulet says, even though I myself am responsible for all the thinking. Hence, the dream is a kind of "strange loop," or "tangled hierarchy," in Hofstadter's terms—"something *in* the system jumps out and acts *on* the system, as if it were *outside* the system" (Hofstadter 1979, 691)—in which the dream I have created seems to be taking place outside of me as an independent reality.

But to return to my fiction: notice what is asked of the brain in the process of inhabiting this "second self," this I/Not I. I begin with a mental image of Sarah sitting on the sofa in tears. (If I have not met her earlier in the story I will simply supply a generic or facsimile Sarah from my memory of "Sarah" possibilities which I will amend as her character and appearance become established.) But immediately, I am *reminded*, through certain cues, of Aunt Julia who recalls what Edgar said on the afternoon of his death. In other words, Aunt Julia, in some sense, momentarily replaces Sarah in my mind's eye, though Sarah remains, so to speak, "on hold" in my attention; but abruptly Edgar replaces Aunt Julia and there is probably even a "flash" on my peripheral mental landscape of a scene involving a car accident somewhere on a highway.

All of this is very effortlessly negotiated by the brain. Of course, we are still debating what sort of images the brain conjures in such a sequence—they are perhaps what Nelson Goodman calls "invisible pictures" (Goodman 1984, 23), or concept-pictures, or what Edward Casey calls images of "pure possibility" (Casey 1979, 36–7)—but it certainly amounts to a center of mental energy wherein an image of Sarah, or of Sarahness, *gives way* fleetingly to an image of Julia and Edgar and a wrecked car of some sort. A cinematic version of the scene would probably achieve the effect through a dissolve in which the scene would shift to the kitchen and the quarrel (?) with Aunt Julia and Edgar, and then back to the scene between the narrator and Sarah, probably with some sort of ripple-effect to suggest the pastness of it all.

In short, in the space of two sentences, the brain has been caused, at some quasi-pictorial level, to replace one scene with another and to hold the sense of several scenes in a simultaneous or oscillating suspension, or what Reichschaffen might call double-mindedness. What textually directs all this mental traffic are the two constructions,

"I was *reminded*" and "I can *still* hear Julia say," which form an associational bridge, so to speak, into the past, whereby the "I" of the narrative and the I/Not I of the reader are able to visualize and make sense of the sequence without bizarrely bunching everybody together on a sofa as a car comes crashing through the kitchen wall. They function like similes in poetic imagery in that they keep the hierarchy from becoming tangled: that is, "I was reminded" serves as a *like* or an *as* that says, in effect, "Sarah, here on the sofa, *resembles* Aunt Julia on that fatal afternoon in the kitchen." In any case, as Poulet says, we have "become the prey of language":

> The universe of fiction is infinitely more elastic than the world of objective reality. It lends itself to any use: it yields with little resistance to the importunities of the mind. Moreover—and of all its benefits I find this the most appealing—this interior universe constituted by language does not seem radically opposed to the *me* who thinks. (1980, 43)

I hope my example can be taken as an elementary instance of the elasticity of fiction and the capacity of human consciousness to shift scenes and focal points on linguistic cues, to convert a purely verbal world into a half-reality taking place in one's head. One would hardly call this transaction bizarre or distorted because it involves a normal "daytime" mental operation (being reminded of something else) that is as common as seeing a face in a bush or remembering your high school prom while overhearing a song. Yet—and this of course is my point—the mental process involved in such re-mindings is no different from the process by which dreams negotiate similar cross-associations, and in doing so produce both "realistic" and "bizarre" images. The only difference is that in dreams there is no text to mediate the experience or to preserve a conscious awareness that the association is *only* an association posited in a fictional universe rather than a part of dream-reality as it appears to the dreamer in the dream state. In a dream based on our story, Sarah would suddenly be Aunt Julia; or what is more likely, the essence of one would contaminate the *image* of the other, or Sarah-Julia might even turn into a familiar stranger, possessing inseparable attributes of both, somewhat as yellow and blue produce the color green when mixed or brought into close proximity.

Indeed, that is what often happens in a dream, and I suspect that the high frequency of strangers in dreams (four out of ten dream characters are strangers, according to Calvin Hall [1966, 30]), or the sudden confusion of a known person with a stranger, may have to do in part with the problem of representing in a single image a charge brought on by an overload of multiple associations. How, after all, is the dream able to move from Sarah to Aunt Julia without an equivalent of the literary device in the simile, a simile being nothing more than a verbal means of maintaining difference in the resemblance? In a dream such a transaction would necessarily occur as a metaphor rather than as a simile, meaning that the two (or more) images would not be held apart by a *like* but would be fused as one.[2] There is simply no other way such a transaction could occur outside of reflective consciousness. A person having this dream, on awaking and telling it to another person, would probably say, "Suddenly, Sarah disappeared and I was with Aunt Julia in her kitchen and Edgar came in." And it would all seem "bizarre." Yet the bizarreness (in this case anyway) was a consequence of limitations—or, could we not say, if we were thoroughly rid of our "normalcy" bias, a consequence of imaginative enhancements—imposed by the condition of Reichschaffen's singlemindedness or, if you prefer, Koestler's passive bisociation?

Of course this is all somewhat beside the point because it is unlikely that such a story would be possible in a dream, or that a dream could tell a story that required the deviation to another prior and as-yet-undreamed story element. A dream cannot deal in flashbacks in the sense that waking fictions almost require them in order to explore what goes on in the minds and pre-story history of their characters. This is one of the distinguishing features of dream stories: they are flat out and one-directional; a dream may *have* a flashback (to a scene from the dreamer's childhood), but thereafter the flashback becomes the focus of the narrative. Moreover, just as dreams, like all imagined objects, are (as Casey says) "ineluctably front-sided" and have "no displaceability of standpoint" (p. 92), they also have no agency comparable to the omniscient narrative voice of fiction, which is capable of virtually infinite expansion or reduction of story perspective or temporal sequence. A dream might easily represent a fictional transaction such as "John had never noticed how frail mother had become" as long as John is the dreamer to whom the thought occurs. But I don't see how a dream could negotiate such hierarchical detours as those called for (for example) in a verbal construction such as "Meanwhile, across town Sidney had left his apartment to buy Felicia a birthday present, having remembered how he had disappointed her last year and how Mother had admonished him at the party for forgetting something that had always been so important to his sister."

One of the consequences of this rigidity, this absence of a hierarchical "stacking" principle, is the occasional production of "bizarre" images which are no different in kind from other images (all dream images being, at bottom, condensations or composites)[3] but whose associational "logic" does not survive the dream state. No one can be sure what brings on a noticeably bizarre image but outside of cases of drug-induced hallucination, sleep deprivation, fatigue, psychosis, or high body fever (and the like), it must occur as a kind of blending or collision of associational priorities that are simply beneath determination. This is not, of course, a collision from the dreamer's point of view: no matter how "bizarre" the image may be, it is experienced as normal and the dreamer has no choice but to believe it. Indeed, in this respect dreams approximate living conditions in the waking world: they are author-less, unmediated by language, and they unfold intrepidly in a world no different from the waking world with respect to the authenticity of the experience. As Boss and Globus have said, the dreamer is thrown into the dream as *Dasein* is thrown into the everyday world (Boss 1977, 175ff; Globus 1987, 91ff). But as dreamers we have lost a crucial capacity of waking thought—reflective awareness, or the capacity to "stand back" and assess our experience as we have it. In its place, however, we have gained a capacity to rearrange the contents of the real world according to a nonhistorical, extratemporal, and subjective directive and at the same time to perceive this new content as being in every sense a reality in its own right.

The reliability or recognizability of dream shapes according to a waking standard of coherence is therefore not a relevant consideration in dream imagery, any more than it is in nonrealistic fiction and art. The dream state is not reflective (in the waking sense) but *reflexive*, meaning that it is in constant reaction to its own productions, continually self-departing, continually creating representations that "slide smoothly from like idea to like idea," as Mary Warnock puts it, "and . . . continue in any course once set, producing more and more similar ideas according to the principles of association" (Warnock 1978, 133). The one restriction on the dream's inventive power is that it is bound by the rule of metaphoric advancement. It cannot get out of its topic any more than *Dasein* can get out of the world—unless of course by waking or by death, two forms of "story" termination that paradoxically amount to the same thing: exile from a reality in which one has been utterly absorbed.

Still, one thing must be said about the absence of the reflective capacity in dreams. If I have lost the power to assess my experience during the dream as being "only a story," as Reichschaffen puts it (p. 99), I have not lost the power to reflect on what happens *within* the dream and to bring to bear on my dream experience the same forms of awareness—or what we might call dream double-mindedness—available to me in the waking state. I can perfectly assess my dream experience just as well as I can assess my waking experience. It may be that I will produce what I will later regard as gibberish, or I may develop an intimate conversation with an animal or a deep fear of shrubbery, or a faith in the power of a bathtub to get me across an ocean; but who is to say that these "bizarre" things don't have their own validity and "logic" in the dream world, had we but the means to trace the clash and fusion of graphic priorities to their source in the neuronal memory banks? Furthermore, I am not sure how my accepting them as natural in the dream is any different from my acceptance of stationary bathtubs and speechless animals in reality, or for that matter, from talking animals, menacing trees, and such things in the world of fantastic fiction and Disney movies. In short, the so-called "willing suspension of disbelief" that we undergo in the waking aesthetic mode of thought differs from involuntary suspension of disbelief in the dream state only in degree rather than in kind.

Another way to state the problem is afforded in J. T. Fraser's concept of the *Umwelt* (developed first by Jacob von Uexkull early in this century). *Umwelt* is a "species-specific universe" in which an organism's capacity ("receptors and effectors") to receive and act upon the things of its environment determines "its world of possible stimuli and actions":

> What is not in a species' *Umwelt* must be taken as nonexistent for the members of that species. For instance, ultraviolet patterns of certain butterflies exist for other butterflies but not for vertebrates: vertebrates have no sense organs through which they could read those patterns. What an earthworm cannot know might kill it but it still won't know what hit it." (Fraser 1980, 148)

Applying the notion of *Umwelt* to dreams we may say that the dreaming brain has certain "receptors and effectors" through which it performs its unique process of converting mental stimuli from the memory into a sequence of narrative images. Why or how it does this we do not know, just as we do not know why or how ultraviolet patterns are necessary to certain butterflies and not to others or to organisms of other species. But the process is, in a manner of speaking, a species-specific operation, at least to the extent that the dream process can not only imagine a world of images (as the waking brain can) but make the imaginer one of that world's inhabitants. This process can be assessed in retrospect by the (same) waking brain, but the dreaming brain cannot, in its turn, "know" that it is in any way contained within the larger *Umwelt* of its waking "host," any more than the earthworm can know of the existence of the fisherman's hook. What is not in the *Umwelt* of the dream "must be taken as nonexistent," which is simply to say that the dream knows only the dream-*Umwelt* and all of its unique operations—however "foreign" to the *Umwelt* of the waking brain—must be conceived as being necessary and natural to its livelihood.

Let us consider this idea of *Umwelt* as it might operate from a stylistic perspective in the fiction of the supernatural. Here is the opening of Poe's *Fall of the House of Usher*, a story that would certainly qualify as containing bizarre or uncanny events:

> During the whole of a dull, dark, and soundless day in the autumn of the year, when the clouds hung oppressively low in the heavens, I had been passing alone on horseback through a singularly dreary tract of country. At length I found myself, as the shades of evening drew on, within view of the melancholy House of Usher.

This passage has nothing to do with impossible events or distortions of the laws of nature as we know them in waking life. In what respect, then, does it belong to the bizarre? Certainly the bizarreness is not to be found in the words themselves in the sense that a reader, having read this far in the story, would be apt to say, "How bizarre!" It is rather present as a potentiality and an expectation. As Kenneth Burke might put it, the passage establishes the tale's scene/act ratio, or the sense in which the quality of the scene implicitly contains "the quality of the action that is to take place within it" (1962, 6–7). In this case, the bizarreness inheres in a certain monochromatic quality that is the hallmark of the Poe world. Altogether it may be described as a condition of morbidity ("dull . . . dark . . . soundless . . . oppressive . . . melancholy"). More important, however, is the narrator's passive acceptance of this mood, as if nature on this particular day, even though "singularly dreary," were nothing generically out of the ordinary. To change the whole quality of the passage, imagine the addition of a sentence that might read, "How I longed for the sunlight and cheerfulness of my native city!" or "So foul a day I'd never seen." Such a sentiment would effectively drive a qualitative wedge between the "I" describing the scene and the scene itself, suggesting that the narrator had come from, or at least knew, a world in which such morbidity was strikingly out of the ordinary. It would be, in short, a product of double-minded thinking in that it would demonstrate Reichschaffen's "reflective or evaluative stream" of thought through which the narrator was placing the scene in some normative perspective.

Tzvetan Todorov would call this a moment of "hesitation." In his view, hesitation is the distinctive feature separating the literature of the fantastic from overlapping genres such as the uncanny and the marvelous, a point we need not debate here. Hesitation is marked by the character's inability to explain an extraordinary event as obeying the laws of our normal world, on one hand, or as an "illusion of the senses, . . . a product of the imagination," on the other. It is the reaction of "a person who knows only the laws of [waking] nature, confronting an apparently supernatural [or bizarre] event" (1975, 25). Hesitation is a species-specific reaction and for our purposes may be considered as another form of double-mindedness, in Reichschaffen's sense of the term: to hesitate involves the power of reflection.

But there is no such moment of hesitation in the Poe passage, just as there is no such moment in a dream. The Poe narrator creates and then inhabits a Poe-like world where only Poe-like things can happen. Even though the sentence directly following reads, "I know not how it was, but with the first glimpse of the building a sense of insufferable gloom pervaded my spirit," we have not so much a change to a new emotional state as an atmospheric intensification. Overall, there is a collusion between this world and the self encountering it. Thus the passage is a virtually perfect example of literary single-mindedness and the best word to describe it is *dreamlike*. Here at the very opening of Poe's tale the atmospheric conditions necessary for the advent of the uncanny events to follow are metonymically established through a kind of stylistic "greenhouse effect." And the sense of "impenetrable gloom" that pervades the narrator's spirit pervades the reader's as well; the reader is "on loan to this gloom, which graphically exposes the world-preconditions in which (in due course) a sister will "naturally" rise from her tomb, die (again) simultaneously with her brother, and the great "melancholy house of Usher" will topple from the precipice and disappear, as though in sympathetic remorse, into the "deep and dank tarn" naturally situated below it.

Bizarreness, then, does not simply erupt in uncanny or fantastic fictions but is conditioned and prepared by the possibilities of the scene. And this is the case in dreams as well, though for "scene" and "style" we must substitute terms like *mode* and *medium*; for the dream, unlike fiction, has only one available style and that, as we have seen, is the single-minded style in which bizarreness is the constant behavioral norm. We see this everywhere in dreams in subtle textural ways. Natural and architectural proportions, even when "realistic," are somehow unreliable (more "elastic," in Poulet's word): stairways rise and descend differently; rooms are furnished differently: bathrooms (when you can find them) are either nonfunctional or crowded with people drinking cocktails; car doors open differently, and inside the car seat-ing arrangements are always inadequate, and heaven help you if you decide to drive in traffic or shift into reverse and then try to find the brake. Even bodily motion is different in dreams: everything is either more difficult (try getting out of harm's way or back to your hotel room in a busy city) or much easier to do (flying, skiing, running), as the theme of the dream dictates.

In short, bizarreness in dreams is everywhere and in everything, unquantifiable and pandemic; it is the enzyme that causes the dream image to shimmer with instability and otherness. And this level of bizarreness is precisely what does not survive in dream reports, however fresh and detailed (except perhaps in statements like "Everything was so strange!"), and what encourages us to make a categorical distinction between realistic and bizarre imagery. That this distinction can be more or less accurately made in the light of day is not at issue here; nor am I implying that quantitative studies of bizarreness are not useful, if only in identifying classes of dreamers who, for one reason or another (superior creative abilities, good spatial balance, etc.),[4] manifest a higher order of bizarreness in their dreams. I'm simply suggesting that bizarreness should not be regarded only as obvious visual deformation but as a continuous and ever-dynamic process that is virtually synonymous with imagination itself—at least in the sense that imagination is the power of the mind to decompose received conceptions and experiences and to recombine their elements according to a creative association. It is very helpful that cognitive psychologists have discovered a connection between bizarreness and creativity. As with many such discoveries, however, the observation becomes almost tautological after the fact, rather like saying that imaginative people tend to dream more imaginatively.

Looked at from the standpoint of the microdynamics of the dream image, then, bizarreness is the means by which the dream represents objects, persons, or experiences that cannot—in the single-mindedness of the dream state—be isolated from the dreamer's history in time and space. In the dream state we re-create the diachronic world from the standpoint of its synchronic coherence as established in a unique memory. I have no idea whether the function of dreams is to correlate new and old experience or to process new information with old, as John Antrobus (1977) and others (e.g. Evans 1984) have suggested. But it seems an unavoidable conclusion that the dream state somehow enhances the correlational powers of the brain by means of a relaxed cooperation of discrete and qualitative expressiveness—or between a more or less "realistic" representation of a specific subject (say, one's sister) and its membership in a thematic history. We do not know why the dream does this, but we do know that one of the brain's primary activities is to categorize knowledge around part-whole divisions.[5] Therefore, shouldn't the law of parsimony suggest —until we have proof to the contrary—that the distortion of real experience in dreams should be approached as a useful brain function designed to recover a certain "field" of congruity that lies beneath awareness (like the butterfly's ultraviolet patterns) to which the experience itself stands in a synecdochic (or part/whole) relationship?

Hobson would place dream bizarreness at the whim of a chemical substance called acetylcholine and claim that it "is not only gratuitous but even possibly hazardous" (p. 258). I have no expertise in neuroscientific matters and I have no doubt that acetylcholine figures in the dream process, but it is difficult to see why the brain should routinely produce useless and harmful images, especially since these images seem to bear so relevantly on our psychic life. Moreover, if acetylcholine is responsible for bizarre dream images, then it must play a similar role in the formation of bizarre images that occur to me in the waking state. Or, if not, why not? (Was Poe's or Kafka's acetylcholine discharge especially copious?) As Gerald Edelman has cautioned, "It is a long way from acetylcholine to the incest taboo, and great care must be exercised in relating physiological states to the contents of conscious states in language-bearing animals" (1989, 212). Finally, should we not consider that the dream may be as focused, for its own purposes, as most forms of waking thought and that it is making the best of an impossible situation (instantaneous fiction!) by pitching its narrative on the frequency of resemblance, jumping, as Shakespeare's Chorus puts it in *A Winter's Tale*, "o'er times [and] turning the accomplishment of many years" into a single image that (for the time being) represents the accomplishment "cubistically"—that is, not only the frontality (or appearance) of the experience but its spatial and temporal depth as well. The consequence may be an ostensible deformation in the image but the image was not, after all, formed for our understanding any more than the heart beats so that we may hear it.

In saying all of this, I am hardly denying that dreams are capable of representing real life situations in more or less faithful terms. My concern is not to delimit the behavior of dreams but to determine why they so persistently produce images and narratives that fly in the face of waking reality. I am suggesting, in sum, that a key parallel may be found in the images of poetry and fiction which routinely thrive on the bizarre. For example, if we take the lines "My love is a red red rose . . . ," or "Your thighs are appletrees whose blossoms touch the sky," we are not apt to think of them as bizarre, at least in the context of the poem we are reading. And the reason we don't is that our state of reflective double-mindedness anesthetizes a graphic reading of the image and allows us to "see" it as metaphorically intended rather than as literal and grotesque.[6]

The possibility also emerges that the function of dreaming is not simply to create a narrative *about* the dreamer's problems and waking experience—as if the dream were a sort of self-tribunal or confessional—but to use the problems and experience to create a narrative, the narrative being the *final* cause, the problems and experience simply the *material* causes out of which the narrative is made. To take the case of the artist: a novelist may write from one of two standpoints—out of a need to express a social or personal theme in displaced or fictional form, or simply to write a novel. And of course these are not mutually exclusive motives. However, can we say that one motive is more urgent or deeply rooted in the psyche than the other? Some of us create narratives and all of us read the narratives of others because, among other things, they seem to satisfy a universal need for a unified, closed, and imaginary analogue to life in an open-ended and accident-prone world. I am not trying to promote one motive over another, only to suggest that a comprehensive theory of dreaming might consider dreams and fictions as differentia of a common genus and that the procedures and possible motives of one might be seen, *mutatis mutandis*, as operating in the other.

At least one corollary follows from this speculation. If we can see the dream as springing in any sense from a creatural need to make narratives as *ends in themselves*, as a way of "scripting" the possibilities of experience—somewhat as scholars create models and systems that "script" nature, history, etc.—we might extend to the dream the same practice of creative freedom that is enjoyed by the novelist who is always thinking in what we may call a hypothetical, or "what if?," mode. For example, a novelist—the better to create a behavioral horror—would have no scruples whatsoever about using her mother's gentle and loving manner to characterize the victimization of prison inmates by a sadistic "motherly" guard.

So, too, I dream about my friend Paul hypothetically. I dream Paul possibilities—not just likely possiblities (though these are probably the most frequent), but improbable possibilities, even impossibilities. It is far from likely that Paul would betray me in real life. But should the theme of betrayal somehow arise when I am dreaming about Paul, the dream would not hesitate to cast him in the role of betrayer. And he would betray me *as* Paul: that is, in Paul's voice, Paul's wit, Paul's quiet considerate way. Really an improbable Paul, but Paul even so. And what such a dream might be doing for me, thematically, is not revealing an unconscious fear that Paul is capable of betraying me or that he is a displacement of someone else whose potential for betrayal I have repressed. Rather the dream exposes the paradox that is the persistent topic of literary tragedy—as summed up succinctly in Caesar's famous line, "*Et tu, Brute!*"—that the world's potentiality is most thoroughly demonstrated in its capacity for unexpected reversal, or the terminal discrepancy of the *peripeteia.* In short, my dream of Paul—"*Et tu, Paul!*"—would be a version of one of the oldest story plots in the world.

So the dream may, as one of its possible functions, be doing much the same thing as the fiction writer who makes models of the world that carry the imprint and structure of our various concerns. And it does this by using real people, or "scraps" of real people, as the instruments of hypothetical acts (a bit of mother here, a confusion of father and mother there, a friend cast as foe, and voila! a Frankenstein). As we all know, most dream narratives are mundane, rather like life: Paul and I are playing tennis; Paul wins or I win, or the dream, having something else up its sleeve, takes us both to lunch. But now and then, a dream becomes extraordinary: Paul and I are playing tennis and we are interrupted by the dancing bears I saw on the TV two nights ago. In the perfect vacuum of the dream's metaphor chamber there is nothing to keep dancing bears and dancing tennis players apart once the association has occurred. As we say: bizarre! But would it be bizarre if during a real tennis game, being played on a real court at mid-morning, Paul should suddenly do something bear-like that reminded me for an instant of the same dancing bears? Obviously not. Unless of course real dancing bears should thereupon suddenly appear on the court. Now that would be bizarre, cause for a radical "*hesitation*": something happened in one *Umwelt* according to the natural laws of another—which is simply to say, a dream come true.

Notes

1. Lucid dream theorists will certainly challenge my assumptions in what follows. My problem is that outside of certain tantalizing experiences on the hypnopompic fringe I have never experienced what I could seriously call a lucid dream; and since my approach here is substantially phenomenological—that is, based on my own perception of dreaming—it is difficult to know how to deal with something I haven't experienced at first hand. Basically, I have the same reservations about lucid dreams as Gordon Globus: any

reflective or lucid act performed during sleep—such as awareness that "This is only a dream"—is necessarily carried out within the condition of dreaming; otherwise, one would be awake within the dream, a patent impossibility. "The lucid dreamer," Globus says, "does whatever he or she decides to do, and wherever he or she decides to do it, *within that dream horizon*, and that horizon is clearly not the horizon for [waking] phenomenological reflection" (1987, 88). I add hastily that these reservations are unexamined and based on a pronounced degree of ignorance about lucid dream research on my part. Therefore, rather than deny the possibility that lucid dreamers are experiencing genuine and full "reflective awareness" (double-mindedness) within the "dream horizon"—as I am defining these things here—I will simply withhold judgment in the hope that my position on bizarreness may contribute to the debate on dream consciousness. I am really trying to isolate certain differences between waking consciousness and dream consciousness as they relate to the phenomenon of bizarreness. If lucid dreaming falls somewhere between the two states it would be extremely interesting to know, among other things, precisely how "bizarre" dream events are perceived by a lucid dreamer: single-mindedly or double-mindedly?

2. Much has been written about the role of metaphor in dreams, but of particular relevance here is an essay by Montague Ullman which discusses dreams as "rapidly changing presentational sequences which in their unity amount to a metaphorical statement." Since metaphor "involves the use of word or image in an improbable context," they are apt to be attended by "incongruity of elements, inappropriate relations, [and] displacement" (p. 697). Indeed, Ullman goes on, "The task before the dreamer is to express relations he has never before experienced" (p. 699). "Dreaming as Metaphor in Motion," *Archives of General Psychiatry* 21 (December 1969), pp. 696–703.

3. I take up this question in the chapter on "Metaphor" in *The Rhetoric of Dreams* (Ithaca: Cornell University Press, 1988), pp. 125–149.

4. See Harry T. Hunt, "The Multiplicity of Dreams," *ASD Newsletter* 7 (no. 5) (Sept.-Oct., 1990), pp. 9–11, which discusses the relation of bizarreness to spatial balance. For a review of work that has been done on the correlation of bizarreness and creativity in general, too numerous to list here, see also Hunt's *Multiplicity of Dreams: Memory, Imagination, and Consciousness* (New Haven and London: Yale University Press, 1989), pp. 8–14 and *passim*. Like Globus's *Sleep Life, Wake Life*, Hunt's book is indispensable to an understanding of the whole question of dreaming and imagination and the peculiar freedoms and limitations in mentation that arise from the dream state. Some of my own ideas here, though substantially developed prior to reading their work, are prolongations of theirs, aimed at a closer examination of similarities in the poetic and dream processes.

5. George Lakoff discusses part-whole relations in *Women, Fire, and Dangerous Things: What Categories Reveal About the Mind* (Chicago and London, University of Chicago Press, 1987), p. 47 and *passim*.

6. I deal more fully with this process of de-literalizing of the poetic image in "Dreaming and Storytelling," *Hudson Review* 43 No. 1 (Spring 1990), 21–37.

References

Antrobus, John S. "The Dream as Metaphor: An Information-Processing and Learning Model." *Journal of Mental Imagery* 2 (1977), 327–338.

Boss, Medard. *"I dreamt last night . . . ."* New York: Gardner Press, 1977.

Burke, Kenneth. *A Grammar of Motives and a Rhetoric of Motives.* Cleveland and New York: World Publishing Co., 1962.

Casey, Edward S. *Imagining: A Phenomenological Study.* Bloomington and London: Indiana University Press, 1979.

Crick, Francis and Graeme Mitchison. "REM Sleep and Neural Nets." *Journal of Mind and Behavior* 7, nos. 2–3 (1986), 231.

Edelman, Gerald M. *The Remembered Present: A Biological Theory of Consciousness.* New York: Basic Books, 1989.

Evans, Christopher. *Landscapes of the Night: How and Why We Dream.* New York: Viking, 1983.

Foulkes, David. *Dreaming: A Cognitive-Psychological Analysis.* New Jersey and London: Lawrence Erlbaum, 1985.

Fraser, J. T. "Out of Plato's Cave: The Natural History of Time," *Kenyon Review* (Winter, 1980), 143–162.

Globus, Gordon. *Dream Life, Wake Life: The Human Condition Through Dreams.* Albany: State University of New York Press, 1987.

Goodman, Nelson. *Of Mind and Other Matters.* Cambridge, Mass.: Harvard University Press, 1984.

Hall, Calvin S. *The Meaning of Dreams*. New York: McGraw Hill, 1966.

Hobson, J. Allan. *The Dreaming Brain*. New York: Basic Books, 1988.

Hofstadter, Douglas R. *Godel, Escher, Bach: An Eternal Golden Braid*. New York: Random House, 1979.

Koestler, Arthur. *The Act of Creation*. London: Macmillan, 1969.

Poulet, Georges. "Criticism and the Experience of Inferiority," *Reader-Response Criticism: From Formalism to Post-Structuralism*. Edited by Jane P. Tompkins. Baltimore and London: Johns Hopkins University Press, 1980, 40–49. Also in *The Structuralist Controversy: The Language of Criticism and the Sciences of Man*. Edited by Richard A. Macksey and Eugenio Donato. Baltimore: Johns Hopkins, 1972, 56–72.

Reichschaffen, Allan. "The Single-Mindedness and Isolation of Dreams," *Sleep* I (1978), 97–109.

Todorov, Tzvetan. *The Fantastic: A Structural Approach to a Literary Genre*. Translated by Richard Howard. Ithaca: Cornell University Press, 1975.

Ullman, Montague. "Dreaming as Metaphor in Motion," *Archives of General Psychiatry* 21 (December 1969), 696–703.

Warnock, Mary. *Imagination*. Berkeley and Los Angeles: University of California Press, 1978.

3. Real Dreams, Literary Dreams, and the Fantastic in Literature

Laurence M. Porter

Manifestations of the paranormal—to say nothing of the super-natural—in literature seem to paralyze critics' faculties so that they become unable to make clear generic distinctions. Anything that violates what we consider to be natural laws, or what a philosopher might call our sense of nomological necessity, is usually called "fantastic." Myths, fairy tales, surrealistic narratives, fantasies, utopias, the art story with supernatural content, and dream narratives are all lumped together under this rubric.

Once we go beyond the feature unifying such stories—they all refer to a state of affairs that is patently unreal—we find that dream narratives occupy an anomalous position. They present images that lead us through experiences such as flying or metamorphosis or time travel, and yet dreams are an everyday occurrence. Fantasy and the fantastic, in contrast, depict an unprecedented adventure, a one-time event that never can be repeated (as the didactic impulse waxes stronger, as in C. S. Lewis's *The Chronicles of Narnia*, Tolkien's *The Lord of the Rings*, or Frank Herbert's *Dune Chronicles*, the fantastic world that serves as its vehicle becomes increasingly routinized and is reencountered). "Dreams," moreover, refer to something either real or literary, whereas the fantastic refers only to something in a book or other artistic medium. Comparing dreams and the fantastic in literature should help us understand the role of dreams as part of a work of art.

The Ancient Greeks' two words for "dream" reveal a clarity of interpretation that we no longer possess, as well as a greater importance for the dream than we are willing to grant it today. *Enypnion* meant any quasi-visual event in sleep, one that could be caused by indigestion, a troubled mind, or memories. *Oneiros* meant a dream that entered our mind through the ivory gate, a message from the gods. Today, four distinct sleep events—ordinary dreams, nightmares, night terrors (apparently nonvisual), and the recurring dreams of post-traumatic stress syndrome—have been correlated with differences in brain chemistry, but in everyday speech we rely upon the feeling tone rather than any formal features to allow us to distinguish, say, between dreams and nightmares.[1] We tend to distinguish bland or pleasurable ordinary dreams from anxiety dreams (akin to the literary mode of the uncanny) and from nightmares (with a feeling tone of panic akin to that of the literary fantastic in the strict sense that I shall develop below).

The real dream must, of course, be distinguished from the literary dream. The real dream seems to consist of a stimulus provoking one level of distortion: the translation of the initial stimulus into images. How and why this translation occurs is open to dispute. Freud believed that unconscious desires, forever straining to emerge into consciousness, were blocked by the censor (the inhibiting function of the superego, or moral sense), and could find expression only in disguised form after undergoing condensation, symbolization, and displacement. They would emerge as the symptoms of physical or mental illness, as *parapraxes* (saying, writing, or doing things we did not intend; accidents, mislaying, forgetting, and so forth), and as dreams. Recently, Hobson and McCarley speculated in their "activation-synthesis" hypothesis that electrical impulses from the brain stem during sleep produce patterns of colored dots inside the retina, out of which our brain then attempts to make sense by gathering from the day residue and other memories any materials that it can. Bert O. States even more recently summarized the hypothesis that the brain, like a computer, needs the "down time" of sleep in order to process the floods of information that it has encountered during the day, and also speculated that dream imagery may, as hypnotic imagery does, serve the purposes of rehearsal and practice for everyday tasks.[2] Freud's repeated claim in *The Interpretation of Dreams* that "a dream is a [disguised] fulfillment of a [repressed] wish" has not been supported by modern research,[3] but Hobson and McCarley have not explained either why the sleeping brain makes one kind of sense—one kind of selection—rather than another.

To place the question of the nature of the literary dream, and its relationship to the fantastic, into sharper focus, it would be well to begin with a real dream. Here is one of mine, with the sentences numbered for ease of reference. Expressions in brackets did not appear in the manifest dream (in the first version I wrote down), but have been added for clarification:

1. I am walking along the road with my [older] brother.

2. We see the cast-off skin of a huge poisonous snake lying in the grass.[4]

3. The snake is heading the same way we are.

4. A cyclone fence to our left separates us from the road.

5. The snake comes around the end of the fence [ahead of us], and attacks us.

6. I have a stick or rod in my hand.

7. I hit the snake in the head [with the rod].

8. It is wounded, and draws back.

Notice, first of all, the simple one-clause sentence structure, a pattern broken only in 5 and 8, with the briefest possible additional verbal phrase. The vocabulary is simple and concrete. There are no verb tenses other than the present tense, and no modals (wish, hypothesis, necessity).[5] There are no adverbs (indicators of intensity). The few adjectives in the manifest content (in 2 and 4) are heavily loaded with emotional connotations. When a snake casts off its skin it becomes bigger; it is reborn. "Huge" and "poisonous" enhance the threat; "cyclone" once again suggests something powerful and overwhelming. Finally, the dream is quite short; only 67 words. In years of recording my dreams, I never have needed more than 500 words. The manifest content of the dream accurately renders the effect of a timeless series of discrete images.

In practice, the real dream represents an example of knowing more than you tell. Even after I have eliminated from this present chapter the details of the therapeutic situation and many associations from my personal history, the flow of meanings that occur to me remains abundant. I shall provide dates in parentheses to convey a sense of the mosaic quality of the references in the dream. At the time of dreaming (1985), my older brother, an autistic (1934–1980), had died five years before. Being with him is on the one hand simple wish fulfillment—we were walking down the road hand in hand—and on the other hand a closer association than I can feel comfortable with, since my identification with him cuts me off from the world of "normal" people. Walking along the road symbolizes moving with the irreversible flow of time (by the time I have the stick in my hand, my brother has disappeared from the dream); by aging, I have "caught up with" a younger relative, a replacement for the lost brother, but that person has also caught up with me by presenting anew the threat of alienation.

The only poisonous snake I have ever seen in the wild was a large copperhead, sunning itself on a path (1943). The ugly brownish colors and lumpy shape of the dream reptile remind me of excrement; "copperhead" was chosen because of its resemblance to "copro-", the combining form of a Greek word meaning "excrement" (a detail learned sometime between 1953 and 1963). The snake is a "shithead." Mental illness messes up your head. The snake, as detached phallus, also suggests castration; my brother never could have sex with a woman, to say nothing of getting married or having children, and I know that he suffered from that incapacity. If I became mentally ill, the same thing (castration) could happen to me. I suddenly realize in the dream that mental illness is my destiny (the snake is going the same way that I am, and my autistic brother is my traveling companion), and then I immediately feel fenced off from normal people on the road (3 and 4). The fence is both cause (the destructive natural disturbance of the cyclone) and effect (separation from others). You can see through a cyclone fence (see others), but not get through it (communicate with others). It is associated in my mind with a cyclone fence I once saw when walking outdoors during a fall hurricane (1956). It stood between the edge of a park and a lake. The rushing torrents of a five-inch rain had plastered dead leaves all over the four-foot-high fence, transforming it into a dam over which the flood waters from the elevated regions of downtown were pouring violently. I wondered whether the fence would stand up against the pressure. I fear mental illness; it's probably hereditary in my family; a younger cousin is also autistic. But then the fence (5 and 6) provides a defense. "Stick or rod" represents an ambiguous, unresolved image complex, divided between nature (the stick) and culture (the rod), or internal and external resources. As often in real dreams, ambiguity poses a question here: "Can I make it (ward off madness) on my own?" To the extent that the rod comes from the fence it represents the metal lithium (used to medicate some forms of mental illness), and the doctor's phallic hypodermic needle (containing within itself both cause and effect: Moses' rod and the water that gushed forth from the rock he struck with it). If we cannot turn the tables by wounding mental illness in the head before it can wound us in ours, at least we can hold it at bay, like the Son of Man who crushed Satan's head beneath his heel (extensive Bible readings, 1958). My anxiety concerning mental illness has reemerged just now to incite the dream because a beloved younger relative has recently been diagnosed as having a bipolar ("manic-depressive") disorder, and has been medicated with lithium. Reborn in this close relative like a snake with a new skin, hereditary mental illness has reappeared in my life to threaten me once again. But this time there is a hope for cure that did not exist with my brother. The threat has been mitigated by the implied revelation of a solution.

How does a literary dream relate to a real one? Just as the bright images of the real dream communicate a moment of special potential insight, a privileged moment in the dark world of sleep, so the literary dream from earliest times can bring us a revelation. But the form of the literary dream tends to be radically different. One concrete example is worth a thousand abstract words. This dream, like mine, was overtly inspired by anxiety. It was dreamt by the fictional Dimitri in Dostoevsky's *The Brothers Karamazov*.[6]

> Some one is hunting me, some one I'm awfully afraid of . . . he's hunting me in the dark, in the night . . . tracking me, and I hide somewhere from him, behind a door or cupboard, hide in a degrading way, and the worst of it is, he always knows where I am, but he pretends not to know where I am on purpose, to prolong my agony, to enjoy my terror. (p. 572)

This recurrent dream is almost exactly the length of mine, but it differs from the real dream through its melodramatic qualities. The feeling tone (ordinarily recuperable only from the associations to the real dream, and not from its manifest text) is repeatedly specified by Dimitri: "awfully afraid . . . degrading . . . agony . . . terror." The emotionality of the account is further enhanced by word repetition and otiose (in terms of the practical exigencies of communication) synonymity ("some one; hunting; dark/night; hide; agony/terror"). The entire dream is rendered in one complex, hypertactic (that is, composed of interlocking clauses), intellectually processed sentence. Uncharacteristically for most real dreams, the motives of the antagonist are specified (in the manifest content of my real dream, we had no notion why the snake was attacking), and the concept of pretense associated with Dimitri's persecutor distinguishes between two levels, appearance and reality. Both these details introduce into the literary dream a dual perspective in contrast to the unvarying single viewpoint of the real dream.

Moreover, real dreams simply appear before our eyes abruptly once we begin the REM phase of sleep, with its identifiable pattern of brain waves. The literary dream, in contrast, typically relies on heavy-handed labeling and framing to distinguish itself from its context. Dimitri is being interrogated by his prosecutors in an investigation into the murder of his father, Fyodor Pavlovich. This experience has been making him feel like a hunted animal, and he tells his dream to explain why he feels reluctant to speak in response to his examiners' questions. The explicit framing words have been emphasized:

> "You see, I listen to you and am haunted by *a dream. It's a dream* I have sometimes, you know . . . I often *dream it—it's* always the same . . . [the dream account quoted above follows] That's just what you're doing now. It's just like that [explicit interpretive connection]!"
> "Is that the sort of thing you *dream* about?" inquired the prosecutor.
> "Yes, *it* is. Don't you want to write *it* down?" said Mitya, with a distorted smile.
> "No; no need to write *it* down. But still you do have curious *dreams* "
> "It's not a question of *dreams* now, gentlemen—this is realism, this is real life! I'm a wolf and you're the hunters. Well, hunt him down!"

In addition to the repeated labeling of part of the text as "dream" either with that word itself or with the pronoun "it," the recurrence of the pronoun "you" (three times just before the dream account, and five after) stresses the communicative situation. The language of Dostoevsky's framing makes it clear that his literary dream is an entity that is in the process of being communicated by the dreamer to other people, whereas the real dream is a message for the dreamer alone. At the end of chapter 8 of the same book, Dimitri's more famous dream of the weeping babe (too long to analyze here) is again framed before and after it appears by the notation of a change of state of consciousness, by the label "dream," and by a sense of dissociation from waking reality:

> . . . instantly *fell asleep.* He had a *strange dream,* utterly out of keeping with the place and the time. [dream account follows]
> "What! Where?" he exclaimed *opening his eyes,* and sitting up on the chest, *as though he had revived from a swoon* . . . *he did not hear Nikolay Parfenovich. . . .*
> "I've had a good *dream,* gentlemen," he said in a *strange* voice, with a new light, as of joy, on his face. (pp. 615–16)

And the beginning of the next chapter explains that Dimitri has come to accept his punishment in the spirit of Christian resignation, because he is innocent of the deed, but guilty of the intention, to murder his father.

Leaving aside the question of whether any particular literary dream has a real dream as its ultimate source, we can therefore distinguish three major differences between literary dreams and real dreams. First, as Freud explained, the [manifest] content of the [real] dream is much shorter than the thoughts for which it is a substitute: it is condensed and laconic. Primary elaboration is the unconscious process that finds ways of representing feelings and thoughts via visual images. Secondary elaboration is the largely unreflective translation of these images into a verbal dream account by the dreamer, who during this process unwittingly eliminates anomalies and papers over discrepancies. In literary dreams, in contrast, secondary elaboration becomes not only the inevitable by-product, but also the conscious aim of the reporting of fantasies. Rather than abridging, it expatiates, to the point that the literary critic Albert Sonnenfeld proposed the term "tertiary elaboration" to distinguish the linguistic encoding of literary dreams from that of real dreams. Repeatedly, for months, years, or decades (as with Goethe's *Faust*), the author masks the original subconscious sources of his fantasy with layers of elaborate detail, carefully selected, lovingly expanded, harmoniously patterned. In therapy, tertiary elaboration is the collaborative product of the client and the therapist, and it leads back to the root feelings so that they can eventually be recognized and assimilated into the conscious psyche. In writing, tertiary elaboration continues unchecked by dialogue (like the compulsive talking of the client who uses it as a form of defense), to generate an enormous superstructure of rationalization and concealing patterns. The foremost guideline in the literary maze, however, is the same as in the therapeutic one: it is the axiom that the point of greatest distortion betrays the point of access to the strongest affect.

Second, literary dreams are surrounded in the adjacent text by explicit labels, framing, and interpretation. We must at once point out, of course, that such labels are most untrustworthy. How do you recognize a true literary dream when you see one? In therapy, if a client reports a "dream," one can usually take the label at face value, rather than needing to examine whether the supposed dream narrative is not really the account of something read, or of someone else's dream, or of something actually done by the client. But in literature before the Romantic period, and frequently thereafter, the author announces a "dream" when she really means that we are about to encounter a different level of meaning such as allegory, divinely inspired visions, encounters with the supernatural, and so forth. The label "dream," like the label "joke," may actually serve mainly to allow an author to express embarrassing or controversial thoughts more safely, evading responsibility and social disapproval. In practice, literature tends not to distinguish between dreams, fantasies, hallucinations, and visions; but a frequent clue to the onset of an implicit literary dream is the notation of gathering darkness, followed by a description of artificial light or moonlight. This corresponds, so to speak, to illuminated images coming onto the screen of our closed eyelids in real dreams. Sometimes a description of wordless sound is introduced as well to suggest a meaning as yet undefined but one which may gradually gain in clarity. And the dream narrative, in accordance with its fundamental subjectivity, tends to be reported in the first person.

The literary dream proper also tends to be morally ambiguous: it has not yet been filtered through the superego. Like the real dream, it protects the dreamer from fearsome or repellent tendencies of his own personality by the doubling or splitting off of characters. The literary dream commonly employs the layering of narration, implying psychic regression by suddenly shifting to an earlier period or periods, with or without a change in the identities of the characters. The resulting structure corresponds to the psychologist's layer-cake model of the psyche, where an adult personality overlays multiple strata of adolescent, childhood, and infantile selves, which remain dynamically active throughout life. Finally, the archetype of conversion transforms the previous evaluation of experience to suggest an understanding transformed by the irruption of the unconscious into the dream narrative. So we may be told that sleep is creativity, madness is insight, disgrace is triumph, and death is liberation. This interpretive gesture integrates the literary dream account into the overall aesthetic structure, by connecting it to an overarching network of meanings.

And third, the latent content of the literary dreams of deceased authors, or authors lacking the time or patience to be interviewed by us, is inaccessible by direct means. It is fashionable to deride those who would speculate on the "hidden" sentiments and motives of fictional characters: their feelings "are not real feelings, but fictive, linguistic feelings: that is to say, feelings which are exhausted by the totality of utterances by which the narration *signifies* them." If one refers the acts of characters to a "deeper" reality (one constituted, most plausibly, by the historical author's life or other works, or both), one is psychoanalyzing the author or the reader—in other words, the reverberations of the text outside the domain of its own discourse.[7] Well and good, but any message needs interpretants (the elements of common and personal knowledge that allow us to infer what something means) in order to be transmitted. In any interpersonal communication, we find the "deeper" meanings by appealing to our responses to others' verbal and nonverbal gestures. It is true that when we confront a [dream] text, we cannot expect it to respond to our questions as a person could respond, denying or confirming the validity of the connotations it evokes in us.

Finally, the unconscious life (as consciously known to the author) of a literary character or implied author may be revealed by linguistic features that make the text superdetermined (repetition, punning, syllepsis, conflation) or underdetermined (ellipsis, antithesis, preterition, litotes). When my excellent typist made only two mistakes in twenty pages of an article—both on the word "infidelity"—I knew that something was up. Gaps and inconsistencies in the text provide clues to the latent content of the literary dream, and the motivation for such discontinuities, fear of self-knowledge, usually is implied in the immediate context.

For example, the narrator of Nerval's *Aurélia* (the greatest work in French visionary Romanticism) has been allowed to install his possessions in his room at the asylum where he is being treated. As he goes through his papers, he discovers old love letters to "my only love," who has since rejected him and then, even more perversely, died. He has the following dream:

> Then I thought I found myself in the middle of an enormous slaughterhouse where world history was written in letters of blood. The body of a gigantic woman was painted opposite me; only, her various parts were sliced off as if by a saber; other women of various races and whose bodies piled up higher and higher, formed a bloody, tangled heap of limbs and heads on the other walls. It was the history of all crime.[8]

Aurélia is unusual because it has the status of a great *work* of art, yet it grew out of the dreams and fantasies which Nerval was encouraged to write down as part of his inpatient therapy. At this time, he also made drawings and sculptures of the mystical world presided over by his former love in the form of a goddess.

The text literally breaks off with an ellipsis after the phrase "my only love," referring to Aurélia. The text earlier told us she is dead. Here the apocalyptic vision of universal destruction, related to the author's preoccupation throughout the work with lost civilizations and lost gods, betrays his secret wish to end a world where he has been defeated, so as to substitute a new order. In "A Case of Paranoia," Freud comments on such fantasies:

> The patient has withdrawn from the people in his environment and from the external world generally the libidinal cathexis which he has hitherto directed on to them. Thus everything has become indifferent and irrelevant to him. . . . The end of the world is the projection of this internal catastrophe; his subjective world has come to an end since his withdrawal of his love from it. . . . The delusional formation, which we take to be the pathological product, is in reality an attempt at recovery, a process of reconstruction.[9]

The ellipsis dissociates Nerval's narrator from his own unresolved anger. He has to repress it, or otherwise he will lose his self-image as an ideal lover, selflessly undergoing ordeals and seeking no reward. If he allows himself to feel angry, he will feel undeserving. The gigantic woman's body is not only Aurélia's in disguise, but the heaps of bodies together with hers suggest all society, which like Aurélia has rejected the narrator by declaring him insane. At the same time, the fragmentation represents his feeling about his own shattered identity. The introductory "I thought," as with frequent other uses of terms referring to belief and to appearance in Nerval's work, stakes out a domain intermediate between the objective and the subjective, a domain which is neither entirely dream nor waking, but which represents "the overflowing of the dream into daily life," as Nerval puts it earlier in the same work.

The phrase "I thought" introduces indirect discourse (the verbal representation of the thoughts or words of a fictional character, without quoting her verbatim) clearly ascribed to the fictional character and therefore suspect of subjectivity. In the fantastic narrative, in contrast, free indirect discourse (lacking the explicit identification of the perceiving character and of the mode in which the message is presented) creates an ambiguous zone between author and character, into which either may move. In Michel Tournier's *The Ogre*, for example, the title character has ideas of reference: he thinks that everything in the cosmos is directly related to him. He is convinced that his school burned down to spare him from punishment for running away; that World War II started in order to save him from being imprisoned because of a false accusation of rape; and that the fall of Nazi Germany occurred to free him from captivity there in order to fulfill his destiny. When he first reaches the concentration camp for French prisoners of war in eastern Prussia, the text comments:

> Tiffauges felt a strong bond uniting him to the place. To begin with—and perhaps for a long time—he was its prisoner, and it was his duty to serve it with his whole body and with his whole heart. But this would be only a probation period, a betrothal; afterward, by one of those fundamental inversions that ordered his life, he would be its master.[10]

The first sentence provides what the French would call a focalization: it reveals who is experiencing the events, and from what point of view—here, from an instinctive feeling. The latter two sentences, in represented (free indirect) discourse, blur the distinction between the subjective protagonist and the objective implied author, who throughout the novel shares narrative authority with the former. Thus the delusions of the protagonist seep through into the world view of the omniscient narrator. The mad certitude of the ogre, Abel Tiffauges, that he stands at the crux of history and that he will be able to raise Prussia "to a higher power" (p. 180), contrasts sharply with the anxiety and doubt attendant upon most modern literary dreams.

So the mentions of world history which frame the dream narrative cited previously from Nerval's *Aurélia*, for example, introduce an alien totalization into the dream, a self-conscious relationship with tradition that represents an attempt to reconstitute an identity by gathering together fragments from all periods and religious traditions. And the saving final clause, "It was the history of all crimes," dissociates the narrator from his anger by ascribing it to others, and then condemning it morally. The emotional impasse, however, never is resolved because the perpetrators of these crimes (since they are the narrator in disguise) never are identified and dealt with. The vision breaks off with another abrupt transition.

In many respects, then, the literary dream appears to be nearly the opposite of the fantastic. I consider the fantastic to be a subclass of fantasy, which is in turn a subclass of fiction. To begin at the beginning, in nonfiction the subject is ostensibly part of the real world. The subject of realistic fiction is not presented as part of the real world, but the fictional world still conforms to our sense of what is physically possible. In hypothetical fictions such as pastoral, science fiction, utopias, and fantasies based on a single, clearly stated eccentric premise (examples being Marcel Aymé's man who could walk through walls in "Le Passe-Muraille," or the phantom girl child called into being on the high seas by a sailor's longing thought in Jules Supervielle's "L'Enfant de la haute mer"), the subject can be easily extrapolated from the world we know. In the uncanny, usually a mood of anxiety builds steadily without any identifiable cause. Other subclasses of fantasy contain multiple violations of plausibility, which they each explain in different ways: through the cultural conventions of a familiar genre such as the fairy tale or legend, fable or myth (the marvelous); or through the arbitrary choice of the implied author.

What distinguishes the fantastic proper, as I understand it, from all other forms of fantasy literature, is that the possible supernatural intervention is an unprecedented event; it is not explained, and so indeterminacy is preserved until the end of the narrative.[11] If indeterminacy is nor preserved, we modulate into a form of hypothetical fantasy such as in Gaston Leroux's *Phantom of the Opera*, where the strange events are at last explained through the title character's preternatural (but not supernatural) skills as a musician, architect, and ventriloquist. The fantastic usually disrupts the narrative chain in the middle with a peripety of category—a reversal of the binary oppositions that shape our experience and help us make sense of ourselves and the world: such oppositions as self and other, divine and human, human and animal, innocence and experience, male and female, living and dead, animate and inanimate, past and future, here and elsewhere. Perhaps the most common form of such disruption is the "living dead" in Poe's *The Fall of the House of Usher* and many other tales. The fantastic event immediately constitutes an emergency and all the energies of the protagonist are mobilized in an attempt to deal with it. In contrast, the literary dream may create category confusion from the beginning, but such perceptual blurring is taken for granted and, as in real dreams, the protagonist tends to be carried passively along or flees rather than actively resisting his or her fate.

Fantastic narratives and many fantasies in general, unlike the dream, rationalize their unnatural transformations with a host of transitional devices lacking in the real or literary dream. The major classes of such objective correlatives for ontological change are the costume, the magical object, the threshold, and the journey. The costume is more typical of the marvelous rather than of the fantastic proper. When hyperbolized to metamorphosis it can become parodic, as in Lautréamont's sixth *Chant de Maldoror* where the protagonist as master criminal can become a cricket or a cloud of mist at will. In dreamlike works such as Kafka's "Metamorphosis," however, the initial transformation functions in a way similar to a hypothesis that is not questioned. In works of fantasy other than literary dreams, magical objects often generate secondary rationalizations for why they have become available to or inflicted on the protagonist. The myth of the magical object's origins, for example, generates a parasitical narrative chain. This secondary narrative provides a conventional or pseudo-explanation for the transformation. The cohesion of this secondary metonymic chain that results (a description of an effect that in turn becomes the cause of the next effect, and so forth, in a virtual linking that is the primary illusion of narrative) can restore the illusion of continuity in the disrupted primary chain by being juxtaposed with it. The coherence of the secondary narrative is then transferred to the primary narrative by virtue of the magical principle of contagion.

In Goethe's *Faust*, for example, the hero is rejuvenated by thirty years after sealing a pact with the Devil. The transition between the story of the fifty-year-old Faust and that of the twenty-year-old Faust is effected by the Devil, but the Devil must seek help, for he cannot by himself rejuvenate. His assistants, the witches, prepare a potion; but these witches are in turn aided by the technical equipment of the elaborately depicted kitchen. And there a third level of personified transitional agents, simian familiars (the first two levels being the Devil and the witches), work as scullions. Thus to overrationalize an already-accepted myth, of course, amounts to undercutting it through tacit irony.

In a more explicitly dreamlike setting, Charles Nodier's *Crumb Fairy* effects a transition to the central narrative through a fourfold progression. Twilight falls (a change of lighting is a widespread Romantic device for indicating a change of perception); the frame narrator falls asleep; his valet Daniel (his imagination personified) suggests a journey across the water to Scotland; and there the frame narrator visits a madhouse where he hears the central dream narrative from a narrator who got there himself via a fantastic voyage. Such a self-conscious accumulation of artifice, used to provide a doorway to the literary dream, characterizes the earlier periods of Romanticism.

Unlike the literary dream, which is heavily framed but still localized, the literary fantastic makes its effects felt throughout the narrative with what one might call pervasive or supersegmental transitions. I would characterize such textual elements as "metonymic debris." It is as if the explosion of causality in the central disruptive transformation had thrown shards of fragmented connectedness through the work, in the form of foreshadowings (such as the footfall and a child's distant cry during the governess's first night in the isolated mansion of *The Turn of the Screw*), or of traces such as the horse's hoofprints, fallen hat, and shattered pumpkin that are all that remain of Ichabod Crane at the end of Washington Irving's "The Legend of Sleepy Hollow."

What most prominently characterizes the fantastic, in my opinion, as it characterizes the detective novel, is the foregrounding of the "hermeneutic code," which means everything in the text (starting, nearly always, with the title) that poses riddles, raises questions, and then deals with attempts to answer them and with the outcomes of such attempts to answer them. The detective gathers clues—traces of the criminal's activity—and reconstitutes the past event with reliable methods that always sum to a solution. Detective fiction exalts the methods by which we learn the truth. Being unprecedented and incomprehensible, the fantastic also foregrounds the hermeneutic code, but it does not resolve the enigma; it prolongs it. Indeed, a number of works such as Balzac's "The Elixir of Long Life" or *The Wild Ass's Skin*, Maupassant's "Le Horla" or Villiers de l'Isle-Adam's *Future Eve* (featuring Thomas Edison, who makes a mechanical woman), emphasize the defeat of science and the experimental method in the face of the fantastic: they mock the pretensions of nineteenth-century positivism and scientism. In both the detective story and the fantastic, however, on the quest for understanding hangs the story. The presence of a protagonist who persists in trying to figure things out creates a secondary effect of cohesion that compensates for the primary disruption characteristic of these genres. Whereas the hero of a fairy story never stops to wonder why animals speak, fairies grant wishes, and dragons breathe fire, and the hero of a literary dream never wonders at the sudden changes of time, place, and identity that he encounters without warning, the heroes of detective or fantastic tales spend most of their time puzzling over why things are happening as they do. In mysteries and in suspense stories the cultural code—tried and true methods of investigation and detection—works to resolve the hermeneutic problem. But in the fantastic the cultural code works against a solution, since everything that the protagonist already knows will prove useless. By presenting an answer immediately the literary dream, in contrast, tends to short-circuit the hermeneutic code; it is often a privileged moment of insight that synthesizes. Note, for example, the accumulation of verbs of cognition (emphasis added) in the dream expressing Winston's survivor guilt in *Nineteen Eighty-Four.*

> Winston was dreaming of his mother [who disappeared together with his baby sister when Winston was ten or eleven; a paragraph of description of his family follows]. . . . He was out in the light and air while they were being sucked down to death, and they were down there *because* [emphasis in original] he was up here. He *knew* it and they *knew* it, and he *could see the knowledge* in their faces or in their hearts, only *the knowledge* that they *must* die *in order that* he might remain alive, and that this was part of *the unavoidable order of things.*[12]

Being saved by the interposition of a female body will form a major strand of Winston's identity theme (for example, only Julia and not he is struck by the Thought Police when they are arrested), a vignette that will be reenacted many times. Of these instances, Winston's cry "Do it to Julia" when he is about to be devoured by rats is only the most notorious. In other words, not only is this literary dream framed in certitude in its immediate context, but it also possesses an explanatory power that carries over into many other parts of the host novel.

This fact points to a final and important resemblance between the literary dream and the fantastic. Whereas the marvelous and the detective story follow familiar, and sometimes even formulaic lines, the text of most recent (nonallegorical) literary dreams and of fantastic tales describes an event (mental or exterior) that is as unprecedented as a poem. You might say that each is an example of the hapax (a term used to describe a word that appears only once in all the known literature of a given language). Therefore the frame for both these forms is essential for creating a transition from the ordinary to the unique. The frame narrator so often found in the fantastic fulfills the same function as the framing words of the literary dream; they both anchor the vision to a known category.

Labeling something as a dream in literature tends to enhance the stature of the character who has dreamed. That character either recovers his or her mastery of events ("it was only a dream"), or else brings back from the dream a moment of special insight. In contrast, the label of the fantastic tends to imply a peculiar blindness or deflation of the character, who cannot cope with events and who becomes expendable. The fantastic tends to foreground possibly supernatural *beings* who, if they are not real, are unrecognized psychic projections; the dream narrative tends to foreground extrarational thought *processes*, manifest in the metaphorical discontinuities of free association. The motivation of such supernatural beings, however enigmatic, appears consistent; James's ghosts in *The Turn of the Screw*, if they are real, keep trying to get at the two children; whereas the transitions into and out of the literary dream, and the movement within it, remain unpredictable and capricious.

Notes

1. See Ernest Hartmann, *The Nightmare: The Psychology and Biology of Terrifying Dreams* (New York: Basic Books, 1984). He provides recent biochemical and psychological information on the various types of dreams, thus superseding Ernest Jones's landmark 1931 study.

2. See J. Allan Hobson and Robert W. McCarley, "The Brain as a Dream State Generator: An Activation-Synthesis Hypothesis of the Dream Process," *American Journal of Psychiatry* 134. 12 (December 1977): 1335–48; and the telling refutation by Gerald W. Vogel, "An Alternative View of the Neurobiology of Dreaming," *American Journal of Psychiatry* 135. 12 (December 1978): 1531–35. A recent popularization of this issue is offered by Edward Dolnick, "What Dreams Are (Really) Made Of," *The Atlantic* 266. (July 1990): 41–61; and more extensively by Bert O. States, *The Rhetoric of Dreams* (Ithaca, N.Y.: Cornell University Press, 1988). See also David Foulkes, *Dreaming: A Cognitive-Psychological Analysis* (Hillsdale, N.J.: Lawrence Erlbaum, 1985).

3. Freud, Sigmund. "On Dreams," *The Standard Edition of the Complete Psychological Works.* Translated and edited by James Strachey. Assisted by Anna Freud, Alix Strachey, and Alan Tyson. Vols. 4–5. London: The

Hogarth Press and the Institute of Psycho-Analysis, 1900a. 640–641; Laurence M. Porter, "*The Interpretation of Dreams*": *Freud's Theory Revisited* (Boston: Twayne, 1987), 48–63 and 115.

4. The day residue provided this detail. I'd just been teaching a French novel by Balzac called *The Wild Ass's Skin* (the French name of the animal is a pun on the word for "grief"). The French expression "se faire peau neuve" (to make oneself a new skin) means to renew oneself. In Balzac's novel, the demonic reverse of renewal occurs. Each time the hero makes a wish, the skin shrinks, and when it disappears, he dies. In my dream, in contrast, a new skin for the snake means a renewed threat to me.

5. Applying modals to the unvarnished account of the real dream provides much leverage for the therapist. For example, taking the first statement of my dream, "I am walking along the road with my brother," a neutral declarative mode, and knowing from my associations that he was dead, your natural instinct would be to reflect that "You would like to be with your brother," the optative mode of straight wish-fulfillment. A more canny approach would be to reframe the optative as "Is there a [living] brother with whom you would like to be?" Your probing would elicit the disclosure that I have another brother at an unknown address in Denver. I had felt close to him during his adolescence, but he had cut off contact with the family some seventeen years before the dream; when he called the family in 1980 after the death of our older brother, it was the first time I had heard his voice since 1963. The apodictic mode (of command or necessity), "You feel you should be with your brother," would lead to my admission of a twofold guilt: guilt at having not paid more attention to my brothers and at not having been kinder to them during the time that they were, respectively, alive and available; and survivor guilt at having largely escaped the psychological problems that crippled both of them. The hypothetical mode, "You might be with your brother," produces an admission of the fear that I too might be mentally ill.

6. Fyodor Dostoevsky, *The Brothers Karamazov*, trans. Constance Garnett. Book 9, Ch. 4, (New York: The Modern Library, 1950) 572.

7. Gérard Genette, "Vraisemblance et motivation." In *Figures II* (Paris: Editions du Seuil, 1969), 86n.

8. Gérard de Nerval, *Oeuvres*, ed. Henri Lemaître (Paris: Garnier, 1958), 815 (part II, chapter 6). Translation mine.

9. Freud, Sigmund. *The Standard Edition of the Complete Psychological Works*. Translated and edited by James Strachey. Assisted by Anna Freud, Alix Strachey, and Alan Tyson. 24 vols. London: The Hogarth Press and the Institute of Psycho-Analysis, 1953–74.

10. Michel Tournier, *The Ogre* (New York: Pantheon, 1972), 168.

11. See Laurence M. Porter, "Taft Lecture: Redefining the Fantastic," *Cincinnati Romance Review*, 8 (1989), 1–12.

12. George Orwell, [1948] *Nineteen Eighty-Four* (New York: Signet, 1981), 27–28.

4. In Defense of Nightmares: Clinical and Literary Cases

Jane White-Lewis

Qualitatively different from other dreams, nightmares are universal intrapsychic events that impact dramatically on our lives. The essence of the nightmare is primarily fear and at a body level we feel the fear. Although relatively infrequent for most dreamers, these intense combinations of image and affect demand our attention and are difficult to ignore or forget. Some nightmares imbued with archetypal power are so memorable and arresting that they color our experience of our lives and ourselves for years. Some stay with us for a lifetime. Similarly, when we encounter nightmares in literary form, we, as readers, are engaged imaginatively and physiologically by the compelling intensity of the images. We identify with the terror; we feel the anxiety. Like our own nightmares, a literary nightmare may prove unforgettable and become a part of our imaginal life.

Considering that so many memorable dreams in literature are nightmares and that all nightmares are personally and clinically significant, one wonders why these dreams have received so little attention. The two major dream theorists of our time, Freud and Jung, were not particularly interested in nightmares and neither developed a theory of nightmares. Although numerous other twentieth-century dream theorists have written about nightmares, the focus has been on their pathology. Nightmares are generally considered negative psychological events which torment us and disrupt our sleep. Sometimes there are efforts to understand the causes of nightmares, but usually the emphasis is on mitigating their effects, reducing their frequency, or eliminating them entirely. Psychiatrists recommend medication. Behaviorists speak in pathology-oriented terms and suggest "treatment" strategies for nightmare "sufferers." "Lucid dreamers" advise altering the images and "resolving" the conflicts in the dream

(LaBerge 1985). No theorists have fully appreciated the psychological importance, symbolic value, and teleological potential of these powerful intrapsychic experiences.

Nightmares, like all dreams, live in that domain somewhere between psychology and literature, between nonfiction (day-residues and psychological history) and fiction (creative imagination). Because of the essential dramatic effect of nightmares these dreams have a special relationship to literature. This kinship suggests that some understanding of the psychology and imaginal field of nightmares can enliven and contribute to discussions of nightmares in literature. And vice versa.

What is a nightmare? The most familiar definition is a "dream arousing feelings of intense inescapable fear, horror, and distress" (*The American Heritage Dictionary of the English Language*, 1981). Used metaphorically, a nightmare refers to an inner or outer event, situation, or condition having the character of a terrifying dream. "Nightmare" is also defined as a "demon or spirit thought to plague sleeping people", that is, an incubus or succubus.[1] Although this definition may seem archaic to the modern reader, it may imaginally capture the experience of the nightmare "victim."

The word "nightmare" has a long history; the first recorded usage of the word in English occurred in 1290. The etymology of "nightmare" is interesting as well as somewhat surprising. Whereas the derivation of "night" is obvious and straightforward, the source of "mare" is not. "Night" comes to us via the Old English word *nigh/neaht* and is originally derived from the Indo-European root word for night, *nekut*. *Nux* (Greek), *nox* (Latin), *Nacht* (German), and *nuit* (French) have the same origin. The "mare" of "nightmare," however, is not related to a female horse or mare as is generally assumed, but rather is derived from a Middle English word for succubus, *nihtmare*, which in turn comes from the Old English *mare/maere* meaning goblin or incubus. To go back even farther, *mare* is understood to have descended from the Indo-European root *mer* (to rub away, harm), and is cognate with words for biting (mordent, morsel), disease (morbid), and death (mortal, murder).

The fact that "nightmare" is associated with and visualized as a female horse in the collective imagination is, of course, not psychologically insignificant as Ernest Jones argues in his classic work *On the Nightmare* (1931). In the chapter entitled "The Mare and the Mara: A Psychoanalytical Contribution to Etymology," Jones draws on mythology, folklore, superstition, and literature, and cites numerous examples of the "rich sexual symbolism of the horse . . . connected

point by point with the corresponding myths of the night fiend."
Jones also points out some confusion between nightmares as female
night fiends and witches. Probably by the late Middle Ages, *mara*
(incubus) was assimilated with *mare* (female horse), so that Shakespeare could use the term "Nightmare and her ninefold." In *King
Lear*, Edgar in his charm to avert the nightmare says:

> Swithold footed thrice the 'old;
> He met the nightmare, and her nine fold;
> Bid her alight
> And her troth plight,
> And aroint thee, witch, aroint thee![2] (III. iv. 112–6)

In any case, a "nightmare" can be understood imaginally as a disturbing dream experience which rubs, bites, and sickens our soul, and
has an undercurrent of horse power, lewd demons, aggressive orality,
and death. It is not surprising that these universal and disturbing psychological events have continued to fascinate, perplex, and challenge
humankind to understand and make sense of them.

The question, "What causes nightmares?," has spawned hundreds of theories, many as fantastical as the nightmare experience
itself. Undoubtedly, because of the vividness of these dreams, the
primitive mind tended to experience them as objective reality. The
return of a dead parent or the visit of a demon or hostile neighbor in a
bad dream was experienced as real and threatening. Nightmares, as
well as other dreams, were often thought to have been sent by a divine
agency—a god or gods—or by demons. Jones speaks of the "very multiplicity and protean nature of the 'causes' to which the malady has
been attributed and lists many examples of fanciful theories (Jones
1931, 29). Paracelsus, for instance, stated that the "menstrual flux
engendered phantoms in the air and that therefore convents were
seminaries of nightmares" (p. 45). Other bizarre explanations include
an elongated uvula, certain phases of the moon, and the ingestion of
West Indian alligator pears (p. 29).

Numerous medical hypotheses were suggested to account for the
origin of nightmares. Gastric disturbances, a hypothesis orginally proposed by Galen, is one of the earliest, most popular and long-lived
theories (p. 31). In medieval dream theory, for instance, dreams in the
early dawn (after digestion had taken place) were often considered
more prophetic, more "pure," because the soul was less disturbed and
contaminated by "lower" body processes. Even as recently as 1941, a
nightmare was defined in *Webster's Collegiate Dictionary* as "a condi-

tion brought on in sleep, commonly by digestive or nervous disorders and characterized by a sense of extreme discomfort or by frightful dreams."

It was Freud who was primarily responsible for a dramatic shift toward an understanding of nightmares as purely psychological events of intrapsychic origin. Freud claimed that nightmares were caused by psychic conflict and not lewd demons, "humours," or indigestion. Freud did not write much about nightmares per se (there are only two references to nightmares in the index to his *Collected Works*); he generally referred to the phenomenon as "anxiety dreams." Nor did he develop a separate theory of nightmares or anxiety dreams, but struggled to fit such dreams into his general theory.

The keystone of Freud's theory of dreams was, of course, his concept of wish-fulfillment (Freud 1900). Forbidden libidinal impulses and wishes seeking expression were the energy behind dreams. In order to safeguard sleep these unconscious contents, which were threatening to the conscious mind, were censored and disguised ("dreamwork"). Because anxiety dreams did *not* have the quality of wish-fulfillment and clearly failed to preserve sleep, they seemed to contradict Freud's theory. At first Freud argued that anxiety was caused by an excess accumulation of repressed sexual tension, which rendered the censoring agent ineffective in its sleep-preserving function. Later, as Freud shifted to a more complex understanding of intrapsychic conflict, he revised his theory of anxiety (Freud 1926). Instead of anxiety resulting from repression, it became the cause of repression. According to Freud, the ego experiences anxiety as a signal of external or internal threats (based on earlier experience) and utilizes defenses of repression to protect itself. In nightmares, therefore, anxiety was a signal of threatening forbidden wishes and was evidence of the failure of the ego defenses.

Ernest Jones developed Freud's concept of intense intrapsychic conflict as it relates to the generation of nightmares and claimed that these dreams were caused by those thoughts, feelings, and images that are most distressing to consciousness: incest desires (Jones 1931). Whereas Jones accentuated the importance of oedipal conflict in producing nightmares, subsequent theorists have tended to stress earlier developmental (preoedipal) phases in the genesis of nightmares. This shift reflects a changing emphasis in psychoanalytic theory.

From a current psychiatric/psychoanalytic perspective, nightmares are caused by a variety of external and internal determinants such as physiological factors, stressful life situations, traumatic memories, instinctual drives and unresolved developmental issues (Mack

1970). The emphasis is clearly on *causes*: there is no concern about the *purpose* of a nightmare or interest in the nightmare as an imaginal experience in an archetypal context. We must turn to Jung to enrich the relatively "thin" formulation of nightmare theory based on a personalistic psychology.

Other than his comments on the etymology of "nightmare," Jung wrote little on the phenomenon and, apparently, did not think that it was necessary to differentiate nightmares from other dreams or that it was important to develop a separate theory of nightmares. Undoubtedly he assumed that nightmares could be understood and treated as other dreams. It is possible, however, to piece together and construct a Jungian theory of nightmares from Jung's scattered comments about nightmares as well as from his general theory of dreams.

A fundamental concept in Jung's dream theory is the compensatory function of dreams. Jung claimed that dreams reveal the inevitable one-sidedness of our conscious life and focus on those aspects that are not sufficiently within our field of awareness. Dreams always tell us something we do not know and suggest new ways of dealing with our neurotic impasses. According to Jung, "The more one-sided [the] conscious attitude is and the further it deviates from the optimum, the greater becomes the possibility that vivid dreams with a strongly contrasting but purposive content will appear as an expression of the self-regulation of the psyche" (Jung 1948, par. 488).

In a nightmare some "corrective" is coming into consciousness and is threatening the ego. This new content frequently appears as an intruder or attacker as in this dream of a woman in her mid-thirties:

> It is night and I am home alone. I think I can hear a man trying to break into my house and I am panicked. I can hear him try to open the door, but it is locked. Feeling terror throughout my body, I run to hide under the bed. I realize that he has found a window that is unlocked. I wake up panicked.

In this nightmare some unknown shadow aspect of the psyche is trying to break into this woman's awareness and is threatening to her status-quo-loving ego. The ego structure is under attack. There is no judgment here about the shadow—that is, whether it is positive or negative. By interpreting the dream, by "befriending" the image (as James Hillman would say) or by means of "active imagination," the dreamer will probably discover that this intruder has an important new message to convey.

In discussing dreams, Jung spoke often of both objective and subjective interpretations. If I dream of my mother raging at me, the dream may refer to something about my mother's anger of which I am not aware, or something about our relationship that is awry. Or the raging mother image can be understood subjectively and intrapsychically as an aspect of my own psyche, as an actor in my own psychological drama. As Jung wrote, "The whole drama is essentially subjective, and a dream is a theater in which the dreamer is himself, the scene, the player, the prompter, the producer, the author, the public, and the critic" (Jung 1948, par. 509). This approach to understanding dreams is particularly valuable in discussing nightmares. If the raging mother figure or the intruder or attacker is an aspect of myself, then I can understand this image or energy as a split-off part of my psyche that is coming into consciousness, my own split-off rage, or in the language of object relations theory—an internal "bad object."

In one reference to nightmares, Jung focused on the energy charge of repressed contents as a factor in the formation of these distressing dreams.

> Anything that falls into the unconscious takes on a more or less archaic form. If, for example, the mother represses a painful and terrifying complex, she will feel it as an evil spirit pursuing her— a "skeleton in the cupboard," as the English say. This formation shows that the complex has already acquired archetypal force. It sits on her like an incubus, she is tormented by nightmares. (Jung 1931, par. 62)

This "archetypal force" is also felt in "big dreams." Originating in the collective unconscious, a "big dream" is "chiefly a mythological structure" (Jung 1935, par. 249). Usually these dreams have few or no personal associations and are accompanied by feelings of awe, uncanniness, or horror. Certainly nightmares, with their underlying archetypal patterns, have a "big dream" quality about them.

In this archetypal dimension the nightmare leads Jung to the negative face of the Great Mother. On several occasions Jung speaks of nightmares in connection with the Negative/Terrible /Devouring Mother (Jung [1911–12] 1952, par. 577; Jung 1954, par. 157). The fullest discussion of the connection between the Terrible Mother and the nightmare is found in the chapter "Symbols of the Mother and of Rebirth" in *Symbols of Transformation*. As Jung speaks of Lilith, The Lamias, and the "whale dragon," it becomes clear that—for Jung—the bottom line of the nightmare experience is the all-devouring nightmarish Negative Mother (Jung [1911–12] 1952, 207–73).[3]

Jung's comments on incest also appear in *Symbols of Transformation*. It is interesting that both Jung and Jones connected the nightmare with incest, but, of course, their understanding of incest was very different. In fact, this critical difference was an important factor in the break between Jung and Freud. In this seminal volume, Jung reinterpreted Freud's concept of the Oedipus complex—interpreting incest symbolically as uroboric incest, a preoedipal, retrospective longing to be one with the Mother. Jung insisted that Freud's view was too literal, that Freud confused the regressive pull of the psyche with the desire for the personal mother. According to Jung,

> The so-called Oedipus complex with its famous incest tendency changes at this [regressed] level into a Jonah-and-the-Whale complex, which has any number of variants, for instance the witch who eats children, the wolf, the ogre, the dragon, and so on. Fear of incest turns into fear of being devoured by the mother. The regressing libido apparently desexualizes itself by retreating back step by step to the presexual stage of earliest infancy. (Jung [1911–12] 1952, par. 654)

Even if the archetypal base of the nightmare experience is the Terrible Mother of death and dissolution, Jung insists on the possibility of healing and renewal in this deep place in the psyche. According to Jung, if the libido can "tear itself loose from the maternal embrace," there is the possibility of returning to the "surface with new possibilities of life" (par. 654–55). In a nightmare, a tension exists between a regressive pull back to the source of renewal (the Great Mother) and a progressive thrust toward greater consciousness and the self-regulation of the psyche.

The feminist reader may be uncomfortable with Jung's insistence on the connection between Death and Mother, between the nightmare experience and the Terrible/Negative/Death Mother. Is Jung's position another unexamined patriarchal construction? It may be helpful to differentiate between regression and the nightmare experience. One can argue that regression for both women and men *does* lead back to the mother, to helplessness, to the womb, to nonbeing; certainly each of us must contend with intrapsychic Negative/Death Mother energy. But are all nightmares an expression of this archetypal force? What about the Terrible/Negative/Death Father? Nightmares often include male attackers and intruders and the primary fear may be rape or abuse, rather than death. These considerations, which go beyond the scope of this essay, raise interesting questions about the nightmare differences between women and men. Jung's neglect of incest with the father and his concentration on incest with the dark, threatening, devouring Mother may well reflect his own unresolved mother complex. Despite the skewed personalistic pattern of his focus on the Negative Mother, however, Jung clearly appreciated the symbolic significance and transformative potential of nightmares.

Nightmares are also important diagnostically. From a clinical point of view, a nightmare is *always* a significant psychological event; it makes a dramatic statement about the acute distress of the psyche in the present moment. If an individual seeks therapy because of a nightmare or reports one early in treatment, the therapist is given a valuable gauge and diagnostic tool for determining the state of the psyche. The occurrence of nightmares may, in fact, indicate the onslaught of a psychotic episode. Detre and Jarecki (1971), for instance, cite nightmares as a diagnostic symptom in the onset of an acute schizophrenic episode. In any case, nightmares are especially valuable in giving a clear indication of the strength of the ego and the ego's capacity to deal with threatening unconscious contents. In the following two dreams from my clinical practice I got a sense of the fragility of the ego and the need to proceed cautiously in therapy.

1. I see a volcano beginning to erupt. I try to run but I am not fast enough and realize that I might be killed by the hot lava.
2. I see a pack of wolves and am paralyzed with fear. I am helpless and think that they are going to devour me.

In the context of therapy, the nightmare is not only a gauge but is also Psyche's invitation to go directly to the core complexes. It is an expression of the teleological thrust of our psychological development—what Jung called "individuation." The nightmare has an "intention." That intention, it seems to me, is to communicate and to express the acute distress of the psyche in the most dramatic form possible and—what is especially important—to suggest a way out of the fear or the complex. The nightmare has the potential to awaken us both literally and psychologically

If the dreamer is in therapy, this psychological context is of utmost importance. Therapy is a peculiar undertaking with a special interpsychic and intrapsychic intensity. Out of the countless dreams, fantasies, thoughts, actions, and interactions that occur during a week, those experiences that are recounted in a therapy session are especially significant. It is, of course, possible to consider anything that is brought into a therapy session as either a conscious or unconscious communication to the therapist. If a patient reports a nightmare, s/he is telling the therapist—either consciously or unconsciously—that something is threatening, something is awry. The psyche is panicked and in pain and is feeling helpless. The psyche is crying out for help.

The first thought of the therapist should be, "Is the message for me?" Is the disturbing dream a "compensation" or corrective for the therapy? Does some aspect of the therapeutic relationship feel unsafe and is the nightmare pointing to a failure on the part of the therapist to provide a secure holding environment? Has the therapist unconsciously violated the therapeutic container and, if so, is this event a replay of the patient's earlier experiences of inadequate parenting? Certainly the intense combination of image and affect suggest that important psychic material has been touched and that the earliest wounds and darkest terrors are surfacing. Has the therapist unwittingly tormented or abandoned the "Self," the inner child of the patient as Lilith kidnaps or Lamia destroys the newborn infant?

Understanding the important connection between nightmares and a safe therapeutic container will enable the reader to appreciate certain relationships between a nightmare in a novel and the work as a whole. Consider the following dream of a professional woman in her late forties:

> I am standing on an elevated platform waiting for the train. There are many other people on the platform, like a scene I have seen in movies about Nazis where people are being loaded onto trains for the concentration camps. I am a little girl about eight years old with a huge heavy backpack with a frame that goes above my shoulders and drags on the ground behind my feet so that it bends me forward. I am wearing a lovely wool coat that is a green and black tweed with a felt collar. My mother is on the platform standing behind me but not paying any attention to me. I go to the edge of the platform to see if the train is coming and when I lean over to look the weight of the backpack topples me off the platform onto the concrete waiting area below and I am crushed by the heavy backpack. I lie there broken apart and bleeding and knowing that I am going to die. I wake up in terror.

The context of the dream was the following: after several years of therapy, the dreamer stopped regular sessions when she moved several hours away, but kept in touch with her therapist, meeting occasionally when some issue would arise. During a particularly stressful time in her life, she was meeting her therapist irregularly and sometimes speaking to him by phone. It was under these conditions that she had the nightmare. The distressing dream expressed a cry for help. Just as she had been overburdened as an eight-year-old child carrying too much responsibility because of an extremely difficult and chaotic family situation, now she was collapsing, threatened by the weight of regressive feelings and memories that had been surfacing during the present life crisis—with no safe therapeutic container to hold her. Her inner mother pays no attention to her just as her real mother had not "seen" her. As a comment on the therapy, the dream points to lack of safety in the therapeutic container. By focusing on this understanding of the dream, the dreamer and therapist were able to recognize the importance of a safe holding environment and the necessity of meeting regularly during this phase of treatment.

The response of the therapist to a nightmare is of critical importance. If the therapist is uncomfortable with these troubling images (ignoring, avoiding, or giving an overly positive interpretation as a way of defending against the affect in the dream), the patient will sense that the therapist cannot deal with this powerful psychic material and that the therapeutic container is not safe. If, however, the therapist does attend carefully to these affect-laden images, a deepening of the analytic work is possible.

Turning to research, we discover another perspective on nightmares. Aserinsky and Kleitman's discovery in 1953 of REM sleep led to a remarkable interest and increase in sleep research. Of special interest is Ernest Hartmann's work on nightmares (1984). Hartmann has been able to bridge the gap between laboratory research on sleep and clinical work with patients. Concerned with the question of who has nightmares, Hartmann has done a series of studies on nightmare "sufferers." Each subject of his studies was given an in-depth interview as well as a battery of psychological tests, including the Minnesota Multiphasic Personality Inventory (MMPI). On the MMPI, in what Hartmann described as his most "clearcut findings," his nightmare sufferers scored "significantly higher" than other groups on the so-called "psychotic" scales—paranoia and schizophrenia—as well as on the F scale (a validity scale and measure of unusual answers). Low K scale (a correction scale which measures test-taking attitude) scores were also reported (pp. 15–17). According to Hartmann:

> A high F score combined with a relatively low K score, characteristic of our subjects, is taken as a measure of openness or willingness to admit to problems, to quirks, to unusual experiences. In this sense, the nightmare subjects as a group are "unusual," more open to suffering, more willing to admit to problems than are the two comparison groups . . . .The most striking finding is not the formal psychopathology of some, but rather the openness and defenselessness of almost all the nightmare sufferers. They have not developed the usual defenses and protections that

most people have. They are not "armored"; they are vulnerable in many respects. (pp. 83, 85, 103)

Hartmann described his group as having "thin" or "permeable" boundaries:

Having thin boundaries can be an advantage in allowing insight into one's mental content and mental processes, and presumably those of others, making one a better writer, painter, teacher, therapist, negotiator. Scientific as well as artistic creativity requires "regression in the service of the ego" implying an ability to regress to a point where different realms of thought are merged, to temporarily ignore boundaries in order to put things together in a new way. This regression may be easier for people with a tendency to thin boundaries. (pp. 168–9)

In fact, many of Hartmann's subjects were "musicians (both composers and performers), painters, poets, writers, craftspersons, teachers, and therapists"—that is, people who were more open to unconscious processes and relationships and not heavily defended against such experiences (p. 65).

Although at times Hartmann seems to appreciate the giftedness of his subjects, his conclusion is that the "formation of unusually thin boundaries, starting in early childhood, is an important predisposing factor in the development of frequent nightmares, schizophrenia and certain kinds of artistic or scientific creativity" (p. 130). Even though Hartmann's subjects were clearly not schizophrenic, but rather "persons living in society, working to support themselves or in school—usually graduate students," he emphasizes the correlation between schizophrenia and nightmares rather than that between creativity and nightmares, and concludes that his subjects "constitute a group specially vulnerable to schizophrenia" (pp. 65, 107).

Throughout his work, Hartmann wavers between a medical model which views nightmares as pathology and a symbolic model which sees meaning and value in them. Trained as a psychoanalyst, Hartmann understands nightmares as primarily an expression of "early childhood fears and helplessness" (p. 184). By emphasizing the pathology of nightmares, Hartmann does not do justice to the richness of the imagery and tends to miss the symbolic significance and transformative potential of these upsetting dreams.

Clinically, if one focuses on pathology rather than on the symbolic meaning and teleological thrust of a nightmare, a valuable opportunity is lost. It seems to me that a similar loss is experienced if the reader does not recognize the centrality of a nightmare in a literary work. With some appreciation for the psychological dynamics, the imaginal associations, and archetypal dimensions of nightmares, let us consider two well-known nightmares in literature: Raskolnikov's dream in chapter 5 of Dostoyevsky's *Crime and Punishment* and Lockwood's dream in chapter 3 of Emily Bronte's *Wuthering Heights.*[4]

Crime and Punishment begins with our hero, the student Raskolnikov, sneaking out of his dingy garret to avoid meeting his landlady. Crushed by poverty, he is unable to continue his studies at the university and is heavily in debt to his landlady. Agitated and distraught, Raskolnikov contemplates robbing and murdering Alyona Ivanova, the avaricious pawnbroker, as a solution to his desperate situation. He decides to "rehearse" the murder, and with "a sinking heart and a nervous tremor," goes to visit the pawnbroker. Immediately after suffering through the transaction of pawning an old watch for a few rubles, Raskolnikov is filled with self-loathing at his thoughts of murder, the "filthy things" in his heart. "Tormented by a burning thirst" he enters a tavern for the first time in his life and meets Marmeladov, a likeable drunk who proceeds to describe the details of his hopeless situation. On helping the drunk man home, the student witnesses a distressing scene—a thin little girl in a ragged dress trying to comfort her trembling, weeping seven-year-old brother who has just been beaten by Marmeladov's rageful, consumptive wife. The next day, after waking up from a fitful sleep feeling ill-tempered, Raskolnikov receives a lengthy guilt-inducing letter from his long-suffering, self-sacrificing mother. She describes the difficulties that she and Raskolnikov's sister, Dounia, have suffered in their attempts to support him in his university studies. Dounia has even agreed to marry an odious man whom she does not love in hopes that he will assist her brother. Tortured by the letter, a frenzied Raskolnikov goes off into the street where he notices a young girl, an "innocent creature" who is intoxicated and disheveled and has probably been abused. He enlists the aid of a policeman in helping the girl, and then, unexpectedly, changes his mind and distances himself. Once again he seeks relief in a tavern where he consumes some vodka. On his way home, he feels the effect of the alcohol, becomes drowsy, and finds a protected spot off the road where he lies down and immediately falls asleep . . . and dreams (pp. 1–50).

Raskolnikov dreams that he is a child of "about seven" back in his native village walking with his father to the graveyard where his grandmother and infant brother are buried. Passing the local tavern, a place of "dread" to the young child, he and his father see that a festivity of some sort seems to be taking place with lots of gaily dressed peasants singing and all "more or less drunk." A large, heavy cart stands outside the tavern. In the shafts of the cart is a "thin little sorrel beast"—not a powerful "cart-horse" who would ordinarily pull such a cart. At the invitation and encouragement of Mikolka, the owner of the little mare, drunken men pile into the cart, laughing at Mikolka's claim that the small animal can pull the cart. Mikolka shouts in reply "I'll make her gallop!" and begins flogging the mare who, tugging with all her might, can barely move the cart. When others join in the beating, the child, crying and upset, rushes to the horse to try to stop the cruelty. No one listens. The brutality escalates when the mare begins feebly kicking in protest. Mikolka attacks the animal with a thick shaft and is furious that he cannot kill her. When someone in the crowd shouts "Fetch an axe to her! Finish her off!," the angry peasant seizes an iron crowbar. Other drunken peasants seize whips, sticks, and poles and join Mikolka in beating the mare to death. The child runs to the dead mare, puts his arms around and kisses her bleeding head. His father grabs him and carries him out of the crowd. The boy sobs, "Father! Why did they kill the poor horse!" "They are drunk. . . . They are brutal . . . it's not our business!" the father replies. Sobbing and choking the little boy puts his arms around his father and tries to cry out. Raskolnikov awakens feeling terrified, gasping for breath, his hair soaked with perspiration: "darkness and confusion were in his soul." "Good God" he cries out, "can it be, can it be, that I shall really take an axe, that I shall strike her on the head, split her skull open?" Moments later he renounces the "accursed" dream and experiences relief. After hours of anguish and a significant "co-incidence," however, Raskolnikov proceeds to murder the pawnbroker (pp. 50–71).

Given what we know about nightmares, what would we as a reader/analyst make of Raskolnikov's dream? Considering that there is no dream without a dreamer, let us imagine that Raskolnikov finds his way to the consulting room. We would meet an agitated, distraught young man who is in acute psychic distress and is obsessed with thoughts of murder. Hypersensitive to his surroundings and flooded by unconscious contents and obsessional thoughts, Raskolnikov is defended against neither external stress nor internal chaos; his boundaries are too "permeable." Yet if we are not focused on his pathology, we can imagine a creative potential in this sensitivity and permeability. Sensing Raskolnikov's intense inner conflict, we might be struck by the appropriateness of his name: *raskol* in Russian means "split."

Given Raskolnikov's character and situation, it is not surprising that he would have a nightmare. There are certainly external "causes." He is stressed physically—he has not been sleeping well, has had little to eat, and has been drinking vodka. He is under a good deal of strain because of his financial circumstances and the alarming news of his sister's impending marriage. In both the text preceding the dream and the dream text, Dostoyevsky has given the reader numerous clues to the internal "causes": the instinctual drives and unresolved psychological and developmental issues of his protagonist.

Interestingly, the dream, coming so early in the novel, has the feeling of an "initial" dream. Jungians consider the "initial" dream, the first dream brought into therapy, especially significant. It is thought to reflect what the patient is bringing, psychologically, into therapy; the dream imaginally describes the core issues and suggests the psychological work or purpose of the analysis. Although most initial dreams are not nightmares, often someone will seek therapy because of an upsetting dream or recurrent nightmare and will relate these dream experiences to the therapist early in the treatment. When an initial dream *is* a nightmare, the dream underscores the urgency and importance of the issues. It is as though the unconscious is demanding to be heard, turning up the volume, and blasting the ego with images and affect which cannot be ignored. In a novel, one can imagine that a nightmare near the beginning of the work serves (can serve, should serve?) a similar purpose of pointing immediately to the core issues. Certainly Raskolnikov's nightmare does both indicate his intense mind-body split, which is a central theme of the book, and suggest the psychological determinants of this conflict.

It is Dostoyevsky's genius of representation that the nightmare feels real and psychologically convincing; it does not seem like a literary device. Not only has Dostoyevsky offered his reader causes and a context that would generate and explain Raskolnikov's having a nightmare, but the author's use of day residues in the dream is masterful. The dream is woven out of experiential fragments and images from Raskolnikov's current life—e.g. the tavern, an "innocent creature," an abused seven-year-old boy. The themes of brutality, abuse, helplessness, anxiety, and drunkenness fill the pages of text preceding the dream.

What does the dream mean? What is the dream trying to say? There is, of course, no definitive interpretation of any dream. The most that can be hoped for is enlivening the imagination, moving the psyche. With such a caveat in mind, let us consider the dream. In the dream Raskolnikov is back in his native village and is about seven years old. If the dream can be understood as a read-out from the unconscious reflecting where the dreamer is psychologically placed at the time of the dream, one can say that there is something about Raskolnikov's current life situation which resonates with this earlier time in his life. That is, Raskolnikov's "stuckness" or unresolved issues are being replayed and are impacting on his current life situation. If the dream is considered subjectively, all of the dream images can be seen as aspects of Raskolnikov—not only the little boy but also the mare, Mikolka, the peasants, the father. The story and action of the dream are also aspects of Raskolnikov—his intrapsychic dynamics and unconscious conflicts.

In the dream the inner child feels helpless, upset, despairing. No one listens to him; his protestations have no effect. Although the dream ego is immature and in emotional pain, it is not overwhelmed. As reader/analyst we sense that Raskolnikov can survive the conflict and has the capacity to suffer his fate. The best that his father can do is carry him away from the scene. The father does not intervene and confront Mikolka; he makes no effort to stop the brutality of the group of drunken peasants. He just wants to flee from the conflict. Up to this point in the novel, the reader has heard nothing of the father; he is a shadowy figure who has apparently died. Raskolnikov has neither a real living father nor a strong, supportive inner-father introject, but seems emotionally immersed in the world of his mother and sister both externally and internally. The inner father cannot take a stand against the destructive, sadistic Death energies that attack the instinctual side of Raskolnikov's nature, the "little sorrel beast."

Just as the mare cannot pull the burden of the heavy cart filled with drunken peasants, so Raskolnikov is over-burdened in his life by the responsibilities of supporting himself and family, of saving Dounia from a bad marriage. It is worth noting that Raskolnikov could certainly have dreamed a brutal scene in the present, but, since it is set in the past, the dream underscores the historical dimension, the repressed issues, his psychological stuckness. It is a psychological burden that is unbearable and is the primary motivating force of this dream and the murder.

The dream can be seen as a compensation, in Jung's sense, for a conscious attitude which focuses too narrowly on the external life situation and which neglects the unconscious dimension. Whereas Raskolnikov professes his love for his mother and sister, he is unconscious of the murderous rage he feels toward them. What is the cause or source of this rage? The guilt-inducing letter written by Raskolnikov's mother gives some indication of the psychology of the mother and the symbiotic relationship between mother and son. Dependent on her for both financial and emotional support, he is deeply enmeshed in his mother complex and is rageful at being tied in knots and knotted to his mother.

We can imagine that the father was not emotionally available to the mother and that she thus turned to her son. This oedipal configuration leads to the land of psychological incest and reflects Ernest Jones's insistence that incestuous desires are the source of nightmares.[5]

The image of the mare resonates with numerous folkloric and psychological associations cited by Jones (pp. 248–272), and suggests a universal and archetypal dimension to the dream. From a Jungian perspective, the death of the mare in the realm of death (the vicinity of the grandmother's grave) points to the regressive pull of the Negative Mother, the Death Mother. Here, according to Jung, is the place of regression and dissolution that has the potential for transformation.

In an analysis, managing and containing these chaotic and powerful energies is the responsibility of the analyst. Shifting lenses from reader/analyst to author/analyst, we see in a novel that it is the author who must balance the tensions and provide a container for the unconscious dynamics and nightmarish forces that have emerged. As *Crime and Punishment* unfolds, it becomes clear that Dostoyevsky—with his intuitive psychological genius and with the help of his nonjudgmental, analyst-like character Sonia (wisdom)—is able to contain the chaos and the tension of opposites out of which Raskolnikov's transformation becomes possible.

When we turn to another nightmare in literature, Lockwood's dream in *Wuthering Heights*, we find a complicated interplay of psychology and literature. The novel begins with Lockwood's describing his first visit to Wuthering Heights and his first encounter with Heathcliff, his landlord. "Wuthering," we are told, is a provincial word meaning "atmospheric tumult." When Lockwood goes to pay a call, the reception is far from cordial. Badly treated by both the dour, peevish, old servant Joseph and the morose Heathcliff, "a dark-skinned gypsy in aspect, in dress and manners a gentleman," Lockwood is also attacked by Heathcliff's dogs and then rescued by a "lusty dame," the servant Zillah.

Lockwood presents himself as a foolish, unaware man who is insensitive to the feelings and needs of others. He boasts, for instance, of gaining the "reputation of deliberate heartlessness" by pursuing and then rejecting a young woman he met at the seacoast. Although aware that Heathcliff "evidently wished no repetition of [his] intrusion," Lockwood inconsiderately returns the next day just as a snow storm is beginning and once again experiences "churlish inhospitality." On this visit Lockwood meets the other two members of the household—the beautiful and sullen "Missus" (Catherine Heathcliff) and the rough and haughty Hareton Earnshaw. Struggling to understand the various relationships, Lockwood blunders and assumes that Catherine is Heathcliff's wife, then Earnshaw's wife; she is, in fact, the widow of Heathcliff's son, Linton. Heathcliff makes an ambiguous reference to his own wife as the "ministering angel" of Wuthering Heights. In an atmosphere of tension and antagonism among the inhabitants of Wuthering Heights and of appalling rudeness to the guest, Lockwood's requests for someone to guide him home through the snow are ignored. Grabbing a lantern, he starts off on his own, which prompts Joseph to set the dogs on him for stealing the lantern. To the obvious displeasure of Heathcliff, Lockwood has to spend the night. Zillah escorts him upstairs to an unused bedroom, urging him to be quiet and hide his candle because the master has an "odd notion" that the room should not be used.

In this "off-bounds" room, Lockwood discovers a window seat with a pile of books marked as belonging to Catherine Earnshaw and with the names—Catherine Earnshaw, Catherine Heathcliff and Catherine Linton—repeatedly scratched in the paint. Lockwood discovers that one of the books is, in fact, Catherine Earnshaw's journal written in an "unformed childish hand" and dated twenty-five years earlier. In leafing through the journal, Lockwood learns about the special relationship between Catherine and Heathcliff and the harsh treatment of Heathcliff by Hindley, Catherine's brother, after the death of their father. In one passage Catherine describes an "awful Sunday" when she and Heathcliff shivered in a cold attic and were subjected to one of the servant Joseph's three-hour sermons while Hindley and his new wife enjoyed themselves in front of a warm fire. When Catherine and Heathcliff protested having to read some religious books thrust on them by Joseph, Hindley punished Heathcliff severely. As Lockwood starts to nod off, he notices a volume entitled, "Seventy Times Seven, and the First of the Seventy-First. A Pious Discourse delivered by the Reverend Jabes Branderham in the Chapel of Gimmerdon Sough," and falls asleep. And "Alas, for the effects of bad tea and bad tempers" has the worst dream of his life (pp. 3–26).

Lockwood's nightmare is in two parts, a rare phenomenon in literary representation of dreams. In the first section, Joseph, who seems to be escorting Lockwood home through the snow, reproaches him for not bringing a pilgrim's staff and takes him to the chapel "near a swamp, whose peaty moisture is said to answer all the purposes of embalming on the few corpses deposited there." Although in reality this chapel is unused because the congregation is too cheap to pay for a pastor, in the dream a large congregation is attentively listening to Reverend Jabes Branderham preach from the text of "Seventy Times Seven"—an endless sermon discussing 490 sins. When Lockwood rises to protest, he is accused of being a sinner and attacked by the congregation. Weaponless, he struggles with Joseph for his staff; the rest of the congregation is at each other's throats. As Branderham "poured forth his zeal in a shower of raps on the boards of the pulpit," Lockwood awakens—and discovers a fir-bough scraping against the window.

Drifting back to sleep, Lockwood dreams that, in an effort to silence the branch, he attempts to open the window and finds it soldered shut.

> "I must stop it, nevertheless!" I muttered, knocking my knuckles through the glass, and stretching an arm out to seize the importunate branch; instead of which, my fingers closed on the fingers of a little, ice-cold hand! The intense horror of nightmare came over me: I tried to draw back my arm, but the hand clung to it, and a most melancholy voice sobbed, "Let me in—let me in!" "Who are you?" I asked, struggling, meanwhile, to disengage myself. "Catherine Linton," it replied, shiveringly (why did I think of *Linton*? I had read *Earnshaw* twenty times for Linton); "I'm come home: I'd lost my way on the moor!" As it spoke, I discerned, obscurely, a child's face looking through the window. Terror made me cruel; and, finding it useless to attempt shaking the creature off, I pulled its wrist on to the broken pane, and rubbed it to and fro till the blood ran down and soaked the bedclothes: still it wailed, "Let me in!" and maintained its tenacious grip, almost maddening me with fear. "How can I?" I said at length. "Let me go, if you want me to let you in!" The fingers relaxed, I snatched mine through the hole, hurriedly piled the books up in a pyramid against it, and stopped my ears to exclude the lamentable prayer. I seemed to keep them closed above a quarter of an hour; yet, the instant I listened again, there was the doleful cry moaning on! "Begone!" I shouted, "I'll never let you in, not if you beg for twenty years." "It is twenty years," mourned the voice: "twenty years. I've been a waif for twenty years!" Thereat began a feeble scratching outside, and the pile of books moved as if thrust forward. I tried to jump up, but could not stir a limb; and so yelled aloud, in a frenzy of fright (pp. 26–30).

Lockwood's shout brings Heathcliff, agitated and furious at being awakened and finding his tenant in the forbidden bedroom. After recounting to him the dream about Catherine Linton, Lockwood leaves the room but overhears Heathcliff wrench open the window, burst into an "uncontrollable passion of tears and grief-stricken intensity," and sob, "Come in! Come in! Cathy, do come. Oh do— *once* more! Oh! my heart's darling; hear me *this* time, Catherine, at last!" (p. 33).

What can be said about the dreamer Lockwood and his bipartite nightmare? In contrast to Raskolnikov, Lockwood is not—according to Hartmann's description—a typical "nightmare sufferer." Lockwood's "boundaries" are far from "permeable"; he is presented as a well-defended, unperceptive, insensitive man whose name reflects and underscores the rigidity of his personality. Given the strange setting and the abusive social interactions, however, it is certainly not unlikely that even a well-armored Lockwood would have a nightmare.

Like Raskolnikov's nightmare, Lockwood's is the first dream recounted in the novel and appears early in the work. This "initial" dream gives the reader important information about the complex relationships between the characters and points to the central "mystery" of the book. Lockwood, as well as the reader, is puzzled by the dream; the meaning becomes clear as Mrs. Dean, the other narrator, tells the story. To understand this dream is, in fact, to understand the story of *Wuthering Heights.*

Like Dostoyevsky, Bronte has also presented a psychologically convincing dream composed of an interweaving of day-residues. The first part of the dream clearly emerges from Lockwood's having read Catherine's account of the "awful Sunday" as well as from his own ordeal as a visitor at Wuthering Heights. Heathcliff's comment about the "ministering angel" coupled with Lockood's experience in Catherine's shut-off bedroom provide the stimuli for the second segment of the dream.

Although the dream feels, to the reader-analyst, like a "real" dream, something about the second part feels unauthenic. It has the feeling of a literary device intended to reveal secrets about the past before the novel begins, and to set a particular emotional tone. This more distressing portion of the dream is not convincingly a product of Lockwood's psyche; rather it would be more plausible presented as Heathcliff's dream. The first section of the dream does feel like Lockwood's dream, reflecting a repressive, judgmental, grim, and rageful inner world. Perhaps Lockwood keeps this dream to himself, rather than recount it to Heathcliff, because he recognizes his own psychic material surfacing. The "Catherine Linton" dream, however, he "gives" ("gives back") to Heathcliff.

Considering Heathcliff is not heavily defended against unconscious processes, he would be more likely than his guest to have such an upsetting nightmare. It is Heathcliff who knows the significance of Catherine Linton, the name which signifies Heathcliff's tragic loss. It is Heathcliff who really suffers the dream and is distraught on hearing it. The power of the images, such as skin rubbing over broken glass, suggests Heathcliff's torment and helps to explain his behavior in the previous pages. Catherine's return seems to be in response to Heathcliff's repeated supplication: "Hear me *this* time, Catherine, at last." The dream has profound meaning for Heathcliff; for Lockwood it is a "ridiculous nightmare." And it is Heathcliff who ultimately, at the end of the novel and the end of his life, returns to the window seat as he prepares to die and thence to meet his Catherine.

Some basis exists, however, for claiming the dream as Lockwood's. Catherine can be understood as a soul figure that has been abused and rejected, and the dream as a reflection of a faulty relationship to both inner and outer female figures. The reader is already aware of Lockwood's difficulties with relationships from his account of "heartless" treatment of the young woman on vacation. In that brief passage, Bronte gives such a skillful portrait of a mother-complexed man that his comment in the dream narrative, "Terror made me cruel," seems in character. Furthermore, this dramatic and emotional nightmare could be considered as compensatory, in the Jungian sense, to Lockwood's pedantic, measured, rigid, two-dimensional approach to life. His defended armored attitude toward the unconscious can be heard in his response to the intrusive dream figure: "I'll never let you in."

Even if Lockwood could have dreamed this dream, one wonders why Bronte would have given this "big dream" to a minor character. Although Lockwood is one of the narrators, and in that role is important, he really stands outside of the drama. The nightmare's potential to "awaken" the dreamer/character is wasted on Lockwood; Bronte is not interested in his development. It is Heathcliff who is touched and changed by the nightmare experience.

Perhaps Bronte intended to underscore the blurring of boundaries and enmeshment of psyches that pervade the novel. That is, being in Catherine's room in Heathcliff's house, Lockwood has Heathcliff's dream. This permeability is also felt in the strong incestuous tenor throughout the book and is illustrated by the complex and sometimes confusing interrelationships: the adopted Heathcliff and

Catherine Earnshaw are raised as brother and sister; after Catherine marries Edgar Linton, Heathcliff elopes with Edgar's sister, Isabella Linton; Edgar and Catherine's daughter Catherine Linton marries the son of Isabella Linton and Heathcliff (Linton), after whose death she marries Catherine Earnshaw Linton's nephew, Hareton Earnshaw.

Containing the energies unleashed in the nightmare becomes an enormous task for the author, and at times *Wuthering Heights* teeters on the edge of chaos. Bronte is, however, able to provide a container or structure through her use of the two narrators (Lockwood and Mrs. Dean) and her careful attention to such details as chronology.

The archetypal dimension is felt not only in the "Catherine Linton" part of the dream, but also in the novel itself. A current of death, dead sons and mothers, and Death Mother energy runs throughout *Wuthering Heights*. We feel the presence of the past, of dead ancestors, from the moment Lockwood first enters the house and notices "Hareton Earnshaw, 1500" inscribed above the door. In the first few pages the reader learns that Heathcliff's wife and son have died. The nightmare is filled with death images—from the peat bogs "embalming" the corpses to the soul who has been wandering for twenty years. And, of course, there is the powerful and irresistible regressive pull on Heathcliff to join Catherine in death.

To appreciate fully the centrality of both Raskolnikov's and Lockwood's nightmares, the reader might try to imagine the novels without these dramatic psychological events. Not only would important information about the characters be lost, but the breadth and depth of the novels would be considerably diminished. From the moment we and the characters are "awakened" by the nightmare, we are not the same. We feel the impact of the dream; we carry a memory of the nightmare and an awareness that unconscious nightmarish energies underlie all surface events. In addition to a dimension of depth the nightmare emphasizes a time dimension. From an agonizing present, the nightmare pushes back to emotionally charged childhood memories and forward into the future as it shapes the development of the novel. One can trace the "intention" of the nightmare and note the ripples throughout the book.

After considering the centrality of a nightmare in a novel and after looking at nightmares from a literary perspective, we can return to psychology with a fuller appreciation of the valuable function of nightmares in an analysis. And ask some questions. If the memory of a nightmare shapes a novel, how does it shape an analysis? If ripple effects of a nightmare are felt throughout a literary work, how are they felt in analytic work? Just as it is difficult to imagine *Crime and Punishment* and *Wuthering Heights* without Raskolnikov's and Lockwood's nightmares, what is an analysis without a nightmare?

Notes

1. An incubus is a male evil spirit believed to descend upon and have sexual intercourse with sleeping women. The word is derived from the Latin word *incubus* (to lie down upon, hatch). A female demon desiring intercourse with a sleeping man is a succubus. This word comes from *succuba* (a late Latin word for prostitute), which in turn is derived from *succubare* (to lie under). *The American Heritage Dictionary of the English Language* (Boston: Houghton Mifflin Co., 1981).

2. " 'old": wold, an upland plain; "aroint thee": be off with you. This is Shakespeare's only use of the word "nightmare" despite the fact that most dreams in Shakespearean drama, even the comedies, are "troublous."

3. Following Jung, Erich Neumann also makes the connection between nightmares and the Terrible Mother. See E. Neumann, *The Great Mother* (Princeton: Princeton University Press, 1974), 149.

4. Fyodor Dostoyevsky, *Crime and Punishment*, trans. Constance Garnett (New York: The Modern Library, 1950); Emily Bronte, *Wuthering Heights* (New York: The Modern Library, 1950).

5. It is worth noting in this context that the Russian word for "crime" is *prestuplenie*, which includes the meaning of transgression, crossing of boundaries, violation (*pre* means "across," *stuplenie* "stepping"). This sense of crossing boundaries, which indeed pervades the novel, is lost in translation. "Crime" in English has a different etymology coming from the Latin *crimen* meaning verdict, judgment.

References

Bronte, Emily. *Wuthering Heights.* New York: Modern Library, 1950.

Detre, Thomas and Henry Jarecki. *Modern Psychiatric Treatment.* Philadelphia: J. B. Lippincott, 1971.

Dostoyevsky, Fyodor. *Crime and Punishment.* Translated by Constance Garnett. New York: Modern Library, 1950.

Freud, Sigmund. *The Standard Edition of the Complete Psychological Works*. Translated and edited by James Strachey. Assisted by Anna Freud, Alix Strachey, and Alan Tyson. 24 vols. London: The Hogarth Press and the Institute of Psycho-analysis, 1953–74.

——. [1900] *The Interpretation of Dreams*, SE 4 and 5.

——. [1926] "Inhibitions, Symptoms and Anxiety", SE 20.

Hartmann, Ernest. *The Nightmare: The Psychology and Biology of Terrifying Dreams*. New York: Basic Books, 1984.

Hillman, James. *Insearch: Psychology and Religion*. New York: Charles Scribner's Sons, 1967.

Jones, Ernest. *On the Nightmare*. London: Hogarth Press, 1931.

Jung, C. G. *The Collected Works of C. G. Jung*. Translated by R. F. C. Hull. Princeton: Princeton University Press, Bollingen Series, 1953–1979.

——. ([1911–12] 1952) *Symbols of Transformation*, CW 5.

——. [1931] "Mind and Earth", CW 10.

——. [1935] "The Tavistock Lectures", CW 18.

——. [1948] "General Aspects of Dream Psychology", CW 8.

——. [1954] "Psychological Aspects of the Mother Archetype", CW 9i.

LaBerge, Stephen. *Lucid Dreaming*. New York: Ballantine Books, 1985.

Mack, John. *Nightmares and Human Conflict*. Boston: Little, Brown, and Co., 1970.

Neumann, Erich. *The Great Mother*. Princeton: Princeton University, 1974.

PART II

Historical, Political, Cultural, and Social Aspects

A stance shared by all of the contributors to this volume is that all dreams, whether of "real" people or "imaginary" characters, are embedded in historical, political, cultural, and social contexts. While universal, archetypal forms may shape dreams cross-culturally, across time, and even across levels of reality, more fruitful pursuit is made in this volume of particular cases, events, and moments in time. In Part II the spotlight is not on a dream or a dreamer, but on some of those other members of the oneiric population whose primary interest in dreams is theoretical or political rather than aesthetic.

John Brennan describes the interpretive methods of official Chinese diviners. He shows how they approached dreams as important messages about the social and political order and how dreams (or at least the styles and techniques of interpreting dreams) changed as the cultural landscape changed. The interpreter had tremendous power by being in the position of one who allegedly knew the unknown and this power could readily be translated into politically expedient versions of dream meaning.

Ken Frieden shifts emphasis from the theories to the theorist himself when he looks at Freud's obfuscation of sources in the Hebrew tradition which he surely knew and apparently used in the establishment of psychoanalysis. And Frieden hints at the psychological, as well as political, motives that might have prompted Freud to neglect crediting certain of his predecessors who wrote on dreams.

Carol Schreier Rupprecht contributes to the historical knowledge of dreams one overlooked but original and valuable text, Girolamo Cardano's *Sommiorum Synesiorum* (1562). In doing so, she draws attention to sixteenth-century Europe both as a site of great oneiric activity and as a turning point when dreams lost their connection to a primarily spiritual realm and moved to association with a primarily secular and medical realm, where they remained in the oneirics of Western Europe and the United States until well into the twentieth century.

Finally Kay Stockholder asks us to examine Shakespeare's *The Merchant of Venice* as if it were the dream of a central character. This strategy forces us to consider the societal implications of the play—the role of the economy and concomitant attitudes toward women and Jews, for example—while also taking account of psychological and interpersonal aspects of the character/dreamer.

5. Dreams, Divination, and Statecraft: The Politics of Dreams in Early Chinese History and Literature

John Brennan

The use of dreams as historical documents was commonplace until relatively recent times in both China and Europe (Steiner 1983, 8). The dreams treated here were accepted as history, but they also constitute a history of early Chinese dreams. This history of dreams records changes beyond predictable reflections of changes in material culture. Dreams that convey a message to the dreamer through ordinary language are prominent in early Chinese records. "Message dreams" with similarities to those of early China are found in ancient Near Eastern texts (Oppenheim 1956, 176–206), the Bible (Priest 1988, 59–60) and in Greek sources (Dodds 1951, 102–121). Despite the great differences in culture, language, and religious beliefs among these civilizations, all shared to some degree the belief that dreams conveyed the intention of the noumenal world to the phenomenal (Priest 1988, 59). In Chinese texts the message dream loses status and is cited less frequently as a historical document in sources that date from the Han dynasty (206 B.C.–A.D. 220) or later. It has been suggested that similar changes in types of dreams have taken place in the cultures of Europe (Dodds 1951, 102–5).

Most of the records of dreams found in the earliest Chinese sources are in books of history. These accounts are presented by Chinese writers as if they were authentic records of dreams and presumably they would have been accepted by a broad class of Chinese readers as actual accounts. Dream accounts in early Chinese historical works primarily concern persons who are known to have lived. In addition to accounts in works of history, however, there are also dreams recorded in poems found in the earliest anthology of Chinese

73

poetry, the *Book of Odes* or *Shi jing*.[1] These poems occur in the *Xiao ya* or *Lesser Odes* section of the anthology and traditional Chinese commentators have treated these poems as odes composed in honor of specific historical occasions and the dreams themselves as genuine events. Among early philosophical texts, only the *Zhuang zi*, a Taoist work dating from the fourth or third century B.C., contains references to dreams. The *Zhuang zi* usually presents dreams as parables and does not treat them as history.[2]

The focus of this inquiry, however, is on dreams, whether considered "literary" or "historical," that offer significant insight into the role of what we might label the irrational in social and especially political life. The dream records of early China were produced in a cultural setting that assigned importance to the recording and interpreting of dreams. There is evidence that perhaps as early as the middle of the second millennium B.C. dream interpretation was an official function of the ancient Chinese state. The nature of the earliest dream accounts in Chinese literature is profoundly influenced by official ritual and statecraft. The earliest surviving Chinese writing consists of thousands of texts and textual fragments inscribed on tortoise plastrons and the scapula of oxen. Most of this material dates from the Shang (or Yin) dynasty (sixteenth to eleventh centuries B.C.) It is known that these earliest records are the results of divinations performed for official purposes. The word dream (*meng*) is found a few times among these fragments, but unfortunately none of these inscriptions relates the content of a specific dream or its interpretation. Although the few fragments which mention dreams are too incomplete to provide a record of an ancient Chinese dream, they do suffice to show that the linkage between dreams, divination, and statecraft was an element of Chinese political organization since the Shang dynasty.

The *Zhou li*, (*Rites of Zhou*, also known as the *Zhou guan* or *The Officers of Zhou*), a work that describes the structure of officialdom during the period of the Zhou dynasty (eleventh century to 221 B.C.), lists dream divination as a bureaucratic function of the ancient Chinese state and provides a table of organization for officers involved with divinatory practices.[3] The *Zhou li* divides officials into six groups under the following rubrics: Heaven, Earth, Spring, Summer, Autumn, and Winter. Divinatory officials are classed among the Spring officials, who are charged with maintaining state ritual. The Grand Diviner (*da bu* or *tai bu*) was a high official who had comprehensive responsibilities for all divination. Directly under the Grand Diviner were four upper-ranking officials called Divining Masters (*bu shi*) and eight middle-ranking officials called Diviners (*bu ren*) (*Zhou li* 17.5). The Grand Diviner had general charge of all methods of divination including tortoise shell and bone cracks, milfoil stalk, geomancy, and animal movements, as well as dreams (*Zhou li* 24.6–7). A separate position called the Examiner of Dreams (*zhan meng*) held by two middle-ranking officers is also mentioned in the list of officials (*Zhou li* 17.6).[4] This office is the same rank as the Diviners and may in fact be a specification or subdivision of the Diviner officials.

The *Zhou li* states that the Grand Diviner is responsible for the three methods of dream divination (*san meng zhi fa*). Although these methods are named in the text, their exact nature is unknown (*Zhou li* 24.6). The first method is called *zhi meng*, which, according to the Zheng Xuan commentary written in the Latter Han (A.D. 25–220), means "where the dream is leading." It could also mean simply to explore or explicate the dream. Zheng Xuan says second and third methods, *ji meng* and *xian zhi*, refer to archaic methods of the Yin and Zhou dynasties. The commentary notes that *ji meng* refers to "what is obtained of the dream," and *xian zhi* refers to "obtaining all of the dream."[5]

There is also reference in the same section of the *Zhou li* to the ten main movements (*yun*) and ninety submovements of dream divination.[6] Zheng Xuan states that this methodology had already been lost by his time. The movements and submovements would seem to refer to an analytical scheme or framework, possibly a method with a numerological structure or basis, like the binary numerology that underlies the method of the *Book of Changes* or *Zhou yi*.[7]

The Examiner of Dreams is charged with divining the good or ill fortune of the six types of dreams, taking into account the positions of the sun, moon, and stars, distinguishing between the yin and the yang, observing the conjunction of heaven and earth according to the seasons (*Zhou li* 25.1). The six types of dreams are given as:

1. Regular or restful dreams (*zheng meng*)
2. Startling or disturbing dreams (*e meng*)
3. Reflective dreams (*si meng*)
4. Daydreams (*wu meng*)
5. Happy dreams (*xi meng*)
6. Frightening dreams (*ju meng*)

This is the first typology of dreams encountered in Chinese literature. There is no correspondence between the type of dream and whether it is divined as auspicious or inauspicious. Startling or frightening dreams, though unsettling, can be favorable omens and happy or restful dreams may be unlucky. The *Zhou li* does not state how this typology was significant in divination, nor how it relates to the three methods of dream divination.

The first two categories seem to be based on the affective nature of the dream itself, i.e. whether the dream is peaceful or disturbing. The last four categories are based on state of mind or activity just previous to the dream. *Si meng* or reflective dreams are based on thoughts a person experiences during the day. *Wu meng* or daydreams are based on things that have been heard while conscious. Happy dreams and frightening dreams occur when the dreamer is or has been in a happy or frightened state (*Zhou li* 25.1–2).[8]

Some ritual functions of the Examiner of Dreams are also mentioned in the *Zhou li*. There was an annual rite before the new year to foster auspicious dreams for the ruler and dispel inauspicious dreams, but the exact nature of this rite is unknown (*Zhou li* 25.2).[9]

The *Zhou li* is generally thought to be the product of the Warring States period (475–221 B.C.). The information it yields on dream divination during this period is sufficient to show that the practice was considered an important ritual function. The details of this ritual function and the methods of the dream diviners from this era are lost, but the place dream divination held in the institutional hierarchy of the *Zhou li* seems only slightly less important than that held by divination using the *Book of Changes*.[10] The analytical schema of the ten movements and ninety submovements suggests an organized framework for dream divination of comparable complexity and sophistication to the eight trigrams and sixty-four hexagrams of the *Book of Changes*.

The six categories of dreams named in the *Zhou li* also indicate an interest in the dream phenomena themselves. The method of categorization is not based on divination as such, since a dream of any category can be either auspicious or inauspicious. The final four categories—reflective dreams, daydreams, happy dreams, and frightening dreams—are based on the prior mental or emotional state of the dreamer. This type of categorization presupposes some type of underlying recognition, based perhaps on simple observation, that there is a relationship between dreams and the mental state of the dreamer. The first two categories—restful dreams and startling dreams—recognize that dreams themselves give rise to affective states which are real. But this typology of dreams cannot be said to presuppose a theory of dreams and their causes. Early dream records and accounts of divinations do not seek the cause or the meaning of dreams in the mental state of the dreamer. The lack of linkage between the typology of dreams given in the *Zhou li* and the divinatory significance of dreams strongly suggests that the basic meaning and cause of dreams is not to be found in the mental state of the dreamer, but in a broader, impersonal system of signification and causality such as that which underlies the *Book of Changes*. In addition, the possibilities for divination are increased and the role of the diviner enhanced by discarding the intuitive notion that happy dreams are favorable signs and frightening dreams are warnings of evil to come.

Structure and content of dreams are not treated in the *Zhou li*. The earliest recorded dreams[11] are the accounts found in two poems in the *Xiao ya* or *Lesser Odes* section of the *Shi jing* or *Book of Odes*, the first collection of Chinese poetry. The composition of the *Xiao ya* section is thought to date from the ninth through the eighth centuries B.C. The first of these poems, *Si gan*, describes the building of a palace. The closing half of the poem is as follows:

> Level is the courtyard, straight are the pillars; pleasantly comfortable are the front rooms, ample are the obscurer parts; that is where the lord is at peace.
> Below there are rush mats, over them are bamboo mats; peacefully he sleeps there, he sleeps and he rises; and so (he says): "Divine my dreams!" Which are the auspicious dreams? There are black bears and brown-and-white bears, there are snake brood and snakes. The Great Man (chief diviner) divines them: "Black bears and brown-and-white bears, they are good omens of sons; snake brood and snakes, they are good omens of daughters."
> And so he bears sons; they lay them on a bed, they dress them in skirts, they give them as toys jade insignia; they cry shrilly; their red knee-covers will be brilliant, (they will be) rulers of hereditary houses.
> And so he bears daughters; they lay them on the ground, they dress them in wrappers, they give them as toys spinning-whorls; they shall have nothing but simplicity; only to the wine and the food shall they give their thoughts; they must not give sorrow to father and mother. (Karlgren 1950, 131)

Traditional commentaries have associated the chief diviner (*da ren*) mentioned in this poem with the Grand Diviner (*da bu* or *tai bu*) mentioned in the *Zhou li*. The commentary of Zhu Xi (A.D. 1130–1200) presents the reasonable suggestion that this poem was an ode upon the completion and dedication of a new palace for King

Xuan of Zhou (827–782 B.C.). The dream is concerned with royal progeny and the continuity of the family line. The sons will inherit the political realm and the daughters will serve the family.

Chinese historical sources are filled with dreams concerning noble progeny, especially dreams prefiguring the births of dynastic founders, several of which will be discussed later. The dream in the poem *Si gan* is remarkable in that it does not serve as a model for later dreams of the same type. In later sources the vast majority of dreams concerning births are very specific and refer to the birth of an individual rather than a line of progeny. These later dreams are almost always experienced by the mother of a special offspring. The imagery of the dream in *Si gan* which associates sons with bears and daughters with snakes is singular.[12] Although the *Book of Odes* is a source of imagery, metaphor, and symbolism that remained in use for more than two millennia, the bear and snake imagery of the dream in *Si gan* is not taken as a prototype for later dreams about male and female progeny. The suggestion of totemism linking the male line with bears and female descendants with snakes lends the poem and the dream it contains an archaic tone that distinguishes and perhaps isolates it from later dream literature.

The next poem in the *Lesser Odes* section is called *Wu yang*, which means "No Sheep." This poem concerns the prosperity of a kingdom and is also associated with the reign of King Xuan of Zhou. *Wu yang* contains the dream of a herdsman:

> Who says that you have no sheep? Three hundred form the herd; who says that you have no cattle? Ninety are those which are seven feet high; your sheep come, their horns are crowded together; your cattle come, their ears are flapping.
>
> Some descend from that sloping hill, some drink in the pool; some are sleeping, some are moving; your herdsmen come, they carry rush cloaks, they carry bamboo hats; some carry on their backs their provisions; thirty beasts form a color category; your victims are thus full in number.
>
> Your herdsmen come, with firewood, with brushwood, with female game, with male game; your sheep come, they are vigorous and strong, they are not defective, they do not collapse; the herdsmen wave to them with their arms, they all come; and now they have gone up into the fold.
>
> And the herdsman dreams: there are locusts, there are fishes, there are tortoise-and-snake banners, there are falcon banners; the Great Man (chief diviner) divines it: There are locusts, there

are fishes—that is rich years; there are tortoise-and-snake banners, there are falcon banners—your house will be multitudinous.
(Karlgren 1950, 131–2)

The concern of the poem and the dream it contains is the wealth
and prosperity of the king and the existence of ample stocks of animals required for ritual sacrifice. It is significant that the dream or
dreams divined are not that of the king, but of his herdsmen. The
herdsmen, though in the employ of the King, are functionaries of
minor importance with menial duties. That their dreams are given
official attention at court indicates that the function of the chief
diviner was not limited to the dreams of the royal family and high
officials. The world that is described in the poem is centered on the
king, but it is extensive in scope. The chief diviner's function is still
clearly related to the needs of the royal household and polity, but
dreams can be worthy of attention even though they occur to humble
or low-born persons.

Although dreams belong in a personal sense to the dreamer, in
the context of this poem and in the poem *Si gan* they take on a supra-
personal significance and belong to the kingdom and its ruler. In the
idealized view of the Chinese state embodied in Confucian and to
some extent Taoist philosophy, the kingdom is a reflection of a larger
natural order. A well-run kingdom or polity is in harmony with the
natural order and nature favors it with good auguries. An improperly
run polity is in conflict with the natural order and nature issues warnings and portents in the form of natural disasters and other calamities.
The two poems *Si gan* and *Wu yang* treat dreams as elements of this
larger order rather than as personal psychological phenomena. Just as
the dreams of both king and herdsman share a common end or ultimate significance that relates to the fate of the kingdom and royal
house, they seem to have a common cause or origin that lies outside
the dreamer.

The dreams in *Wu yang* and *Si gan* consist of animal images, or
pictures of animals on military banners, yet the presentation of the
images in both dreams is completely static. There is no action or narrative development in either dream.

These two poems are praise songs on narrow and specific topics,
the building or completion of a palace and the state of the royal herds.
The structure of the poems is conventional and the language used is
concise and elliptical. Nevertheless, none of these genre limitations
dictates that the dream images be static. There is movement, simple
narrative action, in both poems, but none occurs inside the dreams.

The dreamer is the recipient of an image and not a participant in some dream action. The images are cryptic and unfamiliar and have a group or universal significance rather than a personal meaning for the dreamer. The images are subject to interpretation based on specialized knowledge, a hermeneutic tradition, similar in scope and complexity to that known from the *Book of Changes*. Thus the dream conveys a message to the group and its interpretation is a codified social process, making the entire event a matter of historical rather than personal importance.

Conclusions about the earliest layer of recorded Chinese dreams cannot be drawn with confidence on the basis of the limited information available from the *Zhou li* and *Book of Odes*, but the following generalizations can be made:

1. The causes and significance of dreams are external to the dreamer.
2. The dreamer is a passive participant in the dreams.
3. Dream content and structure are static and consist only of images.
4. Meanings are conveyed through images which have group, rather than personal, significance. In the case of the *Book of Odes*, these images have a totemistic character.

For additional insight into the place of dreams in early Chinese texts we must turn to the *Zuo zhuan*, the richest source of dream records predating the unified imperial system instituted by the Qin dynasty in 221 B.C. The *Zuo zhuan* is an elaborate commentary on the *Spring and Autumn Annuals*, a terse listing of events concerning the reigns of various rulers of kingdoms in China between the years 722 and 481 B.C. The *Zuo zhuan* provides a detailed narrative of certain events throughout the entire span of the *Spring and Autumn Annals* and covers an additional seventeen years ending in 464 B.C. There are 26 accounts of dreams in the *Zuo zhuan* that are supposed to have happened between the years 656–469 B.C. (Fraser 1930, 90).[13]

The primary concerns reflected in the dreams found in the *Zuo zhuan* are fundamental social phenomena—war, death, affairs of government, birth, succession of leadership, and illness. These concerns are predominantly political. Even when dreams deal with extremely personal matters there is always an important political dimension. All of the dreams concerning birth, death, and illness in the *Zuo zhuan* involve the fates of political or military leaders. Almost all of the dreamers are important figures of their times and are identified by name. The few dreams of common or anonymous individuals that are recorded have a specific relation to affairs of state. The *Zuo zhuan* is a narrative and provides a vehicle for fuller exposition of dream content, interpretation, and consequences than the *Book of Odes*, but some dreams are given extremely cursory treatment. The language used in the *Zuo zhuan* is succinct. There are few words or constructions that are used in the roles of adjectives or adverbs. Nevertheless, the expository prose of the *Zuo zhuan* is far more complex and elaborate than that found in the other commentaries on the *Spring and Autumn Annals*, the *Gongyang zhuan* and the *Guliang zhuan*, which are more didactic, less digressive, and generally less interesting.[14] The expanded expository approach of the *Zuo zhuan* marks it as an advance in prose style. Its dream accounts are sufficiently varied and detailed to provide a good basis for analyzing the shape and social importance of dreams during the Spring and Autumn period.

The themes of birth, posterity, and succession to leadership are closely connected and occur together in several dreams. The *Zuo zhuan* contains an imbedded account of a dream of birth that supposedly occurred at the beginning of the Western Zhou dynasty, approximately 1122 B.C.

> When Queen Yijiang, the wife of King Wu of Zhou, was pregnant with Dashu, she dreamed that the Di, the Lord of Heaven, said to her, "I decree that your son shall be named Yu. Tang which is ruled by the constellation Shen shall be given to him. He will have many descendants." When the child was born he had the character Yu written on his hand. And he was named in accordance with the decree of Di. When King Cheng of Zhou destroyed the kingdom of Tang, he invested Dashu as ruler. Therefore the constellation Shen contains the ruling stars of Jin (which was the State formed from the kingdom of Tang). (Legge 1935, 580)[15]

This is the protoype of dreams prevalent from Han times onward of the births of future rulers or great men. It is totally different in content from the dream of royal posterity that occurs in the *Book of Odes*. The dreamer is a woman, the mother of the future ruler. She receives a message or a sign from heaven which is an explicit indication of some great event about to occur. In this case she receives both a message in the dream and a sign after the dream when the child is born with the character for the heaven-ordained name written on his palm. The structure of the dream itself, however, is not totally different from that found in the *Book of Odes*. The dreamer is essentially passive; she listens to a message. She is present in the dream only as an auditor. The figure speaking to her is a spiritual being, a numinous being, not a contemporary living human.

This imbedded dream account is set 400 years before the beginning of the Spring and Autumn period, yet embodies patterns that are characteristic of the dream accounts in the basic narrative of the *Zuo zhuan*.[16] Several characteristics of these patterns differ from those of the two examples from the *Book of Odes*. First of all, the dream is primarily auditory rather than visual. The import of the dream is conveyed through a direct message in plain language. Second, the speaker is a spirit. In later cases it is often an ancestral figure, or a person who has died in the recent past. Third, the dream has a specific, discrete impact on actual affairs, usually involving the fates of particular individuals.

The dream also makes use of cosmological correspondences, in this case the linkage between Yu and the constellation Shen. This element is rare in dreams found in the *Zuo zhuan*, but becomes an important part of similar dreams in Han dynasty records.[17]

A dream of Yanji, the concubine of Duke Wen of Zheng, prefiguring the birth of the future duke has a structure that is almost identical with the dream of Queen Yijiang of Zhou. The dream is supposed to have occurred in 606 B.C.

> Duke Wen of Zheng had a low-ranking concubine named Yanji. She dreamed heaven sent a messenger to her who gave her a fragrant herb called *lan*. The messenger said, "I am Bochou, your ancestor. Take this *lan* as your son's name. Since the *lan* has the 'fragrance of the kingdom' (symbolizing outstanding virtue) men will follow and love him in like manner." A short time afterward, Duke Wen received her, gave her a *lan* and slept with her. She said, "Your concubine is unworthy. If I should be blessed with a son, it would not be believed (that I was bearing your son). Might I dare to use this *lan* as a sign (that it is your son)?" The Duke agreed.
>
> She gave birth to the future Duke Mu, who was named Lan. (Legge 1935, 294)

The detailed similarities between the dream of Yanji and the dream of Queen Yijiang are striking. Both are visited in a dream by a spirit. In the case of Yanji the dream visitor is an ancestor of her clan. The *Zuo zhuan* identifies the ancestor, Bochou, as an emissary from heaven. He delivers a message concerning the birth of a son who will be a future ruler and dictates the name of the child. There is also a physical token of the special name in both events, but in the dream of Yanji the token is presented in the dream. In the same manner as the dream of Queen Yijiang there is an actual physical manifestation of the special token or sign after the dream. Although the action of passing the token occurs in the dream, Yanji is still primarily a listener and passive participant.

Dreams of political succession are sometimes similar to birth dreams. A pair of linked dreams in the *Zuo zhuan* prefigures the birth of a future ruler of the state of Wei. These dreams are primarily concerned with the future composition of the government of Wei and occur to two men who are leading figures of that state.

> Jiang, the wife of Duke Xiang, had no children, but his favorite, Zhou E, gave birth to Meng Zhi. Kong Chengzi dreamt that Kang Shu[18] said to him, "Appoint Yuan as successor (the younger brother of Meng Zhi, yet unborn at the time of the dream, the future Duke Ling of Wei). I will have Yu, the grandson of Ji (i.e., the great-grandson of Kong Zhengchu) and Shi Gou serve him as ministers."
>
> Shi Chao also dreamt that Kang Shu said to him in a dream, "I decree that your son Gou and the great-grandson of Kong Zhengchu, Yu, will serve Yuan as ministers."
>
> When Shi Chao met Kong Chengzi and told him of his dream, they learned that their two dreams were in agreement. (Legge 1935, 619)

Although these dreams do not have a close structural resemblance to birth dreams that occur to women, they do share some general features. As in the dreams of Queen Yijiang and the concubine Yanji, the dreamers are passive auditors of a message delivered by a spirit. The spirit in the dream also names an individual yet to be born. This is not done in the manner of a decree, but as foreknowledge that the spirit possesses. There is a decree in the dream of Kong Chengzi calling for Yuan to be appointed successor.

Although the import of the two messages presented in these paired dreams is the same—both describe the composition of the government of Wei under a future duke—the wording of the messages is specifically designed to meet the needs and expectations of the dreamer. The message to Kong Chengzi emphasizes the role that Yu of the Kong family will play in a government under Yuan. The emphasis of the message is apparent in the order of delivery, which mentions the role of Yu before that of Shi Gou and the relative informality or intimacy in the use of Kong family names. The emphasis is reversed in the dream of Shi Chao.

The appearance of Kang Shu in two separate dreams in which he delivers individually worded messages on a common topic to two individuals with separate interests in the topic illustrates the important role that dreams play as a subtle and precise mechanism for communication between spirits or ancestors and the living. In the four examples of dreams prefiguring births there is a very large overlap if not a total identity between the spirit realm and the dream realm. All of these dreams provide access to the spirit realm, but the dreamer is recipient of only a special, delimited aspect of this realm. The dreamer has no power to initiate action and no means to gain knowledge from the spirit realm except that which is specifically imparted to him. Spirits or ancestors, friendly or hostile ghosts, can direct and inform men and women through dreams, but recipients can only accept or ignore the message.

The fifth and final dream relating to birth in the *Zuo zhuan* is different from the others in both content and structure. It is a dream that deals with posterity and continuity of the family line rather than the birth of a specific individual. It is one of only two examples of dreams in the *Zuo zhuan* that contain no anthropomorphic figures.[19]

> Meng Xizi met with Duke Zhuang of Zou [Zhu] and they made an alliance at Jinxiang, pledging to foster good relations, in accordance with the Rites.
>
> There was a woman in Quanqiu who dreamt that the draperies of her chamber formed a curtain over the ancestral temple of the Meng clan. Afterward she sought out Meng Xizi and her companion followed her. They made a pledge at the shrine of Qingqiu saying that if they had sons they would not contend with one another.
>
> Meng Xizi sent them to serve the concubine of a man of the Wei family. On his return from Jinxiang, he stayed at the house of this man. [Later]Yizi and Nangong Jingshu were born to the woman of Quanqiu. Her companion had no children, but was assigned to care for Nangong Jingshu. (Legge 1935, 634)

The images in the dream are inanimate, but undergo a transformation. The message conveyed by the images is clear and straightforward and requires no interpretation by a third party or specialized diviner. The transformation of the woman's curtains in her private chamber to a covering for the Meng clan temple is a sign that she will give birth to sons of the Meng line who will preserve the sacrifices to their ancestors. Although this dream concerns a theme that is shared by the other dreams of birth in the *Zuo zhuan* and the dream of royal posterity in the *Book of Odes*, in relation to other dreams in the *Zuo zhuan* it is unique in structure.[20]

The messages contained in birth dreams are clear and require no special interpretation. Dreams concerning war, the outcome of battles, and death are not always so easy to understand. Although dream content accords perfectly with dream significance in the dreams of birth, this is definitely not a general rule. The principle in the typology of dreams in the *Zhou li* that separates dream content from significance is clearly illustrated in the *Zuo zhuan* when dream accounts other than birth dreams are considered. Content itself does not always provide the key to meaning. This key is often to be found outside the dream itself. The key to interpretation is the connection between the dream experience and the state of the spirit or noumenal world. The *Zuo zhuan* offers methods for finding this connection. Dreams can be interpreted by use of milfoil or tortoise-shell divination, or by shamans, spirit mediums who can commune directly with the spirit realm to find the cause of a dream. These are all external operations which largely ignore the dream as a text. The content of a dream is not revealing unless the cause or concern of the spirit noumenal realm that occasioned the dream accords with the content. In the case of birth dreams in the *Zuo zhuan* there is a perfect correspondence between the dream content or message and the concern of the spirit realm, but in other dreams there is sometimes no correspondence at all.

Two examples of dreams which deal with military matters—a nightmare on the eve of battle and a cryptic dream that occurred near an eclipse—show the extremes of attitudes concerning the importance and goal of dream interpretation and the role of content in the analysis of dreams. In both examples the content of the dream holds no clear message for the dreamer. The nightmare of the Marquis of Jin demonstrates that the significance of dreams cannot be treated dismissively even when the process of dream interpretation is cynically manipulated.

> The Marquis of Jin dreamt that he was struggling with the Viscount of Chu (King Cheng). The Viscount of Chu knelt down over him and sucked his brains out and drank them. This dream made the Marquis of Jin afraid. Zifan said, "The dream is auspicious. We are in accord with heaven (because you are on the ground facing the sky) and Chu is kneeling as if to acknowledge its crimes. Moreover we deal with Chu gently (gentleness being signified by the softness of brains). (Legge 1935, 209)

The commentary on this passage by Du Yu, written during the Western Jin (A.D. 265–317), clearly recognizes this interpretation as expedient nonsense invented by Zifan. Du says, "Zifan determined that circumstances were favorable for an attack, therefore he interpreted the dream with carefully considered words."[21] Nevertheless, Zifan has provided correct advice and properly dismisses the frightening aspect of the dream. Jin defeats Chu in the upcoming battle and the

Marquis of Jin suffers no harm. Although the skepticism of Zifan produces a favorable result in this instance, skeptical dismissal of dreams is not the norm in the *Zuo zhuan*. They are usually taken as serious and important signs of political, military, and personal fates.[22]

Although the comments of Zifan on the dream of the Marquis of Jin are specious and contrived, they do focus on elements within the dream and attempt to analyze factors that seem to represent defeat and death as signs that are in fact favorable. The Marquis seems to have had his fears allayed by this analysis and the battle against the forces of Chu does take place. Zifan's treatment of the dream is based on his estimate of the military facts. He views the dream as a hindrance to the will and resolve of the Marquis and succeeds in nullifying its effect. All of this seems both practical and pragmatic and has little to do with the spirit or numinous world and its concerns or directives. The adoption of a cynical and manipulative interpretation is actually a recognition of how seriously dreams were taken by the society at large. Although Zifan wished to neutralize the paralyzing effect of the dream on the Marquis, he could not do so by merely dismissing the dream as insignificant. He was forced to adopt a strategy that explained the dream in a manner that fitted his practical objectives and satisfied the doubts of the Marquis.

The concerns of the spirits and ancestors can never be totally ignored in the social context of the Spring and Autumn period and the messages received in dreams cannot be lightly dismissed. A sentiment repeated in the *Zuo zhuan* declares that victory and defeat are in the hands of the spirits. Although practical concerns may dictate the outcome of a battle, participants in the warfare of this period can never leave supernatural concerns totally aside. At the very least, most of the participants believed that victory was only possible if it accorded with a heavenly will and sanction.[23]

A cryptic dream that occurs at the time of a solar eclipse and presages conflict offers a contrasting view of the relationship between content and interpretation. While Zifan was not constrained in shaping his interpretation to meet pragmatic goals, here the divination process is taken very seriously, yet dream content is totally irrelevant to analysis and interpretation. In this example the dreamer requests an interpretation from a court historian and the historian offers an erudite prognostication that includes a precise timetable of future military events.

> The Twelfth Month, on morning of the day *xin hai*,[24] there was an eclipse of the sun. Zhao Jianzi dreamed of a small boy, who was naked and swayed while he sang. On the next day he asked the historian Mo

to divine it, saying, "I have had this dream and today there is an eclipse of the sun. What is to be made of this?" The historian replied, "Six years from now, in this month, the State of Wu will invade Ying (the capital of the State of Chu), but in the end it will not be victorious. Wu will enter Ying on the day *geng chen*. The sun and the moon will be in Sagittarius. On the day *geng wu*, the influence of the sun will begin to change. The element of fire will overcome that of metal. Therefore Wu will not be victorious."(Legge 1935, 738)[25]

The most fascinating part of this explanation is that none of it deals with the content of the dream. The image of the naked boy singing is not mentioned at all in the interpretation offered by the historian. Although Zhao Jianzi is interested in the relationship between his dream and the eclipse of the sun, the answer he is given indicates that the content of the dream itself is not significant. The fact that the dream occurred near the time of an eclipse is important, but the details of the dream are not. The dream itself is only a small reflection of greater changes occurring in the nonmaterial realm that hold the key to future events. The analytical tools used by the historian are based on astrology and the five-phases (*wu xing*) theory.[26] Although the final interpretation of the historian is clear and precise—Wu will invade Ying, but will not succeed—the method is cryptic. It is impossible to reproduce the reasoning or schema that leads to the interpreted result and impossible to assess what role, if any, the dream may have contributed to the interpretation. This is the most detailed interpretative exercise recorded in the *Zuo zhuan* related to a dream, yet dream content appears totally immaterial to the interpretation.[27]

The professional and abstruse style of interpretation exemplified by the historian Mo and the amateur, expedient analysis of Zifan represent two poles of personal attitudes towards dreams and their significance. Dreams are generally taken as bearing special meaning and, with the exception of dreams which seem to have transparent significance such as the birth and succession dreams discussed above, interpretation is usually taken as a weighty matter in the *Zuo zhuan*.

Although a number of personages in the *Zuo zhuan* manage to determine the significance of dreams correctly, especially dreams that contain spoken messages from ancestors or spirits, there is always a danger of misinterpretation as the following story illustrates.

Sometime in the past, Shusun Bao left his clan in Lu and was seeking refuge in Qi. He came to Gengzong. There he met a woman who served him, giving him food and a place to sleep. She asked about his journey. When he told her [that he was fleeing his home], she cried and saw him off. He went to Qi and married a woman of the Guo clan. They had two sons called Mengbing and Zhongren.

Shusun Bao dreamed that the sky was pressing him down and he could not resist it. He saw a man, dark-skinned, hump-backed, with deep-set eyes and a mouth like a pig's. He called out to him saying, "Niu, help me." [And with his help] he was able to overcome the pressure of the sky. The next day he called all his retainers, but there was no such man among them. Then he said, "Make a record of this."

When his elder brother Shusun Qiaoru also came to Qi to seek refuge, he fed him. Shusun Qiaoru said, "Because of my past service to the State of Lu and for the preservation of [sacrifices] to our ancestors, you will certainly be summoned to Lu. If this happens what will you do?" Shusun Bao said, "For a long time I have desired such a thing." Lu did summon him and he returned without informing anyone and was appointed to office [as chief minister of state].

The lady from Gengzong who had given him shelter presented him with a pheasant. He asked her if she had any sons. She replied, "I have a big boy who was able to carry this pheasant and follow me here." He called for the son and when he saw him, he was just like the person he had seen in his dream. Without asking his name he called out the name, Niu. The boy replied in acknowledgment. Shusun Bao called all his retainers in to view the boy and made him an attendant. (Legge 1935, 598–9)

Niu proves to be a treacherous and faithless servant, intriguing against Shusun Bao and his sons, even trying to deprive him of certain honors in his funeral arrangements when he died. Du Yu says, "The *Zuo zhuan* is telling us that it is not necessarily auspicious to act in accordance with a dream."[28] It is difficult for the dreamer to be the judge of the transparency or accuracy of a dream message. Though professional or expert interpretation or divination can be wrong, to dispense with it can be dangerous.

Because interpretation of dreams is often linked to important matters of warfare or statecraft, the responsibility of the interpreter is heavy. The following dream foretells the downfall of the State of Wei and prefigures the death of the sons of the Marquis of Wei. A historian is asked to interpret the dream by means of milfoil stalks, but conceals its true meaning. A second interpretation is done by means of tortoise shell that describes future events in accurate detail. Given the unfavorable nature of the dream and the eventual fate of the Marquis, the historian is understandably reluctant to divulge the true meaning of the dream.

Marquis Zhuang of Wei dreamed that he was at the northern palace and saw a person climb the observation tower on the Kunwu hill. This person had long trailing hair and facing to the north yelled out, "Climbing this hill of Kunwu, the gourds are beginning to grow. I am Hun Liangfu, and I call to heaven that I am innocent."

The Marquis asked that the historian Xu Mishe divine the dream by means of the milfoil. Xu said, "It is harmless." The Marquis gave him a city, which he abandoned and fled to the state of Song.

Then the Marquis had the dream divined by the tortoise shell and the oracular text read:

> Like a fish with a red tail
> Cross-current and unable to reach the edge
> A great state will destroy him and he will flee.
> The gates will be closed and the openings will be shut
> And he must jump over from behind. (Legge 1935, 850)

The subsequent fate of the Marquis is exactly foreshadowed in this oracular text. He is deposed by the army of the state of Jin, but he returns to Wei. He continues his arrogant and rapacious ways and is forced to flee over the back wall of his dwelling during a popular uprising. He attempts to seek refuge, but is killed by a man whom he had wronged. Thus the dream divination in all its parts is fulfilled. The divination is remarkable in its specificity concerning future events. The content of the dream strongly suggests that the Marquis will die as a consequence of his past evil deeds, but there is no specific linkage between the dream content and the details of the oracular text concerning the dream.

Hun Liangfu is a ghost or spirit with a specific grievance against the Marquis. For his help in bringing the Marquis to power he had been promised virtual immunity from execution. Unfortunately he had earned the enmity of the son of the Marquis, Ji, by not clearly supporting him as heir. Ji contrived a plot that would result in his execution and did have him killed in the same year that this dream occurred. Given this background the dream suggests that Hun Liangfu, as a ghost, might seek vengeance and become an agent of destruction, perhaps bringing about the death of the Marquis and his son Ji, but this is not the case. The linkage between the dream and the interpretation is broader and more tenuous than that found in other dreams concerning avenging ghosts. Hun Liangfu is a messenger who merely hints that the Marquis will not escape the consequences of past misdeeds. The significance of the dream as revealed by the tortoise-plastron divination is political rather than personal destruction. Although the appearance of Hun Liangfu in a dream of the Marquis would appear to be a sign of danger, the *Zuo zhuan* record indicates that the Marquis believed and rewarded the historian Xu Mishe for pronouncing the dream harmless.

In contrast to the words in dreams of birth and succession, the speech heard in this dream is not readily understood. The self-identification of Hun Liangfu and his proclamation of innocence are clear, but the significance of the gourds is obscure.

The *Zuo zhuan* is a single text, but its dream material is rich and complex. The modern reader, however, may feel that the dreams are lacking in variety. Indeed, apart from a few dreams that contain startling features, the dream records do not display the imaginative possibilities that our modern cultural context assumes is inherent in dreams. This view of the dream as a form without limitations in structure or content is not itself modern[29] and may in fact have been shared by the men and women of the Spring and Autumn period. In both style and content, the dream records of the *Zuo zhuan* display a broad range of concerns and though the selections of the author have been made on the basis of their historical, social, and political importance, the dreams themselves touch on broad major themes of human life: birth, death, illness, success, and failure. It is not lack of variety, but lack of expected variety that strikes the reader as odd.

The dreams of the *Zuo zhuan* reflect the cultural understandings and patterns of a society not only different from contemporary norms, but also different from later Chinese society. The dream records of the Spring and Autumn period strongly suggest that this was an age in which people firmly believed that the dead and other figures of spiritual authority spoke to the living in dreams. Dreams were not considered the psychological property of the dreamer. They were events that created a bridge between the dreamer and a larger unseen world in which the everyday world was subsumed. Dreams were a form of one-way communication from this larger realm to the sphere of mundane existence. The form of communication used was often direct speech.[30]

The notion of a dream that is primarily an auditory experience does not accord with common preconceptions, but the *Zuo zhuan* provides ample evidence that Chinese readers of the Warring States period not only found such dreams ordinary and believable, but considered them perhaps the most important type of dream.

The text of the *Zuo zhuan* introduces direct speech in dreams in two patterns. The first is "person X dreams of figure Y who says, 'Z.' " In Chinese this pattern reads: "X *meng* Y. . . . *yue*: 'Z.' " The second pattern emphasizes the role of the dreamer as intended auditor in the form, "person X dreams of figure Y who says to him, 'Z' " ("X *meng* Y *wei ji*: 'Z' "). There are also two examples in which the dream figure who speaks is identified as a someone "sent by heaven" ("X *meng tian shi . . . yue* (or *wei ji*): 'Z' ").

Although the concept of direct communication through dreams with spirits of the deceased or with certain spiritual powers can only command disbelief in the modern reader, the phenomenon is recorded in the ancient literatures of many nations other than China. A single example from the *Iliad* is representative of an entire class of dreams found in Homeric and other early Greek literature. It occurs to Agamemnon at the beginning of Book 2.

> Dream stood then beside his head in the likeness of Nestor, Neleus's son, whom Agamemnon honored above all elders beside. In Nestor's likeness the divine Dream spoke to him "son of wise Atreus breaker of horses, are you sleeping?
> He should not sleep night long who is a man burdened with counsels and responsibility for a people and cares so numerous.
> Now listen quickly to what I say, since I am a messenger of Zeus, who far away cares much for you and is pitiful. . . ." (Lattimore 1967, 76–7)

Dreams of this type are common enough in Greek literature to constitute an identifiable and named class of dreams, *chrematismos*. E. R. Dodds noted, "Most of the dreams recorded in Assyrian, Hittite, and ancient Egyptian literature are 'divine dreams' in which a god appears and delivers a plain message to the sleeper, sometimes predicting the future, sometimes demanding cult" (1951, 109). A. Leo Oppenheimer in his study of ancient Near Eastern dreams calls them message dreams (1956, 185). The classification of dreams posited by Macrobius also included a similar distinct category, the *oraculum*. The difficulty of the modern reader in recognizing this type of dream experience has been noted by several authors (Spearing 1976, 10–11), but the records in the *Zuo zhuan* support the proposition that this type of dream should be given credence in its own time and cultural context.[31]

This context differs considerably from both Homeric Greece and the ancient Near East. China of the Spring and Autumn period was not a culture with either hieratic religious beliefs, or well-developed notions of an afterlife. Theistic beliefs of any sort are generally lacking in early Chinese culture. Figures that appear in *Zuo zhuan* dreams with cult importance such as Kang Shu are the spirits of departed ancestors, not gods. The dreams mesh with the practice of honoring ancestors in state or clan temples and though the practice was universal, the ancestral figures themselves are only of importance to a given clan, state, or region. Even Di, the Lord of Heaven, who appears to rulers in dreams, does not appear to be an object of widespread veneration. He is a figure in state ritual sacrifice, but he remains a vague undefined supernatural presence in early sources. In this cultural context it is far more reasonable to believe that the dream records of visitations are a reflection of actual beliefs and events, rather than an attempt by a given author to support an established belief system through interesting literary embellishments. Unlike the ancient Near East there is no indication that certain types of dream records were censored from Chinese historical records.[32] The spirits were a fact of life in the Spring and Autumn period, but not one which demanded support or justification. Discursive treatment of the topic is limited until the Han dynasty and later. Records of the Spring and Autumn period, Warring States period, and the former Han, when they acknowledge the spirits at all, offer broad statements concerning their presence and significance, but little detail or speculative probing concerning their nature or the unseen realm they inhabit. As Confucius noted to one of his disciples when asked about the meaning of wisdom, "He who . . . by respect for the spirits keeps them at a distance, may be termed wise" (Waley 1938, 120).

In ancient China, in contrast to some other early civilizations, there is no evidence of the practice of incubation, i.e. the use of regimens to induce dreams for the purpose of obtaining visions or communicating with spirits (Strickman 1988, 40).[33] The *Zuo zhuan* indicates that direct contact with the world of gods, ghosts, and spirits was a function assigned to the shamans, who could somehow enter the unseen realm through trances.[34] The shamans could also enter the dream space, but there are no accounts of shamans using dreams as a means to enter the spirit realm. Although the record is clear that the social and cultural context of the Spring and Autumn period supported a belief in spirits and ghosts, there is no evidence that ordinary individuals desired direct contact with superhuman authority figures or ancestors through dreams. Given this background there is no reason to assume that the inclusion in the *Zuo zhuan* of dream records of encounters with ancestors or spirits is related to a desire to confirm an established orthodoxy.

The genuine variety of the dreams recorded in the *Zuo zhuan* is illustrated by the difficulty of making generalizations about them as a whole. The prominence of ancestor, spirit, and ghost visions is a distinguishing feature of the group, but other types of dreams also occur. Almost all are mantic dreams, but there are exceptions.[35] Many of the dreams have transparent meanings, but some are cryptic and require specialized interpretation.[36]

A diachronic perspective casts a clearer light on the special characteristics of *Zuo zhuan* dreams. In comparison with Han records, the following features are characteristic of the *Zuo zhuan* dream records, but less prominent in later sources.

1. Auditory dreams with direct messages to the dreamer.
2. Dreams with visitations with ancestors or benign spiritual beings.
3. Dreams where content plays no part in interpretation.

Although dreams with these features are primarily mantic dreams, they do not operate as signs or signals to the dreamer. They are events, external events, in which the dreamer participates, though this participation is mostly passive.

Zuo zhuan dreams rarely contain ordinary places or spaces. What is dreamt is not an obscure version of reality where locations are supranormal or distorted. There simply are no locations. There is a special sphere, where a passive auditor, the dreamer, confronts a spirit or messenger. Dreams tend to come to people where they are sleeping, much in the manner that Dream comes to Agamemnon in the *Iliad*.

When people are met in dreams they are often recognizable people, though they can undergo abnormal transformations, such as the Viscount of Chu sucking the brains from the Marquis of Jin, or a man putting his severed head back on.[37] These may be startling images, but they are not difficult to comprehend as dream images.

The dream records in the *Zuo zhuan* show that the passive auditory dream was still considered normal during the Spring and Autumn and Warring periods, but its relative rarity in later records suggests that it is an archaic element. Symbolic keys based on organized systems of cosmology and astrology had some bearing on dream interpretation, but this methodology on which all "dream books" rely is not common until the Han dynasty and later times (Drege 1981, 213–233).[38] The detailed use of such theories by the historian Mo, in the example cited above, indicates that the mechanism for using symbolic keys based on cosmological theory was available. Nevertheless, taking elements from dream content and analyzing them by use of such symbolic keys is done on only an extremely limited basis in the *Zuo zhuan*. Correspondence theories, where the appearance of an object or an event in a dream indicates the meaning of the dream, do not appear to be a significant means of dream interpretation during the period of the *Zuo zhuan*.

The *Zuo zhuan* contains archaic dream patterns that appear less frequently in the Han period and gradually disappear over the centuries. To a lesser extent it also contains the seeds of dream patterns that were to become dominant during the Han dynasty and throughout subsequent centuries. Although this discussion has dealt only with the *Zuo zhuan*, the few sources that seem contemporary with the *Zuo zhuan* include dream accounts similar in nature to those discussed above.[39]

The rise during the Han dynasty of codified cosmological thought making use of extensive systems of correspondences based on five-phases theory, Yin-Yang theory, numerology, and astrology changed the way in which dreams were interpreted in later times. The first discursive speculation on the nature of dreams also appears in sources shaped or modified during the Han dynasty. The pre-Han *Zhuang zi* suggests all phenomena may be a dream, but does not analyze the dream as a phenomenon. The first analytical treatment of dreams and dream divination is found in the *Lun Heng* by Wang Chong (A.D. 27–c. 97) (Forke 1962, 182–249). Correspondence systems for dream analysis are the basis for most popular dream lore and dream books of later times. The earliest reference to the use of simple symbolic keys to interpret the meaning of dreams seems to be in the *Bowuzhi*, an anthology of exotic lore compiled by Zhang Hua during the third century A.D. This book contains the following two items that would fit into any book of popular dream lore: If a person wears a sash while sleeping, they will dream of snakes. If a bird takes hold of a man's hair in its beak, the man will dream of flying (Ning 1980, 110).[40]

The speculative philosophy of the Han also laid the foundation for the understanding of dreams as a psychological phenomenon. The *Qian fu lun* of Wang Fu (A.D. c. 85–162) introduces a typology of ten classes of dreams which clearly identifies the causes of some dreams as within the dreamer (Strickmann 1988, 27–8). These developments during the Han are part of a new cultural context that seems to have superseded the era of direct communication with spirits characteristic of the Spring and Autumn period.

The changes in dream accounts recorded before and after the Han dynasty are merely a single phase in an ongoing process. The fundamental proposition that dream texts change through history and therefore what we know of dreams changes over time is true in China and in other cultures and literary traditions. Nevertheless it is common to treat the dream in literature as a motif outside history whose variants may be linked to developments in literary genres. This approach is not accurate in the case of Chinese literature. Variations in Chinese historiography as a genre cannot be used to explain the changes that continue to occur in Chinese dream accounts found in the histories written from the Han to the Tang dynasties. Chinese historical texts, in particular the so-called orthodox histories, are a literary form that was essentially stable for centuries.

The chapter is intended as a contribution to the historical and comparative study of dream accounts. The material found in early Chinese records raises the fundamental question as to whether diachronic literary and linguistic analysis of dream accounts can explain the dynamic changes in such accounts over time. The intriguing possibility remains that essential changes in patterns of dreaming, beyond mere changes in the structure of texts, may have occurred and that such basic changes may not have been confined to a single cultural context.

Table of all dream accounts in the *Zuo zhuan* and *Shi jing*, with an index to accessible translations.

Shi jing (Book of Odes or Book of Songs)

Karlgren Page	Waley Page	Name of the Dreamer	Date (B.C.)
129–131	282–284	King Xuan of Zhou?	VIII C
131–132	167–168	King Xuan of Zhou?	VIII C

Legge	Watson	*Zuo zhuan*	
142	23	Duke Xian of Jin	656
209	59–60	Marquis of Jin, (Duke Wen of Jin)	632
210	63	Cheng Ziyu	632
219		Duke Cheng of Wei,	629
294		Yanji (Concubine of Duke Wen of Zheng)	606
328	107–108	Wei Qi of Jin	594
345	114	Han Jue	589
357		Zhao Ying	584
374	120–121	Marquis Nou of Jin (Duke Jing of Jin)	581
374	121	Servant of the Marquis of Jin	581
397	133	Wei Qi of Jin	575
404		Gongsun Yingqi	574
478		Xun Yan	555
580		Yijiang (Wife of King Wu of Zhou)	XII C
599		Shusun Bao	538
616		Duke Zhao of Lu	535
617		Marquis Biao of Jin (Duke Ping of Jin)	535
618		Some People of Zheng	535
619		Kong Chengzi	535
619		Shi Chao of Wei	535
634		woman of Quanqiu	531
668		Han Xuanzi of Jin	525
711		Duke Yuan of Song	517
738		Zhao Jianzi of Jin	511
814		man of Cao	488
850		Marquis Zhuang of Wei (Duke Zhuang of Wei)	478
859		Qi (brother of De of Song)	469

ℵotes

1. All Chinese words are given in *pinyin* romanization.

2. *Zhuang zi* contains several references to dreams, including the most famous dream in early Chinese literature in which Zhuang zi dreams he is a butterfly and upon awakening seems to be himself, but speculates that he might now be a butterfly dreaming it is Zhuang zi. The dream tales within the *Zhuang zi* are generally similar to the famous butterfly dream and are for the most part not presented as historical and will not be treated here.

3. All references are to the *Zhou li Zheng zhu, Jiao yong huai tang* edition. This edition contains only the commentary of Zheng Xuan (A.D. 127–200) of the Latter Han. References to this and other traditional Chinese volumes will be given by *chuan* number followed by a period and page number(s).

4. Examiner of Dreams (*zhan meng*) could also be translated Diviner of Dreams.

5. Later exegesis by Zheng E of the Song dynasty in his *Zhou li quan jie* elaborates on the meaning of the three methods, but he and other later commentators such as Wang Yuzhi of the Song in the *Zhou li ding yi* discuss these methods in terms of types of dreams and do not explain what interpretive methodology might have been used.

6. A gloss of Zheng Xuan indicating *yun* should be read as "halos" or "bright emanations" assumes an interpolation in the text and is not followed here. For a translation that follows Zheng Xuan see Wagner 1988, 19.

7. Exact parallel passages concerning methodological schema follow the main reference to each method of divination in the *Zhou li*. For example, the Grand Diviner also has responsibility for divination by the methods of the three changes (*san yi*), including use of the *Book of Changes* or *Zhou li ding yi*. The *Zhou li* then provides the following methodological schema: "Its trigrams are eight and its subdivisions are sixty-four."

8. These observations are based on the Zheng Xuan commentary.

9. Zheng Xuan says that this rite consisted of offering up all the auspicious dreams of the highest officials from the past year to the ruler and dispelling the inauspicious dreams to the four quarters.

10. *Zhou li* 24.11 states that all important affairs of state were divined by milfoil. No similar claim is made for dream divination. However, the officials in charge of milfoil divination were of the same rank as the Examiner of Dreams and each position was filled by two officials of this rank.

11. The *Shang shu* or *Book of History* is a corrupt text, parts of which date from the Western Zhou period (eleventh century–770 B.C.), that contains an account of a dream of Emperor Wu Ding (fifteenth–fourteenth centuries B.C.) of the Shang or Yin dynasty. The section of the text containing the account is thought to be a late forgery, perhaps dating from the Eastern Jin (A.D. 317–420).

12. *San Guo zhi (Chronicle of the Three Kingdoms)*, Zhonghua ed. 810, contains a reference to a dream of a snake with feet. The account notes that a dream of snakes is ordinarily an auspicious omen concerning women, but the dream of a snake with feet is interpreted as a portent of the death of women bandits. Most other later snake dreams contain similar negative imagery. I have been unable to locate any subsequent reference to bears as an auspicious omen of male offspring.

13. The total number of dreams, including fabricated accounts, clearly identified in the text of the *Zuo zhuan* is 27. In addition there is an apparition that is referred to as a "strange dream" in a separate entry.

14. There are no dreams in the *Gongyang zhuan* or the *Guliang zhuan*.

15. All translations from the *Zuo zhuan* have been made with reference to Legge, 1935. Translations will be cited as Legge even when they have been extensively reworked. The basic Chinese edition used was the *Chun Qiu jing zhuan ji jie (CQJZJJ)* version of Du Yu, *Shang tai Yue shi* edition. Only references to the Du Yu commentary will cite the Chinese text.

16. This dream occurs approximately 500 years earlier than the first actual dream account in the *Zuo Zhuan*, which is found in an entry concerning the year 632 B.C.

17. There is only one other example of a dream in the *Zuo zhuan* that employs the elements of cosmological correspondence theories as images within the dream. This is the dream of Wei Qi, found in Legge 1935, 397. There is also an example of cosmological correspondence theory used to interpret a dream (p. 738), but the dream itself does not make use of such elements.

18. Kang Shu, the ninth younger brother of King Wu of Zhou, was invested as the first Duke of Wei. He is the primary ancestor for the Dukes of Wei. He would have been dead more than 500 years at the time of these dreams.

19. The other dream appears in Legge 1935, 617. The dream of the woman of Quanqiu is the only example in the *Zuo zhuan* of a dream that contains only inanimate images.

20. Dreams that contain only objects or substances do occur in Han and later times, but represent a small fraction of the recorded dream accounts in premodern Chinese.

21. *CQJZJJ* 7.7b.

22. The commentary of Du Yu states that the *Zuo zhuan* contains a warning against excessive belief in the import of dreams (*CQJZJJ* 21.8ab). There are also examples of the negative consequences of accepting reports or interpretations of dreams with excessive credulity. But most dreams in the *Zuo zhuan* prove true.

23. A clear example of the danger of skepticism and reliance solely on pragmatic concerns is found in the story of Cheng Ziyu of Chu in Legge 1935, 210.

24. *Xin hai, geng chen* and *geng wu* are designations for days in the traditional calendrical cycle.

25. A convoluted explanation of all this follows in the Du Yu commentary using five-phases theory, numerology, and astrology (*CQJZJJ* 26.19b–20a).

26. The five phases, *wu xing*, are water, fire, wood, metal, and earth. Five-phases theory considers these to be the basic constituents or phases of matter.

27. In the *Zuo zhuan* there are seventeen interpretations of events using the system of hexagrams in the *Book of Changes*. None of these milfoil interpretations deal with dream events.

28. *CQJZJJ* 21.8b.

29. The same sentiment is found in Cicero *De Divinatione* 2:71, "Nihil tam preropostere, tam monstruose cogitari potest quod non possimus somnare." ("There is no imaginable thing too absurd, too involved, or too abnormal for us to dream about it.") Translated by W. A. Falconer, New York: Loeb Classical Library, 1922.

30. Fourteen of the twenty-seven dreams in the *Zuo zhuan* include important elements of speech; nine consist only of speech.

31. Spearing notes: "Of Macrobius's five types (of dreams), the *oraculum* alone now seems completely obsolete, and it will be worth pausing for a moment to consider why this should be so. It is perhaps true that in our time few people have dreams in which an authoritative figure such as a parent or priest gives advice; and yet Macrobius saw this as a recognizable category of dream, and it is one to which many literary dreams of classical and medieval times belong. One might suppose that this category was a mere literary convention, a convenient way of dressing up didacticism to make it more interesting and convincing. But there is also the possibility that dreams do not follow a constant pattern throughout the ages, and that this may be a respect in which dreaming habits have changed." The same sentiment is expressed in even more positive form in Dodds 1951, 102–8.

32. The *Zuo zhuan* contains misleading, false and frightening dreams of the type Oppenheimer says were excluded from Mesopotamian texts. See Oppenheimer 185.

33. Strickmann notes that Chinese Buddhist texts from the sixth century A.D. contain instructions for dream incubation. I have not found any earlier reference to the practice.

34. See Legge 1935, 374 and 478.

35. See the dream of Wei Qi of Jin concerning an old man who aided him in battle (Legge 1935, 328), the dream of Duke Cheng of Wei concerning sacrifices to Kang Shu (p. 219), and the dream of Han Xuanzi of Jin concerning Duke Wen (p. 617). None of these dreams provides insight into future events.

36. See the dream of Gongsun Yingqi of Lu (Legge 1935, 404), Zhao Jianzi of Jin (p. 738), and the dream of Wei Qi of Jin concerning shooting an arrow at the moon (p. 397).

37. The dream of Xun Yan in Legge 1935, 478.

38. Drege translates the earliest known Chinese dream book based on a manuscript (Pelliot ms. 3908) dating no later than the Tang dynasty discovered in Dunhuang. The manuscript is entitled "The Newly Collected Book of the Explanation of Dreams by the Duke of Zhou." This dream book and similar manuscripts described in Drege (pp. 207–210) follow a scheme of categorical organization also used in Chinese encyclopedias (*lei shu*). The scheme starts with heavenly phenomena—the sun, moon, and stars—and proceeds through a catalog of other physical and human phenomena. The meanings of dreams are given by simple symbolic keys such as "If you dream of ascending to heaven you will give birth to noble offspring."

39. For example the *Yen zi chun qiu* contains two accounts of dreams of Duke Jing of Qi. These accounts are reproduced in the *Gujin tushu jicheng*, ch. 146. The first is a dream of violent spirits and the second is a struggle with two suns. Both accounts share elements with the dream in Legge 1935, 374 and other *Zuo zhuan* dreams.

40. This passage is repeated along with additional material in the *Liezi*, a work included in the Taoist canon which purports to be from the Warring States period, but which probably dates from the same period as the *Bowuzhi*. See *The Book of Lieh-Tzu*, translated by A. C. Graham (London: John Murray, 1960) 66–7.

References

Works in English

Dodds, E. R. *The Greeks and the Irrational*. Berkeley: University of California Press, 1951.

Drege, Jean-Pierre. "Clefs des songs de Touen-houang." *Nouvelles contributions aux etudes de Touen-houang*. Edited by Michel Soymie. Geneva: Droz, 1981.

Forke, Alfred, trans. *Lun-Heng: Philosophical Essays of Wang Ch'ung*. Reprint. New York: Paragon, 1962.

Fraser, Edward D. H. *Index to the Tso Chuan*. London: Oxford University Press, 1930.

Graham, A. C., trans. *The Book of Lieh-Tzu*. London: John Murray, 1960.

Karlgren, Bernard, trans. *Book of Odes*. Stockholm: The Museum of Far Eastern Antiquities, 1950.

Lattimore, Richmond, trans. *The Iliad of Homer*. Chicago: University of Chicago Press, 1967.

Legge, James. *The Ch'un Ts'ew with The Tso Chuen*. Vol. 5, *The Chinese Classics*. Reprint Taipei: Wen Chih Shih, 1972.

Oppenheim, A. Leo. "The Interpretation of Dreams in the Ancient Near East." *Transactions of the American Philosophical Society*, 46, 1956.

Priest, John F. "Myth and Dream in Hebrew Scripture." *Myths, Dreams and Religion*. Edited by Joseph Campbell. Dallas: Spring Publications, 1988.

Spearing, A. C. *Medieval Dream-poetry*. Cambridge: Cambridge University Press, 1976.

Steiner, George. "The Historicity of Dreams." *Salmagundi*, 61, 1983.

Strickmann, Michel. "Dreamwork of Psycho-Sinologists: Doctors, Taoists, Monks." *Psycho-Sinology: The Universe of Dreams in Chinese Culture*. Edited by Caroline T. Brown. Wilson Center: Washington, D.C., 1988.

Wagner, Rudolf G. "Imperial Dreams in China." *Psycho-Sinology: The Universe of Dreams in Chinese Culture*. Edited by Caroline T. Brown. Wilson Center: Washington, D.C., 1988.

Waley, Arthur, trans. *The Analects of Confucius*. London: George Allen & Unwin, 1938.

————, trans. *The Book of Songs*. London: George Allen & Unwin, 1937.

Watson, Burton, trans. *The Complete Works of Chuang Tzu*. New York: Columbia University Press, 1968.

————, trans. *The Tso Chuan*. New York: Columbia University Press, 1989.

Works in Chinese

Chun Qiu jing zhuan ji jie (CQJZJJ) of Du Yu, (A.D. 222–284), *Shang tai Yue shi* edition. Rpt. Taipei: Xinxing shudian, 1981.

Fan Ning, ed. *Bowuzhi jiaozheng.* Beijing: Zhonghua, 1980.

Gujin tushu jicheng (compiled 1725 by Chen Menglei and others). Rpt. Taipei: Wenxing shudian, 1964.

Chen Shou (d. A.D. 297) *San Guo zhi (Chronicle of the Three Kingdoms with commentary by Pei Songzhi* (A.D. 372–451). Beijing: Zonghua, 1959.

Zhou li Zheng zhu (The Rites of Zhou with commentary by Zheng Xuan (A.D. 127–200) *Jiao yong huai tang* edition. Rpt. Taipei: Xinxing shudian, 1979.

6. Talmudic Dream Interpretation, Freudian Ambivalence, Deconstruction*

Ken Frieden

A short chapter cannot do justice to three such unwieldly phenomena as talmudic dream interpretation, Freudian ambivalence, and deconstruction. In any event, this pyramid of catch phrases is not intended to suggest a direct continuity between ancient rabbinic commentary and recent literary criticism. The diversity of talmudic and midrashic texts, not to mention the variety of so-called "deconstructive" writings, should unsettle any claims of full-fledged influence. Nevertheless, there are passages in the Talmud and Midrash Rabbah that do anticipate certain aspects of contemporary literary studies. For example, some rabbinic approaches to dreams are pertinent to the way in which deconstruction, under the influence of Freud, rejected hermeneutics.

Freud's basic assumptions about interpretation resemble those of nineteenth-century philology. Freud even compares the interpretation of a dream to the translation of an ancient text; beneath the surface of the reported dream, he claims, is another layer of meaning. A dream is like a difficult passage in Greek or a message in Egyptian hieroglyphics, elusive yet open to interpretation.

From several standpoints, however, and despite his reliance on philological models, Freud's methods of interpretation differ from nineteenth-century European norms. First, Freud utilizes the dreamer's free associations, insisting that by a circuitous route they guide him back to the hidden meaning of the dream. Second, Freud's interpretations place great emphasis on puns and other wordplays. Third,

---

*This essay, presented in December 1990 at the Modern Language Association Convention in Chicago, expands upon certain elements in my book entitled *Freud's Dream of Interpretation* (Albany: SUNY Press, 1990).

Freudian theory creates the modern myth of the unconscious mind, which he claims is indirectly expressed through dreams.

Freud had more in common with ancient dream interpreters than he was prepared to admit. He does acknowledge that his dreams associate him with Joseph, the central biblical dream interpreter (*Td* 466).[1] Yet when Freud actually addresses Joseph's interpretive approach, in chapter 2 of *The Interpretation of Dreams*, he rejects it as a symbolic method that relies upon the interpreter's insight and intuition. Before turning to Freud, it is helpful to survey the talmudic and midrashic literature on dreams.

Several talmudic opinions and anecdotes relate to dream interpretation.[2] One memorable saying is attributed to Rabbi Chisda: "a dream that is not interpreted is like a letter that is not read" (Berakhot 55b). This analogy suggests several meanings. It indicates that dreams have a hidden message, like the contents of a sealed letter. It also suggests that dreams may be interpreted, as a letter may be opened. Yet Rabbi Chisda neither tells us who is the sender of the dream letter, nor assures us that such letters always contain good news. In some cases, then, it may be advisable to leave the symbolic letter unopened, or the dream uninterpreted.

According to a basic talmudic view, meaning is not merely within the dream, framed as an abstract idea. Rather, the meaning of a dream follows it, in the form of actual events. Hence interpretation may make a great deal of difference—not only to *understanding* what a dream means, but to *influencing* the future. Dream interpretation as depicted in the Talmud is commonly aimed toward the future, attempting to reveal the significance of dreams by discovering their implications. This may be called future-oriented dream interpretation. It is not always *prophetic* because it does not necessarily predict the future, but it is *future-oriented* because it deals with potential consequences.

The biblical model for future-oriented dream interpretation is Joseph. Imprisoned in Egypt, Joseph successfully interprets the dreams of Pharaoh's cupbearer and baker. Subsequently, when Pharaoh needs an interpreter for his own dreams, the cupbearer recalls: "there was with us a Hebrew boy, a servant to the officer of the guard; and we told him, and he interpreted our dreams to us, to each man according to his dream he interpreted. And as he interpreted to us, so it was" (Gen. 41:12–13).

A rabbinic inquiry reinterprets the story of Joseph. This surprising interpretation, or rather association, is contained in Genesis Rabbah, in the midrashic commentary on the biblical passage just quoted.

This midrashic passage deals with Genesis 41:13, in which the cup-bearer tells Pharoah about Joseph, stating that "as he interpreted to us, so it was." The rabbinic text narrates the following story:

> A certain woman went to R. Eliezer and said to him: "I saw in my dream that the second story of my house was split." He said to her: "You will conceive a male child"; she went away and so it was. A second time she dreamed thus and went to R. Eliezer, who told her: "You will give birth to a male child"; and so it was. A third time she dreamed thus and came to him again but did not find him. She said to his students: "I saw in my dream that the second story of my house was split." They said to her: "You will bury your husband," and so it was. R. Eliezer heard a voice of wailing and said to them: "What is this?" They told him the story, and he said to them: "You have killed a man, for is it not written, 'As he interpreted to us, so it was'?" R. Jochanan said: "All dreams follow the mouth, except for wine."[3]

This passage sheds old and new light on the dynamics of dream interpretation. According to a more traditional view, Joseph's interpretations are prophetic in the sense that they predict what is going to occur. The midrashic account diverges from this by stating that "dreams follow the mouth" [that is, it seems, the mouth of the interpreter]. In other words, the interpreter has an active power to change events, the outcome of dreams. If this is the case, then it may be possible to damage a person by offering a negative interpretation. This is the gist of the most extensive story in the chapter on dreams in the Babylonian Talmud.

Bar Hedaya is an interpreter of dreams. He makes a business of his talent: "To one who gave him a fee he interpreted for good, and to one who did not give him a fee he interpreted for evil." The merce-nary, ancient interpreter thus enables his clients to purchase favorable futures. Raba and Abaye, famous rivals, come to Bar Hedaya, the interpreter, saying that they have dreamed identical dreams. In fact, Raba and Abaye most often recount scriptural verses, rather than dream images. Since they claim to have dreamed Scripture, the inter-preter's work underscores the parallel between dream interpretation and biblical commentary.

The rabbis present the same dreams, or verses from the bible, but Abaye pays the interpreter while Raba does not. Following his customary practices, Bar Hedaya interprets Abaye's dreams favorably and Raba's dreams unfavorably. The dream interpreter appears to make dreams mean virtually anything he wishes, and influences the dreamer's future for better or worse. His successes are neither ques-tioned nor explained. Calamities begin to overtake Raba, who has skeptically declined to pay the interpreter's fee. As a result, he changes his tune and starts to believe in the power of dreams and interpretation. After many of Bar Hedaya's unfavorable prophecies have been realized, Raba returns to the interpreter alone. This time he pays the customary fee, and at last he receives favorable interpretations. According to the interpreter's final statement, "miracles will happen to you."

Subsequently Raba and Bar Hedaya travel by boat together. Aware that he has acted badly toward Raba, the dream interpreter suddenly fears divine reprisal. His most recent prediction foretold that miracles would happen to Raba; now he worries that the boat might sink, and that only Raba will be miraculously saved. Trying to make a quick escape, Bar Hedaya drops a book—presumably a manual of dream interpretation. The treatise opens to a page from which Raba reads: "All dreams follow the mouth." After he reads these words, Raba bursts out, "it is all because of you!" He blames the interpreter for the misfortunes that have befallen him, believing that he now knows the secret of Bar Hedaya's destructive interpretations. Raba evidently understands the metaphorical image, "all dreams follow the mouth," to mean: "all dreams' consequences follow their interpretation." According to Raba's way of understanding it, then, "all dreams follow the mouth" implies that the dream interpreter can make a dream mean whatever he says, and so change the dreamer's life.

These biblical, talmudic, and midrashic traditions suggest that although the interpreter may wish to appear unbiased, his work always furthers or hinders vested interests. Biblical dream interpreters such as Joseph and Daniel rise to power through their interpretations, even when the dreamer (as in the case of Nebuchadnezzar) does not benefit from them.

This does not leave us with a single, monolithic rabbinic attitude toward dream interpretation, but with several conflicting opinions. The differences between Raba and Abaye exemplify this. On the one hand, some rabbis express their conviction that dream interpretation can be powerful and effective, even if it is willful and arbitrary. On the other hand, there are intimations that some dream interpreters are mercenary quacks who should not be trusted. Interpretations can be *made good* in spite of their arbitrariness. And this is not always for the best.

Freud was concerned to show underlying meanings beneath the superficial content of dreams. Although he recognized innumerable meanings, calling the dream text "overdetermined" by multiple dream-thoughts, he insisted that he could discover the dream's latent content. On the other hand, Freud employed the method of free association, which at times seems to be as arbitrary as the prophetic mouth of the dream interpreter Bar Hedaya. The talmudic saying, "all dreams follow the mouth," would take on another sense today. In orthodox Freudian doctrine, it might signify that the meaning of a dream follows the dreamer's mouth, through the associations provided by the dreamer.

For a number of reasons, Freud was compelled to repudiate his Judaic forerunners; he both consciously ignored them and unconsciously repressed their insights. On one level, this was part of Freud's effort to gain acceptance for a medical practice that was already being met with considerable resistance. Moreover, Freud associated biblical dream interpretation with simplistic prophecy based on divine inspiration, which would not advance his search for a pragmatic, verifiable method. Finally and most significantly, Freud may have felt threatened by his rabbinic precursors. There was real "anxiety of influence" in his case, and not merely because of Freud's status as a latecomer to the Jewish tradition. Freud the skeptic met his match in talmudic and midrashic passages that deal with dream interpretation. Especially tractate Berakhot shows the dream interpreter, Bar Hedaya, for what he is: a dangerous charlatan who ruins the lives of innocent people. Freud had reason to keep his distance from such an opposing opinion.

How much did Freud know about dream interpretation in the Talmud? Enough to feel uneasy over what he knew. Freud's most provocative reference to dream interpretation in the Jewish tradition occurs in a footnote, which he added to the third edition of *The Interpretation of Dreams* in 1914. Reviewing the prior, "scientific literature on the problem of dreams," Freud writes: "Almoli (1848), Amram (1901), Löwinger (1908), and most recently—with consideration of the psychoanalytic standpoint—Lauer (1913) deal with dream interpretation among the Jews" (*Td* 32). While the latter references to essays by Löwinger and Lauer are easily traced, the first two are enigmatic. Solomon Almoli published his important Hebrew work, *Interpretation of Dreams (Pitron chalomot)*, in about 1516. Why does Freud refer to an 1848 edition that he almost certainly never read? What is his source for this reference? The reference to Amram is even more obscure; which text does Freud mean, and why does he cite it? This bibliographical footnote turns out to be a smokescreen.[4]

Freud's primary source of information on Judaic dream interpretation was apparently the short essay by Chaim Lauer, published under Freud's editorship in the first volume of the *International Journal for Psychoanalysis and "Imago"* of 1913. Lauer hedges his bets when he writes at the outset: "In the following treatise, we wish only to show that—from the standpoint of the historical development of the doctrine of dreams—already in the talmudic-rabbinic literature, views find expression that are in part similar to the Freudian direction of thought, and in part contradictory" (Lauer 1913, 459). He also makes a point of dismissing the issue of originality, apparently so as not to offend his editor, Freud. He states that the laurels go not to the person who "conceived a new scientific theory" but to the one who brings it to prominence. Lauer then reviews the central rabbinic positions concerning dreams and their interpretation. It is significant that in or before 1913 Freud was aware of these rabbinic thoughts on dreams; yet he never quoted them or responded to their contributions. Among numerous references to the Babylonian Talmud, tractate Berakhot, and to the Palestinian Talmud, Ma'aser Sheni, Lauer cites the following opinions:

1. "R. Hisda says: an uninterpreted dream is like an unread letter";
2. "The fulfillment of the dream rests in many ways upon a suggestion by the interpreter";
3. "All dreams are fulfilled in accordance with the interpretation and, in this manner, from a single dream 24 interpretations may be correct";
4. "Talmudic dream interpretation is often based on wordplay, as in the story of Cappadocia." (Lauer 1913, 462–65)

The final assertion is especially relevant, since Freud himself relied heavily upon wordplay as one of his interpretive techniques. Lauer specifically alludes to a talmudic dream that mentions the city of Cappadocia. In tractate Berakhot, after hearing several unfavorable interpretations, a dreamer reports, "I dreamed they were telling me: Your father has left you money in Cappadocia" (Berakhot 56b). R. Ishmael first confirms that the dreamer has no money in that city, and that his father never went there. He then treats *kapadokia* as a bilingual signifier, and interprets on the basis of linguistic clues. *Kapa* means either "beam" in Aramaic or "twenty" in Greek. *Dokos* means "beam," and *deka* means "ten," both in Greek. R. Ishmael interprets: "*Kapa* means 'beam' and *deka* means 'ten.' Go and examine the beam [*kapa*] which is at the head of ten, for it is full of coins."[5] Freud interprets numerous dreams in exactly this fashion. For example, he explains his dream of the nonsense-word *Autodidasker* by separating it into *Autor* (author), *Autodidakt* (autodidact), and *Lasker* (a proper name).

Adolf Löwinger, in his 1908 essay mentioned by Freud, also discusses the element of wordplay. He refers to examples in which homonyms facilitate rabbinic interpretation, and he remarks that the rabbis also rearranged letters: "As needed, they had recourse to separation of the word, the so-called *notarikon*, or they combined two words to form one, which produced a certain sense" (Löwinger 1908, 31). Löwinger compares this rabbinic strategy to the method employed in a legendary Greek story concerning Alexander the Great. After the military leader dreamed of a satyr, his interpreter Aristander reportedly explained this dream by dividing *satyr* into the composite words, *sa* and *tyros*, meaning "Tyre is yours." Alexander then attacked the city and conquered it. Freud, in a 1911 footnote to *The Interpretation of Dreams*, calls this "the most beautiful example of a dream interpretation that has been handed down to us from antiquity" (*Td* 120). Yet Freud conspicuously omits the similar rabbinic examples provided by Löwinger.

Freud owed at least two specific debts to Löwinger's article. First, Löwinger's analysis of *notarikon* refers to the work of Almoli (Löwinger 1908, 28), which is one of Freud's mysterious references. Second, Freud probably drew what he called "the most beautiful example" of wordplay in ancient dream interpretation from Löwinger's book on *Jewish* dream interpretation. It seems that Freud was impressed by this element of rabbinic dream interpretation, but he chose to ascribe *notarikon* solely to the Greek tradition.[6] Freud's footnote on the Judaic background of dream interpretation remains entirely general, lacking specific examples of the kind that are most relevant to his own techniques.

I am less concerned with Freud's borrowings from ancient sources than with his persistent efforts to avoid such influence—or to avoid the appearance of such influence. In other words, my work deals with textual strategies of evasion, which Harold Bloom discusses from a more psychological standpoint in his book *The Anxiety of Influence*. I emphasize the anxiety—discernible in textual evasions—rather than the overt influence.

In some respects, Freud was not skeptical enough about his operative methods. The irony is that, while Freud was skeptical about ancient Jewish dream interpretation, in fact the Talmud contains sophisticated methods as well as highly skeptical opinions. Had Freud carefully studied the talmudic discussion of dream interpretation he might have been forced to take more seriously its challenges to the presumed validity of interpretation. Freud believed that he had surpassed his forerunners in every respect, but tractate Berakhot shows itself to be even more sensitive to the hazards of interpreting dreams. For instance, Berakhot shows an awareness of the power of interpretation over the dreamer's future. This power is intrinsically related to what Freud viewed as the therapeutic value of dream analysis. An inevitable element of future-orientation characterizes even the most scientific interpretations attempted by psychoanalysts. Freud had to renounce this quasi-prophetic style while still claiming to play a future-oriented, curative role.

Freud was an unwitting mediator between rabbinic and deconstructive interpretation: his ambivalence toward ancient Jewish dream interpreters enabled Jacques Derrida and others to discover these forerunners indirectly. Freud himself denied or disavowed them, thus preparing the way for a return of the repressed. Hence deconstructive readings sometimes make explicit what was implicit in Freudian dream interpretation.

Freud's radical method of free association derives virtually endless meanings from texts grafted upon texts in a series of displacements. Post-structuralist critics among Derrida's followers draw from this approach without always realizing that it is the oblique expression of a Freudian denial, Freud's avoidance of the rabbinic tradition.

Notes

1. *Td* refers to Sigmund Freud's *Die Traumdeutung* (*Td*) in the edition of the *Studienausgabe*, vol. 2, ed. Alexander Mitscherlich, Angela Richards, James Strachey (Frankfurt am Main: S. Fishcher, 1972). All translations are my own.

2. Most of these references come from the Babylonian Talmud, tractate Berakhot, and will be indicated by standard page numbers.

3. Genesis Rabbah 89:8. This translation is based on the second critical edition of Chanoch Albeck, *Bereschit Rabbah* (Jerusalem: Wahrman Books, 1965). An alternative English translation is contained in *Midrash Rabbah*, 3d ed., ed. and trans. H. Freedman and Maurice Simon (London: Soncino, 1983), 2, 825.

4. For Freud's 1925 and 1930 revisions of *The Interpretation of Dreams*, most pertinent of all would have been a note to Alexander Kristianpoller's bilingual edition of many talmudic passages pertaining to dream interpretation. It was printed in Vienna in 1923.

5. Compare Gen. Rab. 68:12, Lam. Rab. 1:1:17, Sanhedrin 30a, and the Palestinian Talmud, Ma'aser Sheni 4:6; all contain versions of this popular Cappadocia story. Compare Marcus Jastrow, *A Dictionary of the Targumim, the Talmud Babli and Yerushalmi, and the Midrashic Literature* (1903;

reprint edition New York: The Judaica Press, 1971), 288 and 1398. The preceding paragraph is modified slightly from my book, *Freud's Dream of Interpretation*, chapter 3.

6. Freud is not alone in this; Saul Lieberman makes a similar ascription in his book, *Hellenism in Jewish Palestine* (New York: Jewish Theological Seminary, 1950), 47–82.

References

Bereschit Rabbah, ed. Chanoch Albeck. Jerusalem: Wahrman Books, 1965.

Bloom, Harold. *The Anxiety of Influence: A Theory of Poetry*. New York: Oxford University Press, 1973.

Derrida, Jacques. *L'écriture et la différence*. Paris: Editions du Seuil, 1967.

Freud, Sigmund. *Die Traumdeutung*. In the *Studienausgabe*. Vol. 2. Edited by Alexander Mitscherlich, Angela Richards, James Strachey. Frankfurt am Main: S. Fishcher, 1972.

Frieden, Ken. *Freud's Dream of Interpretation*. Albany: SUNY Press, 1990.

Genesis Rabbah. In *Midrash Rabbah*. Vols. 1–2. 3d ed. Edited and translated by H. Freedman and Maurice Simon. London: Soncino, 1983.

Lauer, Chaim. "Das Wesen des Traumes in der Beurteilung der talmudischen und rabbinischen Literatur." *Internationale Zeitschrift für Psychoanalyse und "Imago"* 1 (1913), 459–69.

Lieberman, Saul. *Hellenism in Jewish Palestine*. New York: Jewish Theological Seminary, 1950.

Löwinger, Adolf. *Der Traum in der jüdischen Literatur*. Leipzig: M. W. Kaufmann, 1908.

The Talmud: Berakhoth. Edited by A. Zvi Ehrman. Vol. 4. Jerusalem: El-'Am, 1982.

7. Divinity, Insanity, Creativity: A Renaissance Contribution to the History and Theory of Dream/Text(s)

Carol Schreier Rupprecht

A reader of the scholarship on dreams from the past five centuries would invariably conclude that the European Renaissance produced no dream theorist of the stature of the ancients or even of Artemidorus or Macrobius.[1] These are the two theorists most readily invoked to read literary dream texts and other cultural phenomena of the sixteenth century whenever scholars are not resorting to twentieth-century theorists of dreams for interpretation by hindsight. Neither approach takes account of the abundance of dream treatises —original works as well as editions and translations of earlier treatises—produced during the Renaissance. Such productions, and the ubiquity of dream representation in literature, demonstrate that dreams were as significant in the cultures of fifteenth- and sixteenth-century Europe as they had been in previous periods of Western literary production.

And, indeed, Renaissance dream theory and poetry form a significant benchmark in the still-incomplete narrative that now constitutes Western oneirological history. Early Renaissance oneirics is a serious omission from this narrative because the period marks a turning point in dreaming, from its long-standing principal alliance with divinity toward a greater alignment with insanity. From the sixteenth century to our own, dreaming has a diminishing association with gods (or demons) and shifts away from the early primacy of its prophetic function. Instead there is an increased association with the irrational, defined as mental illness, and a shift to a diagnostic function. A view of dreaming as a process of external origin with intimations for an often collective future gives way to an increasing sense of dreaming as an internally generated phenomenon tied to the personal past of the individual dreamer. At the turn into this century Freud articulated

112

unequivocally the latter stance toward the dream's trajectory in time when he noted:

> By picturing our wishes as fulfilled, dreams are after all leading us into the future. But this future, which the dreamer pictures as the present, has been moulded by his indestructible wish into a perfect likeness of the past. (Freud 1953, V: 621)

The first aim of this chapter is to open exploration of this drama of transition in the focus of oneiric thought by looking at the life and work of one of its most significant actors, the original and influential Italian Renaissance theorist of dreams, Girolamo Cardano (1501–1576). Readers may wish to consult other writings in which I have considered the meaning this transition had and continues to have for the study of dreams today. But even those making Cardano's acquaintance for the first time here will be able to deduce from the following commentary many of the most significant implications of his treatise.[3]

Cardano had even greater stature in his time than many of his better-known oneirological predecessors had in theirs (Thorndike 1923–58, V: 563–79). However, while he has been an object of sustained scientific inquiry, principally for his work on mathematics, he has been unaccountably ignored, and even denigrated, elsewhere. Thus his major work on dreams, *Somniorum synesiorum, omnis generis insomnia explicantes, libri iiii [About Synesian dreams, dreams of all kinds set forth, in four books]* (Basel, 1562), is little known among Renaissance scholars in literature and related disciplines and is seldom invoked by them.[4] And unlike Artemidorus's *Oneirocritica [The Interpretation of Dreams]*, Macrobius's *Commentary on the Dream of Scipio*, and even Synesius of Cyrene's *On Dreams*, Cardano's dream book has never been translated into English.[5] Such neglect has continued well into the twentieth century despite Cardano's impressive reputation among and acknowledged influence on not only certain notable Renaissance figures including Vesalius, Alciati, John Cheke, and Shakespeare, but also on Sir Thomas Browne, Robert Hook, John Locke, Leibnitz, Goethe, Jung, and Michel Foucault.

Cardano was a Milanese physician, philosopher, astrologer, mathematician, and interpreter of dreams whose collected works at his death in 1576 ran to thousands of folio pages. The 1663 edition of his *Opera Omnia*, reprinted in 1967 with the texts in double columns, takes up ten volumes. Throughout his lifetime, as well as in the late sixteenth and early seventeenth centuries, his works went into several editions and many were translated from the Latin into German, French, and English. Unfortunately, however, the historians of science who have been the main custodians of Cardano's reputation have totally ignored the shaping force of dreams on his thought. In fact, his major text in natural philosophy, *De Subtilitate*, was instigated by a dream. His psychologically astute autobiography, *De Propria Vita*, shows how fully dreaming dominated his perspectives in all fields. And it is hard not to see connections between his famed treatise on algebra, *Ars Magna*, with its mathematical computations of probability and chance as related to his interest in the predictive powers of dreams.

It is true that some early twentieth-century readers were outspoken admirers of Cardano. Focusing almost exclusively on *De Propria Vita*, they did extol his virtues as a multiply talented "Renaissance man." However, Jean Stoner, the first translator of his *Vita* into English, revealed the problematic ground of their estimation in citing with approval a 1909 study of the autobiography: "Cardano is among the first manifestations of what we term the scientific spirit." (Stoner, trans. 1930, ix) Even these admirers "read" right past the oneiric dimensions of the life story, neither sharing nor seeming to understand Cardano's valuing of dreams, starting with his own. This inattention to dreams is especially revealing since these scholars also labeled him "the first psychologist." This label meant for them, however, that he was a "scientist deeply interested in the brain and nervous system, and their relation to the physical and intellectual life, and at a date when the existence of such a relation was by no means clearly established" (ix-x). Ironically, we had to wait for a mathematical physicist, Markus Fierz, to provide in 1980 a truly inclusive view of Cardano's contribution to Renaissance thought generally and to the study of dreams specifically. Fierz was the first modern to gauge accurately the impressive representativeness of Renaissance thought constituted by Cardano's work.

> The voluminous corpus of Cardano's writings embraces all the major ideas of his time, and thus conveys an authentic picture of the intellectual life of the High Renaissance. His writings contain rudiments and ideas pertaining to almost every scientific and philosophical doctrine developed during the seventeenth century. (Fierz [1980] 1983, xii)

Fierz was also the first to re-recognize the interdependence of all of Cardano's multidisciplinary ventures, including the much acclaimed, edited, and translated autobiography and the four-volume dream treatise. Yet, Fierz notes, with the exception of his prominence in the field of mathematics, Cardano has "practically been forgotten, in much the same way that the imaginatively comprehensive thought of the Renaissance has been generally forgotten" (Fierz [1980] 1983, xii).

Ultimately, the argument for restoring Cardano to a position more consonant with the one he held in his own time is precisely this "imaginative comprehensiveness." As new historicists have convincingly argued, our view of the past has been selective in many ways that must now be called into question. And that selectivity in Western habits of thought has led to the substantial privileging of Cardano's logical, rational, "prescientific" writings and to the fragmentation, marginalization, and finally denigration of his writings on aspects of culture like dreams and of his belief in the sympathy of all things in the universe. This pattern of response to Cardano is especially ironic since his famous immediate successor in philosophy, René Descartes (1596–1650), "the father of modern philosophy," appears to have derived the impetus for his central system of thought and his life's work from his own early visionary dreams.[6]

Even in his lifetime, Cardano was becoming a kind of emblem of the disintegration of a holistic view of knowledge based on acceptance of the sympathy and interdependence of all parts of the universe. Already in the sixteenth century, he was simultaneously admired and scorned. Many of his contemporaries divided Cardano into part genius and part madman, a dichotomous view that has persisted and has strongly influenced the reception of his ideas. There is little to differentiate certain appraisals made of Cardano in the 1500s from those made in the 1900s. Gabriel Naudé, in a very negative "judgment" on Cardano affixed to the 1663 printing of the *Vita*, quoted Auguste de Thou (1553–1617) describing Cardano's horoscope of Christ as "evidence of his utmost madness, nay, of his impious rashness" (Shumaker 1982, 60). Other distinguished contemporaries, however, such as Andrea Alciati and Andreas Vesalius, had great respect for Cardano's inventiveness, intellect, and judgment.

In the *Dizionario biografico degli Italiani*, the author of a very extensive piece on Cardano done in the 1970s describes his subject as "geniale ma caotica, alternante un acuto spirito critico a una credulitá infantile, minata nel suo equilibrio da un temperamento psicopatico." ("genial but disturbed, alternating a keen critical sensibility with an infantile credulity, his equilibrium menaced by a psychopathological temperament.") The charges of credulity and psychopathology allude at least partly to Cardano's writings about dreams, since only glancing mention is given to the *Somniorum Synesiorum* in this long, detailed and otherwise laudatory article (Istituto della Enciclopedia Italiana 1976, C:762).

At this coming turn of the century, dreams and dream researchers as well as Renaissance scholars have much to gain if what has been accepted and valued in Cardano's thought is balanced by recuperation of the ignored and disparaged rest. To him and to many of his contemporaries, his writings on astrology (including a horoscope of Christ), metoscopy (telling fortunes by the appearance of a person's face), and dreams were phenomenologically of the same order as his work in mathematics and natural philosophy; all were interdependent and equally valorized.

Only a brief introduction can be provided here to the conceptual richness of the *Somniorum Synesiorum*, but it is possible to get a sense of Cardano's range, originality, sense of tradition, and acuity of observation. The treatise contains four books of greatly varying length and worth with the first book, having sixty-eight chapters, being the longest and richest. It offers a general theory of dream interpretation and is a veritable encyclopedia of phenomena which appear in dreams. That is, of course, all the phenomena in the universe from plants, animals, and people to cities, houses, and artisans; the parts and conditions of the body; the weather; clothing and jewelry; food and drink. Gods, usually pagan deities from Greek and Roman mythology, are prominently featured. And a vivid picture of sixteenth-century life and habits of mind is evoked in Cardano's exhaustive compendium.

This first chapter also provides theories, categories, and rules for interpreting dreams, sixty-three basic rules, to be exact. There is a typological scheme to all of this as well as to the other three books; they are united by several principles that define Cardano's world view, including his preoccupation with the immortality of the soul, which also appears in his philosophic writings.

Chapter IV is uniquely intriguing because of its autobiographical nature. It treats principally Cardano's own dreams. As Synesius had recommended, Cardano was a scrupulous keeper of a dream journal or "night diary." Chapters II and III, though generally ignored, are highly suggestive for the literary scholar and the oneirologist. They treat the formal, narrative characteristics of dreams and their relation to language—a rhetoric of dreams—as well as the absolute interdependence between the dreams and the dreamer's personal life circumstances. There is also an implicit, complex theory of memory and many other heuristic observations.

A few salient characteristics of the mind at work in the text emerge immediately. First is Cardano's clear awareness of his place in oneiric tradition, starting with the title of his treatise. The Synesius to whom it refers was a fourth-century bishop, Synesius of Cyrene, a converted Catholic, neoplatonist, and student of the philosopher

Hypathia as well as author of a treatise on dreams. Cardano alludes to and often cites his other predecessors such as Aristotle, Hippocrates, Artemidorus, and Galen, whose writings all became available during the cinquecento in new Latin translations. But he saw them all in the context of his unique revisionist mission: to be the first to approach the subject of dreams with a theory and a method. For example, he believed that Artemidorus was too caught up in detail; Synesius especially was too unsystematic; and Aristotle, Galen, and Vesalius were too inconsistent. He was to use a similar approach in composing his life story several years later: engage in continuous self-scrutiny; rely on experience and observation; read all the authorities, but put everything you read to the test of evidence from direct observation and experience.

One of the major surprises of the treatise is the complete absence of reference to Macrobius and the *Commentary on the Dream of Scipio*. Cardano makes an apparent allusion to Macrobius's *Saturnalia*; otherwise the omission is total. Another major surprise is the objectivity about religion and Cardano's persistently secular orientation. Although undoubtedly nominally a Catholic, Cardano presents no overtly Christian context for the subject of his treatise. For one thing, he speaks about all religions with equal distance—"I Giudei, I Christiani, I Maomettani" (Jews, Christians, Muslims)—as if he were an observer of all and participant in none. For another he asserts a view of futurity that is exclusively centered, like that of his Graeco-Roman predecessors, on personal fame among posterity based on his own achievements during his lifetime. No explicit eschatological concerns surface, although belief in a Christian god seems at times to be an operating assumption.

Cardano's own dreams, usually about his domestic and professional preoccupations, gave predictions or at least reassuring anticipations of earthly fame. From one impressive dream that he interpreted as testimony to his coming fame he chose to have a medal cast with an image from the dream and the Greek word for message dream: *ONEIPON [Oneiros]*. (It would be interesting to know if his bronze is unique among Renaissance medals in deriving its engraving from a dream.) Cardano was in fact obsessed with immortalizing himself through his work, even before the loss of his two sons (one to death and one to a dissolute life) precluded continuing the family name through his progeny.

Cardano did retain a strong conviction of the divinatory power of dreams, but it was a naturalized and secularized version of the traditional view. Actually he held what is in the tradition an extreme position about the oneiric transmission of foreknowledge. He asserted that "*all* dreams to some extent relate to the future (*tutti i sogni si riferiscono in qualche misura al futuro*)" (Cardano 1989, I:viii). He did not, however, impute the cause of this futurity to divine inspiration despite his awareness of the centrality of such a belief among his predecessors. Instead he asserted that dreams have this function of futurity not because they come from a god or gods but because they come from nature. Foresight was as natural to dreams, he felt, as growing was to plants: "It is evident that the foresight deduced from dreams is not only true, but also derives from a natural cause, as do plants and the other works of nature (*e evidente che le previsioni ricavate dai sogni non sono solamente vere, ma derivano anche da una causa naturale, come le piante e le altre opere della natura*)" (iv). And indeed for Cardano God and nature often seem synonymous although nature is always more prominently featured.

Significantly, the reason the future interests Cardano is that it hasn't yet taken place and thus has the potential to be altered. This strong sense of personal instrumentality is considerably at odds with previous senses of predestined or fated futurity in dreams and the individual dreamer's place in oneiric temporality. There is virtually no religious coloration to his ideas from either a denominational orthodoxy or a general set of tenets. Though he makes frequent statements that appear to express very conventional attitudes toward God, Cardano does not distinguish between a classical polytheism (*dei*) and a Christian (or Arabic) monotheism in the sections where he treats divinities in dreams. And his examples come more often from other ancient texts than from the Bible, even though he includes the by-now-formulaic references to Joseph and Daniel.

The absence of any overt religious context is highly unusual for oneiric texts of the time; in its stead is what scholars have called in his other writing a "prescientific" approach. His confidence in the efficacy of "rational" explanation and the capacity to discover the truth through systematic investigation is a theme throughout the four books. Alice Browne identifies both the richness and the problematics of this effort as his attempt to write a "comprehensive handbook of dream interpretation" while staying "conscious of the individualism and variability of meanings" (Browne 1979, 75). She might have added that Cardano had the extra challenge of his intense self-consciousness, his active awareness that all his perceptions were very influenced by his personal experience.

Such in brief is Cardano's dimension of the oneiric "divinity" in the title of this chapter. His version of oneiric "creativity" is as rich, complex, and suggestive. The amount of emphasis on textual and linguistic issues in dreams in the *Somniorum Synesiorum* is almost in inverse proportion to that of his predecessors, perhaps precisely because his sense of divinity is so generalized and unproblematic. This allows him to avoid spending time in endless tautological discussion about whether or not dreams come from the gods, pertain to the future, etc. He also took an unequivocal stand on another aspect of the historically intense dream debate by asserting that *all* dreams have value. Only after presenting various theories of signification (I. xiv) and criteria for interpretation (I. xi), does Cardano turn to a system of categorization. Then he composes an encyclopedia of dream symbolism rather than a value-laden taxonomy or an irresolvable debate.

Using the energy previous writers had expended on circular controversies about dream origin and function, Cardano speculated on many other dimensions of dreaming. In doing so he generated a fascinating if rudimentary dream aesthetic, as can be seen in the following paraphrase of both his original statements and Browne's descriptions of the text. A key feature is the indistinguishability among states of perception, the inability to remember if a certain experience occurred in waking reality or appeared in a dream or was read in a book or seen in a picture (Browne 1979, 130). He suggests some principles about dreams of fictional objects and notes that some things can be represented in the art in a dream—like thunder or a cat's wagging its tail—that can't be represented in art otherwise (p. 134). Cardano, no doubt influenced by the emblem book of his friend Andrea Alciati, said dream images work like emblems; his method of analyzing the composition of dreams was analogous to methods of art criticism. (p. 62).

Many of these concepts seem to stem from the fact that, like his learned contemporaries, Cardano was well read in ancient and medieval literature. It is typical of his general eclecticism that his two favorite authors were Petrarch and Pulci; one the author of highly crafted lyric love poetry and a Latin epic, the other author of a sprawling political epic in the vernacular with giants as the protagonists. Cardano quotes readily—it seems from memory—Horace, Catullus, Martial, Virgil, and Juvenal, as well as writers on rhetoric such as Quintilian whose methods of composition he sometimes seems to be following. Also like his contemporaries, he is serious about and preoccupied with his own use of language and structure of argument (p. 32).[7]

The rhetoric of dreams is a consistent theme in oneirological history, partly because so much rhetorical strategy was concerned with arrangements designed to foster memory in the orator as well as to have certain effects on the auditors. Obviously, if a dreamer does not have both memory of a dream and the ability to reconstruct it in words, then oneirology has no subject. And recording dreams, as Cardano did in his own dated dream diary, was considered an excellent way to hone one's prose style. A final indication of Cardano's aesthetic interests are the horoscopes he cast of people he admired, among them Erasmus, Petrarch, and Albrecht Dürer.

Cardano himself wrote creative pieces in addition to his scientific and mathematical ones, notably in the genres of the consolation, autobiography, and dialogue. The *Comforte*, or consolation, had special appeal in England where it went into two translations and several editions in the years following his death. In fact the 1573 edition, translated by Bedingfeld, had in its time one rather remarkable claim to fame: it was thought to be the book Hamlet is reading as he passes along the corridor en route to his "to be or not to be" soliloquy. Since the *Comforte* is Cardano's self-consolation after the death of his oldest son and is a moving meditation on sleep, dreams, and death, the claim has a certain credibility, which may yet be further substantiated by research into Cardano's work and its reception. One passage reads:

> Most assured, it is, that such sleeps are most sweet as be most sound, for those are the best where like unto dead men we dream nothing. The broken sleeps, the slumber and dreams full of visions, are commonly in them that have weak and sickly bodies. (Ore 1953, 42)

Forging an aesthetic link between art and dreams is certainly not a Cardano innovation; virtually all early writers on dreams noted the relations between dreams and literary texts and pondered the similarities and differences between the imaginal life that underlies both. In *On Divination*, for example, Cicero put into the mouth of Quintus this view: "Now, even though all this may be nothing more than the product of the poet's imagination, yet it is not inconsistent with the forms dreams often assume" (Cicero 1892, 21). In fact, although the Socratic dialogue in which Quintus participates is an attack on and defense of divination, the central frame of reference is literary; the majority of Cicero's examples of successful or failed oneiromancy are drawn from literary texts.

And in Cardano especially we begin to see the promise realized of the oneriocriticism that has always underlain dream talk. As divinity retreats and insanity advances as the dominant subject in the long Western discourse about reason and non reason, creativity sustains its long-standing association with dream and provides a channel for the intense energy of the oneiric to continue in the cultures of Europe and the New World. Conceptualizing the dream as a poetic text and the poem as dream thus deflects or at least defers decision about dream etiology and function. The oneiric in and of itself, rather than the larger systems of culture in which it is embedded, becomes of central interest. The sixteenth-century shift of focus from divine to human concerns leads to the foregrounding of the creative even as it opens the way to pathology. The dream, like the Bible, becomes a text to be read rather than the inviolable given Word of God that must be grasped by the dreamer or the person of faith. Dreamer, reader, and Biblical exegete are all now dealing with linguistic constructs to be interrogated, interpreted, enjoyed, and even translated. Indeed, Cardano savored dreams and this sentiment carried through in everything he wrote. He is a model for the hospitality of the individual to the creative potential in dreaming. His life is also, unfortunately, a model for the shift toward the "insanity" in the title of this chapter.

The "insanity" part of the oneiric equation being explored here belongs entirely outside of Cardano's own views. His many often self-reflective volumes contain no hint that he saw anything out of the way or unusual in the diversity of his interests or the events of his life, except perhaps his family's extreme ill fortune. There is no discussion of mental disturbance and he himself does not perceive, or at least does not address, any hint of oddity or madness or anything exceptional in his multifarious occupations, preoccupations, vocations, and avocations. Designing a Cardano's suspension (in physics) and coming up with Cardano's cypher and with solutions to algebraic equations (in math) were to him activities neither more nor less substantive or interesting or worthy of pursuit than casting a horoscope of Christ, telling fortunes by the appearance of a person's face, writing detailed accounts of his diet and his sexual problems (impotence) in his autobiography, and exercising his inherited gifts of prognostication. The fact that Leonardo da Vinci consulted Cardano's father Fazio on geometry and other matters seems no more or no less interesting to Cardano than the fact that his father was also known to have been accompanied throughout his life by a "familiar," or personal spirit.

So the label of psychopathology comes from outside and reflects changing attitudes about what we would call the "unconscious" and the workings of the irrational. In fact, Cardano's life story would be of much interest today as a psychological case history. He was an illegitimate child who knew himself to have survived a failed abortion attempt by his mother, a widow who spent much of her life with Cardano's father but may never have married him. Cardano's subsequent personal and professional life was marked by radical swings of fortune; disasters and disappointments alternated with triumphs and successes.

All these experiences he duly recorded and analyzed in his dream reports and in his autobiography. His oldest son was executed for wife murder in 1560 (two years before the printing of the *Somniorum Synesiorum*). Cardano had difficulty attaining academic posts and medical appointments because of his illegitimacy. But he finally achieved academic distinction and grew famous for medical cures that led him to travel throughout England, France, Scotland, and the Netherlands and to be sought after as personal and court physician by some of Europe's leading monarchs, nobles, and clergy.

Late in his life Cardano was imprisoned by the Inquisition. The charges for which he was arrested have been variously identified as impiety, heresy, and atheism. While no explicit link has yet been made by historians or biographers between Cardano's confinement and his insistent public commitment to dreams, his experience suggests that the role of the Inquisition in turning oneiric history around in the sixteenth century may have been a significant one. From his release after several months in prison until his death, Cardano was not allowed to print his writings or to lecture publicly. He was also required to take up residence in Rome, presumably so he could be kept under clerical surveillance.

Thus not only is Cardano representative of all that was subsequently seen as the best of the Renaissance, he is also representative of what might be called, in the Jungian sense, the Shadow of that period: those things from which we became estranged and which we continue to deny, reject, and refuse to acknowledge or value. Central among the dimensions of Western culture that began to be estranged in the sixteenth century was the world of dream; the first step was defusing the powerful energy of the divinatory message dream.

Historically there existed considerable agreement among Greek, Roman, Christian, and even some Arabic writings that the primary function of dreams and their chief, often exclusive, source of interest is divination. Divination usually encompassed notions of foretelling the future, either through admonitions about altering a potentially unfortunate future or through assurance of divine support for ultimately successful outcomes. This congruence of belief systems made easier the Christianizing of "pagan" dream theory, a transformative process that reached its extreme in Macrobius. Macrobius rejected all other types of dreaming by establishing for the five recognized kinds of dreams two distinct categories: those which have divinatory power and hence value and those which have neither. "The two types just described (*enypnion* Gr for nightmare; *phantasma* Gr./*visum* Lat. for apparition) are not worth interpreting since they have no prophetic significance. . . . (they) are of no assistance in foretelling the future; but by means of the other three we are gifted with the powers of divination" (Macrobius 1952, 88–90). And because this function was most often executed through epiphany in dreams of a divine figure, a corollary belief that dreams were messages from a god or gods usually accompanied beliefs in divination.

That such beliefs remain strong in the Renaissance and for centuries thereafter in the popular knowledge cannot be denied. Only what Matlock has called the "learned and poetic traditions" in oneirics are being considered here.[8] Indeed it has perhaps been the powerful persistence of beliefs in dreams outside of elite cultural spheres that accounts for the current resurgence of interest in dreams in so many fields of inquiry.

So Girolamo Cardano's life was as intertwined with issues of divinity, insanity, and creativity as his *Somniorum Synesiorum* was. And his life and the life of that text along with other evidence from his contemporaries shows that in Europe during the Renaissance the dominant strain of oneiric thought ceased to be religious. No apparent intentionality of substitution motivated the removal of the dream from its center in spiritual life, however; writers who challenged the religious view of dream origin and function did not do so with a specific rationale in support of other etiologies and aims for dreaming. But very quickly mental aberration moved into the void left by the departure of the gods. Madness, seen not as creative Platonic furor but only as pathological deviation from the rational, gradually dislodged dreams as an important center of speculation on the nature and function of human mentation. This story can be read in the ambivalent responses to Cardano since his death and the disparate fortunes of his writings.

This claim of the sixteenth century as the site of the transitions described throughout this essay is obviously not original. What is new here is the focus on dreaming as a central issue in the transition. What is unique is the argument for Girolamo Cardano's importance to this moment of social and cultural as well as oneirological history, and the emphasis on the implications of his life and work for research on dreams as well as on the Renaissance.

In *Madness and Civilization: A History of Insanity in the Age of Reason*, Michel Foucault noted that "the quasi-oneiric character of madness" came to be widely recognized in Renaissance culture (Foucault 1973, 101). Foucault's other observation, that up until that time "the sensibility to madness was linked to the presence of imaginary transcendences," also applies to dreams (p. 58). Foucault associates the loss of that link with a new definition of socially acceptable behavior. Any deviance from the new growing social and entirely secular norms came to be seen as a threat that must be contained.

"Indeed, from the fifteenth century on the fact of madness has haunted the imagination of Western man," Foucault argues, because by that century "Madness has ceased to be . . . an eschatological figure" . . . "ceased to be the sign of another world" (p. 5, p. 35, p. 115). This observation also can be made about dreams, with their religious contexts undermined and their primary function nullified or supplanted. Foucault appears to have felt a kinship with Cardano in much of his thinking. At one point he quotes Cardano on crossing the "forbidden limits of knowledge" and facing the challenge of uncovering what is hidden "deep in the bowels of the earth" (p. 22).

Foucault argues that there began in the 1400s a separation of liminal states of mental activity from any relation to transcendence. The labeling of the mad and their forced separation from general society, Foucault says, began with the transportation of deviants on the "ships of fools." This way of handling mad people was followed and eventually superseded by the opening of asylums. These asylums became an established part of society as "hospitals" for the "mentally ill," grounding the deviants and settling them in the midst of society while simultaneously isolating them from it.

Foucault extends his provocative analysis in ways that are suggestive for the discussion of creativity as an oneiric function. When he asserts the intensifying constriction and isolation of madness's place in society, he uses not social but literary examples. And those examples are from the last period of time in which "madness and non-madness, reason and non-reason are inextricably involved" (p. x)—the Renaissance:

> Madness was thus torn from that imaginary freedom which still allowed it to flourish on the Renaissance horizon. Not so long ago, it had floundered about in broad daylight: in *King Lear*, in *Don Quixote* (p. 64).

That such changes as Foucault describes are paralleled in dream history can be seen everywhere in the sixteenth-century world of dreams and especially in a single exemplary life and work: Cardano's. Further, study of the *Somniorum Synesiorum* also can lead us to to other oneiroloical treatises of the times which, like Cardano's have remained unedited, untranslated, and hidden away from the modern, and postmodern, dream researcher. Among the Italians are Auger Ferrier (or Augerius Ferrerius: 1513–1588) *Liber de somniis*, Lyon, 1549; Benito Pereira (or Benedicti Pererii: c. 1535–1610) *Adversus fallaces & superstitiosas artes, id est de Magia, de observatione Somniorum, & de divinatione astrologica*, 1592 [actually printed bound with Cardano's *Somniorum Synesiorum* in a 1654 Amsterdam edition]; Tommaso Garzoni (1549–1589) *Il Serraglio de gli stupori del mondo*, 1580s; Alessandro Carreri (or Alexander Carrerius: 1543–1626) *De somniis deque divinatione per somnia*, Padua, 1575. Also of interest in this regard is an anonymous pamphlet, "Descrizione del canto dei sogni," which appeared in Florence in 1566 and has been attributed to Cosimo de Medici (1519–1574). And much can be learned about the intercultural, intertextual history of oneirics in the *Oneirocriticon* of Achmes (Achmet ibn Sirin): "a Greek book written by a Christian using Arab sources, of uncertain date, except that it must be between 813 and 1176 when it was translated into Latin by Leo Tuscus" (Browne 1971, 28). The treatise was also translated into French in the fourteenth century and into Italian in 1525.

In the sixteenth century then, when a person had a dream, no single criterion could be comfortably or systematically invoked to assess its origin. Since no one could confidently posit a divine external authority, gods disappear and the demon moves inside, becoming one's own human tendency toward the irrational, or, aesthetically considered, toward the imaginal.

Dream theorists invented complicated strategies to circumvent, ignore, or deny any conflict in their inherited views, and their speculations ranged widely. Some writers clung to oneiromancy despite the contradictions that it presented and the clear challenges to its credibility given even by themselves in different works. Some evaded the question of prophecy by associating dreams and astrology with a new external celestial force—stars and planets—or with an extremity of intrapsychic existence such as madness, or with a nonnatural, external, suprahuman force like magic.

Thus they removed dreams altogether from the realm of the supernatural and shifted oneiromancy into realms that would increasingly be given pejorative labels of the occult, pseudoscience, or superstition. The semantic shift enabled writers to maintain interest in and support for other elements of the dream experience and pay less attention to origin and function.

Some writers on dreams subjected all oneiric exploration to ironic scrutiny, while others, including prominent Jesuits, took a moral perspective that lumped the use of dreams with other divinatory activities like astrology and condemned them all. Many practicing physicians like Cardano followed the tradition of Hippocrates and Galen. They took the medical position that dreams can be symptomatic manifestations of physical pathology and thus can serve as useful tools in diagnosis and even in treatment. This was a kind of in-the-body divination that has resurfaced in cancer studies where analysis of the dreams, as well as the art work, of patients has become a factor in diagnosis and prognosis. And some writers remained tied to the religious tradition, maintaining an insistence on the veracity, authenticity, and visionary status of dreams in the Bible, while arguing that this form of divine communication had been essential in the formative years of the Church, but had gradually become obsolete.

> I confesse the Saints and Martires of Primitive Church had unfallible dreames forerunning their ends, as Policarpus and others: but those especially proceeded from heaven and not from any vaporous dreggie parts of our blood or our braines. (Nashe 1594).

This passage comes from *Terrors of the Night, Or, A Discourse of Apparitions*, by Englishman Thomas Nashe (1567–1601). His dream text is a harbinger of the changed oneiric attitudes of the later seventeenth century. He begins by uninhibitedly disparaging his distant and immediate oneirological predecessors," . . . those that will hearken any more after Dreames, I referre them to Artimidorus (sic), Synesius, & Cardan [Cardano] & many others which onely I have heard by their names" (p. 20). There is evidence to suggest that, despite his disclaimer, Nashe was well acquainted with the works whose authors he spurns.[9] Certainly all were available at that time in England in new editions and translations. His pungent comments on divination mark the distance dreams have traversed since Macrobious: "One may as well by the smoke that comes out of a kitchen gesse what meat is there abroach as paraphrasing on smokie dreams praeominate of future events" (p. 31).

The tension caused by discarding or challenging transmitted categories of oneirics, especially rejection of the function of divination, may form the subtext of a later and more sober English writer's dream text. Thomas Tryon (1634–1703) composed *A Treatise of Dreams and Visions*, which was printed by T. Sowle in London in 1695. He concedes that while God is out of the dream schema altogether now, dreams as communication with higher-than-human powers, for example certain ranks of angels, though rare are not unheard of (Ch. XI). This almost-scholastic splitting of hairs testifies to a certain desperation to salvage the divine connection in dreams. Divination by any level of being occupies a minimal place in Tryon's text, however, despite its full title: *A Treatise of Dreams and Visions, the Causes, Natures, and Uses of Nocturnal Representations, and the Communications both of Good and Evil Angels, as also departed souls to Mankind, Are theosophically Unfolded: that is, according to the word of God and the harmony of Created Beings.* Most important for the argument here about the shift from divinity to insanity as the central focus of oneirological inquiry, he appended to this theosophical treatise a second brief text: *A Discourse of the Causes, Nature and Cure of Phrensie, Madness, or Distraction.* In it he asserts "an affinity or analogy between dreams and madness so that the understanding of one will somewhat illustrate the other; for Madness seems to be a Watching and Waking Dream" (Tryon 1695, 249). This position corresponds with Foucault's; everyone begins now to note that insanity has an eerie resemblance to dream: "Madness is nothing but an erring Sleepifying Power" (Tryon 1695, 288). One notable consequence of this shift of perspective is that madness can be assigned an etiology that is in no way linked to the supernatural. The gods aren't responsible for your madness; you are. It does not come from outside of you from them as dreams once did; it comes from inside of you and is entirely a secular affair, yours and society's.

Tryon, also a practicing physician, gives a purely medical account of the nightmare, saying that while popular thought has hobgoblins jumping on the dreamer's chest, the problem really is internal and psychophysiological. People suffering from the specific malady of melancholia (what we would today probably call depression) are literally all choked up by their intense emotions and their breathing is inhibited. Even Nashe acknowledged that dreams perform a reliable medical function of diagnosis: "Physitions by dreames may better discern the distemperature of their pale clients than by either urine or ordure" (Nashe 1594, 32).

Moses Amyraldus (or Moise Amyraut: 1596–1664), writing somewhat later than Nashe, confronted heartily the question many preceding theorists had so often adroitly eluded, avoided, or defused: How can you truly ascertain the origin of dreams? How could one ever tell whether the dream's source was divine or demonic? It had been believed that receptivity to dreams and the likelihood of their occurrence could be enhanced by certain practices, among them "incubation": going to sleep in a holy place after fasting and prayer. Also, being in a state of grace as cultivated by certain mystics was thought to ensure admittance only of divine spirits.

Like Tryon, Amyraldus acknowledges the possibility that contemporary dreams may feature lower—order supernatural beings ("angelic dreams"). However, like Nashe, he claims God Himself no longer needs to speak through dreams. God was compelled to do this in Biblical times when spreading the faith in the early years of the Church required His active intervention. Thus Amyraldus finds an "out" generally overlooked in the patristic tradition whereby he can honor God-sent Biblical dreams, preserve their uniqueness, and remove any implications they might be seen as having for contemporary and future dream interpretations, theories, or beliefs. His title reveals the whole disposition of his text: *A Discourse concerning the divine dreams mention'd in Scripture together with the Marks and Characters by which they might be distinguish'd from vain Delusions.* And Amyraldus saw the early seventeenth century in which he lived as a dreadful time when "some men look upon all Divine Revelations to be mere Dreams, others mistake their mere Dreams for Divine Revelations . . ." (Dedicatory Letter) His unmistakable conclusion is that the "time for Divine Dreams is now wholly expir'd. Only impostors or fools still claim them" (Ch. V., 113).

Amyraldus could then have gone on to take a position many of the Church Fathers would have preferred, given their fear of dangerous false dreams and illusions, that all post-Biblical dreams are nonsense and should be ignored or rejected. But, like Tryon, Amyraldus is reluctant to go so far. He remains content to place such divinatory dreams irrevocably in the past and in exclusively sacred contexts. In citing certain impostors he appears to be arguing against a popular culture in which, as I have noted, traditional beliefs in divination were frequently retained.

After the seventeenth century, divination as the chief function of dreams and the chief justification for remembering, relating, and studying them never again dominates oneiric discourse in the West. Oneirology continues its turn toward the past and away from the future, toward a theory of intrapsychic retrospective that reaches its inevitable extreme with Freud. Jung's theory of Self and his notion of "prospective" dreams advanced toward mid-century seemed to be leading the circle around again in the direction of pre-Renaissance thought, especially as Jung drew upon many of Cardano's works, including the *Somniorum Synesiorum.* But there are familiar ambivalences and complexities of response in and to Jungian psychology which indicate that the secular and medical constraints of post-Renaissance oneirics are still operative.

Restoration of dreaming to a more appopriately central and natural place in Western culture seems to be occurring lately, however, perhaps as a turn-of-the-century phenomenon like the previous movement signaled by the publication (1899) and self-conscious dating (1900) of Freud's *Die Traumdeutung*. This movement will be enhanced if there is a historical awareness of the centuries-long struggle between the non-sense and the beyond-sense approaches to dreams. Dreams need not be pulled between the two extremes of dismiss and exalt, between the nothingness of now and the everything of the afterlife, between cynical or "scientific" denigration and idealistic overvaluation.

The weight of dream experience and theory should not fall wholly on medical pathology or theologically (or psychologically) based versions of spirituality. And more energy can be fruitfully invested in dreaming's contribution to creativity, both in theories about aesthetics and linguistics and in the practices of art and literature. Comparative study of dreams and oneiric attitudes in other cultures that have experienced no historical devaluation of dreams can help Western researchers avoid the polarizations that have constricted their past discourse, including the major polarization in twentieth-century oneirics: Freud vs. Jung. For whatever its fate in religious, political, medical, or social contexts, dreaming has always thrived in its alliance with creativity and its direct insinuation into the personal life of the dreamer.

Notes

1. Availability of their treatises in accessible editions with good English translations has undoubtedly contributed to scholarly familiarity with these theorists, as well as with Synesius. (Artemidorus Daldianus. *The Interpretation of Dreams*. Trans. Ralph White; Macrobius. *Commentary on the Dream of Scipio*. Trans. Wm. H. Stahl; Synesius, "On Dreams" in *The Essays and Hymns of Synesius*. Trans. A. Fitzgerald.) It has perhaps also, however, led to an exaggerated assessment of the importance of the first two writers for the Renaissance and to a neglect of Renaissance dream texts.

2. On the issue of futurity in dreams, I cite verbatim note 7 from my essay, "The Nightmares of History: Shakespeare's Use of Dreams in the Henry VI Tetralogy," presented to the Fifth World Congress on Shakespeare in Japan in August, 1991: "The question of the predictive or prognosticatory function of dreams has remained a vexing one in oneiric history even after its fall from favor during the Renaissance. The attitude toward dream temporality itself is finally coming to be an object of analysis. Freud's frequent and impassioned denial of any futurity in dreams . . . has finally come to be seen as a defense. . . ." I am currently completing a separate article on the issue which is also treated in sources like Ken Frieden's *Freud's Dream of Interpretation* (Albany, NY: State University of New York Press, 1990), and

an article by S.R.F. Price in the British journal of history *Past and Present*, "The Future of Dreams: From Freud to Artemidorus," 113: 1—37, 1986.

3. The quotations from the *Somniorum Synesiorum* used in this essay have been translated into English by me from the 1989 Italian translation since it is the edition most available to readers. My translations have been checked against the 1562 and 1663 Latin editions and against the translations from the Latin of various passages which Browne and Fierz have made for use in their works on Cardano. Citations are given by book and section number which are identical in all editions.

4. See References for my 1990 article in the *Psychiatric Journal of the University of Ottawa*. This is an international quarterly journal published by the Department of Psychiatry, School of Medicine, Faculty of Health Sciences, University of Ottawa, Ontario, Canada. The journal publishes "scientific papers dealing with all aspects of psychiatry and related medical fields" written in either French or English and has printed selected proceedings of the annual conferences of the Association for the Study of Dreams.

5. An English translation of *Somniorum Synesiorum* is sorely needed. The recent Italian translation is lacking in many respects. Among other things, it has no scholarly apparatus, omits Books II-IV, and is not based on the 1562 edition, the only one printed in Cardano's lifetime and overseen by him.

6. There is major disagreement about the nature and effect of these dreams. We do not have Descartes's original accounts of the dreams but summaries are provided in a biography by Adrien Baillet, *La Vie de Monsieur Des—Cartes* (Paris: Table Ronde, 1946). The bibliography on the controversy is extensive, and includes a fine article by Alice Browne in the *Journal of the Warburg and Courtauldt Institute*, XL (1977) 256–273.

7. A contemporary treatment of this subject can be found in Bert O. States's *The Rhetoric of Dreams* (Ithaca: Cornell University Press, 1990).

8. See Charles Michael Matlock's Ph.D. dissertation in English, SUNY-Albany, 1972, "An Interpretation of Piers Plowman Based on the Medieval Dream Background."

9. Professor John Tobin has supplied me with this information and much additional background on Thomas Nashe as part of his commentary on my work on nightmares in Shakespeare's history plays. See n. 2 above.

References

Amyraldus, Moses. [Moise Amyraut.] *A Discourse concerning the divine dreams mention'd in Scripture together with the Marks and Characters by which they might be distinguish'd from vain Delusions.* 1603 English trans. No other bibliographical data.

Artemidorus Daldianus. *The Interpretation of Dreams.* Translated by Ralph White. New Jersey: Noyes Press, 1975.

Browne, Alice L. "Sixteenth Century Beliefs on Dreams with Special References to Girolamo Cardano's *Somniorum Synesiorum Libri IIII.*" M.Phil. thesis, University of London. 1971.

————. "Religious Dreams and Their Interpretation in Some Thinkers of the Seventeenth Century." Ph.D. diss. University of London. 1975.

————. "Girolamo Cardano's *Somniorum Synesiorum Libri IIII.*" *Bibliothéque d'Humanisme et Renaissance* 41:123—135. 1979.

Cardano, Girolamo. [Jerome Cardan.] *The Book of My Life.* Translated by Jean Stoner. New York: E.P. Dutton & Co., Inc., 1930.

————. *Comforte.* Translated by T. Bedingfeld. London: Thomas Marsh, 1573. Reprint Amsterdam: Theatrum Orbis Terrarum Ltd., 1969.

————. *Opera Omnia.* V. Edited by C. Spon. Lyon, 1663. Reprint New York: Johnson Reprint Corporation. Introduction by August Buck. 1967.

————. [Hieronymus Cardanus] *Somniorum Synesiorum, omnis generis insomnia explicantes, libri iiii.* Basel: Henry Petrie, 1562.

————. *Sul Sonno e Sul Sognare.* Translated by S. Montiglio and A. Grieco. Edited by M. Mancia and A.Grieco. Venice: Marsilio Editore, 1989.

Cicero. *On Divination.* Translated by C. D. Yonge. London: George Bell & Sons, 1892.

Dizionario biografico degli Italiani. 1976. Rome: Istituto della Enciclopedia Italiana. C: 758—763.

Fierz, Markus. [1980] *Girolamo Cardano (1501—1576)*. Translated by Helga Niman. Boston: Birkhauser, 1983.

Foucault, Michel. *Madness and Civilization: A History of Insanity in the Age of Reason.* Translated by Richard Howard. New York: Random House, 1973.

Freud, Sigmund. *The Standard Edition of the Complete Psychological Works.* Translated and edited by James Strachey. London: The Hogarth Press and the Institute of Psycho-Analysis, 1953–74. Vol. V.

Macrobius, T. *Commentary on the Dream of Scipio.* Translated by W. H. Stahl. New York: Columbia University Press, 1952.

Nashe, Thomas. *Terrors of the night, Or, a Discourse of Apparitions.* London: John Danter, Printer, 1594.

Ore, Oystein. *Cardano, The Gambling Scholar.* With a translation from the Latin of Cardano's Book on Games of Chance by Sydney Henry Gould. Princeton: Princeton University Press, 1953.

Rupprecht, Carol Schreier. "Our Unacknowledged Ancestors: Dream Theorists of Antiquity, the Middle Ages, and the Renaissance." *The Psychiatric Journal of the University of Ottawa.* 15. 2 (June 1990) 117–122.

Shumaker, Wayne. *Renaissance Curiosa.* Binghamton, New York: Center for Medieval and Early Renaissance Studies, 1982.

Synesius. "On Dreams." *The Essays and Hymns of Synesius.* Translated by A. Fitzgerald. 2 Vols. Cambridge: Oxford University Press, 1930.

Thorndike, Lynn. *History of Magic and Experimental Science.* 8 vols. New York: Macmillan, 1923–58.

Tryon, Thomas. *A Treatise of Dreams and Visions, the Causes, Natures, and Uses of Nocturnal Representations, and the Communications both of Good and Evil Angels, as also departed souls to Mankind, Are Theosophically Unfolded: that is, according to the word of God and the Harmony of Created Beings.* 2nd ed. London: T. Sowle, 1695.

8. Dreaming of Death: Love and Money in *The Merchant of Venice*

Kay Stockholder

Psychoanalytic criticism over the years has generated a refined understanding of the ways literature renders the complex, dynamic organization of human emotion. However, there are two persistent grounds on which most forms of psychoanalytic literary practice have been censured. The first is that they detach literary portrayals of human complexities from the social and political institutions, conscious values, and cognitive systems in which literature embeds them. In concentrating on a presumed latent content, psychoanalytic criticism tends to ignore the interaction between the unconscious emotions and ideas, those that would derive from the past of persons like those represented, and the present world they are depicted as confronting. By limiting meaningfulness to unconscious motivations, this critical approach depreciates representations of social reality, consciousness, and cognition. The second charge against psychoanalytic criticism is that it fails to account for the formal characteristics and aesthetic dimensions of literature. This omission generates criticism that reduces literature to authorial biography, or to characters' case histories; to projecting screens for its audiences' predilections, or to sets of rhetorical manipulations of its readers.[1]

The mode of criticism that this chapter will bring to bear on *The Merchant of Venice* includes these otherwise excluded dimensions by taking the protagonist as the dreamer of his play.[2] To regard the entire configuration of the drama as the protagonist's dream renders significant all that he confronts as external to himself, and reads the genre form itself as expressive of the dreamer's habitual stance towards his or her emotional life. He is analogous not to us dreaming, but rather to the figure in our dreams that we identify as ourselves when we awaken. As well, the play's conclusion reveals the desire implicit in its

133

beginning, and provides thereby the psychological concomitant to the sense of inevitability that contributes to the aesthetic force of fiction. The play's formal properties, the discourse in which the story is articulated, express the modes by which the protagonist mediates between the demands of unacknowledged desires that shape what he confronts as an external world, and his consciously espoused values. This approach makes appropriate some Lacanian and semiotic vocabulary, that is, to trace the ways in which various aspects of the text, including what one normally thinks of as characters, function as a chain of interlocking signifiers. However, unlike Lacanian approaches it centers the work in subjective human experience. Seeing each component as a signifier that collects the affect of multiple signifieds allows one to trace the changing ways in which aspects of works that are generally the focus of psychoanalytic study are linked to, or signify, the dominant ideas that constitute the social and cultural nexus of the worlds that produce them. The entire work becomes a picture of the protagonist's strategy of signification as he negotiates between the demands of unconscious drives, his conscious value systems, and what he experiences as his external worlds. The work becomes a chain of the protagonist's associations that reveals the way his self-experience is interconnected to the structure of signification that constitutes his culture (Silverman 1983). Therefore, to regard the play as the protagonist's dream keeps us closer to and takes more account of the play's surface than does a conventional psychoanalytic account. It addresses the formal patterns of action without losing sight of an experiencing human consciousness within them. By attending to the relationships between conscious and unconscious states, rather than regarding the products of consciousness as clues to what they conceal, one can ascertain some possible emotional correlates of lives shaped within a historical reality other than one's own.

While in principle one can regard any figure as the protagonist of the play, to choose a figure at the periphery of the action is to read the play as the dream of one who defines himself as observer rather than as participant in her or his world. In tragic or serious literature things fall into place more simply by choosing a figure who is at the play's emotional center, so that the choice of whom to regard as protagonist is relatively straightforward. It is, however, the nature of comedy to obscure its emotional center, and to substitute plot for feeling in a way that renders comedy, viewed in this way, as revelatory of more deeply repressed material than is tragedy. That is, while watching a tragedy we are more engaged in the action as it affects the central characters than for its own sake, while the reverse is so for comedy. Therefore, in comedy one often more deftly penetrates the play's emotional center by attending to whomever or whatever functions as the moving force of the plot, however obscure the figure may seem, rather than by focusing on the most emotionally heightened figure. In *The Merchant of Venice*, the central focus of this chapter, all the action stems from Portia's dead father. He arranges his daughter's marriage, and sets in motion all that flows from it. Therefore I will regard this shadowy figure as the dreamer of the play.

This choice is more heuristic than substantive. That is, one could select any of the characters, Shylock, Antonio, Portia, Bassanio, or even Lorenzo. Ultimately one would be telling the same story from different perspectives; for each figure the others would signify repudiated aspects of his or her emotional configuration. For example, if one chose Portia as dreamer, the dead but still influential father would reveal her ambivalence about the paternal authority that she contests in assuming power over the other male figures. Her psychological drama would be the mirror image of her father's, whose ambivalence about male authority is manifested in his retreat from it and in his substitution of Portia for himself (see note 11, p. 154). However, designating the Father as dreamer draws one in more immediately to the male psychodynamic that generates the play and choosing him rather than one of the other male figures highlights the significance of the plot line that derives from his initial retreat. All the action flows from his move to control his daughter's marriage and the transmission of his wealth.

Therefore to think about the play as the Father's dream relates the central concerns with wealth and money, which shape the figures and actions he defines as external and separate from himself, to the psychological significance of the emotionally heightened aspects that more readily suggest psychodynamic meanings. To bring Portia's father from the obscurity of his grave is to locate in a subject what otherwise appear as textual gaps and breaks, and to read them as links in a semiotic chain that is bounded within the single text. In this way one can penetrate most efficaciously what one might call the play's social psychology, or its political unconscious, in relationship to the more usual concerns of psychoanalytic criticism.

To foreground this occulted figure casts light on otherwise-obscure links between this play and others, some of which I will indicate in the process of the argument that follows. As the attributes of characters combine and recombine into a variety of figures in other plays, Shakespeare adopts different strategies to harmonize the conflicts that in his world inhere in romantic marriage. These links suggest that the concern with money that is so obvious in this play has submerged importance in other plays by Shakespeare, and that the conflicting ideologies of this play were not resolved, but rather were submerged in his later work. However, to move in this way from a textual to an intertextual frame, and to relate the experience of one protagonist to that of another, one clearly must consider Shakespeare to be the dreamer, and the various protagonists as avatars of one who casts himself as an invisible observer to his own vast dream.

To think about Shakespeare as the dreamer does not imply that the plays, like dreams, took shape without conscious intention and craft. Rather, to do so assumes that in addition to conscious decisions about what kind of play to write and what ideas it was to incorporate, an intuitive sense of what was fitting guided Shakespeare in making the myriad of choices from the ways his world made it possible for him to accomplish his goals.[3] Such intuitive choices, ranging from the largest components, such as genre, convention, and dramatis personae, to the smallest details of language, draw on the psychic forces that shape dreams out of the contents of our waking lives. In order to elucidate these links between personal psychology and public ideology, the last part of this chapter will place in their historical context the interrelated concerns with marriage and money that emerge from this study.

Considering Portia's father as the dreamer renders *The Merchant of Venice* like a dream of one for whom only such a radically self-denying strategy as dying could provide a compromise between contradictory ideas and desires. His having dreamt himself dead suggests self-hatred and condemnation so intense that he cannot live with himself. Having thus avoided the challenge to become conscious of his psychic drama, he idealizes himself as a beneficent magical power reaching into the world from beyond the grave. He reveals Portia's centrality to the conflicted emotions from which he retreated by the central role he assigns her. His desires pull in two contrary directions. On the one hand, his desire that she join him in the grave to which he has retreated appears in the world-weariness of her opening words, "By my troth, Nerissa, my little body is aweary of this great world" (I.ii.1–2). She makes a more oblique but more trenchant connection between death and marriage, or death and sexuality, when she says that she would "rather be married to a death's-head with a bone in his mouth" than to her suitors. This grotesque image adds a sexual dimension to Portia's world-weariness, which indicates that the Father has initiated, but not completed, a version of a love-death romance such as is suggested when Lear wants to "crawl towards death" while living with

Cordelia, and is explicit in *Pericles* between Antiochus and his daughter. The Father's concentration on Portia's marriage reveals not only his denied incestuous desires; the fact that his sexuality is expressed through incest connotes his association of sexuality in general with the debasement of family affection, violation, evil, and death. This last association is made through his own dream death, as well as in the risk of death incurred by those who seek Portia's hand.[4] This aspect of his mentality remains submerged, but it is the opposite side to the idealization of Portia, who, once married, becomes the Father's surrogate magical agent to preside over Belmont, which functions as a Neoplatonic alternative to the commercial Venice.

While Portia's language manifests the Father's pull on her, his revulsion from his own desires forces a compromise formation in which he substitutes for his forbidden erotic desires control over her marriage choice and the disposition of his wealth. The tension between these contrary pulls appears in Portia's lament that she "may neither choose whom I would nor refuse whom I dislike; so is the will of a living daughter curbed by the will of a dead father" (I.ii.25–7).[5] The Father justifies his hold on her by defining himself as a benign magus whose power will serve her interests when Nerissa says that only one "who you shall rightly love" (I.i.36) will choose the right casket. By thus idealizing himself as a benign magical force, as Prospero more overtly does later, the Father achieves a sleight-of-hand reconciliation between his craving for control, which functions as a devious expression of and substitute for sexual desire, and a romantic conception of marriage. That is, Portia's father cannot forgo his paternal dominion, which is energized by his denied sexual desire; but he cannot assert it explicitly because his ideology of marriage incorporates romantic love. He exonerates himself by defining his control as a magical emanation from the grave that serves not only Portia's best interests, but also her desires. By these means the Father achieves a trickster's reconciliation of the usually mutually exclusive desires both to control his daughter's will and have her marry for love.

However, marriage based on romantic love conflicts not only with the Father's erotic claims; it conflicts as well with the function of marriage as a means of ensuring the transmission of wealth. The pivotal place of wealth in the Father's psyche first appears when Nerissa rebukes Portia for failing to appreciate the abundance of her fortunes (II.i.4–5). It is inscribed more deeply in the casket device that inaugurates the play's major action. Here the Father expresses both his espoused ideal of romantic marriage uncontaminated by material concerns and his sense of the danger of such contamination. The underlying equation of love and money appears in the elaborate denial of the casket device, which associates Portia with valueless lead and gold with "carrion death." In this configuration the Father radically separates love and marriage from money and wealth, but reveals the hidden links by associating Portia with the golden fleece. On the one hand that image presages Portia's function as representative of spiritual gold, but the denied material desires condition the plot in which Portia is a material golden fleece for Bassanio. Bassanio's need for money in order to achieve status and wealth and Antonio's presumed indifference to the money he has acquired from commerce (that is, from buying cheap and selling dear) show the opposed levels of material concerns sliding into and representing each other. The sleight of hand by which the Father reconciles the competing claims of romance and the transmission of inheritance reveals not only his erotically charged concentration on controlling his wealth, but also the self-hatred occasioned by desires that would destroy his self-image should he espouse them. The only compromise he has found for these convoluted desires has been to retreat into death while designing a fairy-tale world to perpetuate images of himself that defend him from self-hatred and self-condemnation.

As we will see later, the Father's psychological dilemma has its roots in the consequences of a romantic ideology of marriage. While marriage was conceived primarily as a financial arrangement between families, a father of daughters was required to part with some of his wealth for their dowries, but he could substitute for forbidden erotic desires an intense connection to a daughter through controlling her will. If a daughter is to marry for love, then her father loses the compensatory satisfaction of control. As Cordelia later puts it, not only will she give her husband half her heart; her love rather than only her father's choice will determine the destination of the dowry. Portia's father, however, has not only accepted romantic marriage, but spiritualized it. Having rendered it symbolic of transcendent, as opposed to material, gold, he must drive his material concerns into his unconscious where they join the guilt and shame associated with forbidden incestuous desires. Having thus fused love and wealth, the Father becomes an aristocratic version of Shylock's confusion of daughters with ducats.[6]

The emotional strife between desires and the values that render them guilty shapes the two paternal surrogates into which he splits himself, Antonio and Shylock, each of whom becomes the other's alter ego. The self-image generated by his denied desires generates Shylock, the Jew denied by society. His possessiveness of Portia appears as Shylock's of Jessica, while his shame for conflating Portia with wealth appears in Shylock's explicit equation of the two—"My daughter, my ducats." In caricaturing Shylock's ugliness and grasping possessiveness, the Father portrays his repressed self-image and the concomitant self-loathing that forced him to repudiate his desires. Though the Father foregrounds Shylock's hatred of Antonio and his love of money, it is Jessica's elopement with Lorenzo that triggers the climactic action. The play obscures whether it was in jest only that Shylock made the bond with Antonio, but it is certainly only after Jessica's marriage that the jest turns to earnest. The linked sexual and monetary components of Shylock's claim on Jessica also appear when Shylock laments that she has stolen her mother's jewels, in effect stealing the dowry that the court later forces him to give her. This configuration reveals the Father's fears that unless he retains extraordinary powers, his daughter's free choice of a husband will wrest his wealth from him and debase his family.

In a self-splitting more radical than that of King Lear, who victimizes Cordelia while victimizing himself to Goneril and Regan, in the despised Shylock the Father embodies his fierce possessiveness of both daughters and ducats, and in the melancholy Antonio he expresses his grief and drift toward death. This is the emotional consequence of having repressed both his erotic and monetary passions. He also embodies in Antonio a short-circuited quest for a homoerotic alternative to his embattled heterosexuality. However, he associates homoeroticism with a depletion of life energies that is expressed in the loss of money. Antonio betrays the same associations of love with wealth that are expressed in the casket motif. Just as the motif betrays the equation of love with money that it is intended to conceal, so do Antonio's answers to his fellow merchants when they ask why he is melancholy. To their suggestion that he is melancholy because he cannot cool his soup or go to church without bringing to mind the rocks upon which the winds might drive his ships, Antonio denies that all his wealth is at hazard. He denies as well their suggestion that he grieves for Bassanio's imminent departure. But the action belies both denials, for were all his wealth not at hazard he would have been able to meet the bond that he would not in the first place have had to make. And were he not grieving for Bassanio, he would not cast himself as competitor with Portia for Bassanio's love, as he does in the trial scene when he uses his predicament as a means by which to draw Bassanio away from Portia.[7] He explicitly contrasts his self-sacrificing love to Portia's when he tells Bassanio to, "Say how I lov'd you, speak me fair in death; / And, when the tale is told, bid her be the judge /

Whether Bassanio had not once a love" (IV.i.276–78). As well, when
he urges Bassanio to part with Portia's ring, he demands that Balthaz-
ar's "deserving, and my love withal / Be valu'd gainst your wife's com-
mandment" (IV.i.454–55).

The action in which Antonio's coffers are drained by Bassanio's
pecuniary needs associates the Father's homoerotic move with loss of
wealth, which is in turn associated with the loss of the life's blood that
will drain from Antonio should Shylock cut his pound of flesh. The
two are further linked by the image in which Bassanio tells Portia that "I freely told you all the wealth I had / Ran in my veins"
(III.ii.255–56).[8] In Antonio's melancholy, then, the Father expresses
the emotional consequence of having repressed both forms of erotic
satisfaction, along with the desire for money that signifies them both.
Antonio's apparently unmotivated self-denigration as a "tainted
wether of the flock" surrounds his figure with an aura of self-loathing
and death that reveal him as an emanation from the Father's grave.

But the intensity of hatred between the wolfish Shylock and his
natural prey, the flock's tainted wether, Antonio, is so great that it
raises the possibility of another and darker level of homosexuality than
appears in the gentle relationship between Antonio and Bassanio. As
we have seen, in Shylock the Father manifests the repressed conflation of incestuous desire and ruthless greed and consequent self-
loathing that bars his access to heterosexual love. Shylock's remoteness
from his own figure, both socially and in the topography of his dream,
manifests his underlying vision of himself as a social outcast. Having
marginalized Shylock in this way, he also expresses through the intensity of the mutual hatred of Shylock and Antonio, out of which they
forge their "bond," his most deeply buried homosexual eroticism. In
turn, homosexuality is also associated with Shylock's open display of
the greed and possessiveness for which the Father despises himself.
This complex of feeling appears in the configuration created by Bassanio, Antonio, and Shylock, in which he rejects as debasing and disgusting his unconscious desire for his socially outcast alter ego, and
masks it with his attachment to the more socially acceptable Bassanio.
In the figure of Bassanio he asserts his rights to membership in the
aristocratic world in which generosity and insouciance about the
money upon which its display depends is a necessary symbol of rank
and status (Stone 1967). Representing in Antonio the frustration and
self-hatred that surfaces in consciousness only as melancholy and
ennui, he forges a compromise between frustrated desire and fear by
moving towards a nightmare version of sexual fulfillment. In Shylock's
refusal to accept reified money in lieu of Antonio's literal flesh, the

Father desublimates his desire, and in the culminating scene in which Antonio bares his breast to Shylock's knife, he reveals his terror of and desire for an enactment that will simultaneously punish and gratify his guilty desires. Furthermore, by casting Antonio as Shylock's victim with Bassanio as audience he has additional gratification of seeing Bassanio feel guilt for taking his daughter and with her his wealth, while, through Antonio, simultaneously enjoying being the object both of his horrified and loving gaze and of Shylock's terrible intimacy. He assuages his guilt through Shylock's punishment, and through Antonio gets the masochistic reward of being victimized, as well as the delight of being the object of Portia's compassionate concern. In this way the Father's dream exemplifies Freud's depiction of the way the superego taps the resources of the id.[9]

The strategy of splitting enables the Father to keep both his surrogates in the land of the living, but the inadequacy of the compromise appears in the fact that both Shylock and Antonio are in the end comforted only by the wealth, without which they would, in Antonio's words, "view with hollow eye and wrinkled brow / An age of poverty" (IV.i.271–72), an odd conclusion to a play that thematically opposes Venetian reified value to Belmont's spiritual gold. Shylock has only enough money to survive in his bitter humiliation, and the Father generates no fourth female to sweep Antonio into the comedic celebration of multiple marriages. To the end he remains an isolated and melancholy figure. These hidden links between the hero and the villain, two figures who are on the surface so radically opposed, reveal that the Jew is not as alien as the Father would like him to be. The failure to resolve the conflicts that generate the play appears as well in Shylock's unsettling comparison of his rights to Antonio's flesh to the Venetian rights over their purchased slaves. The ambivalence about the commerce that characterizes Venice and that her laws are designed to protect also generates sympathy for Shylock. The underlying sense that Antonio and Shylock are twin births, that Shylock functions as scapegoat for the love of money upon which Venice is founded and Belmont is dependent, wells up in Shylock's assertion of his humanity and justifies his vengefulness.[10] It also reflects the Father's ultimate unwillingness completely to forgo his unacknowledged desires, as well as his underlying rage at having been forced to repress them.

The Father's ambivalence about the ideology in terms of which he conceives his cure fractures the light that plays around Portia and problematizes the play's emotional impact. In order both to inherit her father's mantle and to remain a desirable sexual object, she must demonstrate feminine submissiveness, first to her father's will and then to Bassanio. However, her submission of herself and her estate must be token only; she must be heir to her father's power in order to cure in Venice her father's ills. The virtue that is to be therapeutic or redemptive is compassion, as it is in Desdemona, Cordelia, and Miranda, though they are denied Portia's shaping power. Portia shows her compassion first in her eagerness to rescue Antonio, and later in pleading for mercy that is "as the gentle rain from heaven." However, compassion and mercy are private and quiet virtues; to heal a sick world and the Father from whom that world has issued, these virtues must be wedded to the more active and difficult public virtue of justice. Therefore, while protecting the feminine image by having Portia don male disguise, the Father ascribes to her the wisdom and power by which he defines himself, as well as the trickster mentality that allows him to give the illusion of reconciling the conflicting demands of justice and mercy. But justice is a harsh virtue, one easily confused with cruelty. The cunning Portia inherits from him empowers her compassion, but it also entails a capacity for cruelty that threatens to tarnish her image as advocate of mercy and agent of harmony. This capacity also relates her to Shylock in a way that threatens to merge her image into his in ways dangerous to the entire configuration. Furthermore, since she punishes Shylock for his greed and cruelty, and he functions as a stand-in for repudiated aspects of the father, her punishment of Shylock fulfills the Father's fearful desire for the punishment he thinks justice demands. The Father's misgivings about the only compromise formation he has been able to generate are expressed in the precarious comedy of the trial scene when Bassanio and Shylock in turn celebrate Portia as "a Daniel come to judgment."

Portia's money also links her to Shylock. Shylock's gold allows Bassanio to win Portia and endangers Antonio, while Portia's money is the necessary, though not sufficient, condition for her activity. The final action links the two more closely, when, without explaining the source of her knowledge, Portia informs Antonio that his ships are returned and his wealth secure. This odd circumstance reveals the complicity of the idealized Neoplatonic Belmont with the commercialized Venice to which it is posited as a spiritual alternative. The polarized images of society are represented by polarized images of Portia as at once compassionate and cruel. The split in woman's image is not fully realized here, since both sides inhere in the same figure.[11] In *King Lear* the split is more radical; Cordelia, who will not give love for money, symbolizes a transcendent idealization of traditional order, while Goneril and Regan's greed, and the wealth and status to which

Edmund aspires through them, demonize the actuality. Since sexuality is associated with the evil sisters, male heterosexual desires come to signify desire for every kind of violation, all of which are in turn signified by incest. As we will see later, incest taboos concern the transmission of wealth as do other marital prohibitions.

All of these motifs are inextricably knotted into the pound of flesh around which the action turns. In Freudian terms it is an overdetermined dream element; in Lacanian terms it is a floating signifier hungry for signifieds, which in turn function as signifiers for it. Its most obvious signified is the money for which it is substituted, but money, as we have seen, has been equated with both Portia and Jessica. Therefore, the passion for money is fueled by the desire for woman's body, Portia's "little body," that it also represents. Shylock's desire for it then expresses the Father's denied desire for both money and his daughter, equated with each other. The Father has also associated money with the relation between Antonio and Bassanio. Antonio's denied desires for Bassanio being signified by the money which enables him both to send him to Portia and to call him back. Shylock's refusal to accept money as a substitute for Antonio's flesh expresses the ambivalent homoeroticism with which the Father has tinged Antonio's figure. The fears that render the homosexual element elusive between Antonio and Bassanio appear in the ferocious hatred between Shylock and Antonio. Antonio's willingness to sacrifice his pound of flesh for Bassanio and Shylock's desire for it associate homosexuality with castration. In turn, castration signifies death when Portia exposes Shylock's murderous intent. In the death to which Antonio is so ready to go, the Father expresses both his self-punitive impulses and the desire to kill in Antonio the idealized self-image (generously indifferent to money and unpossessive in love) that renders guilty his desires both for money and for his daughter. At its most general level the pound of flesh represents the reified values of Shylock's Venice, whose laws are designed to protect Antonio's commerce. These values the Father contrasts to those of Neoplatonic Belmont, which express his self-idealization. But the father's dream shows self-condemnation and self-idealization to be two sides of a single coin: the self-aggrandizement by which the Father defends himself against his desires amplifies their power to defile what he defines as sacred.

In the union of Bassanio and Portia, the father envisions releasing Portia from the orbit of his desire into the arms of a younger version of himself, so finding vicarious compensation for his loss. However, his vexation about passing Portia on to another man remains apparent in the thinness of Bassanio's characterization, as well as in the postponement of the nuptial celebration beyond the limits of the text. Not only is the wedding night disrupted by Antonio's letter, but the consummation of their marriage retreats into infinite futurity when the last act substitutes for a conventional romantic reunion a more playful version of the court scene in which Bassanio replaces Shylock as Portia's victim, and is punished for dividing his allegiance between her and Antonio. In Portia's privileged knowledge of her identity, by which she reconciles the dilemma she has devised for Bassanio, the Father repeats, in a lighter vein, the earlier configuration in which his magic reconciled otherwise incompatible values. However, the improbability that defines romantic comedy expresses the father's awareness that the conflicts that generated the configuration are still in place, that he has substituted daydream fantasy for genuine dream resolution of conflicts. The incommensurateness of the conclusion to the magnitude of Shylock's figure reveals the Father's dissatisfaction with his own strategy. Shylock's resistance to containment within the comic frame reveals the pressure of the Father's desires toward fuller actualization, a pressure that appears as well in the exclusion of both Shylock and Antonio from the domestic resolution.

That these conflicts remained unresolved appears in the fact that the sleight of hand by which Portia's father generates an illusory resolution of competing value systems most fully characterizes Prospero, who even more trickily contrives to leave his daughter free to choose according to his will, and then celebrates his cleverness in having stage-managed her rebellion. Whereas Portia's father withdraws into death, Prospero withdraws into his study; whereas Portia's father bathes his world in a quasi-magical aura, Prospero emerges from his study with explicitly magical powers on which he bases the superiority that shapes his self-definition. Like his dramatic progenitors, he has only a daughter through whom to control the destiny of his lineage. Sexual passions remain linked to money, for the ideal commonwealth to issue from Ferdinand and Miranda's union is contrasted to the ordinary world in which Sebastian, Antonio, and Stephano anticipate making commercial capital out of Caliban. Caliban represents the unruly sexuality that renders him at once a lump of deformed flesh and a marketplace commodity.

The persistent, if attenuated, ways in which monetary concerns are woven into later plays suggest that Shakespeare, no more than Portia's father, could not remove the taint of money from his imagination of redeeming love and ideal authority. In various ways in different plays he tried to envision a generative heterosexual love that would inseminate a just kingdom with redeeming nurturing compassion, but he could not prevent grotesque images of cruelty and greed from attaching to the active side of multidimensional female figures. Having only daughters to inherit the considerable fortune he acquired in the process of writing and staging plays that deplored the erosion of the traditional hierarchy by the tide of commerce and related ambitions, Shakespeare himself might well have been overwhelmed by the self-loathing and world-weariness he depicts in characters from his royal merchant to his triumphant magician.

✵✵✵

The momentous psychological importance I have found related to money may seem to contradict a Freudian conception in which the primacy of sexual concerns derives from their infantile sources. But as Freud often reminds his readers, the unconscious knows no time. In his topographical model of the unconscious, temporal precedence does not endow events with more affective power than later accretions to which affect may be transferred, and a literary use of the dream model is necessarily concerned with the dynamic interplay of factors within the textual time frame rather than with conceptual origins. Furthermore, though modern sensibilities may be slow to perceive money and wealth as the locus of severe psychological tension, the picture changes when one allows the plays to give emotional resonance to the relationships that existed in their own time between money, wealth, and marriage. Further to widen the frame of reference in this way, to attach signifieds from the time in general to signifying figures within the plays, is to regard Portia's father and his creator as persons experiencing and shaping the age's conflict-ridden nexus of marriage, money, and traditional wealth and status.

In a general way Georg Simmel facilitates an understanding of the psychological stresses in the Renaissance. He argues that the significance of money is that it "expresses the relativity of objects of demand through which they become economic values" (Simmel 1978, 130). Such a fear that the money nexus erodes a social system that authorizes itself on the basis of absolute value is classically expressed by Gaunt in Shakespeare's *Richard II* when he accuses Richard of becoming "England's landlord, not her king." Gaunt's accusation resonates more deeply in view of Simmel's statement that,

> The powerful character of money . . . appears at its most noticeable, at the least at its most uncanny, wherever the money economy is not yet completely established and accepted, and where money displays its

compelling power in relations that are structurally antagonistic (p. 244).

He adds that the "utilization of such a mysterious and dangerous power as capital necessarily appeared as immoral, as criminal misuse" (p. 244). Lawrence Stone's study of complex interrelations between traditional wealth and the rising tide of commerce shows the relevance of this general comment to sixteenth-century England. Stone discusses the sleight of hand necessary to bring new blood into a hereditary aristocracy, and particularly the ways in which the sale of titles by James I inflated the honours of the established orders (Stone 1967, 54). Though he says that Elizabeth was parsimonious in creating new titles, in her reign the busy market in land sales enriched a large group of people who became contenders to entry into noble ranks in the next reign (p. 76). At the same time that wealth, accumulated in commerce, might through marriage provide entrée into the ranks of the elite, membership in that elite still entailed scorn for the money that had both provided access to elite status, and that remained indispensable for maintaining the display of generosity and grandeur that "served as symbolic justifications of rank and status" (p. 266). The consequences of this dilemma can be seen in the configuration of *King Lear*, in which an idealized version of traditional wealth is represented by Cordelia, the "unprized precious maid," while greed for the luxury on which status depends is represented by Goneril and Regan, whose gorgeous clothing scarcely keeps them warm.

The situation Stone describes is one in which persons of traditional wealth, like Portia's father, might well despise themselves for coveting money. On the one hand they required money to maintain a display that signified their status, while that same status required of them their indifference to the money upon which it depended. Money was clearly important: for the landed aristocrats it was the despised conduit that underwrote their status; for the aspiring it promised access both to status and privileges they both despised and envied; and lacking money entailed the social death envisioned by Antonio and Shylock or experienced by such "poor naked wretches" as Poor Tom. But money can be acquired by any clever trickster, by the worthy and the unworthy alike, and when land is for sale money can buy it, along with the honors associated with its ownership, and the hands of noble heiresses. Furthermore, the confusion of status and money went in two directions and threatened to erode the distinctions among the social orders as the aristocracy participated in commercial enterprise. Stone observes that it was the noblemen "still traditionalist in their views . . . and not social groups more deeply affected by the spirit of capitalism, who provided the economy with just that element of risk money without which it could not have moved ahead" (p. 182). He does not discuss the psychological conflicts possible between absolutist values and financial activities, but the situation he envisions is consistent with the weary psychology of bad conscience I have attributed to Shakespeare's characters and, more hypothetically, to Shakespeare.

Some more intimate dimensions of these economic issues are brought into focus in complementary ways by the work of Georges Duby and Jack Goody. Duby describes the conflict in twelfth-century France between the knights and the priests, or between what he calls the lay model of marriage and the clerical model that gradually gained ascendancy. The knights were engaged in a struggle to build up the wealth that would establish their families as honourable, and straightforwardly looked upon marriage as a means of doing so. In the situation Duby describes, one son only was allowed to contract a legal marriage and to have legitimate offspring. Wives who did not produce offspring were easily discarded, for knights and princes, as well as kings, paid little heed to church regulations. In his discussion of the importance the aristocracy placed on controlling their family lines so that their honor would be inherited by their progeny, Duby comments on the difficulty facing a man who had no sons. The solitary heiress was a "target for matrimonial intrigue" among the disinherited younger sons in constant search for wealthy wives (Duby 1977, 110, 145). In this world a father of daughters might well wish he had magic at his disposal, but would feel no guilt at using whatever means he deemed expedient.

However, two factors combined to bring pressure upon what Duby calls the lay model of marriage. First, the younger sons who could not marry within the system pursued wealthy married women, often trying to abduct them. These marauding young men, who valued adventure and daring exploit and who justified their amours in the name of love, formed, Duby argues, the social base from which arose the ideology and literature of courtly love (Duby 1978, 14). Second, between the thirteenth and sixteenth centuries the Church struggled to establish its authority over marriages. Condemning sexual pleasure, certainly outside of marriage and even within it, the Church defined marriage as instituted by God in order to ensure propagation. It

> emphasized the union of two hearts in marriage and postulated that its validity rested more on the betrothal (*desponsatio*) than on the wedding,

and especially on the consent (*consensus*) of the two individuals concerned. (Duby 1978, 17)

An unintended, and ironic, consequence of the Church's success
was to encourage love matches at the expense of arranged marriages,
for it was by defining marriage as a sacrament performed by consent-
ing partners that the Church gained ascendancy over the knights
(Duby 1978, 17). As the priests became more powerful, they added
"certain acts of benediction and exorcism to all the solemn rites,
whose climax they imperceptibly shifted from the house to the
entrance gate of the Church, and eventually to its interior" (Duby
1978, 19). In the process of rendering marriage sacred in this way, the
Church increased its power to define legitimate marriage. It condemned remarriage, even by widowers, as well as the practice of repu-
diating wives who failed to produce progeny; it undermined paternal
authority over marriage by requiring the children's consent. It opposed
"closed marriage," often involving marriage between first cousins, by
which great families consolidated their fortunes, and asserted its
authority simultaneously extending the range of prohibited relationships and inculcating a deep horror of incest.

Duby emphasizes the long struggle between these competing
conceptions of marriage as the Church gradually shaped men's consciences. In the midst of such conflict a man could maintain his
authority over the will of his children, as well as his rights to put aside
a wife who produced no sons, but he would do so with increasingly
conflicted feelings. A man who had only daughters might well
encounter internal as well as external opposition in the pursuit of a
new wife to give him a male heir; at the same time as his control over
the destination of his wealth through his daughter would be constrained both by the increasingly wide definition of incest, and by
pressure to give some measure of attention to her preferences. By the
time one gets to sixteenth-century England, these develpoments have
merged. The Church's success in redefining marriage as inclusive of
love, which carried over into Protestant England, made it possible for
the Church to gather in the romantic ideals spawned by courtly love.
Furthermore, as Spenser's work makes clear, this combination of
romantic ideals and the Christian ideal of married chastity was further
spiritualized by being merged with the Neoplatonic tradition that had
developed through the Florentine Platonists. One can see in the
progress of Shakespeare's plays, from *The Merchant of Venice* to the late
romances, the enormous significance of marriage as the center of spiritual value for both the participants and the society at large. However,
the economic aspects of marriage were subject to the same tensions

and ambivalence that Stone describes in the economic aspects of status. That is, marriage was at once a sacrament and the means by which great families controlled the transmission of wealth. It was a means of acquiring money necessary to maintain or to acquire status, and an ideal consummation of spiritualized romantic love. In this circumstance, in which the social realities are at cross-purposes both with the ideology of love and marriage and the strong emotions that ideology fuels, the bad conscience of Portia's father is comprehensible, as well as the desire to have recourse to magic to resolve otherwise intractable conflicts.

A further dimension to this murky mixture of love and money is suggested by Jack Goody. He argues that the Church served its own interests in its efforts to Christianize marriage. Its advocacy of mutual affection as the basis of marriage lifted clerical above secular authority. As well, it benefited materially from its success in preventing second marriages, for in the failure of progeny it often was the beneficiary of a dying line. Its efforts to inspire a horror of incest and to broaden its definition were also in its own interests. By complicating and enlarging prohibited degrees of kinship, it interfered with the claims of extended kin over land donated to the Church by a kinsman seeking his soul's salvation (Goody 1983, 153). As well, by acquiring power of judgment over whether a proposed or contracted marriage lay within interdicted degrees of relationship, it also secured the power to grant, and to set the price for, exceptions. Goody concludes,

> For the Church to grow and survive it had to accumulate property, which meant acquiring control over the way it was passed on from one generation to the next. Since the distribution of property between generations is related to patterns of marriage and the legitimization of children, the Church had to gain authority over these so that it could influence the strategies of heirship. (p. 221)

Goody's analysis of the intermingled pecuniary and spiritual motivations behind the Church's strictures on marriage not only supports the argument that as marriage took on the aura of the sacred, the material interests of the parents could be driven underground and rendered guilty by the increasingly powerful clerical definitions. It also follows that those caught in the bad conscience engendered by competing value systems would be aware, in dim or acute ways, that their consciences were being manipulated in the interests of the Church's struggle for power and wealth. Portia's father is like a person who has internalized both value systems and at the same time resents being forced to suffer the consequent bad conscience and its related agonies. Neither Duby nor Goody explores the psychology engendered by these conflicting value systems, but the issues I have discussed in *The Merchant of Venice* and their links to later plays give evidence that both value systems were internalized sufficiently to survive into Protestant England and to torment the consciences of Protestant Englishmen.[12]

✵

　　The assumption of this chapter has been that there are two ways by which Shakespeare drew his psychological landscapes from an inner life shaped by the contradictions inherent in his time. That is, his unique childhood experience within his particular family was conditioned by the social institutions and values governing families at the time, and as he grew his modes of dealing with his personal life were both limited and shaped by the social and cultural milieu he confronted. His way of being an artist was conditioned by the nature of the theater, the dramatic conventions, and literary traditions he inherited. All of these elements became part of the fabric of his plays. It follows from this that the kaleidoscopic recombinations of characteristics into different dramatis personae confronting their various worlds represent strategies to resolve or come to terms with conflicts that have both personal and social dimensions.[13] Approaching literature in the way that I put forward here provides an efficient way to penetrate that which is historically distant, and to capitalize both on what makes us different from those who lived at other times and places, and on what makes us similar to them. Though there must be continuities in human experience in order for us to appreciate and respond to the products of distant times and places, the ways in which people experience common or fundamental human desires must differ in relation to different social realities. Though the dreams of people in Elizabethan England would in some respects resemble those of people living now, in other respects they would differ. Both then and now one's dreams might express resentment of authority, but an Elizabethan person's expression of that resentment would be imbued with the dense emotional matrix of the family upon which political structures were modeled. Such a person might dream of killing the king, or of killing his or her superior in the local hierarchy, but he could not dream of a president failing to win an election. That we have such an option has more psychological significance than one might suppose. Our abstract and depersonalized conception of authority renders objections to and resentment of it less guilty, because less charged with infantile emotion. Both our modern dream of unseating the president, and the older dream of killing the king, may have their roots in animosity towards one's father, but in the modern context that animosity itself involves less psychological stress because the world provides more legitimate outlets for it. There is no way to prove it, but one might well suppose that contemporary dreams reflect our relatively positive attitude towards ourselves as freely aspiring individuals, or even as potential rebels, and show less intense conflict around these issues than those of our forebears. We may dream of losing or stealing or accumulating money, and money in our dreams may express our conflicted attitude towards giving and receiving love. But money in our dreams is unlikely to carry shame so intense as to augment the infantile conflicts that initiated the dream, as it does for Portia's father, and possibly for Shakespeare, who enriched himself and advanced his status by writing plays that condemned undue social aspirations and the mercantile values that nurtured them.

To ordinary ways of thinking there can be no two realms as remote from each other as the values that are inscribed in our political and cultural institutions, and the deeply private images we recall when we awaken from our sleep. But to trace in literature the connections between them brings home to us what postmodern theory calls the social construction of reality. To approach the plays as the dreams of their protagonists is to unite a historical understanding of experience with the emotional immediacy of dreams. In this way the polarity between traditional humanist criticism and deconstruction softens, and the question of meaning is differently framed. What a work means has to do with what the structure, array of characters, language, etc., means to the protagonist, just as a dream's meaning has to do with what the various elements of the dream signify for the dreamer. A fiction, then, is like a dream that contains within itself all associations necessary for its unraveling, and the method of interpretation I have applied to *The Merchant of Venice* does not differ greatly from the way one might think about one's own dreams, if one thinks about them as including the associations to the dream report one has generated later. Without having associations from a dreaming person one would not know how his or her dreams related to the reality of his or her life, but one would know something about the dreamer's self-definition and strategies for dealing with other people. With associations, particularly in connection with the day's residue that occasioned the dream, one starts to know something about the ways in which the actual circumstances of the dreamer's present life signify, for the dreamer, the emotional forms of the past. One starts to know something about the dreamer's structure of signification, just as one comes to know that of a literary character. It is true that most psychoanalytic approaches to dreams deemphasize the manifest content, the aspect of the dream that is usually more present-oriented and more immediately related to the day's residue, in order to concentrate on the latent, or past, content. That is, analysts tend to be interested in early causal traumas, rather than in the linkages that can be traced between past and present forms, or the way in which one's experience of past forms is shaped by the particularities, both personal and cultural, of the present. But in principle, Freud's dream theory does not preclude such an approach, and there is considerable interest and perhaps gain to be had from the angle of vision towards one's life circumstance such a way of thinking engenders.

Finally, a word on the difference between art and dream. I do not want to give the impression that they are the same in my view. They differ not only because, as I have said, literary work incorporates and integrates the author's conscious values into the unconscious or dream dimensions of the creative process. They differ also in that an art work offers itself for judgment by standards that have nothing to do with the process of its creation or its creator. The nature of those standards constitutes a subject beyond the scope of this chapter. However, this chapter does involve the belief that the age-old intuition, expressed first in our culture by Plato, that art and dream have something to do with each other is based on a psychological reality. That psychological reality has to do not only with the process by which artists draw on their unconscious drives to advance their conscious purposes in the specific ways I believe I have demonstrated; it also has to do with the reception of the work. Immersion in a work of art combines in a unique way the unmediated experience that we have while we dream with the conscious, cognitive and esthetic values that we bring to it and judge it by. Therefore to both experience and to reflect upon an art work may be thought of as training us in self-reflection and perhaps increasing our awareness of the devious ways by which we channel, for good or ill, our inward being into the outward world.

Notes

1. There are two exceptions: Jameson clearly attends to political and social dimensions of literary work, but denigrates the personal realm, which he regards as epiphenomenal. Holland (1968) attends to formal aspects of literature, regarding them as defense strategies which simultaneously conceal and reveal the work's core fantasy. Though my theory overlaps with Holland's in important ways, his conception of the formal is less inclusive than

mine, which, by eliminating the latent/manifest distinction, renders all aspects equally expressive of the compromise between competing desires and fears.

2. For a full explanation of and rationale for this mode of criticism see Stockholder, pp. 3–25.

3. As will become clear in the course of this argument, I do not agree with the perspective on Shakespeare's relation to his time favored by most new-historicist critics such as Greenblatt, Cartelli, and Meller. While it may be true, as Cartelli says (25n), that an orthodox Shakespeare was created rather than discovered by Tillyard's school, it is just as likely that a subversive Shakespeare is created, rather than discovered, by the new-historicists.

4. The close parallels between this scene and the one in *Pericles* in which the suitors risk their lives on a correct guess suggest that the death's heads that adorn the chamber in the later play, and the overt incest of Antigonus and his daughter, make explicit what here hovers in the interstices.

5. Freud in "The Theme of the Three Caskets" discusses Portia as a figure representing death for Shakespeare but seeing the play from my perspective renders Freud's insight more specific and relates it to the rest of the play. The father associates Portia with death because it is only in death that he can allow himself to imagine having her.

6. A related approach to the intertwined themes of love and money is taken by Engle, who argues that the theological terms in which economic issues are articulated "also define a system of exchange or conversion which works to the advantage of . . . those who, by religion or social situation, are placed to take advantage of exchange patterns" (Engle 1986, 21). Engle, however, sees no problem generated by the disparate value systems. A view closer to my own is held by Shell who says that "the beautiful marriage bond is not far removed from the ugly bond that made it possible in the first place" (Shell 1979, 91).

7. Engle also believes that Antonio lies here (Engle 1986, 22). He sees Antonio's sadness as a "market-linked phenomenon" (p. 28), and he associates his self-sacrificing stance with homosexuality (p. 24).

8. Whigham equates Bassanio with Shylock as a fellow social climber (Whigham 1979, 102). However, Bassanio's equation of wealth with family blood, as well as the father's apparent approval of him, makes it more plausible to think of him as an impecunious aristocratic younger son. The merchant's love of Bassanio, then, makes him, rather than Bassanio, vulnerable to the charge of social climbing. See below for the significance of this attribution.

9. In "The Ego and the Id," Freud's discussion of the ways in which the superego taps the repressed desires of the id and merges them with the guilt that occasioned their repression seems particularly apt for this play (Freud 1987, 394-50). As well, in the configuration of Bassanio, Shylock, and Antonio, the father nicely confirms Freud's observation that "in mild cases of homosexuality" the identification with an esteemed figure "is a sub-

stitute for an affectionate object-choice," which in turn has substituted for erotically imbued hostility and aggression among siblings (p. 377).

10. The links between Shylock and the Venetian world, and Shylock's role as scapegoat, have been seen in various ways. See Engle, Shell, Whigham, Meller, Cartelli, Sharp, and Girard.

11. To regard Portia as the dreamer would be to see her as one who tries to mediate between maintaining a self-image that conforms to the conventional demands for femininity and repressing rage at men who would control and possess her. Her rage would also contain an erotic component that mirrors her father's association of sex with incest and death.

12. Stone argues that the English clergy's emphasis on sacred marriage functioned similarly as a way to ensure social control (Stone 1977, 144), and Goody argues that despite the reduction of prohibited degrees in 1540, the Reformation had little impact on the English forms of marriage until the mid-seventeenth century (Goody 1983, 152). The persistence of the tensions from these earlier times into a Protestant England where marriage increasingly took on the sanctity that had once inhered in Catholic sacraments, suggested by Barber, is evident in the literature. Whatever gulf existed between literature and social practices, the mental sets that created literary characters formed part of the social ferment. Stone ignores this complexity in his assumption that literary renderings of romantic love had no bearing on people's management of their lives (Stone 1977, 181).

13. I would not, however, claim that one can construct an author's biography from his or her work. We can never know from writings the exact balance and proportion that constitute a lived self, and it should be kept in mind that the simplest person is vastly more complicated than any literary figure.

References

Barber, C. L. "The Family in Shakespeare's Development: Tragedy and Sacredness." In *Representing Shakespeare: New Psychoanalytic Essays*, edited by Murray M. Schwartz and Coppélia Kahn. Baltimore: Johns Hopkins University Press, 1980, 188–202.

Cartelli, Thomas. "Ideology and Subversion in the Shakespearean Set Speech." *ELH* (Spring 1986): 1–25.

Duby, Georg. *The Chivalrous Society*. Translated by Cynthia Postan, London: Edward Arnold, 1977, 110, 145.

————. *Medieval Marriage: Two Models from Twelfth-Century France*. Translated by Elborg Forster. Baltimore: Johns Hopkins University Press, 1978.

Engel, Lars. " 'Thrift is Blessing': Exchange and Explanation in *The Merchant of Venice.*" *Shakespeare Quarterly* 37 (1986): 20–37.

Freud, Sigmund. "The Theme of the Three Caskets," (*Collected Papers*, vol. IV).

———. *Jokes and Their Relation to the Unconscious* (SE vol. VIII, 1905).

———. *Character and Anal Eroticism*, *Collected Papers* vol. II, 45–50.

———. *On Metapsychology: Theory of Psychoanalysis* (vol. II, Pelican Freud Library, 1987) 350–408.

Girard, René. " 'To Entrap the Wisest': a Reading of *The Merchant of Venice.*" In *Literature and Society*, edited by Edward Said. Baltimore: Johns Hopkins University Press, 1980, 100–19.

Goody, Jack. *The Development of the Family and Marriage in Europe.* Cambridge: Cambridge University Press, 1983, 153.

Greenblatt, Stephen. *Renaissance Self-Fashioning: From More to Shakespeare.* Chicago: University of Chicago Press, 1980.

Holland, Norman. *Dynamics of Literary Response.* New York: Oxford University Press, 1968.

Hyman, Lawrence W. "The Rival Lovers of *The Merchant of Venice*," *Shakespeare Quarterly* 21 (1970): 109–16.

Jameson, Fredric. *The Political Unconscious.* New York: Cornell University Press, 1981.

Lacan, Jacques. *Écrits.* Translated by Alan Sheridan. New York: Norton, 1977.

Meller, Horst. "A Pound of Flesh and the Economics of Christian Grace: Shakespeare's *Merchant of Venice.*" In *Essays on Shakespeare*, edited by T. R. Sharma. Meerut, India: Shalabh Book House, 1986, 150–174.

Sharp, Ronald. "Gift Exchange and the Economy of Spirit in *The Merchant of Venice*," *Modern Philology* 83 (1986): 250–65.

Shell, Marc. " 'The Wether and the Ewe': Verbal Usury in *The Merchant of Venice.*" *Kenyon Review* (Fall 1979): 65–93.

Silverman, Kaja. *The Subject of Semiotics.* New York: Oxford University Press, 1983.

Simmel, Georg. *The Philosophy of Money.* Translated by Tom Bottomore and David Frisby. London: Routledge & Kegan Paul, 1978.

Stockholder, Kay. *Dream Works: Lovers and Families in Shakespeare's Plays.* Toronto: University of Toronto Press, 1987.

Stone, Lawrence. *The Crisis of the Aristocracy: 1558-1641.* London: Oxford University Press, 1967.

―――. *The Family, Sex and Marriage in England: 1500-1800.* London: Weidenfeld and Nicolson, 1977.

Whigham, Frank. "Ideology and Class Conduct in *The Merchant of Venice.*" *Renaissance Drama* (1979): 93–115.

PART III

A Dreamer and a Text: Case Studies

The four chapters comprising this section all focus on a single dreamer: Gilgamesh, Hermia, Posthumus, and Henry James. Three are literary characters and one is an author. The texts span more than four thousand years of literary representation and while each dreamer provides each essayist with a unique starting point, there are striking continuities in the dream material.

Bulkley uses the dreams of Gilgamesh, from the Sumerian epic of that name, to advance an argument for the interdisciplinary use of psychological and literary techniques of analysis in reading dreams in texts. In the course of his argument he also shows how modern theory can illuminate ancient texts and how critics who claim to be using exclusively literary criteria are often unconsciously reading psychologically as well.

Holland reviews the process by which literary criticism changes over the lifetime of a critic and how such changes become manifest in that critic's reading. He does this by tracing three kinds of readings he has given to one dramatic episode: Hermia's nightmare in Shakespeare's *A Midsummer Night's Dream*. Since the essay was first published in 1977, we can safely assume that his reading of Hermia's dream has undergone yet another transformation. What direction that transformation has taken may be guessed at by reading Holland's light and enlivening foreword, composed fourteen years later especially for this volume.

Westlund treats one literary dream—by Posthumus in Shakespeare's late and little-known romance *Cymbeline*—that has been much discussed in Freudian terms. He rereads the dream event from the perspective of psychoanalyst Heinz Kohut's self psychology, enriching our understanding not only of this individual character with the suggestive name but also of the whole drama.

Naiburg moves from these comparative, inter- and intradisciplinary readings of literary dreams to consideration of an author's dream which she relates to two paintings. She engages in a subtle blending of autobiographical and aesthetic concerns to analyze the role of dreaming in James's creative process. Naiburg mirrors James's own intersemiotic maneuvering as he dreams, recaptures in memory a significant experience of his childhood, records dream and memory and transmutes both into literary representation.

9. The Evil Dreams of Gilgamesh: An Interdisciplinary Approach to Dreams in Mythological Texts

Kelly Bulkley

If the interpretation of dreams is a difficult pursuit, filled with ambiguity, strangeness, and uncertainty, then the interpretation of dreams in mythological texts would seem to magnify those difficulties to new degrees of intensity. Dreams in mythological texts are generally hundreds or even thousands of years old, from cultures that may have disappeared entirely. We have no way of knowing if the dreams in such texts were ever really dreamed by an actual person, or if the dreams are merely fabrications created by the author to serve as literary devices. And what we now have of the myth has passed through the various hands of oral tellers, scribes, editors, and translators, with an unknown degree of corruption to the earlier versions.

Yet, despite such difficulties, we still find that myths often narrate dreams that move us deeply; across the long ages and through the fragmented texts, something about certain dreams in mythological texts resonates within us. Jacob's revelatory dream vision of the divine ladder spanning heaven and earth, and Penelope's hope-inspiring dream that her husband Odysseus would soon return to vanquish the hated suitors, are two of the most prominent Western examples of dreams in mythological texts that speak to us even now, thousands of years later.

What, then, do we make of dreams in mythological texts? On the one hand it is tempting to view myths as "psychology writ large," and thus to interpret dreams in these texts as we would one of our own dreams. On the other hand, it seems to be simple good sense to admit that dreams in mythological texts are so thoroughly shaped by

literary, cultural, and historical sources that a headlong rush into psychological interpretation would be naive in the extreme.

A literary analysis focusing on linguistic, narrative, and aesthetic
aspects of a text, often referring to the text's cultural and historical
background, and a psychological analysis using one or more modern
psychological theories to interpret the motivation of characters, plot
development, and the overall meaning of a text need not, however, be
opposed to each other. My aim in this essay will be to show that a
careful and reflective integration of these two approaches may in fact
lead to a much fuller, more interesting, and more solidly grounded
understanding of the meanings of dreams in mythological texts. A
study of the ancient Sumerian epic *Gilgamesh* provides an excellent
opportunity to demonstrate the potentials of such an interdisciplinary
approach. *Gilgamesh* is filled with remarkably strange, vivid dreams
that play crucial roles in the unfolding of the plot. While both literary
critics and psychological interpreters have devoted much attention to
the epic, their efforts have been limited by their one-sided nature.[1] If,
however, we work to integrate the findings of the two approaches, we
will find that we enrich our understanding of both the literary and the
psychological meanings of these mythological dreams.

In his classic study, *The Interpretation of Dreams in the Ancient
Near East,* A. Leo Oppenheim argues that most dream accounts in
the ancient Near East conform to certain well-established literary
conventions. Oppenheim's work, which remains the most authoritative analysis of dreams in ancient Near Eastern culture, examines a
wide variety of reports of dreams in mythological, religious, and historical texts and finds that the basic pattern involves the following
standard elements: the dreamer, almost always a king; the description
of the setting of the dream, usually a temple or some sacred place; the
dream itself; and an interpretation. Oppenheim claims that almost all
of these dream accounts have a primarily literary function, serving as
plot devices used deliberately by the authors. Consequently, Oppenheim asserts that psychological inquiry into these dreams is vain, for it
is highly unlikely, and impossible to prove, that these reports are based
on genuine dream experiences (Oppenheim 1956, 185).

Oppenheim's work is a good place to start a study of *Gilgamesh*,
for his literary analysis is detailed, comprehensive, and extremely erudite. Oppenheim finds many signs in the epic of conformity to the
standard ancient Near Eastern patterns, and he concludes that the
meaning and function of the dreams in *Gilgamesh* are basically the
same as in any other ancient Near Eastern text—in short, the dreams
are literary devices used to further the plot of the epic. But a close

reading of *Gilgamesh* reveals that Oppenheim neglects to explore an important question: in what ways do the dreams in the epic *deviate* from the standard forms of the ancient Near Eastern dream accounts? If we look for the unique rather than for the conventional in these dreams, we find a tremendous number of features differing dramatically from the basic patterns that Oppenheim says govern ancient Near Eastern dream reports. Most strikingly, all the dreams in *Gilgamesh* are evil dreams—frightening, confusing nightmares of struggle, violence, and death. Accounts of evil dreams are extremely rare in these texts, Oppenheim notes, and no other ancient Near Eastern work he cites reports anywhere near as many nightmare experiences.

Any interdisciplinary study of *Gilgamesh* needs to explore the various ways these evil dreams depart from, rather than conform to, ancient Near Eastern dream-report conventions. This line of exploration will enable us to reach two important conclusions. First, we will develop a deep appreciation for the masterly and sophisticated literary use of these dreams in the epic. In this regard we will confirm Oppenheim's thesis that the dreams are literary devices, but with even stronger evidence than he himself presents. Second (and much less to Oppenheim's liking), we will find the way open for a legitimate psychological assessment of the dreams in *Gilgamesh*. Having gained a full understanding of the literary influences on the dream accounts, we will be able, with a clear conscience, to draw on modern psychology in order to develop further insight into the meaning of these dreams.

> Gilgamesh rises, speaks to Ninsun his mother to
> untie his dream.
> "Last night, Mother, I saw a dream.
> There was a star in the heavens.
> Like a shooting star of Anu it fell on me.
> I tried to lift it; too much for me.
> I tried to move it; I could not move it."
> (Tablet I.iv; Gardner and Maier 1984, 81)[2]

The first dream experienced by Gilgamesh, the hero of the epic, contains many of the elements common to all ancient Near Eastern dream reports. The dream comes to a king, it contains a message regarding the future, and its content is repeated in a slightly differing second dream. But this dream is more notable for the many unusual features it has: rather than passively receiving a divine message, Gilgamesh actively struggles against the fallen star; instead of joy or satisfaction, the predominant emotions he seems to feel are distress and frustration; and, most importantly, Gilgamesh does not know what the dream means. Instead of the clear, almost stately dreams most ancient Near Eastern kings receive, Gilgamesh experiences a strange, confusing nightmare.

Since most ancient Near Eastern dream reports serve to establish the power and divine favor a king enjoys, the great deviation of Gilgamesh's dream from the standard patterns can only call into question the legitimacy of his rule. If a king is having nightmares, the gods must be angry with him. The closest parallel in the ancient Near Eastern texts to Gilgamesh's first dreams are those of Pharaoh in Genesis Chapter 41. Pharaoh also has two symbolic dreams which he cannot understand. Joseph's success in interpreting these dreams demonstrates how Joseph, and not Pharaoh, has God's support. Elsewhere in the Hebrew Bible the distinction is made between the clear dreams of the Jews and the "dark speech" of the Gentiles' dreams as a way of illustrating the special relationship of the Jews with God.[3] Gilgamesh's dreams, however, take this theme of divine disfavor being expressed through opaque dreams even further. While Pharaoh simply fails to receive a direct message dream, he does not personally experience any fear or suffering in his dreams; Gilgamesh's terrifying nightmare, however, shows that he has somehow earned the gods' active antagonism.

The opening scenes of the epic reveal just what it is that Gilgamesh has been doing wrong. In Tablet I.ii we read "Gilgamesh does not allow the son to go with his father; day and night he oppresses the weak. . . . Is this our shepherd, strong, shining, full of thought? Gilgamesh does not let the young woman go to her mother, the girl to the warrior, the bride to the young groom" (Gardner and Maier 1984, 67). The people cry out in distress to the gods, and the gods agree that Gilgamesh has been abusing his power. Their solution is to create Enkidu, "a second image of Gilgamesh," to counteract Gilgamesh's excesses and return peace to the city of Uruk. Gilgamesh's dreams, then, reflect the fact that he has transgressed the gods' laws; dreams, which customarily establish a king's legitimacy, here reveal instead a king's criminality.[4]

As symbolic dreams these require interpretation, and Gilgamesh's mother Ninsun helps him discover the meaning of his nightmares. Gilgamesh's anxiety that his mother quickly "untie" the dreams stems from the ancient Near Eastern belief that a symbolic dream without an interpretation will have evil consequences (Oppenheim 1956, 206). Oppenheim describes how the original Sumerian word here, *bur*, actually means much more than is denoted by our word "interpret." Included in this term's meanings are the notions of reporting the dream to someone, translating the symbols, and dispelling the potentially evil consequences (Oppenheim 1956, 219). The rendering of this term in the Gardner and Maier translation of *Gilgamesh* as "untie" accurately conveys the cathartic effect that is essential to any ancient Near Eastern dream interpretation. Here, the interpretation/untying is successful: Ninsun discerns the meaning of the symbols, explains their significance for Gilgamesh's future, and tells him what he should do now that he understands the message of the dream.

As with his first dream, the three dreams Gilgamesh has at the Cedar Mountain are also grounded in common ancient Near Eastern patterns. In particular, these dreams make explicit use of the theme of incubated dreams, i.e. dreams invoked by means of rituals, prayers, and/or sleeping at sacred localities. Oppenheim says that incubated dreams provide the basic formula for most ancient Near Eastern dream reports (p. 190). Gilgamesh's dreams at the Cedar Mountain include many of the conventional elements found in all incubated dreams. A king sleeps at some holy place on the eve of a great undertaking; certain rituals are performed and prayers recited;[5] and the king is awakened in surprise with the dream and immediately reports its contents for interpretation.

But again, the few ordinary features of Gilgamesh's dreams only serve to highlight how strikingly unusual the dreams are in general. Once more Gilgamesh receives no clear, direct message dreams but baffling symbolic dreams, an extremely rare result of a dream incubation (Oppenheim 1956, 191). Rather than beneficent expressions of divine confirmation of the undertaking, these dreams are nightmares even more terrifying than the previous two. First Gilgamesh flees from a violent, wild bull, then barely escapes the fearsome collapse of the mountain, and finally has an apocalyptic vision of the heavens crying and the earth roaring.[6] Instead of passively receiving a dream theophany, Gilgamesh dreams of struggling desperately to fight and escape strange, unidentified antagonists.[7]

All three of these dreams fill Gilgamesh with dread and a sense of impending doom. He had just been boasting that he is going to kill the monster Humbaba, that he has no fear of death, and that making a name for oneself is a hero's supreme achievement; now, however, Gilgamesh cannot avoid seeing that the nightmares bode ill for his and Enkidu's venture. He says to Enkidu, "Friend, I saw a dream—bad luck troublesome . . ." (Tablets IV.vi, V.i.; Gardner and Maier 1984, 130, 134). Although the text becomes very fragmentary at this point, we do have records of Enkidu's attempts to "untie" the first two of the dreams. Enkidu dismisses Gilgamesh's fear, arguing that the wild bull actually represents the god Shamash, who will help them in their battle. Of the second dream Enkidu exclaims, "Friend, your dream is good luck, the dream is valuable . . . Friend, the mountain you saw . . . we'll seize Humbaba and throw down his shape, and his height will lie prone on the plain" (Tablet V.iii.; Gardner and Maier 1984, 138).

Enkidu's interpretations are wrong. The validity of his interpretation of the falling mountain is shattered by the simple fact that there is a third dream. It is extremely rare in ancient Near Eastern dream reports for anyone to have more than two dreams (Oppenheim 1956, 208). Having a third dream, then, is a good indication that the message of the first two has not been understood.[8] And not only does Gilgamesh have a third dream, but the contents of this third dream are by far the most intense and terrifying of all. Gilgamesh says, "Friend, you did not call me; why am I awake? You did not touch me; why am I troubled? No god passed by; why are my limbs paralyzed? Friend, I saw a third dream, and the dream I saw was in every way frightening" (Tablet V.iv; Gardner and Maier 1984, 140).

The rare occurrence of three dreams and the increasing intensity of the dreams, culminating in an overwhelming vision of cosmic destruction, confirm the conclusion that Enkidu has misinterpreted them. While Enkidu is right about the victory over Humbaba, he appears to miss the far more important meaning of these dreams, a meaning which only later events reveal: by defeating Humbaba the two heroes rouse the displeasure of the gods, and the gods' response is to doom one to death and the other to a long, sorrowful journey.[9]

Up to the point where Gilgamesh and Enkidu have valiantly killed the Bull of Heaven, however, the heroic quest appears to be a success. The ever-dissatisfied Gilgamesh, on whom the gods have laid "a restless heart that will not sleep" (Tablet III.ii; Gardner and Maier 1984, 115) and who has suffered from a series of evil dreams, is finally able to lie down and sleep peacefully. But it is at precisely this moment, when Gilgamesh appears at long last to have achieved all he has wanted, that Enkidu experiences his own terrible nightmares announcing his impending death. This is a wonderfully effective use of dreams as a literary device, for Enkidu's nightmares not only make a dramatic contrast with Gilgamesh's first restful sleep, but they also signal a fundamental shift in the plot of the story: now that Enkidu is to die, Gilgamesh's quest changes from making a name for himself to trying to understand the meaning of death.

Enkidu's dreams are quite different from Gilgamesh's, both in form and content. Rather than the "kingly" dreams of Gilgamesh, Enkidu has what Oppenheim calls "subjective" dreams, which refer more to the specific conditions of the dreamer's mind, body, and religious status than to royal or national affairs (Oppenheim 1956, 227). The fact that Enkidu has evil dreams of this type, then, suggests that he is guilty of a "sin" of some sort. And indeed, Enkidu's misinterpretation of Gilgamesh's dreams *is* a genuine sin: the accurate interpretation of dreams is an important religious practice, and Enkidu has failed to discharge it. Not only did Enkidu miss the true message, but the meaning he falsely drew from the dreams was the exact opposite of what the gods intended. In this light, Enkidu's misinterpretation appears as a direct insult to the gods.

As with Gilgamesh's dreams, these two dreams of Enkidu also deviate from many dream report patterns in the ancient Near East. First, Enkidu travels about outside his body in his dream to visit other places and realms, rather than passively receiving a more conventional visit from a god. Second, the particular places to which Enkidu makes his dream travels are extremely unusual: to the council of the gods, and to the underworld. Other than Jacob's dream of the ladder spanning heaven and earth (Gen. 28:10–17) and Isaiah's vision of God's throne (Isa. 6:1–13), there are practically no other dream or visionary experiences of such mythical wonder recorded in the ancient Near Eastern texts Oppenheim considers. Third, Enkidu's reaction to his dreams is unique: rather than passively accepting what he has seen and what has been decided for him, he bitterly curses his fate (Tablet VII.iii; Gardner and Maier 1984, 172).

Now it is Gilgamesh's turn to interpret one of Enkidu's dreams, but he can only go so far in untying it. Gilgamesh understands what the dream means, he knows that "the dream is sound. For the living man it brings sorrow: the dream causes the living to mourn" (Tablet VII.ii; Gardner and Maier 1984, 169). But with this dream, understanding its message cannot make the evil go away; Enkidu will die, and there is nothing Gilgamesh can do to stop it.

If we recall the close relationship between sleep, dreams, and death in the mythologies of Babylonia and of many other cultures,[10] we may justly describe the rest of the story as Gilgamesh's attempt to interpret death, to untie its effects. When Enkidu finally dies, Gilgamesh cries out, "What is this sleep that has taken hold of you?" (Tablet VIII.ii; Gardner and Maier 1984, 187); his long journey culminating in his meeting with the mysterious, immortal Utnapishtim is a quest to interpret this most impenetrable and most terrifying of

nightmares. This quest ends in the realization that there is no interpretation of death; there is no way to untie its effects. While Enkidu
made a wrong interpretation, Gilgamesh has come up against something that cannot be interpreted at all.[11]

Once Enkidu has died, Gilgamesh sets out on a journey to find
Utnapishtim, an immortal man who may be able to tell Gilgamesh
something about death. As he begins his journey, Gilgamesh again
asks for divine guidance and sanction by means of an incubated
dream: "I lift my head to pray to the moon god Sin: For . . . a dream I
go to the gods in prayer: . . . preserve me!" (Tablet IX.i; Gardner and
Maier 1984, 196). As he did at the Cedar Mountain, Gilgamesh is
here invoking an acknowledged prerogative of ancient Near Eastern
kings, using an incubated dream to initiate a major undertaking and
establish its legitimacy. Here, however, Gilgamesh is not even warned
by terrifying nightmares; here he receives no dream at all. ". . .
Though he lay down [to sleep], the dream did not come" (Tablet IX.i;
Gardner and Maier 1984, 196). If the nightmares signified that the
gods were angry with Gilgamesh, at least that meant that the gods
still cared enough about what he was doing to warn him against it.
Now it seems that the gods do not even consider Gilgamesh and his
quest worthy of a nightmare. The silence from the gods is clearly far
more upsetting to Gilgamesh than were the evil dreams, as his violent
reaction upon awakening shows: "Gilgamesh takes up the axe in his
hand; he drew [the weapon] from his belt [and] like an arrow . . . he
fell among them. He struck . . . smashing them" (Tablet IX.i; Gardner
and Maier 1984, 196).[12]

This failed dream incubation marks another powerful literary
use of the standard ancient Near Eastern dream report patterns to
highlight a key theme of the story at this point, namely Gilgamesh's
detachment from the world of civilization, order, and status. Gilgamesh is leaving his city, leaving his kingdom, leaving the whole
world as he knows it to seek out Utnapishtim and try to understand
the meaning of death. The failure of his dream incubation attempt
indicates as clearly as possible how Gilgamesh has entirely lost his
status as a king and how his journey is leading him beyond all bounds
of religiously and socially ordered life.

Regarding the final dream experience in the epic, we may not be
sure at the outset if it is actually a dream at all. In Tablet XII Gilgamesh, after prayers to many different gods, finally succeeds in
receiving a visit from the spirit of Enkidu. The great hero Nergal
"opened up a hole now to the underworld. The ghost of Enkidu
issued from the darkness like a dream. They [Enkidu and Gilgamesh]

tried to embrace, to kiss one another. They traded words, groaning at one another" (Tablet XII.iii; Gardner and Maier 1984, 263). While this incident is not explicitly presented as a dream, it bears many strong similarities to other dreams reported in the ancient Near East. Oppenheim points out that the wording of this scene is identical to that used in other texts to describe the appearance of spirits in dreams (Oppenheim 1956, 234). Throughout the ancient Near East there is an intimate relationship between ghosts, spirits, and figures appearing in dreams.[13]

If we do look at this episode as a dream and consider its relations with the various dream report patterns we have been discussing, we make the surprising discovery that in many ways this is the most typical dream in the whole story. The experience has the distinct form of a dream incubation, what Oppenheim calls the paradigmatic frame for most ancient Near Eastern dream reports. It is not an easy incubation, as Gilgamesh must ask three different gods for help, but at least he does finally receive the experience he seeks rather than horrible, enigmatic nightmares or frightening silence. Here a figure comes to Gilgamesh and presents him with a direct message. Gilgamesh receives the message quietly and passively; no special interpretation is needed to help him understand what it means.

With all of these characteristics, this "dream" is unique in the epic, and yet entirely typical in the context of dream report conventions; this is much more the sort of dream one would expect an ancient Near Eastern king to have. As such, it would seem to suggest that Gilgamesh has now returned to the world of order and status he had left. It is a qualified return, for the dream is still somewhat unusual (e.g. the repeated requests, the figure being a recently deceased person rather than a god), and the message is certainly a gloomy one, but at least it is clear and direct. The dream thus serves the literary function of complementing Gilgamesh's return to Uruk in Tablet XI. He comes back to the city not with a triumphant flourish but with a genuine, sobering wisdom about life and death won at the cost of much suffering. Gilgamesh is not the same king now as he was at the beginning of the story—but he is still king, and he does return to the city and to civilized life. After so many deviations from the standard dream report patterns, this final dream with its great conformity to those patterns makes it clear that Gilgamesh is once again king, and further, that his rule is now more legitimately grounded than it had ever been before.[14]

The foregoing analysis of the dreams and nightmares in *Gilgamesh* establishes that they do serve as literary devices. The dreams of

Gilgamesh and Enkidu show many signs of being shaped by the literary conventions of the ancient Near East, and the dreams play a role
(indeed, a highly effective role) in the development of the epic's plot.
But if the dreams in *Gilgamesh* are indeed literary devices, does that
necessarily mean that they are *only* literary devices? In other words,
does that function automatically rule out any psychological analysis of
these dreams?

I would argue that the answer to both questions is no. Literary
and psychological analyses can be integrated so as to greatly enhance
our understanding of the epic as a whole. A literary approach can take
us a long way, but it leaves many important questions unanswered.
Why, for example, does Gilgamesh have such a "restless heart," and
why does he oppress the people of Uruk so? What is the nature of the
deep friendship between Gilgamesh and Enkidu? How has Gilgamesh changed by the end of the story? Questions such as these
involve fundamentally psychological issues. To ignore or deny this is
merely to substitute a covert kind of psychological interpretation for
one that is more open, honest, and self-reflective. And yet a psychological approach that lacks a sufficient understanding of literary qualities cannot do full justice to the epic either. Without a thorough
appreciation of the literary, cultural, and historical factors that shape
the story, any psychological interpretation of *Gilgamesh* risks being an
arbitrary, distorting projection (to use a psychological term) of our
own expectations onto the epic.

If, however, we first take the time to make a detailed study of
the literary dimensions of a mythological work, we may then learn a
great deal by drawing on various psychological perspectives to see
what additional light they shed on the text. Returning to *Gilgamesh*,
we may find much of interest in the studies of sleep researcher Ernest
Hartmann. In *The Nightmare*, Ernest Hartmann makes an exhaustive
study of the biological and psychological factors involved in nightmares. His fundamental conclusion is that nightmare sufferers have
"thin boundaries" in terms of their general personality characteristics:

> The formation of boundaries is part of a child's development of mental
> structures. Partly as a simple matter of neurological maturation and
> partly as a result of interaction with the environment, a child learns to
> distinguish between himself and others, between fantasy and reality,
> between dreaming and waking, between men and women, and so on.
> Each of these distinctions implies mental boundaries around them.
> Boundaries of many kinds are built up and all of them can vary from
> very "thin," "fluid," or "permeable," to "thick," "solid," or "rigid." In
> every sense . . . people with frequent nightmares appear to me to have
> "thin" or "permeable" boundaries." (Hartmann 1984, 137)

Hartmann describes how nightmare sufferers typically have weaker ego structures, less ability to distinguish fantasy from reality, less resistance to intimate interpersonal relationships, a stronger sense of bisexuality, and a greater tendency to think of themselves as child-like or even as animal-like (Hartmann 1984, 138–146). Hartmann states that "clinical summaries, done on a blind basis, describe most of the nightmare subjects as more pathological, more primitive, more vulnerable than the controls. . . . These descriptions characterize the nightmare sufferers as an unusual group with unusual openness and considerable psychopathology" (Hartmann 1984, 94, 88).

All of these discoveries of Hartmann's laboratory and clinical research give striking confirmations of what we have found through a literary analysis of Gilgamesh's and Enkidu's nightmares to be unique qualities of their personalities—both Gilgamesh and Enkidu do indeed have "thin boundaries" in many ways. Gilgamesh cannot maintain an orderly rule of his kingdom, as he oppresses the people of Uruk with his rampant aggressive and sexual urges; in other words, he cannot maintain the boundaries between his office as king and his desires as an instinct-driven human. He forms an intense personal bond with Enkidu almost as soon as he meets him, a relationship verging on total merger of identities.[15] While being a very masculine and fearless warrior, Gilgamesh is also likened to a wife and a wailing woman, he sleeps in the fetal position, and upon beginning his journey to Utnapishtim he covers himself with a dog's skin (Tablets I.v, VIII.ii, V.v, and VIII.iii; Gardner and Maier 1984, 82, 187, 140, and 190). This journey itself takes him far beyond the ken, beyond the boundaries, of the civilized world.

Enkidu, of course, begins his life in a state devoid of any boundaries whatsoever. He is raised out in the wilderness by animals and never entirely adapts to civilization. He addresses one of his most moving speeches not to a person, but to a door (Tablet VII.ii; Gardner and Maier 1984, 170). In addition to his fluid relations between the wilderness, civilization, and the world of inanimate objects, Enkidu also visits the divine council and the underworld; from one end to the other, the universe literally has no boundaries for Enkidu.

These are only a few of the many examples in the epic indicating that the notion of thin, fluid, or permeable boundaries accurately characterizes the personalities of both Gilgamesh and Enkidu. Hartmann's sleep-laboratory investigations and clinical research provide strong evidence for the contention that Gilgamesh and Enkidu suffering harrowing nightmares makes psychological sense. We have already noted the literary basis for their nightmares, the way their "evil dreams" clash with the standard dream-report conventions in ways that add important meaning to the story. Here we see that there is also a psychological basis for their nightmares: given the many signs that the two heroes have thin psychological boundaries, we expect that this quality of their personalities would also manifest itself in their dreams, in the form of nightmares.

Other psychological theories can add still more to our understanding of the epic. Jung's theory of dreams as compensations for the excesses of consciousness can illuminate some important aspects of the nightmares in *Gilgamesh*. The portrait of Gilgamesh's rule in the first few episodes of the story indicates that he is abusing his powers, that his behavior as a king is excessive and out of control. His proud boasting in anticipation of the battle with Humbaba gives us the impression of an overbearing arrogance and self-confidence; he exorts Enkidu to "stand, friend, . . . Let your heart grow light in battle. Forget death, fear nothing" (Tablet IV.vi; Gardner and Maier 1984, 130). But Gilgamesh's nightmares show him in an entirely different light: as impotent, frustrated, fearful, in need of help. In his first nightmare he is unable to lift the fallen star off of himself, no matter how hard he struggles; in the three Cedar Mountain nightmares he is helpless in the face of the wild bull, the falling mountain, and the roaring of the earth.

These nightmares present mirror images of his waking behavior and attitudes. In Jung's terms, they may be seen as the attempts of Gilgamesh's unconscious to balance the unstable, destructive forces dominating his consciousness. Jung claims that the unconscious tries

> to restore our psychological balance by producing dream material that reestablishes, in a subtle way, the total psychic equilibrium. . . . Dream symbols are the essential message carriers from the instinctive to the rational parts of the human mind, and their interpretation enriches the poverty of consciousness so that it learns to understand again the forgotten language of the instincts. (Jung 1979, 34, 37)

Given what we have already learned of Gilgamesh's kingship from a literary analysis of the epic, we may now add to our understanding by applying Jung's dream theories here. Seen in the light of the compensation theory, Gilgamesh's nightmares do indeed make sense as efforts to balance his conscious excesses. His first nightmare startles Gilgamesh, as he experiences within it difficulties he cannot overcome; since his behavior in the city of Uruk has been entirely without control or limitation, this is deeply troubling to him. With the help of Ninsun's interpretation, Gilgamesh understands that he will soon meet with a figure, a "companion," who will help check his excessive behavior and achieve a more balanced rule. But the mere appearance of Enkidu does not end the restlessness of Gilgamesh's heart or the one-sidedness of his attitudes. Indeed, Gilgamesh appears to corrupt Enkidu to the point where Enkidu shares his inflated ambitions. Thus when Gilgamesh has the three nightmares at Cedar Mountain, which clearly warn him against this reckless pursuit of heroic glory, Enkidu is unable to help him with the interpretation. Seen from this perspective, it is the failure of the heroes to heed the compensating imagery of their nightmares that results in the tragedy of Enkidu's death and Gilgamesh's sorrowful journey.

We may also find that some of Freud's psychological insights can be helpful in discerning the significance of the final "dream" of Enkidu's spirit. Freud considers the process of mourning to be crucial in all psychological development. When we lose an object, be it a person, an ideal, or an age, Freud states that we react by trying to take that object into ourselves, by introjecting it. The result of this introjection is the creation of psychic structure, and a general strengthening of the personality (Freud 1957).

If we set the experiences of Gilgamesh in this context, it seems that by losing his intimate friend Enkidu and embarking on his frightful quest, Gilgamesh slowly develops psychic structure, maturity, and control over his impulses. In this sense the latter half of *Gilgamesh* could be seen as a symbolic portrayal of the mourning process. The dream of Enkidu's spirit would accordingly mark the successful internalization of Enkidu into Gilgamesh's psyche. This psychological reading finds strong support in the literary evidence we have already considered. The dream of Enkidu, because it conforms to the more conventional type of the incubated dream, indicates that Gilgamesh has now returned to the traditional world of an ancient Near Eastern king.[16] He has gone back to his city, sadder but with a deeper understanding of life. The loss of Enkidu has tempered his grandiose ambitions, has made him admit his own mortality, and yet has not entirely crushed his vigor or vitality. When he returns to Uruk he still proudly describes the city to his companion Urshanabi: "Go up, Urshanabi, onto the walls of Uruk. Inspect the base, view the brickwork. Is not the very core made of oven-fired brick? Did not the seven sages lay down its foundations?" (Tablet XI.vi; Gardner and Maier 1984, 250). All of this behavior corresponds remarkably well with Freud's belief that maturity consists of the honest acceptance of our limitations, a resignation to the laws of nature, and a modest faith in human will.[17]

These brief excursions into the psychological interpretation of *Gilgamesh* should make clear three points regarding the interdisciplinary study of dreams. First, it is legitimate, despite Oppenheim's view, to use psychological theories to analyze dreams in mythological texts. Second, our use of such psychological theories becomes vastly richer when we combine their insights with a thorough literary analysis of a given mythological text. And third, we need not restrict ourselves to the confines of one particular psychological model, but may effectively draw upon a number of different psychological perspectives. In using limited selections from a variety of psychological theories we must, of course, strive to be fair and accurate with each of them; but granting that, there is no reason not to refer to any theory that can promote our understanding. Indeed, if psychological theories are to have any value in the interdisciplinary study of dreams, the use of such limited selections is a practical necessity.

❀

Too often the discussion of how to read mythological texts, and in particular how to understand the dreams they portray, degenerates into a fruitless argument over which single approach is most legitimate. Some, like Oppenheim, will maintain that only a literary analysis is truly justified and that psychological speculations merely confuse matters without being able to prove anything conclusively. The psychoanalyst Erik Erikson encountered this same resistance as he researched his psychobiography of Martin Luther, and Erikson's response to other biographers applies just as well to our dispute with Oppenheim: "it is necessary . . . to point out that biographers categorically opposed to systematic psychological interpretation permit themselves the most extensive psychologizing—which they can afford to believe is common sense only because they disclaim a defined psychological viewpoint. Yet there is always an implicit psychology behind the explicit anti-psychology" (Erikson 1962, 35–36). Other interpreters, though, among them many in both the Freudian and Jungian camps, treat mythological works as mere illustrations of their psychological theories, and rest satisfied as soon as they have boiled the text down to its oedipal or archetypal "core." But this kind of psychological reductionism, which inevitably involves groundless speculation, historical blindness, and procrustean simplification, is just as injurious to our understanding as is an antipsychological literary analysis.

This chapter has been an attempt to demonstrate the value of taking an interdisciplinary approach to mythological texts. An examination of the evil dreams in *Gilgamesh* in its literary context reveals that these nightmares make a very subtle and sophisticated use of the narrative patterns of conventional ancient Near Eastern Dream reports. Many of the most important details and nuances of Gilgamesh's and Enkidu's nightmares emerge only when set within this literary context. At the same time, however, psychological reflections show that besides being masterful literary devices these dreams are also highly accurate representations of genuine psychological experience. These are not the clumsy, stylized sorts of pseudodreams that Oppenheim finds in such abundance in the ancient Near Eastern literature, where an author seems first to decide that a character will have a divine experience and then, almost as an afterthought, frames the experience as a dream. On the contrary, contemporary psychological thought on dreams suggests that the evil dreams in *Gilgamesh* are utterly true-to-life; and further, that the descriptions of these dreams cohere in every way with the personalities of Gilgamesh and Enkidu as presented in the story.

Thus the discussion shifts from debating which single approach is better to asking what we may learn from an integration of a variety of different approaches. Insofar as we have discerned both literary and psychological dimensions of meaning in the nightmares of *Gilgamesh*, we may conclude, in a Freudian key, that these dreams are truly "overdetermined" in their meaning.

Notes

1. Among the scholars who have studied the literary, linguistic, and cultural nature of the *Gilgamesh* epic are A. Leo Oppenheim, "The Interpretation of Dreams in the Ancient Near East", in *Transactions of the American Philosophical Society* (1956), vol. 46, pt. 3; Alexander Heidel, *The Gilgamesh Epic and Old Testament Parallels* (Chicago: University of Chicago Press, 1963); and Jeffrey H. Tigay, *The Evolution of the Gilgamesh Epic* (Philadelphia: University of Pennsylvania Press, 1982). Among the psychologists who have attempted interpretations of the epic, C. G. Jung is the most prominent: see *Tavistock Lectures (1935)*, Lecture IV, in *The Collected Works of C. G. Jung*, trans. R. F. C. Hull, (Princeton: Princeton University Press, 1970), V. 18, 105–107, para. 235–239. In the *Tavistock Lectures* Jung begins his interpretation of *Gilgamesh* with the words, "Translated into psychological language this means: . . ."

2. Gardener and Maier translation of *Gilgamesh* used throughout. Roman numerals indicate tablet number in original; page numbers are also given for the translation.

3. For example, compare the symbolic dreams of the Egyptian butler and baker (Gen. 40), Pharaoh (Gen. 41), Nebuchadnezzar (Dan. 2 and 4),

and the two Midianite soldiers (Jud. 7) with the direct message dreams of Abraham (Gen. 15), Samuel (1 Sam. 3), and Solomon (I Kings 3). This is a very consistent theme in the Hebrew Bible: people not favored by God have opaque, symbolic dreams that require interpretation; people favored by God have clear, direct dreams in which God's message requires no interpretation to be understood.

4. There is an interesting parallel between Gilgamesh's nightmare and the nightmare of King Dasaratha in the Indian epic The Ramayana. Dasaratha reports to his son Rama, "Yet, O Rama, fearful dreams have visited me this night, and, in the midst of tempests, meteors fell from heaven attended by the crash of thunder! Further, O Rama, the star of my birth is held captive by formidable planets, such as the Sun, Mars, and Rahu; those versed in divination speak of this as an evil augury that portends either the death of a king or the visitation of some grave calamity" (Shastri 1985, 168). In both Gilgamesh's and Dasaratha's dreams the falling of stars makes for powerful symbols of coming disaster to their rule over their kingdoms, indicating that cosmic order has been profoundly and dangerously disrupted.

5. The two heroes ceremonially dig a pit, pour food into it, and pray, "Mountain, bring him a dream, do it for him." (Tablet V.iii; Gardner and Maier 1984, 138).

6. For the content of the first and second of the dreams at the Cedar Mountain I am drawing on the other Gilgamesh texts Gardner and Maier include in their notes (pp. 134–5, 139).

7. Even the surprise Gilgamesh expresses upon awakening from these dreams seems to have an ironic intention of showing how disturbing and unusual these dreams are. While the dramatized "surprise" attributed to the kings in most ancient Near Eastern dream reports is a formulaic indicator of the fact that a dream did occur (cf. Oppenheim 1956, 191), we can readily imagine that Gilgamesh really and truly is surprised by his dreams. These are not the pleasant, consoling dreams of encouragement most kings have—these are howling nightmares with dramatic and violent imagery.

8. The only other instance in the ancient Near Eastern texts of a series of three dreams is in 1 Samuel 3:1–18. Yet it is the exact point of this passage that having the three dreams is unusual and indicates that the first two were not heeded. The Deuteronomistic historian who wrote this part of the Hebrew Bible had as one of his main purposes to emphasize the theological distinctions of the Israelite faith over against the other religions in the ancient Near East. One of the key differences was that Yahweh is an independent and omnipotent god who controls human destiny, and not a god from whom people can receive knowledge, possessions, and power only if they perform the right rituals—for example, in dream incubation rituals. The Deuteronomistic historian illustrates this point in his description of Samuel's dream: Samuel sleeps inside the temple, in the very presence of the ark of God; a more holy place, and a more likely place for a dream theophany to occur, could not be found. And yet God has to call him three times before Samuel realizes who is calling—this is a powerful expression of the belief

(also hinted at in Genesis 15 and 28) that dream theophanies cannot be provoked or expected, because the Lord speaks in dreams when the Lord chooses. This writer and the author of *Gilgamesh* thus use the standard ancient Near Eastern dream conventions in the same way, as foils for their own special points; both use the device of a third dream to emphasize how the first two dream messages had not been understood.

9. In many myths and stories the making of a mistaken interpretation such as this is a terrible, even a fatal, mistake. In the book of Daniel, King Nebuchadnezzar declares to all his magicians that "if you do not make known to me the dream and its interpretation, you shall be torn limb from limb, and your houses shall be laid in ruins" (Dan. 2:5). In Shakespeare's *Richard III* the gullible Clarence fails to recognize how in a dream his brother Richard pushed him over the side of a ship to his death, and Clarence pays for his naiveté with his life. The whole of the *Tibetan Book of the Dead* could be read as a testament to the dangers of misinterpreting visions, dreams, and other signs. In *Gilgamesh*, the three dreams at the Cedar Mountain clearly warn Gilgamesh and Enkidu not to continue their grandiose quest; yet Enkidu convinces Gilgamesh that the dreams are actually good omens. Insofar as this incident sets off the chain of events which leads to the battle with the Bull of Heaven, the confrontation with the goddess Ishtar, and finally the fateful decree by the council of the gods, Enkidu's misinterpretation does lead to his own death. Like Nebuchadnezzar's court magicians, Enkidu ultimately pays for his misinterpretation with his life.

10. For example, Hesiod's *Theogony* states, "And Night bore frightful Doom and the black Ker, and Death, and Sleep, and the whole Tribe of Dreams" (D. Wender, trans. [Bungay, Great Britain: Penguin Books, 1986], vv. 212–213).

11. Enkidu's dreams bear an intriguing resemblance to the myth of a dream of Tammuz (discussed in Oppenheim 1956, 246). Like Enkidu, Tammuz dreamed of his own impending death, and like Enkidu, he would not accept it. Tammuz fought and struggled, argued and pleaded, but in the end he could not avoid the destiny revealed in his dream. If we assume that the audience of *Gilgamesh* was familiar with his myth (and given the fact that there is reference in the text to another myth of Tammuz, that of his marriage with Ishtar, this assumption seems reasonable), the parallels between Tammuz's dream and Enkidu's would only intensify the tragic atmosphere of Gilgamesh's quest to understand death. Gilgamesh may have avoided one of Tammuz's fates, as Ishtar's husband, but the audience senses as soon as Gilgamesh begins his journey to "untie" Enkidu's death that he will inevitably confront the same fact Tammuz did: the inscrutable yet inexorable reality of death.

12. The fragmented nature of this text means that we do not know the identity of the "them" that Gilgamesh attacks.

13. (Oppenheim 1956, 234–35). The kinship between the spirits of the deceased and the spirits in dreams appears in many other cultures as well. In both the *Odyssey* and the *Iliad* the same words are used to portray the

dream figures and the souls of the departed. At the end of the Indian epic, the *Mahabharata*, all the warriors who were killed in battle emerge at night out of the sacred river Ganga in a "celestial vision" to visit their grieving families, and return to their other-world abodes as soon as dawn breaks. The underworld journeys of Er in Plato's *Republic* and Dante in the *Divine Comedy* are framed as dream-like experiences. Given these widespread parallels, it seems legitimate to treat this encounter with Enkidu's spirit as a dream.

14. *Gilgamesh* scholars have argued for decades over the precise relationship of Tablet XII to the preceding eleven Tablets. Our analysis of the "dream" in Tablet XII has some bearing on this issue: insofar as the special qualities of the dream correspond so well with the implications of Gilgamesh's return to Uruk, the dream could serve as evidence for the argument that Tablet XII is a legitimate part of the epic, and not an arbitrary addition without any essential relation to the other eleven Tablets.

15. While I do not have the space to do so here, it would be very interesting to consider Enkidu's and Gilgamesh's relationship in light of the psychoanalyst Heinz Kohut's thinking on narcissism and mirroring or twin transferences. Indeed, Gilgamesh's dreams could, from a Kohutian view, be seen as illustrating the development of narcissism from its infantile to its more mature stages—from the frustrated grandiosity in his first dream of the fallen star to the wise acceptance of death in his final dream of Enkidu's spirit.

16. As Carol Schreier Rupprecht pointed out to me, the evolution of Gilgamesh's dreams suggests that a person's dreams correspond to traditional dream forms when that person is in "sync' with his or her culture. This notion has many ramifications for studying issues in nightmares, socialization, deviance, and psychological development.

17. See, for example, Freud's reflections in *Beyond the Pleasure Principle*, *Future of an Illusion*, and *Civilization and its Discontents*.

References

Erikson, Erik. *Young Man Luther.* New York: W. W. Norton, 1962.

Freud, Sigmund. *The Standard Edition of the Complete Psychological Works.* Translated and edited by James Strachey. Assisted by Anna Freud, Alix Strachey, and Alan Tyson. 24 vols. London: The Hogarth Press and the Institute of Psycho-Analysis, 1953–74.

Gardner, John and John Maier, trans. *Gilgamesh.* New York: Random House, 1984.

Hartmann, Ernest. *The Nightmare: The Psychology and Biology of Terrifying Dreams.* New York: Basic Books, 1984.

Heidel, Alexander. *The Gilgamesh Epic and Old Testament Parallels.* Chicago: University of Chicago Press, 1963.

Jung, C. G., ed. *Man and His Symbols.* New York: Dell Publishing, [1964] 1979.

————. *Tavistock Lectures.* Lecture IV, Vol. 18, *The Collected Works of C. G. Jung,* translated by R. F. C. Hull. Princeton: Princeton University Press, Bollingen Series, [1935] 1970.

Oppenheim, A. Leo. "The Interpretation of Dreams in the Ancient Near East." *Transactions of the American Philosophical Society* (1956) 46: pt. 3.

Shastri, H. P., trans. *The Ramayana of Valmiki* [London: Shyantisdan, 1985], Vol. 1.

Tigay, Jeffrey H. *The Evolution of the Gilgamesh Epic.* Philadelphia: University of Philadelphia Press, 1987.

10. Hermia's Dream*

Norman N. Holland

Literature is a dream dreamed for us.

What could be more imaginary than a dream of a dream of a dream? Yet Hermia's dream is just that. She dreams, but later she decides she was dreaming when she dreamed. Then at the very end of *A Midsummer Night's Dream* we, the audience, are told "You have but slumber'd here": we dreamed that she dreamed that she dreamed.

A dream of a dream of a dream—surely this is what the comedy describes in the lines that tell how

> as imagination bodies forth
> The forms of things unknown, the poet's pen
> Turns them to shapes, and gives to aery nothing
> A local habitation and a name. (V.i.14-17)[1]

The psychoanalyst and the literary critic do the same. In our effort to give imaginary dreams "a local habitation and a name," however, those of us who use psychoanalysis to interpret literature have, historically, used several different approaches. The first is typical of the first phase of psychoanalysis: we would use Hermia's dream as an illustration of someone's unconscious made conscious. In the second phase, we would place her dream within a system of ego functions. Finally—today—we would use this airy nothing to symbolize ourselves to ourselves.

For the moment, though, let me go back to the circumstances that lead up to Hermia's dream. At the opening of the play, Duke Theseus hears a plea from Hermia's father Egeus. Egeus wants the duke to force Hermia to marry Demetrius who loves Hermia and of

---

*Presented on October 20, 1978, as one of the Edith G. Neisser Memorial Lectures of the Chicago Institute for Psychoanalysis.

whom he, her father, approves. Hermia, however, loves Lysander, and Lysander loves Hermia. Theseus nevertheless agrees with Egeus and promises to enforce the law of Athens which provides that Hermia must either marry the man her father has chosen, or die, or vow to live the rest of her life as a nun, abjuring forever the society of men. A dreadful fate for a young lady even in Elizabethan times, but perhaps not so bad a fate when you see what men are available.

Hermia and Lysander decide that the best way to cope with this decree is to run away from Athens. They do so; but Lysander gets lost, and Hermia becomes exhausted from wandering in the wood. They sleep, and Hermia has her dream.

When we first hear the dream, it is still going on. That is, I think she is still dreaming when she first speaks about it. As with so many nightmares, she is having trouble waking.

> Help me, Lysander, help me! do thy best
> To pluck this crawling serpent from my breast!
> Ay me, for pity!

And only now, I think, is she beginning to come out of it—

> Ay me, for pity! what a dream was here!
> Lysander, look how I do quake with fear.
> Methought a serpent eat my heart away,
> And you sate smiling at his cruel prey.
> Lysander! what, remov'd? Lysander! lord!
> What, out of hearing gone? No sound, no word?
> Alack, where are you? Speak, and if you hear!
> Speak, of all loves! I swoon almost with fear.
> No? Then I well perceive you are not nigh.
> Either death, or you, I'll find immediately.   (II.ii.147–156)

In effect, as Hermia tells the dream, she splits it into two parts. In the first, we hear the dream actually taking place. In the second, Hermia reports the dream to us after it is over. In the first part she makes a plea for help, but in the second we learn that Lysander wasn't interested in helping at all—he was just smiling and watching the serpent eat Hermia. Further, if we take the most obvious "Freudian" meaning for that serpent—a penis or phallus— the masculinity in the dream is split between the attacking, crawling serpent and her lover, Lysander, smiling at a distance.

Among the fifty-one topics that Erikson suggests should be considered in a full dream analysis, let me be merciful and select just one—"methods of defense, denial, and distortion"—which might be seen as a variation on another topic—"mechanisms of defense"—itself a subtopic of "ego identity and lifeplan" (Erikson 1954, 144–145). I see in this dream something that I think is fundamental to Hermia's character.

If I go back to the first things Hermia says and look just at her speeches, as an actor would, I see a recurring pattern.[2] After hearing her father, Theseus admonishes her, "Demetrius is a worthy gentleman" (I.i.52), and Hermia replies with her first words in the play, "So is Lysander." (An alternative.) But, replies Theseus, since Demetrius has your father's approval, he "must be held the worthier." "I would my father look'd but with my eyes," answers Hermia (I.i.55-56). Next she begins a long speech by begging Theseus's pardon, wondering why she is so bold, and worrying lest, by revealing her thoughts, she impeach her modesty. But, she says,

> I beseech your Grace that I may know
> The worst that may befall me in this case,
> If I refuse to wed Demetrius. (I.i.62–64)

What's the alternative to Demetrius?

Now I hear in all these speeches a distinct, recurring pattern. Call it a concern for alternatives, for other possibilities, or for an elsewhere: Lysander as an alternative to Demetrius, her judgment as an alternative to her father's, her boldness contrasted with her modesty, or the alternatives the law allows her. We could say that Hermia's personal style or character consists (in the theoretical language of Heinz Kohut) of creating selfobjects (Kohut 1971, xiv-xv and passim). Thus, after her dialogue with Theseus, the lovers are left alone, and Hermia uses a variety of examples and legends from the elsewhere of classical mythology to illustrate and buttress their love. Then, to Helena, who loves Demetrius, she describes how she and Lysander will run away, again looking for an elsewhere, an alternative to Athens, "To seek new friends and stranger companies" (I.i.219). I would phrase Hermia's personal style as the seeking of some alternative in order to amend something closer to herself.

Her last speeches as well as her first show this sense of alternatives. Theseus, Egeus, and the rest have come on the lovers and wakened them. They, however, are not sure they are not still dreaming. Says Hermia,

> Methinks I see these things with parted eye,
> When every thing seems double.   (IV.i.189-190)

Demetrius starts checking reality and asks, "Do you not think / The duke was here, and bid us follow him?" And Hermia, for her last word in the play, offers one final alternative: "Yea, and my father" (IV.i.194-196).[3]

Her dream dramatizes her "parted eye" in all its divisions, in the double telling, in the here and there of Lysander and the serpent, and in the very content of the dream—her effort to save herself by getting the serpent away and bringing Lysander closer. I think I could show the same theme of amendment by alternative if I were to trace through the dream the various levels of this adolescent girl's development: oedipal, phallic, anal, and oral.

Following out the symbols, like that snake, and the libidinal levels of Hermia's dream would be the first and classical way of analyzing Hermia's dream, provided we ground the analysis on the free associations of the dreamer. Alas, however, this being a literary dream, we do not have free associations in the way they usually float up from the couch. Nevertheless, we can analyze the dream in the classic way by inferring Hermia's associations.

I

We can begin by guessing at the day residue of Hermia's dream—a conversation she has with Lysander just before they lie down to sleep.

> *Enter Lysander and Hermia.*
> *Lysander.* Fair love, you faint with wand'ring in the wood;
> And to speak troth I have forgot our way.
> We'll rest us, Hermia, if you think it good,
> And tarry for the comfort of the day.
> *Hermia.* Be't so, Lysander. Find you out a bed;
> For I upon this bank will rest my head.
> *Lysander.* One turf shall serve as a pillow for us both,
> One heart, one bed, two bosoms, and one troth.
> *Hermia.* Nay, good Lysander. For my sake, my dear,
> Lie further off yet. Do not lie so near.
> *Lysander.* O, take the sense, sweet, of my innocence!

> Love takes the meaning in love's conference.
> I mean that my heart unto yours is knit
> So that but one heart we can make of it;
> Two bosoms interchained with an oath,
> So then two bosoms and a single troth.
> Then by your side no bed-room me deny;
> For lying so, Hermia, I do not lie.
> *Hermia.* Lysander riddles very prettily.
> Now much beshrew my manners and my pride,
> If Hermia meant to say Lysander lied.
> But, gentle friend, for love and courtesy,
> Lie further off, in humane modesty;
> Such separation as may well be said
> Becomes a virtuous bachelor and a maid,
> So far be distant; and good night, sweet friend.
> Thy love ne'er alter till thy sweet life end!
> *Lysander.* Amen, amen, to that fair prayer, say I,
> And then end life when I end loyalty.
> Here is my bed; sleep give thee all his rest.
> *Hermia.* With half that wish the wisher's eyes be pressed!
> [*They sleep.*]   (II.ii.35-65)

(Notice, she closes by "alternating" Lysander's wish.)

Their conversation concerns just exactly the question of separation—as in "Lie further off"—and the danger of union—Hermia's fear for her maidenly modesty if Lysander comes too close. If I think about Hermia's dream in the general framework of an adolescent girl's oedipal fears and wishes about the opposite sex, particularly in the light of this conversation, I see her imagining of Lysander in two aspects. First, there is the Lysander physically close to her, and in the conversation they had before sleeping this is a sexual Lysander, one whom she feels as a threat to her maidenly virtue. The other is a Lysander at a distance, and him she associates with love, courtesy, humane modesty, and loyalty. In the dream, she will image this distant Lysander as smiling. Not so the nearer. In the day residue, the Lysander trying to get close proclaims, "My heart unto yours is knit, / So that but one heart we can make of it" (47–48). In the dream, this sexual union of hearts becomes a snake eating her heart "away." The dream separates these two aspects of Lysander, the sexual and the affectionate, but images both as hostile. By her waking cry for Lysander to help her, Hermia tries to put them back together in a more benevolent, pitying way, but reality fails her in this. While she dreamed, Lysander left her for Helena.

The next time we see Hermia, she has managed to track down the missing Lysander by his voice. Lysander, however, has been following Helena, for while he and Hermia were briefly asleep, Puck dropped on his eyes the "love-juice," "This flower's force in stirring love" (III.ii.89; II.ii.69) which made Lysander fall in love with the next being he saw. While Hermia was sleeping Helena came in and woke Lysander up. He promptly fell madly in love with her and followed her off into the forest. Hermia, when she woke up from her nightmare, could not find him.

We have no way of knowing how much Hermia has heard through her sleep of Puck's talk about the charm for Lysander's eyes or of the ensuing dialogue between Helena and Lysander, but I am willing to assume that some of this talk has percolated into her dream. In particular, I think she may have heard Puck speaking about the charm and may have drawn on the idea of a special fluid in representing the oedipal Lysander as a snake with its venom. She may also have heard Lysander declare his love for Helena, and that is why she shows him in the dream as hurting her and as a double person, that is, a person who lies. "Lies" is a key word not only because his name is "Liesander," but also because he made all those puns on "lie" during their dialogue before their little nap. As he said, "For lying so [close to you], Hermia, I do not lie." Puns and lies, in which one word carries two meanings, might have helped Hermia to split and so double her representation of Lysander, especially Lysander as a snake.

In a true free association, the next time we see Hermia she misunderstands Demetrius and thinks he has killed Lysander while he was sleeping. She promptly compares Demetrius to a snake:

> O brave touch!
> Could not a worm, an adder, do so much?
> An adder did it! for with doubler tongue
> Than thine, thou serpent, never adder stung (III.ii.70-73)

In other words, Hermia's free association for falseness while sleeping is a snake, and her free association to the snake is the doubleness of its tongue. As one of the fairies had sung earlier, "You spotted snakes with double tongue" (II.ii.9).

Both in the doubleness and in the "tonguiness," the snake says what Hermia might well want to say about her now-false Lysander. The serpent fits Hermia's thoughts in another curious way. Twice in

Shakespeare's works (although not, as it happens, in *A Midsummer Night's Dream*) we are told that the adder is deaf. So in Hermia's dream, Lysander does not seem to hear her cries for help.

In yet another way, then, Hermia applies her characteristic personal style to the sexual problems imaged in her dream. She separates the oedipal Lysander into two aspects: a sexual, hostile, intrusive being right on top of her and a milder, yet also hostile, man at some distance. In the same way, her dream shifts its sensory mode (to return to another of Erikson's topics for dream analysis). She begins with something touching her—the serpent crawling on her breast. She shifts to looking: "Lysander, look how I do quake with fear" (II.ii.148). Then she looks for Lysander and does not find him, "What, remov'd?" (151). Then she calls to him, but he does not answer: "What, out of hearing gone?" (152). She has moved from the immediate sense of touch to the more distant senses of sight and hearing. Interestingly, Hermia comments on—or if you will, associates to—just this shift when next we see her. The very words she speaks when she finds her lost Lysander are:

> Dark night, that from the eye his function takes,
> The ear more quick of apprehension makes.
> Wherein it [night] doth impair the seeing sense,
> It pays the hearing double recompense.
> Thou art not by mine eye, Lysander, found;
> Mine ear, I thank it, brought me to thy sound.
>
> (III.ii.177–182)

Again, with her doubling and with the ear gaining what the eye loses at night, she shows her characteristic concern with alternatives, particularly one alternative compensating for another.

Sight takes on still more importance if we can imagine that Hermia has unconsciously overheard Lysander's falling in love with Helena. Puck has just dropped the love-juice into Lysander's eyes. Further, when Helena comes upon the sleeping Hermia and Lysander right after Puck leaves, she is complaining that her eyes will not attract Demetrius the way Hermia's eyes do. Then, almost the first thing Lysander says when he awakes and falls in love with Helena is:

> Transparent Helena, nature shows art,
> That through thy bosom makes me see thy heart.
>
> (II.ii.104–105)

Hermia seems to me to take this image of complete truth or candor and dream it into a snake eating her own heart, an emblem of doubleness, treachery, and hostility.

If we were to limit ourselves to the old, rigid, one-to-one symbolism for early psychoanalysis, we would say simply that the snake is a symbol for a penis or phallus. Rather than call it simply phallic, though, I would like to go beyond the symbolic code to a more human meaning for that stinging, biting snake. I can find it in Erikson's modal terms "intrusive" or "penetrating." Hermia expresses that intrusion into her body as eating. In other words, she has built into the oedipal or phallic levels of the dream (the dream considered as an expression of an adolescent girl's attitude toward male sexuality) a regression to earlier levels of development. In yet another way, Hermia has provided an alternative, namely, anal and oral significances to her own oedipal and phallic sexuality.

For example, one of the issues raised by the serpent in Hermia's dream is possession in contrast to true love. The serpent proposes to eat Hermia's heart, to make it a prey, in other words, to possess it. Earlier that day Hermia's father, Egeus, had accused Lysander, "With cunning hast thou filch'd my daughter's heart" (I.i.36), just as he had given her bracelets, and rings, and knickknacks and nosegays. Lysander partly replies by insisting that he has just as much by way of money and land as Demetrius. When Hermia sees that Lysander has fallen in love with Helena, she cries,

> What, have you come by night
> And stol'n my love's heart from him?   (III.ii.283-284)

False love is treating a heart like a possession that can be stolen. In true love, by contrast, hearts fuse and become one, as in Lysander's plea for Hermia to lie down by him: "My heart unto yours is knit, / So that but one heart we can make of it" (II.ii.47-48). Similarly, Helena recalls that she and Hermia were such close friends they had "two seeming bodies, but one heart" (III.ii.212).

Yet it is precisely this fusion of hearts that Hermia refused when she would not let Lysander lie down with her. She left herself open to the other, possessive kind of love. Now, after her dream, she pleads to Lysander, "Do thy best / To pluck this crawling serpent from my breast!" Make an effort to get this repellent, crawling thing away— and I hear the faintest trace of an excremental metaphor: make an effort to push this disgusting thing out of you or me.

"Crawling" she calls it, a word she uses only one other time in the play, much later when Puck has thoroughly befuddled all four lovers, leading them on a wild goose chase through the woods. Finally, each collapses, Hermia saying,

> I can no further crawl, no further go;
> My legs can keep no pace with my desires. (III.ii.444–445)

Legless "crawling" is something less than fully human. "Crawling" images a desire for possession almost disembodied from the human, a desire which in life she has kept within "humane modesty" but which in her dream she feels as overpowering.

At the deepest level of the dream, that desire for possession becomes eating and thus both fusing with and taking away the essence of someone: "Methought a serpent eat my heart *away*" (italics added). Phallic intrusion and possession become a hostile, consuming oral possession. The dominant image of the dream seems to me to be the mouth: the serpent's eating and Lysander's smiling. Hermia's thought moves in the direction of sublimation, from the eating to the smiling, from her being the serpent's "prey," to "pray" in the other sense, her prayer to Lysander to help her. Similarly, in the dream, she moves from being eaten to being looked at: "Lysander, *look* how I quake. . . ." The day before, she had parted from Lysander by saying, "We must starve our sight / From lovers' food till morrow deep midnight" (I.i.222–223). The sight of the beloved is lovers' food. We should perhaps hear a pun in Hermia's exclamation during her dream, "Ay me, for pity!" "Ay me!" includes "Eye me," look at me, as well as "I—me," a blurting out of her dual self. Again, Hermia has defended by setting up alternatives. She deals with the nightmare by saying she is both in the dream and out of it.

In the same way, when she cannot find Lysander, she cries "Alack," and I hear the word in its original sense—just that, a lack: something is missing, taken away, dissociated. Her characteristic defense of providing an alternative can lead to a tragic separation—here it is Lysander's going off after the alternative, Helena.

Doubleness thus takes on a special charge for Hermia because it plays into her characteristic mode of defense and adaptation: the providing of alternatives. Now, finally, I can surmise why, out of all the materials that might have been important to her, her meeting with the duke, her argument with her father, her flight by night, she dreams about the conversation she has with Lysander before they lie down to go to sleep. That conversation hinges on precisely the key issue for Hermia: one and two. Lysander wants them to have "one turf. . . . / One heart, one bed, two bosoms, and one troth," but Hermia finds this idea threatening, not only for the ordinary reasons a young girl of the gentry in the English Renaissance would, but because such a fantasy would deprive her of her customary mode of adaptation. At all the levels of her dream she is working out a theme of love within her characteristic way of dealing with inner and outer reality, namely, by finding alternatives. Union in love is one possibility, but she dreams her fear of it as a deadly possession that would prey upon and eat away her very being. Separation, however, the other alternative, leads to another kind of cruelty through distance and indifference and—alack!—a loss.

The sexual symbolism of her dream thus rests upon a far deeper doubleness, her wish and her fear that alternatives won't work, that she will have to settle for just one thing—one intrusive, penetrating, possessive lover. In a psychoanalytic context, we can guess that the adolescent Hermia is working out with Lysander a much earlier, more formative, relationship with a figure never seen, never even mentioned in this comedy, her mother.

II

When we come to mother, we come to both the beginning and the end of this kind of analysis of a dream. What you have just read is an analysis of this fictitious dream as if I were doing it in 1968. I have been thinking about Hermia's dream mostly as though it were an event "out there" in a play "out there," wholly separate from me. I have been tracing her associations through deeper and earlier phases of her development.

In the earliest years of psychoanalysis, when people turned to invented dreams like Hermia's, they did so for two reasons. Either they were going to use the insight of the poet to confirm the views of the scientist or they were going to use the ideas of the scientist to understand what the poet had done. One could use Hermia's dream to confirm various ideas about dreaming: that associations explain dreams; that dreams express character structure; that dreams work at a variety of developmental levels, and so on. Then one could say, "See, Shakespeare knew this intuitively. Now psychoanalysis has shown it scientifically." Alternatively, the psychoanalytic literary critic might say, "Here is all this scientific knowledge about dreams. If we apply it to Hermia's dream, we shall see what an extraordinarily rich and complex thing it is." In effect the Shakespearean critic got a boost from psychoanalysis, and the psychoanalyst got a lift from Shakespeare.

Both these approaches, however, rest on the assumption that we can treat the dream Shakespeare invented for Hermia like a real dream. We are assuming that a play is an exact representation of reality, which obeys the same laws as reality and to which we can apply the same rules for interpretation that we would apply in real life. We can have free associations and symbols and oedipal, phallic, anal, and oral levels in Hermia's dream just as in any real adolescent girl's dream.

Such an assumption is, of course, one way of relating to a play, and some psychoanalytic criticism is still written this way, but few indeed are the literary critics who would settle for this one way. Since the 1930s and 1940s, literary people have been insisting that literary works are not meant to be looked at as portrayals of some other, imagined reality. Rather they are to be looked at as ends in themselves. They are artifacts, just like paintings or sculptures, but made of words, not paint or stone. This non-representational attitude, furthermore, is part and parcel of the whole twentieth-century concept of art. As Matisse replied to a lady who complained that the arm of a woman in one of his paintings was too long, "Madame, you are mistaken. That is not a woman, that is a picture." So here, Hermia is not an adolescent girl—she is a character in a remarkably artificial comedy, so artificial, in fact, that she states her dream in rhymed couplets. Now how many patients in real life do *that*?

In the 1950s and 1960s, we psychoanalytic literary critics shifted our objective. No longer did we want to treat Hermia like a real adolescent. Instead we wanted to understand her as one part fitted into the total play, as the arm fits into Matisse's painting. Both the character and the play are sequences of words we understand by giving them meaning. Treating Hermia as a real person leads, of course, to one possible meaning, but a very closely limited one, and literary critics prefer to find a larger, more general meaning through themes.

For example, most literary critics treat Hermia's dream as simply "an accurate, if symbolic, account of what has just happened" (Young 1966, 120). In that sense, the dream fits into the play's major theme: revelations through vision, such as watching plays or seeing fairies or falling in love with someone you look at.

At least two Shakespeareans, however, have found their way to larger themes by treating Hermia's dream more dreamily. Professor Marjorie Garber analyzes this dream in her study of all Shakespeare's dreams and dream imagery (Garber 1974, 72–74). She sees Hermia as afraid of the doubleness she represents in the snake. Hermia separates Lysander as beloved from the sexuality and violation she associates with the serpent. Yet, in the context of the play as a whole, says Garber, Hermia should not be afraid of ambiguity or double meanings, for that is what this play is. She should take doubleness rather as a form of creativity, for in this play the dream—and that includes the whole play—is truer than reality.

Professor Melvin D. Faber has analyzed this dream, too (Faber 1972). The strength of his analysis lies in the thoroughness with which he has followed through every symbolic and associative possibility. The limitation comes from resting the analysis on the overly simple one-to-one symbolic equations so popular in the first exuberant years of applying psychoanalytic symbolism. Thus, the snake is Lysander's penis, dissociated from Lysander, thereby making him less sexual, and therefore less dangerous. Hermia's heart stands for her genitals, and the serpent's eating symbolizes (but regressively disguises) genital sex. Thus, concludes Faber, the dream fulfills Hermia's wish for sex with Lysander, and Lysander's smiling expresses his satisfied desire and Hermia's as well.

Faber sees in the play as a whole Shakespeare's effort to establish masculine control over unruly impulses associated with the lack of proper boundaries between male and female. The play establishes control by dissociating the conscious, social part of the mind from the unconscious, sexual, and dreamlike part—as, says Faber, Hermia does in miniature in her dream.

As for my own themes for this comedy, I see the questions of separation and fusion that appear in Hermia's dream permeating the play. That is, *A Midsummer Night's Dream* begins with the separation of lovers. Theseus and Hippolyta have to wait out the four days till their wedding, the fairy king and queen, Oberon and Titania, have quarreled, and, of course, the lovers have tangled up their affections and drawn down the threats of the duke and the father.

The end of the comedy brings all these lovers together and in between, what has happened is *our* dream. Puck says in the epilogue,

> Think . . .
> That you have but slumb'red here
> While these visions did appear.
> And this weak and idle theme,
> No more yielding but a dream . . .   (V.i.424-428)

Hermia's dream is, as we have seen, a dream within a dream, a wish therefore that what she dreams of were a wish like the dream around it, therefore the truest part of the play. What, then, is the truth she dreams? She dreams of the doubleness of lovers and the separation of the two aspects of her own lover. As in our word "duplicity," this doubleness connotes his falseness as perhaps his name also does—"Liesander." One part of him wishes to fuse sexually with her, and she turns to a more separate part of him for help. But, divided this way, both parts of Lysander are cruel, one more physically so than the other.

Cruelty pervades this comedy. As Theseus says to his fiancée in the opening lines:

> Hippolyta, I woo'd thee with my sword,
> And won thy love doing thee injuries.   (I.i.16-17)

You could say the same of Oberon, who humiliates Titania, or of either of our two young men, each of whom deserts and reviles and threatens his future wife. Throughout the play, the ruler, the father, the lovers, the king of the fairies, the amateur actors, and even the audience at the play within the play—they all proclaim love, but they also threaten violence or humiliation. The play within the play focuses this ambivalence: it is a "very tragical mirth" (V.i.55). "The most lamentable comedy and most cruel death of Pyramus and Thisby" (I.ii.11–12). It is both the funniest and the bloodiest part of the play.

This comical tragedy within the comedy comes about because the lover Pyramus, separated from his love Thisby, and confused in the dark (like our four lovers), believes a lion has eaten her. That lion in Renaissance symbology provides the opposite to Hermia's snake.[4] The royal beast takes his prey in the open, by force and grandeur. The low serpent sneaks his prey by stealth and cunning. Thus the lion in the clowns' broad farce causes right before your eyes a bloody fusion of lovers as Pyramus stabs himself over Thisby's bloody mantle and Thisby stabs herself over Pyramus' bloody body. By contrast, the snake in Hermia's dream images a much subtler cruelty, the desertion and indifference of these not-so-courtly lovers.

This is a second way, then, to read Hermia's dream. The first way is as a clinical study of an adolescent girl. This second, larger reading sets Hermia's dream in the whole atmosphere and development of ambivalence in the comedy. We move beyond the nineteenth- and early twentieth-century concern with realism toward a more modernist interest in theme. Instead of treating the various levels (oedipal, phallic, anal, and oral) as aspects of some particular adolescent girl, I would see them all as variations on the comedy's theme of ambivalence, separations that are both loving and cruel.

Yet both these methods treat Hermia or her dream or her play as though they were "out there," as though I were distant and indifferent to them except for a coolly intellectual curiosity. Both readings pretend the dream and the play are not connected to any me "in here" who shapes and recreates both the dream and the comedy to fit my own character or, as I prefer to say, my identity. Rather, an abstractly skilled interpreter finds "the" meaning of the dream and fits it to "the" meaning of the play.

III

Since 1970, when I wrote such externalized dream analyses, many of us in literature and psychology have come to share the interest in the self that has quickened psychoanalytic theory throughout the world: in Paris through the writings of Lacan, in London in the object-relations theory of Milner and Winnicott and others, or in Chicago in the remarkable technical and theoretical studies of Heinz Kohut. Rather than simply look for an abstract theme "out there" in *A Midsummer Night's Dream*, we have become more interested in how a self—my self, for example—uses the text of the play or the dream as an object to establish a self-structuring relation.

Clearly, the kind of level-by-level exegesis you have just read makes up part of that relation: working out the implications of the dream through such schemes as Erikson's for analyzing the interaction of manifest and latent content or the classic psychoanalytic scheme of developmental levels. But this kind of analysis leaves out a great deal. It ignores, for example, my feelings as I hear this dream. It ignores the personal quality of my reading which makes it different from Professor Faber's or Professor Garber's.

In the 1960s, psychoanalytic literary critics cared little about the personal qualities that set one interpretation off from another, partly because we believed there was a best reading ("the" meaning) which would rise to the top as we refined our literary ideas, leaving the other readings, which simply didn't matter very much, in the pot. Partly, too, we left out the personal element because we had no way of talking about it. After 1970, however, we are less confident that there is some best reading, and we have a way of talking about the personal quality of a response.

That is, we have identity theory. We have a way of conceptualizing each new thing someone does as new, yet stamped with the same personal style as all the other actions chosen by that person. Each of us is a mixture of sameness and difference. We detect the sameness by seeing what persists within the constant change of our lives. We detect the difference by seeing what has changed against the background of sameness.

The most powerful way I know to think of that dialectic of sameness and difference is the one suggested by Heinz Lichtenstein (1961): to see identity as a theme and variations like a musical theme and variations. Think of the sameness as a theme, an "identity theme." Think of the differences as variations on that identity theme. That is the way I have read Hermia's character, for example. She creates an alternative that will amend the original possibility. That is her identity theme, and we have seen her work out variations on it in her opening plea to Theseus, in her witty dialogue with Lysander before they lie down to sleep, and above all, in her dream. These are all various ways by which she tries to amend through an alternative.

Now, just as Hermia develops a variation on her identity theme when she dreams, so you and I develop variations on our identity themes when we read her dream. Thus we arrive at a new kind of psychoanalytic method with literature. Our group at Buffalo called it "transactive criticism." We actively create—we *transact*—Hermia's dream and *A Midsummer Night's Dream*. As critics it is our job to articulate that relation explicitly.

For me, the two images of Hermia's dream, the eating snake and the smiling lover, evoke large questions of fidelity and possession between men and women that I find puzzling and troubling as I watch my students struggling to find and maintain stable relationships or as I see in my own generation yet another friend's marriage break up. That is, Hermia's dream, her very presence in the forest with Lysander, builds on the mutual promises she had Lysander make, a contract sealed by a dangerous elopement, a pledge of faith that her lover, at the very moment of her dream, has abandoned. Her dream begins from his infidelity.

As I visualize the dream, I see a small snake at a distance—yes, like a penis in the classic Freudian symbolism. But there is more: I also remember a picture from a book of nature photographs of a snake's wide-open mouth with long, curved fangs under a pink, arched palate, one demonic eye showing behind the furious jaws. The head is all mouth, really, there is so little else besides that act of biting. Hermia describes the snake as "crawling," and we have already guessed at her associations. Mine are to a baby who is all helpless, inarticulate demand. For me, then, Hermia's image of the snake sets up the idea of possession, the way a lover or a penis can make a total demand as an animal or a baby demands food.

Curiously, food comes up again when Shakespeare has his two male lovers explain why they switched partners. When Demetrius announces he is back in love with Helena, he says:

> like a sickness did I loathe this food [Helena],
> But, as in health, come to my natural taste,
> Now I do wish it, love it, long for it,
> And will for evermore be true to it.   (IV.i.173–176)

The first time Shakespeare explains the switching of affections, it is Lysander who has suddenly fallen in love with Helena just before Hermia's dream. He looks at the sleeping Hermia and says:

> For as a surfeit of the sweetest things
> The deepest loathing to the stomach brings,
> . . . .
> So thou, my surfeit and my heresy,
> Of all be hated, but the most of me!   (II.ii. 137–142)

Both times Shakespeare has his lovers refer emotional love to oral appetite, and an appetite of total desire or total rejection, fidelity to one girl meaning disgust at all others—at least for a time.

As we have seen, mouths appear twice in Hermia's dream, once in the serpent's eating and once when Hermia describes Lysander in her dream, "you sate smiling." For me, there is a great cruelty in that smile, just as there is in his radical rejection of Hermia as a "surfeit" that brings "deepest loathing to the stomach." I feel hatred in that smile and in that imagery of disgust, a hatred that psychoanalysis, in one of its hardest truths, asks us to believe tinges every human relationship. As the tough-minded La Rochefoucauld put it once and for all, "In the misfortune of our best friends we always find something that is not entirely displeasing" (La Rochefoucauld 1665, 138).

In other words, if I bring my own associations to Hermia's dream and its context, I begin to read the comedy of which it is a part as a rather uncomfortable hovering between different views of love. In one view, love is a total, consuming desire like a baby's for food. In the other, the relation is less demanding. It admits a change of heart or appetite. Yet so cool a lover may be hateful in his very smiling, just as hateful as the snake is in his eating.

Nowadays people reject the idea that love entitles you to possess another person. I, too, reject that kind of possessiveness—at least I consciously do. Yet the opposite possibility—a cool, distant love—does not satisfy me as a solution. I believe in a fidelity of mutual trust, an exchange of promises that I will be true to you and you will be true to me. I realize that contemporary patterns of marriage and sex deeply question this style of relationship. Many people believe they can and do love more than one person passionately and sexually at the same time.

No matter how contemporary I like to think myself in sexual matters, however, I have to admit that deep down I do not feel that the mutual pledge of loving or of sexual promises is the kind of contract one can negotiate like a lease on an apartment with provisions for termination, renegotiation, or repairs. Nor do I believe one can hold several such leases at once. To be intimate is to risk oneself with another, and it is difficult, for me at least, to feel free to open myself up to another person without being able to feel that that opening up will be one to one, that neither of us will compromise our intimacy by sharing it with some third person. Somewhere inside me I deeply fear that I would be made small and ridiculous, like a child, were my lover to share our one-to-oneness with another lover. Hence I perceive Lysander's smiling as a cruel ridicule.

The comedy, however, like today's lovers, rejects possessiveness. Hermia's father states the theme: "As she is mine, I may dispose of her" (I.i.42). The comedy as a whole moves away from this dehumanizing possessiveness, but what the play will substitute is not exactly clear. At the end Duke Theseus rules:

> Egeus, I will overbear your will;
> For in the temple, by and by, with us
> These couples shall eternally be knit.   (IV.i.179–181)

They will be married, and the power of the duke will knit them together as couples and as his subjects.

Paradoxically, though, the comedy arrives at this knitting by a system of separations and infidelities. At first Demetrius had been in love with Helena, but at the opening of the play he has fallen in love with Hermia. Then, when Lysander's eyes are charmed, *he* falls in love with Helena. Later the same thing happens to Demetrius: his eyes are drugged and he, too, falls in love with Helena. Finally, Puck uncharms Lysander, and the lovers fall into their natural pairs. The Polish critic, Jan Kott, urges us to think of this part of the comedy as a drunken switch party on a hot night in which all the scantily clad lovers are interchangeable objects of desire who do exchange with one another, finally waking up the next morning, hung over, exhausted, and ashamed (Kott 1964, 210–216).

Perhaps Kott takes too extreme a view, but the comedy does seem to say the lovers learn fidelity through their infidelities. Yet very little is said about how this union comes about. After they all wake up Demetrius says of the events of the night before, "These things seem small and indistinguishable" (IV.i.187). And once they are reunited with their proper lovers, the two girls say not another word for the whole long last scene of the comedy.

In other words, the comedy is silent just at the point where I, with my puzzling about fidelity, am most curious. How do these lovers, who now pledge to be true to one another, derive fidelity from their previous infidelity? The play doesn't say. I feel it is up to us as readers and critics to find a solution. One distinguished Shakespeare-an, Norman Rabkin, writes:

> In *A Midsummer Night's Dream* Shakespeare opposes reason to the folly of lovers whose choices are often magically induced and always willful, only to make us realize that those choices are ultimately right and of the same order as that anti-rational illusion-mongering, the perform-ing and watching of plays, which, depending on the charitable suspen-sion of disbelief . . . nevertheless tells us truths of which reason is inca-pable. (Rabkin 1967, 74)[5]

Rabkin suggests a parallel between the lovers falling in love and the way the rest of us give ourselves to plays. Illusions, fancies, fictions—if we can tolerate them—even lies can lead us to a higher truth, a loving experience beyond reason. In psychoanalytic terms, I think this transcending corresponds to the basic trust we must all have developed in translating an imagining of a mother's nurturing pres-ence into a confidence that she would really be there when needed. By not being there, she is unfaithful; but out of that first infidelity, most of us made the most basic of fidelities.

Thus I read Hermia's dream as having three parts. First, the snake preys on a passive Hermia's heart in an act of total, painful, destructive possession—hard on Hermia, but satisfying to that mascu-line snake. That possessiveness is one possibility open to me in relat-ing to a woman or a play.

Second, Lysander smilingly watches the woman he so recently loved being possessed by another. His smile signals to me another kind of cruelty—dispassion, distance, indifference—another way of relating to a play or a lover. The snake is fantastic and symbolic, whereas Lysander presents a far more realistic lover whom I can interpret all too well through our century's alternatives to romantic commitment.

Then there is a third aspect to the dream, as I view it. It is a nightmare. The dream has aroused anxieties too great for Hermia to sleep through. She wakes, and we never learn how she might have dreamed that a loving Lysander plucked away a possessive snake. Instead, we are left with his deserting her for another woman.

For me the sense of incompleteness is particularly strong, because I very much need to see a coherence and unity in human relations. I want a happy ending for this comedy. I want these couples married at the end, but I don't see—I don't trust, really—the way the comedy gets them together. Out of infidelity comes fidelity—but how? Hermia trusts Lysander but he is unfaithful and leaves her alone and terrified: "I swoon almost with fear" (II.ii.154). It is hard for me to trust that there will be a happy outcome despite his cruel and contemptuous abandonment.

When I confess my uneasiness because the dream is incomplete and the play is silent on the creation of trust, I am working through something about myself I have faced many times before. It's hard for me simply to trust and to tolerate uncertainty or absence or silence. I question both Hermia's dream and the sexual revolution of our own time because I need to *know* things, particularly about human relations. I need to feel certain.

None of this, of course, do Lysander or the other lovers say. They talk about feelings of love and jealousy we can all share, but they do so within the conventions of Renaissance marriage. You and I, however, read what they say from a perch in our own culture with its many marital and nonmarital and extramarital possibilities, all challenging the traditional limits on relations between the sexes. Where Shakespeare's lovers proceeded in their own day to a sure and socially structured Renaissance conclusion, now I feel they are opening up all kinds of twentieth-century uncertainties without, naturally, saying much about them. In particular, Hermia's dream images the tension between possessiveness and distance and the—to me at least—unknown way trust will resolve that tension.

Often, I think, we Shakespeareans teach Shakespeare as though we were ourselves unaffected by any of the changes in the relations between men and women that have happened since the days of Queen Elizabeth or A. C. Bradley. We are reading Shakespeare's romantic comedies in the middle of a sexual revolution. It would make sense to come to grips with the way our own feelings about that revolution shape our perception of episodes like Hermia's dream (or, even more drastically, Kate's antifeminist speech at the end of *The Taming of the Shrew*). That assertion of our selves is the new direction psychoanalytic literary criticism has begun to take.[6]

In acknowledging my role in bringing these twentieth-century issues to this comedy of 1594, I am discovering through Hermia's dream how I am unconsciously or half-consciously possessive even though I consciously aspire to an ethic of mutual trust. More generally, I am discovering that Hermia's dream takes its life not from some fictitious dreamer, but from my own concern with relations between men and women in my own time and my own hopes for those relations. I read Hermia's dream as an emblem of two human problems. One is an American problem of the 1970s and after: Can one separate love from trust? The other is a universal human question: How can we establish trust with another being whom we partly trust and partly mistrust? Reading Hermia's dream this way, I—or you and I, if you will go along with me—can go beyond the earlier relations with literature psychoanalysis made possible.

At first we treated the unconscious process in literary characters as though they were fact, not fiction, happening "out there," separate from us dispassionate observers. Then we set the character into an ego process embodied in the play as a whole. We began to acknowledge that we were included in that process, too, as we lent ourselves to the play. Now we have begun to make explicit the self-discovery that was only implicit and silent in those two earlier methods.

We can learn how each of us gives life to Shakespeare's imaginings "out there" through our own times and lives and wishes and fears and defenses "in here." Through psychoanalytic identity theory, we can understand how we are able to talk about the words of another through ourselves and, in doing so, talk about ourselves through the words of another—even if they are as airy a nothing as dream of dream of dream. When we do, we each continue Shakespeare's achievement in and through ourselves. Just as self and object constitute each other in human development, so in the literary transaction the reader constitutes text so that text may constitute its reader. In this mutuality, Hermia's dream is not simply a dream dreamed for us. Rather, we dream her dream for ourselves, and as we know ourselves so we know the dream, until its local habitation is here and its name is us.

Notes

1. Throughout this essay I have relied on the text of *The Riverside Shakespeare*, ed. G. Blakemore Evans (Boston: Houghton Mifflin, 1974), although I occasionally have made changes in the punctuation.

2. For a more elaborate example of this method see "A Touching of Literary and Psychiatric Education" (Holland 1973).

3. Most Shakespeareans regard Hermia and Helena as interchangeable, except for height and hair color (III.ii.290 ff. and II.ii.114). Reading their "sides," though, as an actress would (see Holland 1973), I detect a characterological difference. As in the text, Hermia speaks and acts through "amendment by alternative" (to compress her identity into a theme). Helena tries to cope (I think) by establishing a contradiction or opposition and then seeking to become that opposite. See, for example, her speeches in I.i: "Call you me fair? That fair again unsay" (181); "O that your frowns would teach my smiles such skill" (195). She would give everything, she tells her rival Hermia, "to be to you translated" (191). "How happy some o'er other some can be" (226). All of these statements lead to her explication of the emblem of Cupid as a series of reversals and her decision at the end of the scene to convert Demetrius's pursuit of Hermia in the wood to his presence with herself. Compare her last words in the play, "And Hippolyta" (Theseus's opposite) to Hermia's "and my father" (Theseus's parallel).

4. See the similar juxtaposition of lion and snake threatening a sleeper in *As You Like It*, IV.iii.106–118.

5. See also pp. 201–205 and 234n.

6. For a particularly fine example of this new mode, applied to a number of Shakespearean plays, see Schwartz 1977.

References

Erikson, Erik. "The Dream Specimen of Psychoanalysis." *Journal of the American Psychoanalytic Association* 2 (1954): 5–56.

Faber, Melvin D. "Hermia's Dream: Royal Road to *A Midsummer Night's Dream.*" *Literature and Psychology* 22 (1972): 179–190.

Garber, Marjorie B. *Dream in Shakespeare: From Metaphor to Metamorphosis.* New Haven & London: Yale University Press, 1974.

Holland, Norman N. "A Touching of Literary and Psychiatric Education." *Seminars in Psychiatry* 5 (1973): 287–299.

Kohut, Heinz. *The Analysis of the Self.* New York: International Universities Press, 1971.

Kott, Jan. *Shakespeare Our Contemporary.* Translated by B. Taborski. Garden City, N.Y.: Doubleday, 1964.

La Rochefoucauld, François de. *Maximes.* Edited by F. C. Green. Cambridge, Eng.: Cambridge University Press. 1946.

Lichtenstein, Heinz. "Identity and Sexuality: A Study of Their Inter-relationship in Man." *Journal of the American Psychoanalytic Association* 9 (1961): 179–260.

Rabkin Norman. *Shakespeare and the Common Understanding.* New York: Free Press, 1967.

Schwartz, Murray M. "Shakespeare Through Contemporary Psycho-analysis." *Hebrew University Studies in Literature* 5 (1977): 182–198.

Young, David P. *Something of Great Constancy: The Art of "A Midsummer Night's Dream."* New Haven and London: Yale University Press, 1966.

11. Self and Self-validation in a Stage Character: A Shakespearean Use of Dream

Joseph Westlund

Near the end of Shakespeare's *Cymbeline* the play's central character, Posthumus, has a dream that critics and directors often treat as exterior—as a vision of Jupiter—rather than as the depiction of an interior event.[1] Nevertheless, the appearance of Jupiter and the ghosts of Posthumus's family is the theatrical representation of an interior event within the character who lies sleeping before us on the stage. As such, the dream allows us to speculate about how Shakespeare conceives of the function of dreaming and how he prepares Posthumus and the audience for the imminent happy reunion with Imogen. Posthumus's dream offers an irresistible attraction to anyone attempting to figure out the motivation of this elusive character.

The dream is especially intriguing to psychoanalytic critics, among whom Meredith Skura offers the best and most extensive account.[2] My interpretation differs from hers in large part because my perspective is that of "self psychology," an extensive revision of Freudian theory proposed by the psychoanalyst Heinz Kohut (1913–1981). Kohut offers an unusually effective approach to analyzing dreams in real life—and by extension in literature. One of my aims in this essay is to demonstrate the value of the shift in psychoanalytic assumptions which Kohut and other psychoanalysts propose under the term "self psychology." To put the innovation very briefly, such proponents emphasize the "self" as the central organizing and stabilizing principle of the personality (as different from Freudian emphasis upon conflict among various agencies such as the id/ego/superego, conflict arising from sexual and aggressive drives and culminating in the Oedipus complex).

Kohut's psychology shares with other twentieth-century systems of psychology certain implicit value judgments; for instance, it is better to be autonomous than dependent. Kohut emphasizes the centrality of self-esteem even more than other psychoanalytic theorists do; he often refers to it as "healthy narcissism" so as to stress the value of basic rudimentary self-love. To claim that self-love is essential for an individual may grate upon some Renaissance scholars who feel that in Shakespeare's world one has to lose one's self, and one's self-esteem, to find oneself. The alternative view of self such scholars offer is roughly that of Christianity which de-emphasizes autonomy and the independent individual in favor of dependence upon, and merger with, God. Nevertheless, Christianity, and in particular Protestantism, lays extraordinary demands upon the individual to whom it delegates sole responsibility for personal salvation. It is dangerous to assume that we know for certain what the range of possibilities was for a Renaissance, much less a Shakespearean, conceptualization.

Kohut's theory illuminates an important aspect of Shakespeare. Shakespeare's works are among the very first to contribute to our contemporary perception of the vital role of a sense of self. Shakespeare at once creates and depends upon a heightened awareness of individuality, autonomy and self-fashioning. By scrutinizing the dream of Posthumus we gain further insight into the vicissitudes of the individual as conceptualized during the Renaissance. In Posthumus's roles as heroic soldier, trusting spouse, and repentant murderer he seems unable to perceive himself as a coherent center of initiative persisting over time. In this shaky sense of self he has much in common with Hamlet. Posthumus is also similar to Gloucester's younger son Edgar in *King Lear*; Edgar's antic creation of several roles and disguises strikes some interpreters as a prelude to his self-integration—or, to others, seems a sign of his self-fragmentation.

My interpretation of Posthumus's dream builds upon Skura's excellent account. She points out that Posthumus, unlike other heroes and heroines in the romances, does not find his family members literally alive; instead he recreates them in his dreams. To find himself as a husband, Skura argues, Posthumus must find himself as a son—as part of the family he lacked because his mother died giving birth to him after the death of his brothers and the more recent death of his father. "Posthumus's trouble at the beginning of the play is that he does not know who he is—and this is partly because he does not know who his family is" (Skura 1980, 208). The King, Cymbeline, takes him in and Cymbeline's own family provides the first substitute for the one Posthumus misses. However, Posthumus violates his proper place in this surrogate family when he elopes with Cymbeline's daughter, the princess Imogen. When Posthumus joins a second foster family (Imogen's long-lost brothers and the lord who abducted them), "he takes his proper place: brave, but not over-bearing; accepting his position as a nameless third son, subduing his own ends to those of the little family" (Skura 1980, 209). Skura argues that in this manner Posthumus mends a flaw in his character: the over-possessiveness, derived from Cymbeline's family, which led to his destructive marriage:

> Posthumus's achievement as a husband and a son is crowned by this vision of his family [in the dream]. Dead though they are, they appear physically on stage, breaking into the current action and revealing their implicit presence all along. They appear just when Posthumus finds himself, and the dream is a perfect climax to his story. (p. 210)

Skura concludes that "after his dream, nothing has changed except his state of mind: Posthumus has simply recognized his past and therefore recognized himself" (p. 212).

I want to modify this account by challenging some of its assumptions about dreams and the nature of the change in Posthumus.[3] As far as I can see he has not achieved much success as a husband or a son by the point he has the dream; indeed, he is self-destructive and explicitly suicidal when he falls asleep. Nor is it clear exactly how his state of mind alters; that "he recognizes his past and therefore recognizes himself" suggests some sort of "working through," but I am not certain that such a process can be imagined to occur here.

Skura sees Posthumus as a coherent, autonomous character. This view strikes me as improbable. For instance, he rarely interacts with other characters as if they were entities outside himself; he does not treat them as autonomous "objects" distinct from himself as a "subject." Instead, he continually treats them as what Kohut terms "selfobjects"; that is, Posthumus merges with others and treats them as if they were part of himself. Thus, to me his sense of self is more primitive and incoherent than most interpreters assume; he is less firm in his sense of the boundaries between himself and others. This trait suggests that Posthumus behaves in a way similar to that of real-life persons who were arrested at an early developmental stage; for instance, it suggests a reason why instinctual conflict is not central to his characterization. Skura also concentrates upon matters other than instinctual conflict. Despite his apparently adult behavior during much of the play, Posthumus also exhibits, in my opinion, a chaotic and rather infantile side.

Posthumus's State of Mind Before the Dream

For members of the audience the effect of the dream depends upon what we imagine to be Posthumus's "state of mind" before he falls asleep. This is particularly important given Kohut's insistence upon the need to clarify both the specific and the general *vulnerabilities* of the dreamer having the dream, for he argues that the dream arises from and unconsciously addresses such vulnerabilities.

My view of Posthumus's state of mind before the dream differs from Skura's in several important ways. When Posthumus reappears at the start of the final act he repents having had Imogen murdered (5.1.1–29); nevertheless, I argue that he repents in an antic and radically ambivalent manner. He shifts from his Roman dress into that of a "Briton peasant" (5.1.29–33), and silently vanquishes Iachimo (5.2. stage direction). Then Posthumus reenters "and seconds the Britons"—that is, Belarius and the two princes. In doing so, he saves the king and Britain in a battle scene long on action but short on dialogue (5.2.14–17). Nevertheless, each of the three other defenders speaks, if only, like the two princes, to share a line such as "Stand, stand, and fight!" (5.2.13). Posthumus says nothing during the scene; he simply reenters, fights, and leaves at the same time as the three other heroes leave.

That the text allows us to feel an air of disengagement in Posthumus may be unimportant, for we can assume that he is a compelling physical presence during the scene. Still, that he says nothing forms a pattern. That he reenters once the battle has begun and remains silent during the scene conveys an air of detachment on his part, which the following scene intensifies. Right after the defeat of the Romans there follows a scene in which Posthumus describes the battle to a taciturn cowardly Lord (5.3). At first glance, it seems difficult to guess why Shakespeare put this scene here; we in the audience have just witnessed the battle through our own eyes—and have never before seen the Lord nor will we see him again. As a result, critics often dispute the authorship of the scene. They also grow puzzled about what Posthumus means to say here (see Nosworthy, the New Arden Edition, pp. 148–49).

I suggest that, like the dream itself, this scene is designed to offer a glimpse of Posthumus's inner world. By hearing his own version of the battle, we can reexperience it from his own subjective viewpoint. From this viewpoint, from his own perspective, his deed loses much of its power to validate him as a worthy man. He disavows his heroic role even while he describes the battle on the narrow bridge. Instead of describing his own efforts and success—or simply assuming them with quiet modesty—Posthumus becomes almost overwhelmed with rage. His anger is apparently directed at the coward, but it has an indeterminate, archaic quality: the rage seems far out of proportion to the fact that the Lord was one of the men who fled. Why should Posthumus work himself up to such a state over a coward when the battle was victorious? More to the point, why should Shakespeare want to present Posthumus as beside himself with rage at a moment when we might expect to see the hero attending to other more pressing matters (such as consolidating his gains, or proceeding to repentance)?

Since the audience already knows Posthumus is valiant and the battle won, the scene's effect is to alert us to his overwhelming anger, his vulnerability, and his tendency to be self-defeating. The scene reinforces our sense that the three traits are linked in Posthumus, for we see them flare up elsewhere. For instance, the issue of Imogen's chastity kindles all three responses—as does Iachimo's challenge, apparent success, and the result of this success. Posthumus seems unable to *experience* himself in any positive behavior: as beloved husband, as national hero, as repentant sinner. Instead, he falls prey to fits of bedeviled rage.[4]

In growing angry he silently, ominously, deletes himself from the list of heroes who saved the day. He tells the Lord that there was "an ancient soldier" (Belarius) who "with two striplings" (the Princes) fought off the Romans:

> These three,
> Three thousand confident, in act as many,—
> For three performers are the file when all
> The rest do nothing. . . .   (5.3.28–31)

Since Posthumus was also engaged in the fight, there were four soldiers who defended the bridge, not three. Why does he fail to mention himself? Perhaps he simply intends to be modest (although he might have mentioned some unknown warrior who assisted the others). It seems more likely, however—given Posthumus's excessive and unfocused anger at this point—that Posthumus omits himself because of his sense of disengagement and worthlessness. This interpretation gains support from the fact that once Posthumus has driven the Lord away, he shifts his anger to himself and contemplates suicide.

Many viewers join Meredith Skura in expecting that some healing benefit must result from Posthumus's valor. His heroic deeds offer Shakespeare an excellent reason why Posthumus has an auspicious dream and why he is worthy of reunion with Imogen. However, the text here and in the dream suggests that Posthumus *disavows* his heroism: it apparently means nothing to him for he cannot own it as his. So, too, he gives no sign that he feels at one with Belarius and the young princes (who, Skura suggests, aid in the healing process which culminates in the dream [Skura 1980, 209]). Instead, the scene with the Lord heightens the discrepancy between how we expect Posthumus to react and how he actually views himself.

Posthumus's estrangement from the three Britons and from himself as British hero is underscored in symbolic terms. Once more he changes his clothes. Again, this is not modesty or self-abnegation, for he draws attention to himself by his anger and self-contempt. Since the British are now triumphant, he decides he will no longer be one of them: "No more a Briton, I have resumed again / The part I came in" (5.3.75–76). He assiduously takes on the costume of the vulnerable. First, he dressed as a Briton when the Romans were marching against them; now he changes into Roman garb as soon as the Romans are vanquished. The manner in which he changes clothes, like his disavowal of his heroism, heightens the audience's sense of his self-defeat and desolation; he looks defeated, he sounds defeated, and he focuses on such failings at the very moment he has helped achieve victory.

Posthumus's despair must stem in large part from losing Imogen, but it is more diffuse and global than we might expect from such a loss. For instance, he seems unable to focus upon his loss of Imogen so that he might properly mourn her. He apparently can conceive of no way out of his plight—at least not in waking life.

Even his words of repentance in jail seem forced and rather unconvincing. Many critics assume that he repents, but he tends to confuse the issue in his oblique and tortured rumination. For instance, he addresses himself by saying:

> My conscience, thou art fetter'd
> More than my shanks and wrists: you good gods, give me
> The penitent instrument to pick that bolt,
> Then free for ever. Is't enough I am sorry?
> So children temporal fathers do appease;
> Gods are more full of mercy. (5.4.8–13)

It is not clear to me how the "penitent instrument" death can free his conscience. Death might make conscience irrelevant since God's judgment would prevail; but in this lower world only repentance can assuage conscience. Critics note that he employs traditional language in distinguishing the three parts of repentance (Nosworthy, the New Arden Edition, pp. 155–56). Nevertheless, he undermines his attempts at penitence by his doggedly ambivalent tone. He seems defensive or even truculent when he asks of the gods "Is't enough I am sorry?" Does he mean to praise the gods for their degree of mercy, or to blame them for being less merciful than temporal fathers? When he addresses the gods again, he asks them to take his life:

> For Imogen's dear life take mine, and though
> 'Tis not so dear, yet 'tis a life; you coin'd it.   (5.4.22–23)

His attitude verges on being accusatory. The gods allow all that happens to happen, and thus allowed Iachimo to seduce Imogen; still, Posthumus is also to blame, although he avoids saying so here and in his long soliloquy at the outset of the final act (5.1.1–33). Posthumus resists facing the fact that he is responsible for his deed; without this vital first step, any forms of repentance can mean but little. He devotes much of his energy to accusing the gods of unfairness. He asks that they take his life although it is "light" and not worth much. This characteristic self-devaluation also carries with it an implicit denigration of the gods. He adds the idea that since the gods made him they really ought to accept his life—light though it be. Such baroque and confused reasoning undermines his attempt at repentance. If the gods are meant to be at all like the Christian God, they are not likely to see his soliloquy as an effective step toward repentance.

Self-validation in the Dream

Posthumus now falls asleep on stage. He is in jail, having provoked imprisonment by those whom he had just saved from the Romans. He seems to be at a nadir of self-fragmentation and self-defeat rather than a climax of healing. Critics sometimes assume that he is saved by a vision of Jupiter, by an arbitrary external power. Anything is possible as soon as a deity enters; one might even argue for an analogy to the mysterious workings of Christian grace. Still, it seems more likely that we are meant to see the dream as a dream, and to conceive of it as signaling some positive change from within his own nature and characterization.

For a moment, let me stand back and generalize about his "state of mind" as it is represented to us at the moment the dream begins. He has much in common with real-life persons whom Kohut describes in terms of a "vertical split" of character disorders (as distinct from the "horizontal split" of repression within a unified self which Freudians use to describe neurotics). Posthumus vacillates between two poles: a grandiose self, and an empty or deprived self. His grandiosity manifests itself in presuming to test Imogen, to assume her guilt, and to have her murdered. One might choose other terms than "grandiose" to describe his attitude (such as hubristic, sinful, cruel), but the term is useful in that it refers to a trait which Posthumus reveals in other significant areas of his behavior.

Posthumus also reveals an empty self in direct contrast to the grandiose self: profoundly deprived, he gives the impression of being unable to fulfill his needs by his own deeds. This emptiness manifests itself in his depression and also in his inability to *own* anything as his—whether heroic deeds or wicked ones.

That he is so vulnerable suggests his dream can profitably be interpreted as a "self-state dream." Kohut argues that such a dream differs from the traditional formulation of dreams by psychoanalysts. From a Freudian perspective dreams are assumed to deal with hidden instinctual wishes (mainly sexual and aggressive), with conflict, and with attempted solutions of conflict. For a Kohutian perspective, self-state dreams respond to a crisis in which the sense of self-coherence begins to fragment. Kohut suggests that our scrutiny of the manifest content of self-state dreams can "allow us to recognize that the healthy sectors of the patient's psyche are reacting with anxiety to a disturbing change in the condition of the self—manic overstimulation or a serious depressive drop in self-esteem—or to the threat of the dissolution of the self" (Kohut 1977, 109).[5]

Skura makes some roughly similar assumptions in her deemphasis of conflict and drives, and in her emphasis on Posthumus's need for his lost family. Where we differ is in my focus upon Posthumus's vacillation between grandiosity and emptiness, and in my sense of his extreme vulnerability at the time of the dream. What he needs, and what he creates in his dream, is not simply a family to recognize but a family (and a deity) who mirror his worth and sustain him.

Let me shift more decisively into Posthumus's own perspective on the dream. In doing so I follow one of Kohut's ill-understood but revolutionary clinical precepts: I emphasize the *subjective* nature of the

dreamer's dream, rather than look at it objectively—as most interpreters do without being aware of their stance.[6] Kohut refers to such
attempts as "empathy" and they form the basis of both the data and
the theory of self psychology. At first glance, empathy seems a mild
and sentimental attitude; the term often draws scorn from those who
miss his point, or find his advice difficult to follow. Kohut insists that
the analyst can understand only through experiencing within himself
or herself what the other person is feeling. He stresses this move not
because of a wish to be supportive (although such a move can be valuable). Instead, Kohut uses the concept of "empathy" to confront the
inevitable bias of the interpreter who will inevitably distort the reality
of the other since it differs from his or her own reality. Because of his
awareness of this inevitable bias, Kohut insists upon the need to try
not to look at others from the outside with preconceived theories of
what the person "must really be feeling."

   All theory limits what one can perceive, and this includes psychoanalytic theory. Since theory is unavoidably limiting—and often
just plain wrong—and since every person is intensely different and
individual, Kohut asks that the interpreter try to set aside assumptions
about what goes on in the emotional life of others. Instead, the interpreter should attempt to feel in himself or herself, by a kind of vicarious introspection, what the other person feels. In a clinical setting this
is an attempt on the analyst's part to put himself or herself into the
patient's shoes, rather than to try to be an external observer of events
taking place in an isolated entity out there in what is sometimes
referred to as an intrapsychic apparatus.

   Following the method Kohut articulates, we need to put ourselves in Posthumus's shoes if we wish to understand his dream. We
need to attend to his vulnerability at this point in the play, and set
aside the assumption that he must have derived benefit from his heroism in battle—or from his attempts at repentance. Similarly, we need
to attend to what *he* finds significant, not just what we find significant
or think that he finds or should find significant.

   The dream validates Posthumus in ways which we as outsiders
could barely conceive possible. It should come as a surprise that by
dreaming he gives himself what he has never before been able to give
himself. What he creates is not a family out there—as autonomous
entities from whom he has more or less successfully differentiated
himself. Nor, I think, is it so important that he recognizes them.
What is crucial is that they recognize *him* and validate his sense of
worth. As a dreamer Posthumus focuses upon his family's and his
deity's nurturing relation to himself. We might expect other familiar

figures such as Imogen to appear in his dream, but only his family and Jupiter do so. Members of the audience might very well have expected him to dream about his wife, for his last waking words were "O Imogen, / I'll speak to thee in silence" (5.4.28–29). That he does not dream about her is another sign that we are in the presence of a self-state dream. Posthumus's dream seems to have little to do with such matters as instinctual conflict, guilt, resistance, or possible solutions of conflict. Indeed, his dream seems to ignore his relation to others as objects outside himself—say, to his estranged and murdered wife. The implication is that his sense of self is not cohesive enough to allow for this.

Posthumus dreams not of a murdered wife, nor of an Imogen who was (in wish fulfillment) saved from being murdered. Nor does he "resist" dreaming about her at the manifest level only to do so on the latent level—as psychoanalytic interpreters might suspect. He dreams instead about what most concerns him: not having lost Imogen but being in the presence of an admiring family and deity. He dreams of selfobjects who function as part of himself, literally, for he creates them out of whole cloth. He never has seen them (except, perhaps, for his brothers); thus he cannot technically recognize them in their existence outside his imagination. My point may at first seem pedantic; that it does might well remind us of the need to perceive the dream from his own perspective. We need to look at his dream from the inside, rather than from the point of view of our own preconceived ideas of what must be important. His family and Jupiter serve as selfobjects created by his own sense of need for them. They have no traits other than what he needs to find in them: absolute and convincing support.

Imogen cannot very well enter in his dream, for she would either be disturbing as a reminder of his all-but-disavowed guilt, or intrusive as a reminder of her own (apparent) guilt for adultery. Perhaps we can spot an allusion to her in the shape of his mother, who enters with his father as part of a united couple: enter Sicilius Leonatus "attired like a warrior, leading in his hand an ancient Matron (his wife, and mother to Posthumus)" (5.4.29 stage direction). Posthumus's dream thus seems to hint at his identifying with his father and wishing for his own wife. If we are right to discover Imogen in this wish fulfillment about a united couple, it is appropriate that she should appear in the guise of an all-supportive figure with no traits of her own—such as she would have as his murdered wife—but only as a selfobject to validate his sense of worth.

In his dream, Posthumus creates a deity whose role is similarly restricted. Jupiter comes across as little more than a supportive self-object, as a god who does not seem particularly godlike. For instance, Jupiter states: "No more, you petty spirits of region low / Offend our hearing: hush! How dare you ghosts / Accuse the thunderer" (5.4.93–95). Still, the "hush!"—although peculiar diction for a thunderer—precisely conveys the nourishing, parental tone Posthumus needs from all his dream figures. So, too, Jupiter's explanation sounds rather offhanded even for divine planning: "Whom best I love I cross; to make my gift / The more delay'd delighted" (5.4.101–02). Nevertheless, Jupiter speaks directly to Posthumus's need at this point: not a need for a plausible account of anything in particular but for paternal validation. Perhaps "avuncular" is a better term, for "paternal" has connotations of stern accountability. What Posthumus needs is not confrontation, or forgiveness, or even the sort of stunning theophany which Wilson Knight conjures up in his interpretation of the vision. What Posthumus needs and what he gives himself, in his dream, is comforting reassurance.

All of Posthumus's dream figures speak in ways which offer narcissistic enrichment. They exemplify confirmation of the self, for they demand it for themselves as well as extend it to him. When speaking about his son, Sicilius Leonatus emphasizes that both Posthumus and he are worthy: "Great nature, like his ancestry, moulded the stuff so fair, / That he deserved the praise o' the' world, as great Sicilius' heir" (5.4.48–51). Similarly, the ghosts take care when complaining that they do not undermine Jupiter's dignity; while they chasten him, they also bolster his self-esteem by addressing him as "Jupiter, thou king of gods" (5.4.77). They force him to validate Posthumus as the only way of saving face. In this dream, the dreamer allows no one, much less himself, to suffer a loss of self-esteem.

In such ways the dream serves a benign purpose. Nevertheless, it also reveals troublesome aspects of the dreamer's inner state. The healthy aspects are bound up with the unhealthy ones, as they would be in a real-life dream of someone in Posthumus's position. The dream partakes of that trait in Posthumus which I refer to as his grandiosity. Many dreams in reality and in fiction are full of magical thinking, but Posthumus's dream exceeds the usual: he imagines that ghosts arise from the dead to minister to his needs, and Jupiter descends with a divine plan for his special benefit. In conceiving of such narcissistic support, the dreamer perpetuates his archaic wish to discover validation from *outside* himself rather than from within himself through his own actions. In a word, he still conceives of himself in a merged state rather than as an autonomous individual who can and must fend for himself.

The dream implies that Posthumus's state of mind has changed for the better in that he can conjure up narcissistic supplies. Still, he remains both grandiose and needy; he remains in the state Kohut describes in terms of the "vertical split." For instance, Posthumus has no active role in the events of the dream. He conceives of others who nurture him, but aside from this he does nothing to fulfill his needs. He performs no deeds. His family, not Posthumus, calls upon Jupiter to save him. Since he uses his family as selfobjects he thereby indirectly puts himself into the dream; the figures he imagines in dreaming the dream function, to a great degree, as aspects of himself. Still, it is striking that he should be so absent in his own right from the dream. Perhaps we never think of this while watching the play since he lies before us while the dream goes on around him. Still, in his use of selfobjects Posthumus creates others who do for him what he might be expected to do in his own right were he not so dependent upon them—upon others whom he can experience only as extensions of himself.

The Extent of Posthumus's Change

Kohut's premises are worth invoking at this point in the discussion of the dream. One is to try to put oneself in the dreamer's shoes rather than look at the dream "objectively." Another, to try to find signs of a healthy sector rather than dwell solely upon pathological aspects. As in so much of Kohut's work, these aims may seem obvious and easy to attain. They are not. A psychiatrist who was in training with Kohut, and thus armed with the best intentions, attests to the difficulty of following these simple maxims; he soon reverted to the habit of looking at a patient's dreams from his own perspective—not the dreamer's—and confronted the dreamer with signs of pathology rather than discover healthy aspects peering out from under them.[7]

By searching for signs of the healthy aspect, the interpreter discovers—and thereby confirms—a vital and often disavowed aspect of the dreamer's inner reality. The healthy part is one which has been submerged by pathological parts. The latter are precisely those most accessible to the observer and thus most often, unhelpfully, emphasized by the observer—and by the person himself or herself. The germ of a true but undeveloped self lies arrested in development and hidden within the predominant and more obvious false self.

Posthumus's dream owes much of its poignancy to the glimpse of the healthy sector in him which it allows. The ghosts and Jupiter continually attest to his worth, but other factors even more forcefully indicate a healthy sector hidden within his despairing and self-defeating nature. First, he can *conceive* of such validation at a low point in his career. And second, he can *experience* this benign nurturance as his own and use it, rather than disavow it as he does virtually all his waking experiences.[8]

Dreamers conceive of and make their own dreams. This vital principle can easily be lost even to the most ardent dream interpreters unless we keep reminding ourselves about dreaming's intensely subjective nature. The healthy sector of Posthumus's dream appears, first, in his advance from a position of neediness. When awake he seems unable to get what he wants, but in dreaming he creates it from within himself: he obtains self-confirmation by creating an idealized family and deity. He says immediately upon awakening:

> Sleep, thou hast been a grandsire, and begot
> A father to me: and thou hast created
> A mother, and two brothers; O scorn!
> Gone! they went hence so soon as they were born:
> And so I am awake.   (5.4.123–25)

Characteristically, Posthumus assigns the process of creation to "Sleep" rather than to his own generative and creative capacities. Nevertheless, even Posthumus's deference to grandsire Sleep can be thought of as part of his persistent effort to create for himself a family whose every move is attuned to his needs.

The second principal indication of a healthy sector lies in his being able to experience and use his dream, instead of treating it as though it happened to someone else or as though it were worthy of contempt. Unlike his disengagement from his heroic deed against the Romans, his response to his dream is to own it: he acknowledges and incorporates what the dream gave him into his sense of himself. He owns his need for what his grandsire sleep begot for him, however temporary and however strange. Then he turns to the book with the riddle, and attests to its value even though he cannot be sure what it is:

> 'Tis still a dream: or else such stuff as madmen
> Tongue, and brain not: either both, or nothing,

Or senseless speaking, or a speaking such
As sense cannot untie. Be what it is,
The action of my life is like it, which
I'll keep, if but for sympathy.   (5.4.146–51)

He identifies the riddle with the dream, and with life, as a tangible reminder. And he vows to keep the riddle, the dream, and his life. He cherishes them as significant parts of his experience, rather than disavowing them as irrelevant or insufficient—as would be so easy for him and so typical of him. Posthumus attaches explicit positive value to his dream and links it to his life whatever it may mean: "Be what it is, / The action of my life is like it."[9]

That Posthumus values the dream and riddle as his own signals a benevolent change of mind. Upon awakening from a dream in which others cherish him and his worth, he himself now begins to have a sense of self-esteem. That he should do so strikes me as the first sign of a more viable Posthumus than the one we have seen earlier.

Before the dream occurs, Posthumus is presented as a character who does not seem to have a sense of living his own experiences. He rarely conceives of himself as an autonomous agent in any of his roles: heroic soldier, trusting spouse, repentant murderer. In terms of self psychology, his disavowal suggests an inability to identify with his own experiencing self. He gives the impression that someone else lives his life, as in a way is quite true: one part of him is grandiose and lives in a fantasy world imperfectly attuned to reality. The other part of him—the part who lives in outside reality—seems unable to feel, or experience, or gain much from that life.

Because of the two split-off parts of himself, grandiose or empty, Posthumus appears incapable of giving himself anything or doing anything for himself. He cannot even experience anything as his own. The grandiose self is merged with an archaic other, as for example it is when he tests Imogen. Or the empty self gets nothing it wants since it has surrendered volition to the grandiose self. We have seen this surrender in his scene with the Lord: Posthumus disavows his truly heroic deeds in the battle against the Romans, and instead contrives fantasies of freeing himself from his guilty conscience by suicide.

In dreaming, however, Posthumus gives the impression of having established contact with his split-off empty self; he seems to have connected himself to the kernel of his otherwise disavowed true self. When he creates validating figures he indicates that he can draw upon narcissistic supplies from *within* himself. I stress the significance of this accomplishment as coming from within the dreamer. We in the audience see the dramatization of a dream, which means that we see a stage on which the family and Jupiter may seem to exist outside Posthumus. Still, insofar as the stage dream is the dramatization or the outward realization of an inner psychological event, the dream figures are not external but internal. The character Posthumus—not Shakespeare—peoples his dream with validating figures at a moment when he is empty, depressed, and suicidal, and in doing so gives himself what he needs.

In conclusion, I think that Posthumus reveals contradictory aspects of himself in *Cymbeline*: a self-defeating and near-tragic aspect tinged with grandiosity and neediness, and an aspect which suggests that a healthy kernel of self-esteem can quicken to life when he reunites with Imogen. He begins to seem capable of integrating into his sense of himself aspects to which his family and Jupiter attest: that he is of central importance, that he is brave, noble, and lovable.

The dream serves not so much as a sign of a changed state of mind as the harbinger of such a change. From now to the end of *Cymbeline* when he becomes reconciled to the King and to Imogen, Posthumus tentatively begins to validate his own worth rather than simply conceive of it as being affirmed—or, invalidated—by figures outside himself. Like the regeneration of other protagonists of Shakespeare's romances—Pericles, Leontes, and Prospero—Posthumus's regeneration is more tentative and thus, I think, more poignant than critics have for a long time allowed.

Notes

1. Posthumus himself comments upon what he has witnessed as a dream: "Poor wretches, that depend / On greatness' favour, dream as I have done, / Wake, and find nothing. But, alas, I swerve: / Many dream not to find, neither deserve, / And yet are steep'd in favours; so am I, / That have this golden chance [the book he finds on his breast when awaking]"; he concludes that " 'Tis still a dream: or else such stuff as madmen / Tongue, and brain not" (5.4.127–31, 147–48). Throughout I quote from the New Arden edition of *Cymbeline*, edited by J. M. Nosworthy (1955; reprint London: Methuen, 1979). Nor does Posthumus see what has transpired as a vision brought about by Jupiter; he fails to mention the spectacular appearance of the deity and refers instead to the agency of sleep: "Sleep, thou hast been a grandsire, and begot / A father to me: and . . . / A mother, and two brothers" (5.4.123–25).

G. Wilson Knight demonstrates the Shakespearean nature of the episode despite the doubts of those who find it irrelevant and thus suspect (Knight [1947] 1966. However, Knight treats the dream as a vision or theophany—despite Posthumus's remarks just quoted. J. M. Nosworthy follows

Knight in seeing the episode as a vision. Nosworthy states that "in making him [Jupiter] literally the *deus ex machina* Shakespeare flies in the face of Aristotelian doctrine, but necessity is above precept" since one cannot suppose that the rapid change of fortune at the end is brought about by human agency. I argue that the psychological implications of the dream convey a sense of human agency at work here. (Nosworthy [1955] 1979, xxxiii–xxxvii)

2. "Interpreting Posthumus' Dream from Above and Below: Families, Psychoanalysts, and Literary Critics" (Schwartz and Kahn, 1980, 203–16). Her account for the most part follows Freudian precepts. Also see Arthur Kirsch, *Shakespeare and the Experience of Love* (Cambridge: Cambridge University Press, 1981); he interprets the dream in explicitly Freudian ways and concludes that "the recovery of a childhood literally lost . . . enables him [Posthumus] to reintegrate himself as a man and reunite with Imogen" (p. 167).

3. Can a character be said to possess a state of mind? Many people readily assume that Posthumus does, so lifelike is his representation and so pressing is our need to imagine that characters reflect ourselves. This psychological need is especially pressing when a play is staged and an actor bodies forth the representation. I also raise for a moment the question of whether viewers—or characters—can be thought to possess a unified self of the sort which colors such assumptions. My interpretation of Posthumus and of his dream discovers a divided nature in terms of Kohut's "vertical split," but I still postulate that such unity is inherent in the unfolding of the self when not arrested in its development.

For a long time critics have assumed that the romance genre (in which most place *Cymbeline*) is the polar opposite of "realism" (psychological or otherwise). Posthumus's dream is not the locus of the unreal or of the surreal, for it seems clearly to reveal human agency.

4. On this see Heinz Kohut. Kohut argues that because of the excess of anger beyond what the situation would seem to provoke, "such bedevilment indicates that the aggression was mobilized in the service of an archaic grandiose self and that it is deployed within the framework of an archaic perception of reality" (Kohut 1978, 643).

I think that Posthumus's behavior here is of a piece with his behavior elsewhere. He does not simply "disown" his pride in his heroic behavior as some Renaissance heroes do. Modesty or Christian self-abnegation differ from Posthumus's anger. Instead of being modest or self-abnegating, Posthumus draws extraordinary attention to himself, his presumed failures, and those of others.

5. For a more extended account of this technique, see James L. Fosshage, "Dream Interpretation Revisited," *Frontiers in Self Psychology*, ed. Arnold Goldberg, Vol. 3 of *Progress in Self Psychology* (Hillsdale, N. J.: Atlantic Press, 1988), 161–75.

6. For a lucid account of this controversial view, see Paul H. Ornstein and Anna Ornstein, "Clinical Understanding and Explaining: The Empathic Vantage Point," *Progress in Self Psychology*, ed. Arnold Goldberg (New York: Guilford Press, 1985), Vol. 1, 43–61.

7. See Jule P. Miller, "How Kohut Actually Worked," *Progress in Self Psychology*, Vol. 1, 22–29.

8. Fosshage argues that "dreaming mentation not only serves to maintain organization, but contributes to the development of new organizations, a crucially important dream function that has remained unrecognized with the classical model" (Fosshage 1988, 164).

9. Director Elijah Moshinsky chose this speech as the core quotation of the play for a production that is especially attuned to the play's psychological implications. Moshinsky emphasizes the centrality of this passage: " 'This is a most astonishing line . . . Shakespeare is saying the confusion of the play is like life: it's bizarre and emotionally penetrating and psychologically intense. And very lifelike.' " See Henry Fenwick 1983, p. 26.

References

Fenwick, Henry. "The Production." In the BBC Television Edition of *Cymbeline*. New York: Mayflower Books, 1983.

Fosshage, James L. "Dream Interpretation Revisited." In *Frontiers in Self Psychology*, edited by Arnold Goldberg. Vol. 3, *Progress in Self Psychology*. Hillsdale, N.J.: Atlantic Press, 1988.

Kirsch, Arthur. *Shakespeare and the Experience of Love*. Cambridge: Cambridge University Press, 1981.

Knight, G. Wilson. "The Vision of Jupiter." In *The Crown of Life*. 1947. Reprint. New York: Barnes and Noble, 1966.

Kohut, Heinz. "Thoughts on Narcissism and Narcissistic Rage." In *The Search for the Self: Selected Writings of Heinz Kohut: 1950–1978*, edited by Paul H. Ornstein. Vol. 2. New York: International Universities Press, 1978.

————. *The Restoration of the Self.* Madison, Conn.: International Universities Press, 1977.

Nosworthy, J. M. Introduction to *Cymbeline*, by William Shakespeare. 1955. Reprint. London: Methuen, 1979.

Ornstein, Paul H. and Anna Ornstein. "Clinical Understanding and Explaining: The Empathic Vantage Point." In *Progress in Self Psychology*, edited by Arnold Goldberg. Vol. 1. New York: Guilford Press, 1985.

Skura, Meredith. "Interpreting Posthumus's Dream from Above and Below: Families, Psychoanalysts and Literary Critics." In *Representing Shakespeare: New Psychoanalytic Essays*, edited by Murray M. Schwartz and Coppélia Kahn. Baltimore: Johns Hopkins University Press, 1980.

12. A Challenge to Apollonian Mastery: A New Reading of Henry James's "Most Appalling Yet Most Admirable" Nightmare*

Suzi Naiburg

Ghostly figures stalk Henry James's dreams as well as his fiction, attesting to the power of the unconscious to command attention. "The most appalling yet most admirable nightmare" of James's life (James [1913] 1983, 196)[1] is an intruder dream in which an awful creature threatens and terrifies the dream-ego (the dream's "I"). Startled from his sleep, the dream-ego becomes the aggressor, dismays and dispels his visitant, and emerges triumphantly in the palace of art. James records his dream-adventure in the twenty-fifth chapter of *A Small Boy and Others*, the first volume of his autobiography, which he began to write in 1911. The dream itself is set in the Louvre's Gallery of Apollo—"a wondrous place," "a splendid scene of things" particularly of "my young imaginative life in it of long before" (196–197). Henry was 12 and his brother William 13 when they first visited the Louvre in July, 1855, and it is to the memory of this visit that Henry returns in his nightmare and its text.

Traditionally critics have tried to identify the intruder and have named him variously—as William (Edel 1985, 20–24); as their father (Lichtenberg 1987, 102); as "one who would stand in the way of Henry's artistic commitment" (Tintner 1977, 256) or his claim to glory as an artist (Mackenzie 1978, 24–25); or as the persona of the artist as author who sets out to memorialize William in *A Small Boy and Others* and ends by writing the story of his own life (Cox 1987,

---

*Photographs of Delacroix's "Apollo Destroying Python" and Géricault's "Raft of the Medusa" reproduced with permission from TIME-LIFE LIBRARY OF ART: *The World of Delacroix*. Photographs by Eddy Van Der Veen, © 1966 Time-Life Books, Inc.

217

244).[2] We too can validate the nightmare as emblematic of an aspect of Henry's relation to William and of his empowered assertion of his artistic self, because the interpersonal dynamics of the artist's life and the dream-ego's drama can be matched. I would, however, like to suggest that the nightmare resonates deeply to an archetypal as well as a historical situation and to intrapsychic as well as interpersonal dynamics.[3]

All previous interpretations of the nightmare have allied themselves with the heroic mode and the dream-ego's triumph. While these interpretations can be substantiated, they do not tell the whole story. Eugène Delacroix's painting entitled "Apollo Destroying Python" has adorned the gallery's ceiling since 1851 [Figure 1]. But to read the dream only in terms of plot—either the dream's or the painting's—is to miss a major point exemplified by Greek mythology, depth psychology, and James's short story "The Jolly Corner" (James 1980). That point has to do with the complementarity of the Dionysian and Apollonian in myth, art, and psyche; with the dynamic interaction of the unconscious and conscious; and with Alice Staverton's ability to accept the hideous black stranger that Brydon Spencer rejects as a part of himself. By focusing on the dream's plot and the intruder's identity, which can never be verified without the dreamer's participation, previous interpretations have failed to emphasize the psychological process that the dream demonstrates and Alice understands.

One important clue can be read in James's pairing of opposing terms to describe the Louvre and his dream. In his autobiography James identifies the dazzling effect of all the aesthetic "sources" in the museum at which his "intense young fancy" was to drink as "that of a love-philtre or fear-philtre which fixes for the senses their supreme symbol of the fair or the strange" (p. 198). On his first visit the young Henry hung "appalled but uplifted on the brave Nadali's arm . . . I cling to him while I gape at Géricault's Radeau de la Méduse . . ." (p. 198). James's description of his nightmare as founded in "an act indeed of life-saving energy as well as in unutterable fear" (p. 196) applies equally to the theme of Théodore Géricault's painting [Figure 2]. Reciprocally, the "splendor and terror of interest" (p. 198) that the "Raft of the Medusa" arouses in James also describes the emotional core of his nightmare. Just as the nightmare marks the symbolic center of the autobiography, so James's experience of this painting marks the symbolic center of his young life. The Géricault provokes "*the* sensation" of "that juncture" with how can I say what foretaste (as determined by that instant as if the hour had struck from a clock) of all the fun, confusedly speaking, that one was going to have, and the kind of life, always of the queer so-called inward sort, tremendously "sporting" in its way—though that description didn't wait upon it, that one was going to lead. It came of itself, this almost awful apprehension in all the presences, under our courier's protection and in my brother's company, it came just there and so; there was alarm in it somehow as well as bliss. (p. 198)

Looking back across more than half a century to write his auto-biography, James depicts both the vulnerability and the excitement that he felt on his first visit to the Louvre. He found the great palace of art "the most peopled of all scenes not less than the most hushed of all temples" (p. 199) "where at first [all the forms of style] . . . simply overwhelmed and bewildered" (p. 195). The small boy, who was so permeable to impressions, would discover "the sense of a freedom of contact and appreciation really too big for one (p. 198). From our vantage point, the bewilderment the museum provokes in James seems mild in comparison to the terror his nightmare instills in him. Yet James suggests an intimacy between these two states as well as an equivalent intensity within each by linking them through a series of parallel terms: alarm and bliss, appalling and admirable, fear and love, the strange and the fair, appalled and uplifted, terror and splendor. James's use and interpretation of the nightmare in his autobiography, its setting in the Gallery of Apollo, and Delacroix's and Géricault's art all attest to the Apollonian mastery of turbulent emotion through the formal properties and structures of art. But the emotional extremes— those that the dream and the art arouse in James—testify to the tumultuous mix of affect that art may contain and transform but not always quell.

Whether James's nightmare was his psyche's attempt to reassert his sense of mastery after a long depression in 1910 as his biographer Leon Edel proposes (Edel 1985, 668) or whether it reflected a challenge to his usual style of Apollonian mastery can never be determined, because we can't put the dreamer on the couch. We can, however, amplify the meaning of his dream by drawing on contextual evidence from a variety of sources. The new reading I propose echoes the wisdom of Alice Staverton in "The Jolly Corner" and pays homage to the full emotional resonance of the appalling and admirable that coexist in our lives. Over and over again in his fiction and criticism, James attests to the "terribly mixed" quality of life. In one of the prefaces for the New York Edition of his work, James writes:

Figure 1. Eugène Delacroix: "Apollo Slaying Python"
1850–1851 Louvre, Paris

Figure 2. Théodore Géricault: "Raft of the Medusa" 1818–1819 Louvre, Paris

No themes are so human as those that reflect for us, out of the confusion of life, the close connection of bliss and bale, of the things that help with the things that hurt, so dangling before us for ever that bright hard metal, of so strange an alloy, one face of which is somebody's right and ease and the other somebody's pain and wrong. (James 1962, 143)

Now let's take a closer look at the dream, which Edel believes occurred on the morning of July 21, 1910, more than a year before James records it in his autobiography. James introduces his nightmare by declaring the value of its setting, attesting to the "vividness" of his recall and affirming the "precious part" the Gallery of Apollo played in his recollection of childhood memories and the "instantaneous recovery" of the nightmare.

> The Galerie d'Apollon became for years what I can only term a splendid scene of things, even of the quite irrelevant or, as might be, almost unworthy: and I recall to this hour, with the last vividness, what a precious part it played for me, and exactly by that continuity of honour, on my awaking, in a summer dawn many years later, to the fortunate, the instantaneous recovery and capture of the most appalling yet most admirable nightmare of my life (196).

Notice how the "splendid scene of things" also includes the "quite irrelevant" and "almost unworthy." James leads us to the nightmare's climax by way of further commentary.

> The climax of this extraordinary experience—which stands alone for me as a dream-adventure founded in the deepest, quickest, clearest act of cognition and comparison, act indeed of life-saving energy, as well as in unutterable fear—was the sudden pursuit, through an open door, along a huge high saloon, of a just dimly-descried figure that retreated in terror before my rush and dash (a glare of inspired reaction from irresistible but shameful dread,) out of the room I had a moment before been desperately, and all the more abjectly, defending by the push of my shoulder against hard pressure on lock and bar from the other side. The lucidity, not to say the sublimity, of the crisis had consisted of the great thought that I, in my appalled state, was probably still more appalling than the awful agent, creature or presence, whatever he was, whom I had guessed, in the suddenest wild start from sleep, the sleep within my sleep, to be making for my place of rest. The triumph of my impulse, perceived in a flash as I acted on it by myself at a bound, forcing the door outward, was the grand thing, but the great point of the whole was the wonder of my final recognition. Routed, dismayed, the tables turned upon him by my so surpassing him for straight aggression and dire intention, my visitant was already but a diminished spot in the long perspective, the tremendous, glorious hall,

as I say, over the far-gleaming floor of which, cleared for the occasion of its great line of priceless vitrines down the middle, he sped for his life, while a great storm of thunder and lightning played through the deep embrasures of high windows at the right. The lightning that revealed the retreat revealed also the wondrous place and, by the same amazing play, my young imaginative life in it of long before, the sense of which, deep inside me, had kept it whole, preserved it to this thrilling use; for what in the world were the deep embrasures and those polished floors but those of the Galerie d'Apollon of my childhood? (p. 196–197)

The drama of James's nightmare is that of a typical ghost story. It is "very short; it contains the briefest of expositions; it is almost all 'climax'; there is one ghostly figure, one human mind to comprehend it, one encounter, one ending" (Banta 1972, 137–138). But while the dramatic action of the dream—like that of Delacroix's mural and Géricault's painting—is direct, its presentation—like that of the paintings—is anything but linear. The nightmare's action is presented climax first with the interpretation preceding the story. The climax and its resolution come before the conflict itself is defined. The narrative then moves backward to preceding incident. Reaction ("my rush and dash") comes before affective cause ("irresistible but shameful dread"). The pursuit and retreat of the intruder precedes the report of his intrusion. A second elaboration of the climax is presented just before the initiating point of the action (the attempted intrusion). Once the beginning of the tale is reached, we come to the climax a third time. Picking up the action again midway, we are brought to its conclusion.

How can we interpret the meaning of this complex reordering of a simple dramatic action? First, it highlights the importance James places on the climax; and second, it effectively hides the dream's energetic core within a complex narrative labyrinth, embedding emotion in form, containing affect in art. The dream-ego's "irresistible but shameful dread" is even tucked away in parentheses. The dream's literary text, the parenthetical framing of the dream-ego's dread, James's interpretation, and the dream's setting all serve the same god—Apollo. One of the most interesting aspects of this verbal labyrinth, which characterizes James's late style, is that the narrative of action is subordinated to the action of cognition enfolded within it. The foundation of the dream adventure for James is "the deepest, quickest, clearest act of cognition and comparison." "The lucidity, not to say sublimity, of the crisis had consisted of the great thought. . . ." The triumph of the dreamer's impulse was "the grand thing, but the great point of the whole was the wonder of my final recognition." The dramatic movement of the dream demonstrates how the reflecting consciousness can be active, heroic, and transformative. The dream-ego moves from resisting the terrifying energy that is projected onto the appalling other to claiming that energy in a great and empowering thought. His triumph is not only of "straight aggression and dire intention" but also of affective identification and cognition.

Although all previous interpretations have overlooked this identification between dream-ego and intruder, it is clearly underscored in the dream: the recognition of their common bond of fear defines the climax. The dream-ego does not deny his fear. Instead he acknowledges it and in so doing can see himself as more frightening than the awful agent who frightens him. He knows he is both appalled and appalling. The dream-ego comes to possess the very qualities that are projected onto the intruder. The dreamer's awareness empowers him to surpass his fear with a courageous thrust outward, claiming for himself the intruder's aggressive energy.

James begins and ends his dream text with references to the dream's setting. The Louvre was originally a palace, and the two-hundred-foot-long Gallery of Apollo is the great hall in which the crown jewels and the crown of the first Napoleon were exhibited. Its style reflects the authority of the Second Empire, and Napoleon, who fascinated James, was a symbol of imperial power. James calls the gallery a "bridge over to style," which inspires "a general sense of *glory*. The glory meant ever so many things at once, not only beauty and art and supreme design, but history and fame and power. The world in fine raised to the richest and noblest expression" (p. 196). James is of Hazlitt's persuasion: "art spoke to him of the imperious will, with music of an army with banners" (Trilling 1950, 78). Frightening as the nightmare may have initially been, it confirms James's identity as an accomplished artist, as one who enters Apollo's gallery triumphantly. It also returns him to important childhood memories, especially of his burgeoning awareness of his own artistic sensitivity. On his first visit to the Louvre in 1855, the young James perceived the museum to hold the "secret" of his "future" (p. 191). There he experienced how "the house of life and the palace of art" became "so mixed and interchangeable" (p. 198). "The great rooms of the Louvre" were "educative, formative, fertilising, in a degree which no other 'intellectual experience' of our youth was to know could pretend, as a comprehensive, conductive thing, to rival" (197).

While Edel's assignment of the July 21, 1910, date to the nightmare is strictly conjecture, it is consistent with James's symbolic use of his dream-adventure in *A Small Boy and Others*. Paul John Eakin reads the nightmare as

> a paradigm of the inward drama of the entire autobiography: the dream culminates in an act of self-display that reveals precisely the aspect of the small boy's consciousness that the mature artist sought to dramatize in his autobiographic narrative. . . . The reassuring message of the dream for both the small boy and the autobiographer was that James had it in him to come into his own, to emerge in glory. (Eakin 1985, 81)

On completing *A Small Boy and Others*, James wrote his nephew Harry on January 19, 1913, identifying his work as "the proof of my powers . . . my vitality, my still sufficient cluster of vital 'assets,' to say nothing of my will to live and to write" (Lubbock 1920, 2:289).

In 1909 and 1910 James was depressed by the meager revenues from the New York Edition of his works and by the lack of an appreciative audience that they represented. The failure of the Edition was also linked emotionally to his failures on the English stage climaxing in the closing of *Guy Domville* in 1895. Both had left him "high and dry" (James 1984, 4:553). James's idealization of and affection for the young sculptor Hendrik Andersen also left him wanting. When they met in Italy in 1899, James was instantly attracted (Edel 1985, 489–498). The handsome Norwegian-born American "inspired feelings in Henry James akin to love" (Edel 1985, 498). Gradually James assessed Andersen's character more accurately, and the fire of his early "ardor" cooled (Edel 1985, 632). Undoubtedly, the "progressive disillusionment that dawned on James and the disruption of the idealizing relationship" (Rhead 1987, 277) also contributed to his depression. This was the first relationship in which James lavished—at least verbally—so much passion.

On April 19, 1909, James wrote to Edith Wharton: "I *have* had—to be frank—a bad and worried and depressed and inconvenient winter" (James 1984, 4:518). By July 29, 1910, he sounds a different note: "I am definitely much better, and on the road to *well*; a great gain has come to me, in spite of everything, during the last ten days in particular" (James 1984, 4:547). Although Henry's younger brother Robertson had died of a heart attack a few weeks earlier and William's health was deteriorating rapidly, James once again records red-letter days after July 21, the morning Edel proposes as the time of his remarkable dream. By placing the nightmare near the end of *A Small Boy and Others*, James seems to be "using the symbolism of the dream consciously in his analysis of his earlier identity in a way that parallels its unconscious function in his illness and recovery of 1910" (Eakin 1985, 80).

Clearly, the dreamer and the autobiographer share a feeling of triumph, which is why critics have seen the nightmare and autobiography as therapeutic. Eakin draws a parallel between the Galerie d'Apollon and the "similarly elaborate" autobiographical text because both house "the workings of the boy's imagination in the splendor of a work of art" (Eakin 1985, 81). The placement of the nightmare within the frame of the autobiography is Apollonian. The threatening and appalling forces of the deep unconscious are ordered in prose and placed at a comfortable distance within the controlling frame of art. James's psyche made an exquisite choice in setting his dream-adventure in the Galerie d'Apollon, because Apollo is the god of distance, art, reason, and form; and his gallery epitomized the imperial power of art. Beauty, art, and style were intimately linked for James with history, fame, and power. Style is "dignity . . . memory . . . measure, conscience and proportion and taste, not to mention a strong sense too" (191). All the attributes James ascribes to style are Apollo's, and it is safely under his aegis that James confronts the appalling other of his unconscious.

As the god of prophecy, Apollo "reveals what is hidden and what is yet to be" (Otto 1978, 72). At his temple in Delphi he admonishes, "Know thyself." Such knowledge is not to be gained at the cost of proximity, merger, excess, or intoxication, which are Dionysian modalities. Apollo, like many of James's narrators and James himself, sought clarity and cognition through distance and detached observation (Otto 1978, 78; Hillman 1985, 25). Even as an observer it would be imperative for James to keep his distance. In the autobiography one can trace the problematic issue of distance in Henry's relation to William. "I never for all the time of childhood and youth in the least caught up with him or overtook him. He was always round the corner and out of sight. . . " (7–8). Yet Henry's envy of William and his desire for merger—for example, to live "by the imagination in William's so adaptive skin" (James [1914] 1983, 247)—are only thinly veiled.

James's connection to younger men such as Hendrik Andersen and Dudley Jocelyn Persse, with whom he had a more satisfactory if less tumultuous relation, also evidences his desire to be close. Such a need for intimacy and a desire for connection, which were probably never acted out sexually, emerged more openly for James when he was in his mid-fifties. The lifelong patterns of his personal relations as well as those of many of his characters suggest

> that James's central unconscious conflict . . . centered . . . around the
> fantasy that close relationship evoked both the intense wish to merge

with the other person and the fear of such a disintegrating merger. The ultimate catastrophe was the loss of one's identity and individuality, a loss from which one might be saved by withdrawal into a cold, shy, but narcissistically vulnerable world. (Rhead 1987, 269)

How safe Apollonian modalities would be for James; how threatening Dionysian merger and disruption.

The bow was Apollo's symbol. It could pierce from afar. "The Greeks habitually pictured recognition of what is right under the image of an accurate bow shot" (Otto 1978, 79). Apollo was "the god of archery and heroic excellence" (Stassinopoulos and Beny 1983, 54). In Delacroix's ceiling painting [Figure 1], the sun god stands astride his chariot firing arrows into the dark flesh of the snake-like water dragon. In 1851 Delacroix described his work in detail:

> The god, mounted on his chariot, has already hurled some of his arrows. His sister, Diana, flying after him, hands him his quiver. Already pierced by the arrows of the god of warmth and life, the bleeding monster writhes as it gives forth in fiery steam the last breath of its life and impotent rage. The waters of the flood begin to dry up, depositing dead bodies of human beings and animals on mountain peaks or dragging them in their wake. The gods are aroused at the sight of the earth abandoned to misshapen monsters, impure creatures of the slime. They have armed themselves like Apollo. Minerva and Mercury rush forth to exterminate the monsters until Eternal Wisdom repeoples the solitary universe. Hercules crushes them with his club, Vulcan, god of fire, drives before him night and the impure vapors, while Boreas and the Zephyrs dry the waters with their breath and finally scatter the clouds. . . . More timid gods stand to one side watching this struggle of the gods and the elements. Nevertheless, Victory descends from the height of Heaven to crown Apollo the victor, and Iris, messenger of the gods, unfurls her scarf in the sky, symbol of the triumph of light over darkness and over the revolt of the waters. (Baudelaire 1947, 48–49)

Delacroix portrays Apollo and Python in deadly combat. The dream's plot sets up a similar adversarial relation between dream-ego and appalling other. In Western culture the heroic ego has become the dominant metaphor for the development of consciousness (Neumann 1973). Yet such a model with its concomitant associations to battle and conquest is limited (Hillman 1977, 135; Hillman 1973, 104). At certain times in the personality's development, it is appropriate for the ego to be antagonistic to the unconscious and heroic in its bearing. But at other times such antagonism becomes a defense against development and a sign of the ego's resistance to becoming subordinated to the Self. From the perspective of the threatened ego, however, the intruding other *is* the enemy. The ego's reaction to polarization is "to solve the problem of the opposites and of the psychic tension they create by accepting one side (and identifying with it) and rejecting the other (and repressing it)" (Stein 1983, 138–139). The sense of adversity originates with the heroic ego. The ego feels threatened by the imposition of an opposing force into its psychic field. *"The experience of the self,"* Carl Jung writes, *"is always a defeat for the ego"* (Jung [1963] 1970, 546); and it is often a confrontation with what is alien to the ego that precipitates such an experience.

Let me give you a contemporary example of this dynamic as it was revealed in a dream and the subsequent analysis. A woman dreamed that she was riding on a trolley car. At the stop before the museum, which was her destination, a gang of hoodlums—all young males—boarded the car and started snatching purses and other valuables. The dreamer was frightened and awoke. The dreamer's associations to the trolley car were all positive. She had ridden one as a teenager on her first trip abroad, so it represented the independence of that trip. The museum was seen as a repository of culture, a place to look at art and objects of established value that didn't belong to her and which she couldn't even touch. The hoodlums represent an aggressive energy, a desire to snatch and take valuables even at the cost of breaking the law. In the dream, the dreamer is terrified of the hoodlums, who are so different from her socially acceptable self. They are the threatening and intrusive "others," but they are also aspects of herself. What the dream is presenting is a vital energy that grabs from life what is not given and has to be taken to be acquired. While not particularly complimentary to her ideal image of herself (her ego-ideal), the hoodlums demonstrate an assertiveness that she needed to use on her own behalf.

Not all hoodlum or gangster images in dreams are positive shadow figures. They may represent negative attributes that the ego refuses to recognize in itself. In either case, recognizing what appears to be other as an aspect of the Self pushes the ego beyond its old self-image to new awareness. Yet when the challenge is first presented, the ego usually responds with fear. Both positive and negative shadow figures can instill fear, because the ego may be defended against either type. Claiming unrealized potential, strength, or assertiveness may feel as appalling to the ego as acknowledging its faults. Despite the ego's tenacity in holding its own against change,

the tensions and conflicts that appear in dreams (as in life) are necessary, even essential. The psyche is deeply complicated, and its tensions
are the means by which it moves. The ego-alien others who give trouble to the dream ego, sometimes torturingly, are at the same time making possible the individuating movement. The tension is the grist by
which the psyche works, the manner in which it enlarges and differentiates itself. (Berry 1982, 87–88)

There is no question that a strong-enough ego is the foundation
for psychological development. What is questioned in analytical psychology is the primacy of the ego in the structure of the developed
personality encompassing both conscious and unconscious dominants.
The emphasis in Jungian psychology is much less on putting the
unconscious in service of the ego than it is in creating a collaboration
between ego and unconscious to serve the guiding principle Jung calls
the Self. In Jungian parlance the Self is, paradoxically, both the guiding principle or impetus for personal development *and* the totality of
the personality encompassing all its constituent parts. Individuation,
the process of fulfilling one's unique potential, is predicated on the
ego's confronting its shadow—the unseen, buried, and sometimes
threatening potentials the ego has not yet acknowledged as its own.
What is critical in developing a full appreciation of James's nightmare
is to see the reflective ego and appalling other not simply as adver-
saries but also as complementary aspects of the total personality or the
Self.

The Greeks, among other ancient peoples who were polytheists,
knew of this complementarity. Apollo and Dionysus were half brothers. They shared the Delphic festival year and were worshiped together at Delphi. On one side of Apollo's temple the pediment sculptures
portray Apollo with Leto, Artemis, and the Muses. On the other side
are Dionysus and his delirious Maenads (Stassinopoulos and Beny
1983, 55; Otto 1981, 203). Dionysus represents what seems antithetical to Apollo. His energies are associated with releasing, merging, and
disrupting. Dionysus's symbol is the phallus; his worshipers were
women. Those who denied him were driven mad. In Euripides's play
The Bacchae, he stands for what the Theban culture repressed—the
feminine, sensual, uninhibited, emotional, natural, ecstatic, dark, and
irrational. Dionysus is an apt symbol for the repressed because "the
cult forms present him as the god who comes, the god of epiphany,
whose appearance is far more urgent, far more compelling than that
of any god" (Otto 1981, 79). Python is connected mythologically to
Dionysus (Fontenrose 1959, 375–380; Kerényi 1984, 49–75); and

Dionysus is connected to life and death, the creative and destructive. His realm is

> that of the instinct, exuberance, and intoxication in the rhythmic dance of life. In his manifestations as bull, lion, goat, serpent, his power and masculinity come to the fore; when associated with the feminine force—nature—he was identified with all types of liquids (water, honey, milk, wine) conducive to growth and procreation. . . . (Knapp 1984, 11–12)

The Apollonian spirit in its highest expression of "clarity, discipline and reason" is grounded in the very source of being that Python/Dionysus represents (Stassinopoulos and Beny 1983, 54): Apollo's priestess at Delphi—Pythia—took her name from the snake-like dragon.

William James observed the split between the Apollonian and Dionysian when he noted that "The scientific-academic mind and the feminine-mystical mind shy from each other's facts just as they fly from each other's temper and spirit" (James 1897, 301–303). The emphasis Delacroix gives to Apollo's victory as well as the emphasis literary critics have given to the dream-ego's triumph reflect the psychological reality of modern Western culture's split between Apollo and Dionysus—between light and dark, reason and intuition, conscious and unconscious, spirit and matter, objective and subjective experience. But mythologically and psychologically, Apollo and Dionysus are not as diametrically opposed as this split suggests. Neither are the ego and shadow as adversarial as the ego may feel them to be when the ego is aligned with the heroic Apollonian. In 1888 Ralph Waldo Emerson wrote that dreams

> have a double consciousness, at once sub- and objective. We call the phantoms that rise, the creation of our own fancy, but they act like mutineers, and fire on their commander; showing that every act, every thought, every cause, is bi-polar and in the act is contained the counteraction. If I strike, I am struck; if I chase, I am pursued (Emerson 1888, 12–13).

Both halves of the dream's action, however opposed they may appear to be, belong to the dreamer. "The dreamer," Jung observes, "is the whole dream" (Jung [1953] 1966, 84) making all the characters "valuable subjective entities" (Berry 1982, 69) and parts of a whole.

The composition of Delacroix's ceiling painting in the Gallery of Apollo teaches a smiliar lesson. In an 1880 review of *The Letters of Delacroix*, James writes that Delacroix "saw his subjects as a whole, not as the portrait of a group of selected and isolated objects, but as an incident in the continuity of things and the passage of human life" (James 1989, 184). Delacroix uses the formal elements of art to express and contain the dramatic possibilities of his subject. He spent six months planning and sketching "Apollo Destroying Python" and expanded his palette "from ten basic colors to twenty-eight component hues" (Trapp 1970, 286). Color is a very important organizing principle in Delacroix's art. James saw him as a "singularly powerful and various colourist" (James 1989, 186). If we look at his painting as a composition built around color, then the dramatic oppositions can be more easily seen as complementary. The golden light around Apollo is balanced by the darker tones of Python and his watery domain. Artists employ the shades and shadows of chiaroscuro not only to create depth but also to define structure. Notice the turbulence created within the painting by the figures in motion around Apollo. Light and color are used to blend these swirling forms into a single image.

James thought very highly of Delacroix. He begins his review of Delacroix's letters by declaring the French school as "the most complete" school of modern painting and Delacroix as "the most eminent member. He has passed into the rank of one of the 'glories' of France" (James 1989, 183). In his 1872 review entitled "French Pictures in Boston," James presents another argument for judging Delacroix "more than any painter we know . . . by the total impression: Delacroix's weaknesses are inseparable from his strengths.

> the qualities which charm and those which irritate . . . are so grotesquely combined in his genius that it is nearly impossible to separate them and open a distinct account with each. We may even say that he pleases, in certain cases, by virtue of his errors—by reason, at least, of a certain generous fallibility which is the penalty of his generous imagination. (James 1989, 47)

Géricault's masterwork, the "Raft of the Medusa" [Figure 2], is also a mix of different elements. Géricault depicts a historical incident from the shipwreck of the *Medusa*. One hundred and thirty-nine men and one woman were crammed on a raft and cut adrift by scandalously inept officers. Only fifteen men survived days of exposure to harsh elements and their own savagery, including cannibalism. Géricault combines grisly realistic details with a romantic feeling for the suffering and heroism of the survivors. The canvas covers an impressive area of approximately sixteen by twenty-three feet. The raft is tipped up in a stormy sea and lurches desolate men at the viewer. While the painting captures the extremes of hope and despair, life and death, heroic effort and the unheeding forces of nature, it contains them all in a carefully composed image. In 1868 James wrote that the painting "possesses not only vastness of size, but real power of conception" (James 1989, 39). Tom Prideaux notes that "Géricault achieved his climactic effect by building two stressful pyramids—one based on the falled bodies of dead and dying, topped by the Negro signaling a far-off rescue ship; the other formed by the tilting raft, the guy lines and the mast" (Prideaux 1966, 48–49).

Imagine how a sensitive twelve-year-old boy who had just crossed the sea might react to this painting—to its high drama and brutally realistic details; to the pyramid of muscular bodies and intimately intertwined male nudes; to its strong shadows, its crossing and thrusting diagonals; and to the powerful natural forces about to swamp the survivors like the unconscious itself, which can flood and disable a fragile ego. "In the arts," James writes, "feeling is always meaning" (James 1989, 185). Géricault's painting exemplifies the arousal of strong affect as well as the mastery of turbulent emotion through the formal properties of art.

Dreams, like art, transform the intensities of "emotion into design" (Perera 1990, 45). James's dream text is a further elaboration of this ordering principle because it is a part of a formal work of art. Just to what extent the intricate autobiographic text is a stylistic elaboration on his nightmare as it was recalled upon waking can only be inferred by comparing it to an earlier dream Lady Ottoline Morrell recorded in her memoirs. In April, 1909, fifteen months before the probable July 21, 1910, date of his nightmare, James told Lady Morrell two dreams from his youth. One is strikingly similar to his nightmare and also contains elements that we can identify in his short story "The Jolly Corner" (written in 1906). Although we have only Lady Morrell's record, her simple narrative style is far more characteristic of freshly remembered dreams than James's complex autobiographic text.

> He awoke trembling in a great state of nerves. He had become aware that a terrible beast had entered into the house where he was. He realized that the room in which he was had four doors. He rushed to the first, the second and the third, turning the key; when he arrived at the fourth he was aware that there was something awful behind it, and he began to hold the door to with all his strength. But as he was doing this, he felt a sudden volte-face within himself, and he called out, "What a vile, cowardly creature you are to be afraid." He dashed open the door and determined to pursue the monster; as he opened it he found he was on the threshold of a long beautiful gallery, flooded with sunlight. He rushed out, waving his arms, and at the far end of the gallery there was a monster rushing away, and as he fled after it he woke. (Gathorne-Hardy 1963, 171–172)

James's nightmare reflects the same dramatic pattern as this earlier dream in which the dream-ego is terrified by an appalling other, who in turn is frightened by him. At the center of each drama the dream-ego does an about-face, overcomes his fear, and becomes the aggressor. Each dream introduces similar issues around the ego's relation to an appalling other, embodies the same affect (fear), shares specific details of setting, and repeats the door motif. The long beautiful gallery of the earlier dream presages the nightmare's Gallery of Apollo setting. In each a threatening, disruptive presence intrudes upon the setting of fine art, and in each the dream-ego is triumphant in that setting.[4] The dream-ego's mastery suggests that art has the power to prevail over the threatening intrusion of an appalling other. It is only a short step from making these observations to drawing a hypothesis about James's late style: the intricacies of his complex literary style may be dependent as much on a need to contain emotion in form as they are on a desire to reveal thought in process.

The sinuous surface of James's late style reflects the author's and his characters' way of processing deeply felt experience through complex cognitive modalities. Both the style and the thinking it reflects function to contain and filter whatever threatens to disrupt. Because the contents of the unconscious that erupt into consciousness are affect-laden, the unconscious poses a particular threat to those who maintain their balance primarily by intellectualizing experience. In writing about actors, James exhibits a preference for those who are "disciplined, controlled, reined-in, and yet capable of abundant consciousness" (Jobe 1990, 36). He admired Constant-Benoit Coquelin (1841–1909) for his "command of the effects that lie entirely in self-possession, effects of low tone, indications of inward things." Comparing Coquelin's art to that of a tightrope walker, James notes that his skill is "a defiance of the loss of balance under exhilaration" (James 1957, 204).

On October 13, 1908, James wrote Edith Wharton to recommend a strategy of containment. Wharton was distressed over her difficult marriage to Teddy and her intimacy with Morton Fullerton. James responds:

> Only sit tight yourself & *go through the movements of life*. That keeps up our connection with life—I mean of the immediate & apparent life; behind which, all the while, the deeper & darker and the unapparent, in which things *really* happen to us, learns, under that hygiene, to stay in its place. Let it get out of its place & it swamps the scene; besides which its place, God knows, is enough for it! Live it all through, every inch of it—out of it something valuable will come—but live it ever so quietly; &—*je maintiens mon dire*—waitingly! (Powers 1990, 101)

In drawing this distinction between the immediate and apparent surface of life in which one moves and the deeper, darker unapparent in which things really happen to us, James pays his respects to the influence of the unconscious. But his hope is clearly that the unconscious will learn "under that hygiene, to stay in its place." The degree to which James praises or counsels containment reflects his respect for the disruptive forces that lie like pythons in our watery depths. Moreover, the complexity with which he structures his text seems to be in direct proportion to the perceived danger of losing one's balance.

Like Dionysus, the intruders in James's dreams make a sudden, urgent, and compelling appearance in order to arouse—to throw the ego off balance, to challenge the status quo. They present to consciousness the inferior, unbridled, frightening, and monstrous aspects of the personality that are still hidden or denied. The intruder represents that with which James was not consciously identified. We know from reading James's fiction that ghosts and other shadow figures represent energies that are unwanted, resisted, or repressed but are not inert. These energies are potent, more so by virtue of being repressed and exerting their influence unconsciously. James wrote ghost stories throughout his career. The first was published in 1868 and the last in 1908. They include some of his best and most famous tales: "The Turn of the Screw" (1898), "The Beast in the Jungle" (1903), and "The Jolly Corner" (1908).

Ghostly figures haunt James's nightmare and tales just as they materialize in our own imagination to "insist on admittance into consciousness" (Jaffé 1979,102). Freudians and Jungians share the "notion of the psyche as dynamic" as well as an appreciation that "perhaps the major dynamic conflict . . . is between consciousness and unconsciousness" (Samuels 1985, 8). The appalling other in James's nightmare threatens the dream-ego just as the forces of the unconscious push against the boundaries of our ego-centered consciousness to enlarge our sense of who we are. It is from this perspective that I would argue that the nightmare's essence is intrapsychic and archetypal—that it images the ego's struggle with the eruptions of the unconscious that threaten the ego's position in order to further personal development.

But what is pushing the ego? What is exerting pressure for change? Jung postulated an internal principle of growth, a movement toward wholeness that is inherent in the psyche and intimately related to creativity and the unconscious. He calls the process individuation and the impetus the Self. Max Zeller explains that

Wholeness is the goal of every life process in nature. The seed, the flower, the tree all grow toward fulfillment of an inner law, toward the realization of their innate potentials, which emerge as a single, unique Gestalt. The drive toward completion is a continuous movement, a basic urge that goes through all of life, like a yearning that wants to be satisfied. Man can never stop this eternal impulse, but he can at any time cripple it. (Zeller 1975, 60–61)

Viewing the dream in this context suggests that the dreamer's daylight task is to examine what is presently being overlooked or denied, causing it to force its way into consciousness. In the nightmare the appalling other has to demand the ego's attention by intruding and instilling fear. From the perspective of the Self, the slumbering ego needs to be aroused. But does it need to ward off the intruder?

Alice Staverton would say, "not all the time." In "The Jolly Corner," Alice represents an attitude toward the unconscious that is born of empathy and acceptance. In contrast, Brydon Spencer exemplifies an attitude defined by denial and fear. The story's plot is actually the reverse of James's nightmare. Brydon actively initiates a search to discover "the personality he might have been" had he not lived abroad; (James 1980, 735)[5] "it's only a question of what fantastic, yet perfectly possible, development of my own nature I mayn't have missed" (p. 736). As Brydon's quest to know himself intensifies, a "vain egoism" and "morbid obsession" to discover his alter ego envelops him (p. 735). He stalks this shadow figure in the house on the Jolly Corner as if he were in pursuit of "big game" (p. 741). He thrives on the thrill and imagines himself terrifying his ghost.

But in the intensity of felt emotion, Brydon's confidence is eroded. He feels more like the hunted than the hunter. The tables turn as they do in James's nightmare, but they turn the other way. Brydon is overtaken by fear. When the dark stranger appears, Brydon recoils in horror. His "revulsion" is "immense" (p. 755). Brydon denies any identification with this figure and sees him as "evil, odious, blatant, vulgar" (p. 756). As the specter advances toward him, Brydon collapses in a faint. Later Brydon awakens cradled in Alice's lap.

Alice's connection to the unconscious yields knowledge to which Brydon does not yet have access. Because she "had accepted him" and "knew him," the stranger is "less dreadful" to her (p. 762). Alice even pities him, recognizing that he has been "unhappy" and "ravaged," is "grim" and "worn" (p. 762). Her response is an empathic acceptance even of the most ravaged and forlorn aspects of the Self. The dark stranger appears again in her dreams at the moment Brydon confronts his alter ego alone in the dark house. Thus the stranger comes to her as an ally rather than an adversary to alert her to Brydon's need.

In James's nightmare there isn't a knowing woman to accept the appalling other as there is in "The Jolly Corner." James's dream-ego must face the challenge of the unconscious alone as Brydon does in the empty house on the Jolly Corner. Unlike Brydon, however, the dream-ego does not capitulate in the face of the hideous stranger. So in this sense the dream-ego is more daring in the unconscious fantasy of the dream than Brydon is in James's more consciously crafted tale. But being heroic and warding off the appalling other may not always be the most appropriate response for the strong-enough ego. In his preface James identifies "the idea entertained for 'The Jolly Corner'" to be "that of the strange and sinister embroidered on the very type of the normal and easy" (James 1962, 261–262).

Like James's dream-adventure and the "deafening chorus" of great art he saw in the Louvre (James [1913] 1983, 195), life presents us with a mix of the fair and the strange. This strange alloy exists within our own psyches; dream-ego and appalling other are both aspects of ourselves. At some junctures in our lives, it may be appropriate to rout the terrors of the night. But at others we may, like Alice, find acceptance creates an ally out of the hideous stranger who lurks in the dark recesses of us all. Slaying the dragon as Apollo does with his solar arrows is one way we have to meet the forces of the deep unconscious in which our pythons lie like strange sea monsters. But it is not the only way; nor is it Alice's. Dionysus arouses, releases, and embraces. Delacroix and Géricault express and contain. Alice attends, receives, and accepts. The psyche's repertoire of responses is fuller than any pantheon and richer than any palette.

But it is the pantheon and the artist's palette that remind us of the complementarity of apparent opposites. Looking at the dream as an image rather than as a story leads us to the same point. If we regard Delacroix's painting as an image rather than a narrative in oil, we can see the complementarity of Apollo and Python more easily. Both are needed in the structure of the whole. "The Greek word for dream, *oneiros*, meant image not story" (Berry 1982, 66). In contrast to narrative, which is sequential by nature, an image is characterized by simultaneity. (Berry 1982, 59). If we side with the dream-ego in James's nightmare, then the ghost is terrifying. But if we enlarge our perspective to include the whole image or if we adopt the perspective of the Self, then the dream-ego and ghost can be seen to form a complementary pair. "The two of them together *are* the image" (Berry 1982, 61). Dream-ego and appalling other are part of a larger whole that is both imaginal and psychological. One might even say that it is "natural," psychologically speaking, for the frightened ego to have its ghost and for the ghost to have its "fearful human." With a sense of opposition that is reminiscent of Emerson's 1888 remark, John Weir Perry writes in 1970:

> I therefore see the entire emotional psyche as structured not only in complexes, but in their bipolar systems or arrangements; the occurrence of an emotion requires the interplay of two complexes, and habitual emotions belong to habitual pairs. For every mother complex there has to be a child, and for every princess anima a princely lover, for every awesome father a son, and for every overwhelming monster a fearful human. The problem of conceptualizing the emotional event is a matter of understanding what happens at the interface between the two poles, where the ego adopts and experiences one affect, and relegates the opposite member of the bipolar pair to its "object." I therefore do not visualize a model of the unconscious in which the complexes are randomly arranged, but rather one in which the complexes are arranged in bipolar systems or pairs. (Perry, 1970, 9)

To conclude with an imaginal or aesthetic approach to James's dream and a bipolar model of unconscious complexes invites our appreciation of all the constituted parts of the whole—whether the whole is James's nightmare, Delacroix's painting, Géricault's oil, the dyad of Brydon and his alter ego, or the psyche itself. Each contains elements that appear oppositional, even antagonistic. Yet from another perspective, these apparent opposites may be seen to complement or complete each other. Indeed, the most appalling and the most admirable, the strange and the fair, terror and splendor coexist within us all.

Notes

1. Subsequent parenthetical references to this text will include page numbers only.

2. Other critics who have commented on the nightmare include Martha Banta, Stephen Donadio, Paul John Eakin, B. D. Horwitz, Clifton Rhead, Claire Rosenfield, Saul Rosenzweig, John Carlos Rowe, Cushing Strout, and Lionel Trilling.

3. My work on James's nightmare has developed through a number of stages. My thanks are due especially to Sylvia Brinton Perera for her help at each stage and to those who offered their cogent comments at presentations at the Association for the Study of Dreams 1990 Conference, the C.G. Jung

Foundation of New York, the C.G. Jung Institute of San Francisco, and the C.G. Jung Societies of New Mexico and Seattle.

    4. For a more detailed comparison of James's early dreams with the nightmare and "The Jolly Corner," see my book manuscript, *The Appalling Other in Henry James.*

    5. Subsequent parethentical references to this text will include page numbers only.

References

Banta, Martha. *Henry James and the Occult.* Bloomington: Indiana University Press, 1972.

Baudelaire, Charles. *Eugene Delacroix: His Life and Work.* New York: Lear Publishers, 1947.

Berry, Patricia. *Echo's Subtle Body: Contributions to Analytical Psychology.* Dallas: Spring Publications, Inc., 1982.

Cox, James M. "The Memories of Henry James: Self-Interest as Autobiography." *Southern Review* 22 (1987): 231–251.

Donadio, Stephen. *Nietzsche, Henry James and the Artistic Will.* New York: Oxford University Press, 1978.

Eakin, Paul John. *Fictions in Autobiography: Studies in the Art of Self-Invention.* Princeton: Princeton University Press, 1985.

Edel, Leon. *Henry James: A Life.* New York: Harper & Row, Publishers, 1985.

Emerson, Ralph Waldo. *Lectures and Biographical Sketches.* Boston: Houghton, Mifflin, 1888.

Fontenrose, Joseph. *Python: A Study of Delphic Myth and Its Origins.* Berkeley: University of California Press, 1959 .

Gathorne-Hardy, Robert, ed. *The Early Memoirs of Lady Ottoline Morrell.* London: Farber and Farber, 1963.

Hillman, James. *Archetypal Psychology: A Brief Account.* Dallas: Spring Publications, Inc., 1985.

――――. "The Great Mother, Her Son, Her Hero, and the Puer." In *Fathers and Mothers: Five Papers in Archetypal Background of Family Psychology,* edited by Patricia Berry. Zurich: Spring Publications, Inc., 1973.

――――. *Re-Visioning Psychology.* New York: Harper & Row, Publishers, 1977.

Horwitz, B.D. "Henry James and the Fearful Hero: The Sense of Desolation in Henry James." *Psychocultural Review* 1 (1977): 488–491.

Jaffé, Aniela. *Apparitions: An Archetypal Approach to Death Dreams and Ghosts.* Irving, Tex.: Spring Publications, Inc., 1979.

James, Henry. *The Art of the Novel.* New York: Charles Scribner's Sons, 1962.

――――. "The Jolly Corner." In Henry James, *Stories of the Supernatural,* edited by Leon Edel. New York: Taplinger Publishing Company, 1980.

――――. *Letters.* Edited by Leon Edel. Vol. 4. Cambridge: Harvard University Press, 1984.

――――. *Notes of a Son and Brother.* In Henry James, *Autobiography,* edited by Frederick W. Dupee. 1914 Reprint. Princeton: Princeton University Press, 1983.

――――. *The Painter's Eye: Notes and Essays on the Pictorial Arts.* Edited by John L. Sweeney. Madison: University of Wisconsin Press, 1989.

――――. *The Scenic Art: Notes on Acting & Drama: 1872–1901.* Edited by Allan Wade. New York: Hill and Wang, 1957.

————. *A Small Boy and Others*. In Henry James, *Autobiography*, edited by Frederick W. Dupee. 1913 Reprint. Princeton: Princeton University Press, 1983.

————. *What Maisie Knew*. New York: Oxford University Press, 1987.

James, William. *The Will to Believe and Other Essays in Popular Philosophy*. New York: Longmans, Inc., 1897.

Jobe, Steven H. "Henry James and the Philosophic Actor." *American Literature*. 62.1 (March 1990): 32–43.

Jung, C.G. *Mysterium Coniunctionis: An Inquiry into the Separation and Synthesis of Psychic Opposites in Alchemy*. Translated by R.F.C. Hull. Second edition. Princeton: Princeton University Press, [1963] 1970.

————. *Two Essays on Analytical Psychology*. Translated by R.F.C. Hull. Second edition. Princeton: Princeton University Press, [1953] 1966.

Kerényi, C. "Apollo Epiphanies." In *Spirit and Nature: Papers from the Eranos Yearbook*. Princeton: Princeton University Press, 1954, 49–75.

————. *The Gods of the Greeks*. London: Thames and Hudson, 1951.

Knapp, L. Bettina. *A Jungian Approach to Literature*. Carbondale: Southern Illinois University Press, 1984.

Lichtenberg, Joseph D. "A Memory, a Dream, and a Tale: Connecting Themes in the Creativity of Henry James." In *Psychoanalytic Studies of Biography*, edited by George Moraitis and George H. Pollock. Madison: International University Press, 1987, 85–113.

Lubbock, Percy, ed. *The Letters of Henry James*. Vol. 2. New York: Charles Scribner's Sons, 1920.

Mackenzie, Manfred. *Communities of Honor and Love in Henry James.* Cambridge: Harvard University Press, 1978.

Neumann, Erich. *The Origins and History of Consciousness.* Translated by R.F.C. Hull. Princeton: Princeton University Press, 1973.

Otto, Walter F. *Dionysus: Myth and Cult.* Dallas: Spring Publications, Inc., 1981.

──────. *The Homeric Gods: The Spiritual Siqnificance of Greek Religion.* New York: Octagon Books, 1978.

Perera, Sylvia Brinton. "Dream Design: Some Operations Underlying Clinical Dream Appreciation." In *Dreams in Analysis,* edited by Nathan Schwartz-Salant and Murray Stein. Wilmette, Il.: Chiron Publications, 1990, 39–79.

Perry, John Weir. "Emotions and Object Relations." *Journal of Analytical Psychology.* 15.1 (1970): 1–12.

Powers, Lyall H., ed. *Henry James and Edith Wharton: Letters 1900–1915.* New York: Charles Scribner's Sons, 1990.

Prideaux, Tom. *The World of Delacroix, 1798–1863.* New York: Time-Life Books, 1966.

Rhead, Clifton. "Henry James and the Sense of the Past." In *Psychoanalytic Studies of Biography,* edited by George Moraitis and George H. Pollock. Madison: International University Press, 1987, 263–279.

Rosenfield, Claire. "The Shadow Within: The Conscious and Unconscious Use of the Double." In *Stories of the Double,* edited by Albert Guerard. Philadelphia: J. B. Lippincott Co., 1967.

Rosenzweig, Saul. "The Ghost of Henry James." *Partisan Review* 11 (1944): 436–55.

Rowe, John Carlos. *The Theoretical Dimensions of Henry James.* Madison: University of Wisconsin Press, 1984.

Samuels, Andrew. *Jung and the Post-Jungians.* London: Routledge & Kegan Paul, 1985.

Stassinopoulos, Arianna and Roloff Beny. *The Gods of Greece.* New York: Harry N. Abrams, Inc. Publishers, 1983.

Stein, Murray. *In Midlife: A Jungian Perspective.* Dallas: Spring Publications, Inc., 1983.

Strout, Cushing. "Henry James's Dream of the Louvre, 'The Jolly Corner,' and Psychological Interpretation." *The Psychohistory Review.* 8 (1979): 47–52.

Tintner, Adeline. "Autobiography as Fiction: 'The Usurping Consciousness' as Hero of James's Memoirs." *Twentieth-Century Literature* 23 (1977): 239–260.

Trilling, Lionel. *The Liberal Imagination.* New York: Doubleday Anchor Books, 1950.

Trapp, Frank Anderson. *The Attainment of Delacroix.* Baltimore: John Hopkins University Press, 1970.

Williams, C.K. *The Bacchae of Euripides.* New York: Farrar, Straus and Giroux, 1990.

Zeller, Max. *The Dream: The Vision of the Night.* Los Angeles: The Analytical Psychology Club of Los Angeles and the C.G. Jung Institute of Los Angeles, 1975.

PART IV

Dreams in Texts

The three chapters concluding this volume examine respectively one medieval author's diverse use of dreams as literary devices, and as much more, in his lyric poetry; the use of dreams in one Spanish Golden Age drama; and the function of prophetic dreams in several novels of nineteenth-century Russia. Again readers will be struck by the particularities of literary genre, period, and language at the same time as they become intensely aware of a quality of dreamingness in which all these literary representations, as well as all those which have appeared earlier in this book, participate.

Harriet Goldberg's study of Santillana reveals that dreams appearing initially to be little more than literary techniques providing information or insight needed in the text actually serve many creative and psychological purposes for the author. They help him disguise his meanings, express his ideal hopes, disclose various kinds of narrative transformations, and experiment with different forms of the poetic "I." Thus dreams attain for him the possibility of multiple voices within the personalistic expressiveness of the lyric form.

Frederick de Armas demonstrates how entering a text through its dream elements enriches awareness of the subtlety and complexity of the drama, leading to a revaluation of its aesthetic effectiveness. Writing on a comedia from Spain's Golden Age concerned with the discovery of the "New World," he finds that dreams directly reflect the process of "finding the other" that the first conquistadores engaged in. He explores how the author, through representing differences between true prophetic dreams and false dreams, can simultaneously support and question the whole Spanish enterprise of the New World conquest.

C. Nicholas Lee starts with several Russian literary texts that contain dreams and nightmares and he differentiates a variety of roles oneiric representation plays in the narratives. He then sets these uses of dream in the broader context of dreams in the traditions of European Romanticism.

13. The Marqués de Santillana: Master Dreamer

Harriet Goldberg

Previously I have argued that dream reports in medieval Castilian works are authorial devices employed to depict fantastic, imaginary, or extraordinarily visual material within the constraints of an ordinarily non-visual literary style (Goldberg 1983, 21). To mention just a few examples, Gonzalo de Berceo (ca. 1185–1264) created scenes in which saintly figures instructed their disciples by relating their dreams—*Vida de Santo Domingo, Vida de Santa Oria,* and in *Milagros de Nuestra Señora* the poet-pilgrim falls asleep in a *locus amoenus* and experiences an amorous vision *a lo divino.* Prophecies that permit the storyteller to foreshadow future events were related in a chivalric novel, *El caballero Çifar;* in a pseudohistoriographic account of the Crusades, *La gran conquista de Ultramar;* in *Amadís de Gaula;* and in the national epic, *Poema de Mio Cid* (Goldberg 1983). The anonymous poet of the thirteenth-century *Razón de amor y los denuestos del agua y el vino* wrote a more-or-less conventional amorous vision and linked it with an equally conventional debate vision to create a unified dream report (Goldberg 1984). However, for Iñigo López de Mendoza, the Marqués de Santillana (1398–1458)—a poet whose work bridged the ostensible distance between an earlier period and the advent of "el modo itálico" to use his descriptive term for his innovative poetic style—dream visions seem to have meant something more.

To this end, I propose to examine four of Santillana's dream visions: two that treat literary and political topics—*Coronaçión del Mossén Jordí,* and the *Comedieta de Ponza,* and two that deal with love—*El sueño* and the *Infierno de los enamorados.* The question to be answered, whether Santillana's decision to present his thoughts in the

245

form of dream narratives was merely a stylistic choice, or if he saw the dream as a medium for the transmission of thoughts, is meaningful in itself. We can rule out surface content as a determining factor since each poem was written to convey a quite different message. *El sueño* is an elaborate conceit in which the poetic "I" declares himself to be love's prisoner despite the valiant support of Diana, the goddess of chastity; in *El infierno de los enamorados* he makes a Dantesque trip to witness the suffering of famous lovers and returns mildly chastened and determined to avoid love's pain. Rafael Lapesa sees these two love poems as antithetical, one stating the problem and the second the resolution (Lapesa 1957, 117); and David William Foster thinks the *Infierno* is a continuation of the *Sueño* (Foster 1971, 183). Alan Deyermond reminds us that priority of composition is not the question here; it is their order in the narrative sequence that is significant (Deyermond 1989, 77). In fact, the British hispanist prefers to think of a three-part sequence that begins with *Triunfete de amor*, where the poet falls in love; that continues with *Sueño*, where he is painfully in love; and that ends with *Infierno*, where he is free of love (Deyermond 1989, 86). These are not amorous visions in the tradition of *Razón de amor* where the lovers share passionate moments but rather are examinations of the nature of love.[1]

On the other hand, the *Coronación del Mossén Jordí* celebrates a Valencian poet's ascension to a poetic Parnassus, while the *Comedieta de Ponza* is a dramatic vignette of the events surrounding the receipt of the news of the naval disaster at Ponza near Gaeta, and the subsequent imprisonment of Alfonso V of Aragón and his two brothers—Juan of Navarra and Enrique, Maestre of Santiago.

Given the range of topics among these poems, we must look beyond surface content for the recurrent rhetorical strategy that they share. From Edward Friedman who looks at the structural aspects of dream rhetoric, we learn that rhetorical strategies occupy the space between signified and signifier (Friedman 1988, 35); it is in this space that he locates metaphor and, by extension, dream-as-metaphor. He writes: "Metaphor rests, as does the logocentric world, on the direct relation between signifier and signified, vehicle and tenor" (p. 36). Imagine, if you will, a poet-author with an idea he/she wants to convey (the signified) confronted with the problem of how to convey it (the signifier). From real-life experience, the poet-author knows that dreaming and the relating of a dream to another is an essential part of human intimacy. Therefore, the selection of a dream report to relate allegorical or fanciful matter becomes more than a technique to present the fantastic. The dream report itself (because of its personal nature) enhances the message. The poet-dreamer's narrative touches the reader more closely than if he/she were merely relating an imaginary adventure. Reader and poet have shared a close personal moment.

In John F. Priest's observation about the way dreams work in myths one sees an analogy with the signifier/signified pattern in which the phenomenal is the signifier and the noumenal the signified. He writes: "In either case it is tacitly assumed that the function of the dream is to establish a contact between the noumenal and phenomenal world of sense experienced" (Priest 1970, 48–67). In this way of looking at the "space between," the dream links external reality and the human being's spiritual reality. Furthermore, psychology tells us that even nonliterary people produce "mythic narratives, which are often so basic to human nature that they transcend the individual's concerns and reveal universal truths" (Roth 1987, 181). What, then, do we expect from a remarkable poet gifted with great erudition and insight? At the very least he will have hinted at the nature of the dream metaphor common to his vision poems. Certainly it will become clear that for him dreams are not merely structuring devices.

The first step is to review the nature of the literary dream report. It characteristically begins with the hour, the season, the location in which the dreamer falls asleep, and his/her physical and emotional state immediately before dropping off. The narrative is frequently episodic with abrupt transitions, and not infrequently there are dreams within dreams. Many dreamers recall the moment when they awoke, either joyfully, transported spiritually, or terrified. At times the dreamer makes an on-the-spot report to a companion who is asked to interpret the experience (Goldberg 1983, 23). All of Santillana's dream visions include one or more of these features.

The modern reader must readjust his/her preconceived ideas about the tyranny of medieval style and must recognize that medieval authors felt no obligation to adhere rigidly to a checklist of the circumstantial details necessary to depict a dream report. Indeed, the convention was undoubtedly so well-established that a few touches sufficed to convey the idea that the speaker was relating an oneiric experience, be it waking or sleeping. For example, although Santillana does not say that he is dreaming, Nancy F. Marino concludes that his *serranilla*, (a pastoral poem in which a knight encounters a shepherd woman), the *Vaquera de la Finojosa*, is an account of a dream simply because the poet says he was overcome by sleep after having lost his way in a rough and difficult terrain that is magically transformed into a lovely meadow (Marino 1986, 263).[2] In fact, the line between waking and sleeping dreams is not at all clear. Julian Palley comments on a daydream in *La vida es sueño*: "Segismundo's waking experience in the palace, although not literally a dream, has in all respects the function and structure of a dream in both the psychological and philosophical interpretations, in the life of the Prince and in the unfolding of the drama" (Palley 1976, 149).[3]

Recalling the guidelines for reporting a dream, we turn to Santillana's most completely realized amatory dream vision poem, *Sueño*, in search of the "space between." Despite Alan Deyermond's statement that "less than one-fifth is occupied by an account of the narrator-protagonists's dream" (Deyermond 1989, 82), I hope to show that the Marqués, aware of the phenomenon of dreams within dreams and sequential dreams, was writing a unified dream poem. Typically the doleful poet starts his account with the time of the year and his emotional state immediately prior to sleeping, saying that he had been thinking about how he had had the ill luck to fall in love: "Cruel inhuman Fortune ordered Love, this evil enemy with her huge band of troops, to pursue me."[4] The sleeper is stretched out in his bed in the dead of the night at a specific hour: "I was lying in my bed at the hour when Brutus asked the wise Cato what he should do" (VI:49–54.176).[5] Santillana begins his oneiric narrative: "In that dream I saw myself in a spacious garden."[6] By saying that he saw himself in a dream, he marks this as a dream provoked by waking concerns (neither divinely inspired nor enigmatic).[7] A divinely inspired dream (*ostensio*) would have begun with expressions like: "A sweet dream overtook him so deeply did he sleep" (*Poema de mio Cid* v.405) or "a woman appeared before him in a vision" (*Primera crónica general* 195). If it had begun with "in that sleep he was dreaming" (*Amadís de Gaula* 395) it would have signalled an enigmatic dream that required interpretation.[8] The poet-dreamer gives the astrological time saying that the sun is in Scorpio.[9] His dream journey begins in a *locus amoenus* replete with all the usual features—bright sunlight, fragrant blossoms, and birdsong, but a shift of mood is presaged: "I felt like Theseus when he asked Peirithous why he was remaining in Scythia."[10] In a powerful descriptive passage the scene is transformed. Dark clouds, fierce winds, flocks of menacing birds swirl around him; trees are distorted and twisted; the birdsong is raucous; the birds are now snakes. The harp he played in stanza IX has become a dreadful desert serpent that bites the bewildered poet-dreamer (XI–XIII.177–78). The Marqués, aware of the shifting nature of dreams, has the dreamer move on to a pleasanter place where darkness has been replaced by dawn's light and it seems as though the dream has vanished: "Darkness dissipated, dawn appearing, [at the moment] when a dream turns away and flees to its lair."[11] The dreamer, still within the dream, thinks that he has awakened, but the dream continues (XV.179), a not-uncommon phenomenon.[12] In the same way, in the *Razón de amor*, the dreamer thinks he has awakened. He wants to fall asleep but cannot: "I truly wanted to fall asleep but I saw a dove" and then he begins to narrate a new part of his dream, a debate between wine and water that repeats the symbols of his earlier dream (Goldberg 1984; see also Grieve 1986 and Gornall 1987).[13]

Is it a coincidence that a dream in a pleasance or place of delight is interrupted by a poetic debate between the heart and the mind in *Sueño*, just as a debate between wine and water had interrupted a similar idyll in the thirteenth-century *Razón de amor*? Perhaps such an interpolation had become a part of the literary dream tradition. In any event the poet-dreamer in *Sueño* thinks he has awakened and that he overhears his heart and his brain arguing about the meaning of dreams (XV–XXI.179–81). This disputatious segment links the first relatively passive part of the dream with the subsequent active one.[14]

The dreamer-poet, still vaguely disquieted but determined to understand, is swept along in his journey through a strange dreamscape "through a wilderness and untrod lands" (XXIV.187–88.182) until on the eighth day there appeared before him a wise old man, Teresias the Theban seer, who will be the interpreter of the previous parts of the dream. The unhappy dreamer tells him that he was once tranquil and happy and that now he is in the grip of a dream: "I come from a city called Tranquility and flee a cruel dream that holds me captive."[15] He repeats to a companion the onset of his dream ("I was happily reclining on my bed when I saw myself in that dream" IV.25.175; VI.41.175; VIII.57.176). The dream itself has taken on a new reality; the poet-dreamer speaks within the dream of the dream itself as he acts out an awakening scene. He weeps over love's harsh treatment but now his pain comes from his previous dream just as much as it does from love's pangs. Still asleep he needs Teresias's help to understand "the true meaning of the dream that made me succumb exhausted to such thoughts" (XXX.238–40.185). At this turning point, the seer tells him that he cannot avoid love's battle; he must exercise his free will and must seek out Diana to ask her to turn back love's arrows (XXXI–XXXIII.185–86). A. C. Spearing wrote that passive narrators—"involuntary participants" of poetic dreams—"share in a kind of common dream-personality" (Spearing 1976, 44), but our poet is undergoing a transformation from victim to actor.

Having shed some of his passive dream personality, the dreamer no longer thinks of himself as a victim or prisoner of a cruel dream as he sets out in a frenzied search for Diana (XXXV.186–87). She and her host are impressive in their beauty, their strength (XXXVI–XLIX.281–392.187–92). His new spiritual power stemming from his determination to act has also restored his intellect. Prior to this moment in his dream, classical allusions were simple similes; for example, he searched for Diana with the same diligence as had King Agenor for his daughter Europa (XXXV.186–87). Now that he has taken command of his dream persona, he alludes to the events at Troy as material he has read: "I have read of the enemy hosts that came to Troy."[16] He read of Agamemnon (LI.401.193), "of Ulysses and Polidamas and their deeds as described by the poet" (LII.415–16.193), and of Sarpedon (LIII.417.194). No longer the whimpering "involuntary participant," the poet-dreamer confidently assures the reader that he is not stretching the truth nor relying on Homer when he describes the battle: "I will not speak metaphorically, nor will I gloss the tragic story [of Troy]."[17]

The transformed poet-dreamer is now a reporter on a foreign battlefield who gives a vividly dramatic account of the battle scene. Warriors are everywhere; banners are displayed; trumpets sound and an allegorical battle begins. As befits a man of letters in full possession of his powers, his approach to the inexpressibility *topos* is based on specific literary sources. Not in Statius's *Thebais*, nor in tales of Tisiphone (the avenger of murders), nor in accounts of Procne's vengeance for the horrifying abuse of her sister Philomela, had he read of fury equal to Diana's (LXI–LXII.197). After defeat of the advocate of chastity, the newly self-conscious poet-dreamer compares his poor efforts to those of all the great classical authors, saying with false modesty that if this terrible bloodshed could not have been described by them, then "pues ¿cómo podrá mi mano?" (LXXI.568.201). Finally he, too, lies vanquished on the battlefield, and in the *Finida* he is tormented and in chains (LXXII.201–202).

Now let us compare the waking poet of stanza IV with the transformed dreamer in stanza LXXII. The voice in stanza IV had protested that he could not resist the onslaught of love (IV.32.175). The honorably wounded warrior at the end of his dream journey, however unsuccessfully he had resisted, lay on the field of battle: "Wounded in my chest by a fatal blow, and badly injured, I remained disconsolate, near death on the battle field."[18] He has undergone a dramatic change within his dream experience. Before, he had been a powerless victim, but at the end of his journey, his status is of a battle-scarred veteran whose defeat was only accomplished unfairly when "Venus, Jupiter and Juno with one accord came to the aid of the false Cupid."[19] If we think of levels of reality, then, there are three: the external waking reality of a poet in love (or pretending to be), the reality of a poet who writes a protest about his despair, and that of the poet who couches his protest in the form of a dream adventure. It is my contention that his interior transformation is an intimate communiaction that occupies the "space between" the poet author's intention to write of a love affair, and his desire to describe a personal transformation. Thus his dream report is also an account of a spiritual self-recognition.

In the *Infierno de los enamorados* the Marqués once again says that he has been deprived of his free will, carried off by Fortune "totally powerless; so that I had been deprived of my free will."[20] However, this time, he comes to the experience as a sentient, thinking poet. He will report accurately what he sees: "I do not paint [or color the truth] nor do I gloss poet's syllogisms, but rather I follow straight lines, and will not speak fancifully."[21] However, his journey through a terrifying forest populated by wild beasts is sketched in economically. The beasts are so terrible that he will not speak of them: "of whose deformed features / I will not speak at length."[22] At nightfall, sleep overtakes him "So I stayed tired and was overtaken by sleep [or a dream]."[23] His sleep was troubled: "And I slept fitfully until dawn" (XI.206) when his Dantesque adventures began. Although he does not specifically say that he is reporting a dream, the evidence leads us to suspect that his abduction (he was carried off against his will) is a metaphor for sleep or the loss of conscious thought, so that in this poem Santillana's poet-dreamer relates a sequential dream—the first part takes place after his abduction, and continues as he wanders in the forest until he falls asleep, where the second part begins.[24]

Thus, this second sleep at dawn is a dream within a dream and, because it is a morning dream, it has special meaning.[25] The events after he has fallen asleep in the forest are reported much more vividly than the previous ones. While the previous beasts had been too awful to portray, here three colorful graphic stanzas depict the dreadful wild boar that now attacks him (XV–XIX.207–09). His rescuer and guide is Hippolytus, a youthful victim of his stepmother Phaedra's passion (XXXII.249–52.213). Responding to his guide's query, the poet does not present himself this time as a helpless victim, but as a proud Spaniard who in his youth had fallen in love (XXXVII.289–96.215). What is more, he says defiantly that Fortune is badly deceived if she thinks he will acquiesce passively to her will (XXXIX.216). Hippolytus offers to lead him to a truthful assessment of human love. Unhappy but fearful of reproach, he agrees but doubts he will be convinced because he wants to be in love: "I am happy to follow you sir, not leaving off serving Love to whom my service is pledged."[26] After witnessing the torments of the lovers suffering in the Castle of Love, he is chastened by what he has seen and tells the unfortunate Macías (love's martyr by antonomasia): "Your dreadful torment has wounded me incurably" (LXV.519.20). His return from his mysterious journey is sudden and typical of the abrupt way that many dreams are ended or are interrupted by an awakening. "I returned from whence I had come . . . looking for my abductor."[27] The bewildered poet, in the *Finida*, reacts with incommensurate mildness by declaring his intention to shun love because only a madman would not do so: "Thus I will give up all of love's endeavors; nor do I know of anyone who would not do so unless he is a madman" (545–548.227). The *Infierno* strikes me as an account of a less intensely felt experience than the tale of the anguish experienced in the *Sueño*. This dream was an account of a didactic journey, a sort of fact-finding expedition experienced by a seasoned traveler. One might say that the dream metaphor, or the space between signified and signifier, is occcupied by an intention to relate a lesson learned.

In another vein, two of Santillana's *decires narrativos* are accounts of dream visions that are thematically quite different from the *Sueño* and *Infierno*. The shortest of the two, the *Coronaçión de Mossén Jordí*, is a praise of the Valencian poet Jordí de Sant Jordí (d. ca. 1425). Typically, the dream begins at dawn: "And the night's darkness, as if vanquished fled . . . In my sleep a strange sight appeared to me."[28] This is a *visión*, or in Augustinian terms an *ostensio*, a divinely inspired dream. He says that he saw a procession of beautiful warrior-maidens in the service of Venus in a pleasance. They were leading an elephant topped by a castle in which sat a splendidly arrayed golden-haired woman, the goddess Venus.[29] They set a magnificently adorned throne next to a spring (X–XI.73–88.159–60). The dreamer sees three men not dressed royally nor like courtiers but in the garb of Roman consuls. They turn out to be the three great poets of antiquity.[30] Still insisting that he has really seen this apparition, the dreamer goes on to say that he saw a knight preceding them (XIII.97–8.160). The three classical poets (Lucan, Homer, and Virgil) escort their candidate Jordí at a leisurely pace approaching the throne where they will greet Venus (XIV.161). When Venus is ready to speak, silence falls on the company (XV.113–14.161). She invites them to speak and they present their petition that Jordí be granted the laurel crown of poets

(XVI–XX.121–61.161–63). After the award has been made, the four dream apparitions drift away and the dream ends equivocally: "In this manner they left, all four poets . . . the road they took is not told in my source."[31]

In the *Coronación* Santillana has created an idealized magnificent royal court, peopled by beautiful creatures, governed by a gracious and benevolent monarch who welcomes strangers: "In this my flowery realm, where there are only those who serve me; . . . Who are you? Do not fear that you will be treated discourteously by me."[32] The dream celebrates exquisite manners and civility and courtly behavior more than it does the talents of the Valencian poet. We can conclude that the superficial narrative of a dream of a visit to Venus's court seeking laurels for the poet Jordí is supported by a substructure in which the poet-dreamer imagines a gentle gracious literary court in which appropriate honors are bestowed and where the rhythm of life is slow-paced and temperate.[33]

The second nonamatory poem dream vision is the *Comedieta de Ponza*, characterized by Maxim Kerkhof as a patriotic poem written to glorify the Spanish struggle against the Italians and a panegyric dedicated to the Aragonese royal house (Kerkhof 1986, 41). The *Comedieta* portrays the receipt of the news of the loss of a naval battle near the island of Ponza in 1435. The defeat and the imprisonment in Milan of Alfonso V of Aragón and his brothers, Juan of Navarra and Enrique, Maestre of Santiago, permit the poet to treat a topic of profound interest in fifteenth-century Spain, the role of Fortune in human affairs.[34]

For the reader interested in dream lore, the *Comedieta* is a rich source. It is an account of "the dream events of a single night contained in one unshifting look at what took place before his eyes" (Foreman 1974, 110). The poet supplies many circumstantial details common to both real-life and literary dream reports. The time is late autumn: "The fields have lost their color / and have given up their tribute" (III.17–18.241). This poet-dreamer is a self-aware artist, not directly involved in the narrative as he had been in *Sueño* and *Infierno*. He will speak truthfully and accurately. He will rely on that part of the memory that resides in the "çela de la memoria" [third ventricle of the brain,. according to the *Diccionario de las Autoridades*][35] "putting aside the style of poets who pretend with fictitious vain metaphors."[36] The hour is late: "At the hour when wild beasts leave their lairs to feed and when humankind seeks rest."[37] Sleep deprives him of his will, and he hears mournful sounds (IV.29.242). He behaves as though he has awakened as he turns to see the source of the sad sounds: "Thus awakened I looked about to find from whence the sad mourning came."[38] He sees, as in a portrait [*ut pictura poesis*], the queen mother and the wives of the captives. They are first glimpsed, as if posing, holding the shields of their respective households in their left hands— Albuquerque, Navarre, and León-Castile (VI–VIII).[39] The dreamer then sees the poet Boccaccio (similarly prepared for portraiture) wearing a garland of laurel (X.245). The unhappy women interrogate the dead poet; they want to know if it is possible to know the cause of their sorrows (XII.246), how their misery compares to that of others (XIII.246–47). Finally Doña Catalina, the wife of Enrique, is the spokesperson for the poet's concern with the vagaries of Fortuna in a series of stanzas that imitate the Horatian *beatus ille* ode (XV–XVIII.247–49).

A new segment of the dream in the *Comedieta* begins when the queen mother recounts her personal sorrow (XXII–XLII.251–60). Addressing herself to Boccaccio, she prefaces her account of a prophetic dream with a warning that other signs had presaged the dream: "Do not think, poet, that certain signs and dreams about the future misfortune of the royal family had not come to me."[40] She lists the owl's cry and the appearance of Iris, the messenger of sad news (XLIII.260.341–45). These prophetic signs foreshadow in the poem the dramatic moment when her prophetic dream is fulfilled. Santillana's contemporary audience would have been ready to expect her death as she reads the fatal letter. In fact, the dream and its subsequent fulfillment must have circulated as a local legend in the years following her death.

The royal dreamer gives her pre-dream location and activities: in a pleasant grove near a river, she and her attendants were exchanging stories about classical and mythological persons (XLIV–XLVI-II.261–63). Tired, but stimulated by what she has heard, she returned to her palace at night after the stars had appeared in the sky (L.393.264). She retired, giving the location of the dreamer at the onset of the dream (L.396.264). She names her experience: "In my chamber overcome with sleep, I do not know if I should call it a phantasm or a vision."[41] If her dream were a *fantasma* its imagery would not have corresponded to reality, but if a *visión*, then it would have had the authority of *ostensio* or divinely inspired images (See n. 13). She says that her revelation was unheard of and had never even been hinted at in fiction.[42] Her choice of terms shows that the poet wants to say that this is an externally inspired dream. If this were an internally inspired, enigmatic dream that required interpretation, she would have begun her report with a direct statement like: "I dreamt a dream" or merely "I dreamt I was in a boat" (Goldberg 1984, 24). Giving her dream further authority, she says that her dream rivaled those recorded in classical lore related by Macrobius, by Guido de Colonna, and by Valerius Maximus (LI.264–65).

In her dream experience (within the poet-dreamer's account of his own oneiric experience) Doña Leonor, the queen mother, found herself in a small storm-tossed boat. In contrast to classical dream lore, Neptune and his forces did not come to her rescue; the little boat was shattered by wind and waves, and she fell overboard (LIV.432.266). She describes her misery upon awakening at sunrise when her servants opened her bed curtains. As she comes fully awake she is aware of the sound of lamentation in the palace, and a tear-stained member of her retinue presents her with a letter that informs her of the events at Gaeta (LV–LVIII.266–268). Santillana's dramatic account of the time when they brought the news of this great loss ends with Doña Leonor's death upon reading the terrible missive (LXXXIII.281–82).

Santillana's dream that had commenced at night (LV.242) has continued and (still asleep) he dreams that the night has ended at dawn: "Alecto's mother (Earth) was bathed in dawn's light so that visions were clear and none were unclear."[43] The poet plays with the double meaning of *visiones*: "dream-visions" and "sight." Thus does the poetic "I" introduce the final segment of his own dream with an assurance that it is to be believed as a true account. As he had with his depictions of the royal mourners, he presents a dream portrait of the goddess Fortuna (LXXXV–CVI.673–848.282–97). The royal women greet Fortuna respectfully and she addresses a sermon to them (CVII–CVIII.849–64.298–301), and miraculously all four of the royal captives appear (CXIX.303). It is now really dawn when the Marqués awakens in the *Finida*, and his vision has disappeared: "The great princess and her attendants had disappeared before my eyes" (CXX.956–57.304). He is, however, left consoled that such sad events had ended happily.

We are left with the question of the meaning of the dream metaphor in this intricately designed poem.[45] Its uniqueness lies in the delicate way the Marqués moves his poetic "I" through his dream-scape, making the scene changes appear to be almost seamless. The shifts in scene and tone are portrayed just as they might have occurred in a real dream so that the reader comes away feeling as though he has been peering into a magic scene in a splendid Easter egg with a revolving stage. David William Foster writes that Santillana distanced himself from reality by speaking only in the voice of the poet-dreamer: "The resulting point of view is both superior and distant, removed from both the immediate realm of the event, which is only fortuitous- ly 'observed,' and from the audience, which plays no important role in the hermetically sealed world of the vision (Foster 1971, 23).

We ask then, why distance and removal were required for a poetic account of this highly dramatic moment. First we note that the Marqués lets us know in the first stanza that his topic is Fortune's dominant role in human life (I.240). Keeping this declaration of intent in mind, we find our answer in the fact that there were political reasons as well as aesthetic ones for distancing his own voice from this warning about Fortune with its recommendation of Christian sto- icism: "Because those who endure calmly have a laudable victory over Fortune."[46] The murder of Pedro I and the ascent to the throne of Castile of the Trastamaran, Enrique II, had inspired interest in Castile in the topic of the fall of the mighty and the nature of Fortune (Díaz Jimeno 1987, 41). Prudence might have made the poet decide that the topic was best approached indirectly. Furthermore Castile and Aragón were not to be united until 1479 and it might have been politic to couch the praise of the Aragonese royal house in the form of a dream rather than to have spoken more directly.[47]

On the evidence of the four poems studied here we can conclude that the dream vision in the hands of a poet like the Marqués de San- tillana is a more subtle tool than a mere structuring device used to present fanciful material. We have seen that Santillana's decision to convey his thoughts in the form of dream visions was motivated by a desire to make the dream a meaningful connection between the signi- fied and the signifier.

In the *Comedieta* he created a perfectly organized dream universe where the human side of a dramatic historical event was incorporated into his own dream experience. In this sense, it was an account of an interior voyage in which he said in effect: "I saw, I was there" (Gold- berg 1984, 22), but while some authors used the device to create verisimilitude, his intention appears to have been to enhance the poignancy of his narrative. Santillana shows the compassion he feels by describing the grieving women and by portraying vividly the scene where Doña Leonor, awakened by her maids as the sun streams into her bedchamber, is handed the fatal letter. In the course of reporting this emotional moment, he has also used his own experience to evolve a fully developed theory about the vagaries of Fortune and to present it in an aesthetically pleasing form. At the same time he has skirted the danger inherent in speaking about the fall of the mighty.

In the *Coronaçión* the Marqués availed himself of the dream formula to create an idealized court in which poets were received with civility and gentleness and their efforts were given great honor. The surface content of the dream (signifier) is a poetic coronation witnessed by the Marqués; the signified is a comment on the honor due to poets and the dream is the personal intervention of the Marqués in the polemic.[48]

In the two love poems examined in this study the *Sueño* is the next most fully realized dream vision after the *Comedieta*. Santillana's poetic "I" functions on three levels in this complex episodic dream account: he is a poet in love, a poet who dreamt about his struggle against love in the form of a dramatic oneiric adventure, and a poet who came out of the experience a changed man. On the surface it is an account of an interior journey of a dreamer-poet in search of answers in dreams, who along the way questions the reliability of dreams, until he finally finds himself a helpless prisoner of love. The dream metaphor—justified internally when the heart convinces the brain that truth can be found in dreams—is the means by which the author-poet is able to express his helplessness in the face of love.

The *Infierno*, on the other hand, although it begins with an enamored poet and follows his dream journey to that part of hell where lovers are punished, is different because the suffering is witnessed but not experienced directly by the dreamer. His transformation is a cerebral one, and he returns convinced by what he has seen and heard that love is perilous. Here Santillana has used the space between the surface narrative and the meaning to trace an intellectual conversion, not an emotional one.

Finally, previously I have suggested that credibility was the key word in speaking of literary dream reports in medieval Hispanic literature because it was important to both authors and readers that an idealized perception of events be authenticated (Goldberg 1984, 27). However, in the case of the dream vision poems of Iñigo López de Mendoza, Marqués de Santillana, the dream metaphor itself was an essential part of the message.

Notes

I cite the two volume *Poesías completas* of the Marqués de Santillana edited by Manuel Durán. Each verse line is identified first by the stanza number in Roman numerals, the line numbers and the page numbers (e.g. VII.57–9.176). All translations are mine.

1. They differ from wish-fulfillment dreams where a lover imagines he is embracing his love (Palley 1983, 70).

2. In the *Defunssión de don Enrique de Villena* the Marqués does not say explicitly that he dreamed: "Me vi todo solo al pie de un collado" (IV.29.229); in the *Finida* he writes: "Despues del Aurora, el sueño passado / . . . E vime en el lecho tan encontinente. / Como al pie del monte por mi recontado" (177–80.236).

3. One way a dreamer showed that he might have been daydreaming was to say, for example: "Non se sy uelaua nin se sy dormia" (Micer Francisco Imperial, *Cancionero de Baena* No. 226.413). The *Cancionero de Baena* is an anthology, a compilation of poems written by many court poets. See Ira Progoff on daydreams (Progoff 1970, 176–95).

4. "la cruel, inhumana fortuna / ordenó que me siguiese / esta enemiga malvada / amor con gran mesnada" (IV.27–30.175).

5. See *Pharsalia* II.234–38.175.

6. "En aquel sueño me v[í]a . . . en un vergel espacioso" (VIII.57–9.176).

7. A contemporary poet began his dream report with the same convention: "Una noche yo yasiendo / en mi casa a mi sabor / ante my vy un resplandor, . . ." (*Cancionero de Baena* 295.636). For Macrobius this would not have been an enigmatic dream (*somnium*), nor would it have been prophetic (*visio*), nor oracular (*oraculum*) but rather an apparition that comes in the moments between wakefulness and first sleep (*visum*). It would have been caused by the dreamer's daytime thoughts or emotions *ex parte anime*, not by physical stimuli (*ex parte corporibus*) (Macrobius, *Commentary.* Trans. 1952. 87–88). Nor is it externally stimulated because these dreams were events that came to the dreamer: "uinole en uision" (*Primera crónica general* 195).

8. "un sueño l' priso dulce tan bien se adurmió" (*Poema de mio Cid* v. 405) or "uinole en uision quel paraua delante una muger" (*Primera crónica general* 195) or "en aquel dormir soñava" (*Amadís de Gaula* 395).

9. Although this may be an echo of *Pharsalia* I.655–60 where Nigidius Figulus predicted the terrible consequences of battle, Lapesa believes that Santillana used the astrological reference to allude to the sun's daily progress (Lapesa 1957, 121).

10. (IX.69–72.177). His readers would have expected disaster because they would have known that Peirithous had accompanied Theseus when he went to the underworld to rescue Persephone.

11. "Las tinieblas despendidas / e el alva parescía, / quando al [sueño] se de[svía] / e fuye de las manidas" (XIII.97–104.178–79).

12. See for example the double dream of Fernán González who thought he had awakened frightened only to hear the voice of San Millán in the second part of his dream (sts. 409–11). See Goldberg 1983, 26–27 for a discussion of serial dreams.

13. In the debate segment of the dream, Santillana's heart tells his brain that a diligent search will encounter: "la fantasía / lo que por derecha vía / avino en muchos lugares" (XIX.150–52.181). The choice of "fantasía" is

significant according to St. Augustine: *ostensio*—divinely inspired images, *phantasma*—imaginative imagery not corresponding to reality, and *phantasia*—imagery derived from dreamer's memory (Dulaey 1973, 89–93). Hence the poet is signalling that in this part of the dream he is relying on his memory of what he has read. Fray Lope de Barrientos (1382–1469) writes: "La quinta potencia, la cual está e face sus operaciones en la cámara e parte del celebro que está en medio de la cabeza" (Barrientos 1927, 21). He goes on: "E la propiedad e condición desta potencia es nunca estar queda, dormiendo ni velando" (p. 22).

14. Constance B. Hicatt wrote of the frequent use of dream episodes as linking devices (Hieatt 1967, 11).

15. "De la çibdad / parto, . . . la que es yntitulada / por nombre *Tranquilidad*; e fuyo a la crueldad / de un sueño que me conquiere" (XXVII.217–22.184).

16. "De las huestes he le[í]do que sobre Troy venieron" (L.393–94.192).

17. "non metaforo nin gloso / en el trágico tratado;" (LIV.429–30.194). See also *Infierno* III.21–4.203.

18. De mortal golpe llegado / en mi pecho, e mal ferido / en el campo amortecido / yo finqué desconsolado" (LXXII.569–72.201).

19. "Venus, Júpiter e Juno / socorrieron de consuno / al fraudulento Cupido" (LXIX.550–53.200).

20. "fuera de mi poderío; así quel franco alvedrío del todo me fue [privado]" (I.6–8.202).

21 "Que yo non pinto nin gloso / silogismos de [poetas], / mas, siguendo liñas rretas, / fablaré non ynfintoso" (III.21–4.203).

22. "de sus diformes façiones / non relato por estenso" (VI.44–5.204).

23. "así que finqué cansado / del sueño que me vencía" (X.79–80.206); c.f. *La vaquera de la Finojosa* II.6.51. The *Diccionario de la Real Academia* gives "Acto de dormir" as the first definition and the second as "Acto de representarse en la fantasía de uno mientras duerme, sucesos e especies" [Act of representing, in the fantasy of a person who is sleeping, events and emotions]. Speakers rely on context because there is no other common term for *dream*.

24. David W. Foster believes that *Infierno* is presented as an adventure, not an account of a dream (Foster 1971, 57). Nor does he believe that *Sueño* is an extended dream account. For him, only stanzas 6–14 of *Sueño* are an allegorical dream (p. 49). See also Deyermond's opinion that only a fifth of *Sueño* is a dream narration (Deyermond 1989, 82).

25. Fray Lope de Barrientos wrote that morning dreams were especially spiritual because the dreamer was not subject to the physical effects of the digestive process: "viene cerca de la mañana, después de celebrada la digestión, cuando los vapores della están ya delgados e sotiles en tal manera que no empachan tanto a las potencias de facer sus operaciones" (Barrientos 1927, 57). See also Charles Speroni's comments on morning dreams.

26. "Pagado / soy se[ñ]or, de vos [seguir] / non çessando de [servir] / Amor, a quien me soy dado" (XLI.325–28.216).

27. "Bolvime por do veniera / . . . buscando quien me truxiera / en su guarda e compañia;" (LXVII.529–32.227).

28. (IV-IX.157–59). Elaborate ceremonies designed to honor a political or a literary figure were real occurrences, and Lapesa shows that the Marqués took part in such pageants (Lapesa 1957, 147–8).

29. Lucan is the spokesperson: "—: E dixo:—'El grand eloqüente / Homero e el Mantuano / E yo terçero Lucano'" (XXII.174–176).

31. "En tal guisa se partieron / Los poetas todos quatro / . . .; El Camino que siguieron / Non recuenta mi tractado" (XXIV.186–91.164).

32. " En esta floresta mía, / A do non son otras gentes, / Sinon estas mis sirvientes / Que trayo en mi compañia? . . . Non receledes de mí / de alguna descortesía" (XVI.121–28.161).

33. The conflict between arms and letters was a current topic in Juan II's court (1406–54). See P. E. Russell's essay on Spanish humanism.

34. Santillana, who resented the power of D. Alvaro de Luna in the turbulent court of Juan II, wrote celebrating the fall of the royal advisor the *Doctrinal de Privados. Fecho a la muerte del Maestre de Sanctiago, Don Alvaro de Luna, donde se introduçe el autor, fablando en nombre del maestre* and *Otras coplas del dicho señor Marqués sobre el mesmo caso* (1980:157–89).

35. "Dexado el estilo de los que fengían / Metáforas vanas con dulçe loqüela, / Diré lo que priso mi vitima çela" (III.21–23.241–42).

36. Otis Green studied the late medieval and renaissance attitudes toward pagan mythology particularly with respect to the use of the verb "fingir" [to pretend with fiction].

37. "Al tiempo que al pasto salen de guarida / les fieras siluestres, y vmanidad / Descança o reposa" (IV.25—27.242).

38. "Assí recordado, miré do sonaua / el clamoso duelo" (V.33.242).

39. See John Pope-Hennessy's chapter, "Image and Emblem," for the custom of representing subjects with emblems or objects so that portraits could be commemorative (Pope-Hennessy 1979, 205–36). See also my article, "Personal Descriptions in Medieval Texts: Decorative or Functional?" (Goldberg 1986).

40. "non pienses, poeta, que ciertas sinyales / y suenyos aduersos non me demonstraron / los danyos futuros y vinientes males / de la real casa" (XLIII.337–40.260).

41. "El la qual, sobrada del suenyo y vencida, Non sé si la nombre fantasma o visión" (L.397–98).

42. "Me fue demostrada tal reuelaçión / Que nuncha fue vista, ni menos, fengida" (L.399–400.264).

43. "La madre de Aleto las nostras regiones / Dexara ya claras al alua lumbrosa, / Assí que patentes eran las visiones / Y non era alguna que fuesse dudosa."

44. Cf. her portrait in Boccaccio's *De Casibus*, the Spanish translation *La caída de principes*, and Fray Martin de Córdoba's *Compendio de la fortuna*. See Goldberg 1978.

45. Kerkhof bases his observation that the structure of *Comedieta* is like a series of nested boxes on an analysis made by A. J. Foreman (Foreman 1974, 40).

46. "Ca los que pacientes sufren la crueza / Han de la Fortuna loable victoria" (LIX.469–70.269).

47. The Marqués wrote in a letter sent on May 4, 1444, to Violante de Prades that she was the first person to see the poem and that he had begun to write it after the battle of Gaeta (ed. Durán 237–39). Kerkhov dates the letter in 1443 because Juan de Mena, writing early in 1444, had already read *Comedieta* (Kerkhof, ed. 1987.277).

48. In Santillana's *Querella de amor* the poet dreamer cites Macías's words, declaring that the dying poet's voice might have been stilled by death but his words would endure (VII.76–79.142).

References

Amadís de Gaula. Edited by Edwin B. Place. 4 Vols. Madrid: CSIC, I, 1959 y 1971; II 1962; III 1965; IV 1969.

Baena, Juan Alfonso de. *Cancionero de Baena.* Edited by José Maria Azáceta. 3 Vols. Madrid: CSIC, 1966.

Barrientos, Fray Lope de. *Tratado de sueños (Tratado de dormir).* Edited by Fr. Luis G. A. Getino, *Vida y obra de Fray Lope de Barrientos.* Salamanca: *Anales salmantinos*, 1927.1–85.

Deyermond, Alan. "Santillana's Love-Allegories: Structure, Relation, and Message." In *Studies in Honor of Bruce W. Wardropper*, edited by Dian Fox, Harry Sieber, Robert Ter Horst. Newark, DE: Juan de la Cuesta, 1989.75–90.

Diaz, Jimeno Felipe. *Hado y fortuna en la España del siglo XVI.* Madrid: Fundación Universitaria Española, 1987.

Dulaey, Martine. *La rêve dans la vie et la pensée de Saint Augustin.* Paris: Études Augustiniennes, 1973.

Foreman, A. J. "The structure and content of Santillana's *Comedieta de Ponça.*" *Bulletin of Hispanic Studies* 51 (1974). 109–24.

Foster, David William. *The Marqués de Santillana.* New York: Twayne, 1971.

Friedman, Edward H. "Deconstructing the Metaphor: Empty Spaces in Calderonian Drama." *South Central Review* 5 (1988):35–42.

Goldberg, Harriet. "The Dream Report as a Literary Device in Medieval Hispanic Literature." *Hispania* 66 (1983):21–31.

————. "Fifteenth-Century Castilian Versions of Boccaccio's Fortune-Poverty Contest." *Hispania* 61 (1978):472–79.

————. "Personal Descriptions in Medieval Texts: Decorative or Functional?" *Hispanófila* 87 (1986):1–12.

————. "The *Razón de amor* and *Los denuestos del agua y el vino* as a Unified Dream Report." *Kentucky Romance Quarterly* 31 (1984):41–9.

Gornall, John. "Dreaming in traditional lyric." *Corónica* 16 (1987):138–44.

Green, Otis H. "*Fingen los poetas*—Notes on the Spanish Attitude toward Pagan Mythology." In *The Literary Mind of Medieval & Renaissance Spain: Essays by Otis H. Green,* edited by John E. Keller. Lexington: University of Kentucky Press, 1970.113–23. (Rpt. from *Estudios dedicados a Menéndez Pidal.* Madrid, 1950.)

Grieve, Patricia E. "Through the Silver Goblet: A Note on the 'Vaso de plata' in *Razón de amor.*" *Revista de Estudios Hispánicos* 20 (1986):15–20.

Hieatt, Constance B. *The Realism of Dream Visions. The Poetic Exploitation of the Dream-Experience in Chaucer and his Contemporaries.* The Hague: Mouton, 1967.

Horace. *The Odes and Epodes of Horace.* Translated by Joseph P. Clancy. Chicago and London: University of Chicago Press, 1960.

Kerkhof, Maxim P. A. M. Ed. Santillana, Marqués de. *Comedieta de Ponça.* Madrid: Cátedra, 1986.

La gran conquista de Ultramar: Edición crítica. Edited by Louis Cooper. 4 Vols. Bogotá: Instituto de Caro y Cuervo, 1979.

Lapesa, Rafael. *La obra literaria del Marqués de Santillana.* Madrid: Insula, 1957.

Libro del Cauallero Çifar. Edited by Marilyn A. Olsen. *Hispanic Seminary of Medieval Studies* 16. Madison: University of Wisconsin Press, 1984.

Lucan. *Pharsalia. Dramatic Episodes of the Civil Wars.* Translated by Robert Graves. Baltimore: Penguin Books, 1957.

Macrobius. *Commentary on the Dream of Scipio.* Translated by William Harris Stahl. New York: Columbia University Press, 1952.

Marino, Nancy F. "*The Vaquera de la Finojosa*: Was She a Vision?" *Romance Notes* 26 (1986):261–68.

Palley, Julian. *The Ambiguous Mirror: Dreams in Spanish Literature.* Albatros Ediciones 27 Valencia - Chapel Hill: Hispanófila, 1983.

———. "The Love-Dream Lyric in the Spanish Renaissance." *Kentucky Romance Quarterly* 29 (1982):75–83.

———. " 'Si fue mi maestro un sueño:' Segismundo's Dream." *Kentucky Romance Quarterly* 23 (1976):149–62.

Poema de Mio Cid. Edited by Ian Michael. Madrid: Clásicos Castalia, 1973.

Poema de Fernán González. Edited by Alonso Zamora Vicente. Clásicos Castellanos. Madrid: Espasa-Calpe,1963.

Pope-Hennessy, John. *The Portrait in the Renaissance.* Bollingen Series XXXV 12. Princeton: Princeton University Press, 1979.

Priest, John F. "Myth and Dreams in Hebrew Scripture." In *Myth, Dreams and Religion*, edited by Joseph Campbell. New York: Dutton, 1970, 48–67.

Primera crónica general. Edited by Ramón Menéndez Pidal. 2 Vols. Madrid: Gredos, 1955.

Progoff, Ira. "Waking Dreams and Living Myth." In *Myth, Dreams and Religion*, edited by Joseph Campbell. New York: Dutton, 1970, 176–95.

Razón de amor. Edited by Ramón Menéndez Pidal. *Revue Hispanique* 13 (1905):602–18.

Roth, Sheldon. *Psychotherapy: The Art of Wooing Nature.* Northvale, N.J.: Jason Aronson, 1987.

Russell, Peter E. "Las armas contra las letras: para una definción del humanismo español." In *Temas de "La Celestina" y otros estudios.* Letras e Ideas: Maior 14. Barcelona: Ariel, 1978.207–39.

Santillana, Marqués de. *Comedieta de Ponça.* Edited by Maxim P.A.M. Kerhkof. Clásicos castellanos. Madrid: Espasa-Calpe, 1987.

————. *Comedieta de Ponça. Sonetos.* Edited by Maxim P.A.M. Kerhkof. Madrid: Cátedra, 1986.

————. *Poesías completas, I: Serranillas, cantares y decires. Sonetos fechos al itálico modo.* Edited by Manuel Durán. Madrid: Castalia, 1975.

————. *Poesías completas, II: Poemas morales, políticos y religiosos. El proemio e carta..* Edited by Manuel Durán. Madrid: Castalia, 1980.

Spearing, A. C. *Medieval Dream Poetry.* Cambridge: Cambridge University Press, 1976.

Speroni, Charles. "Dante's Prophetic Morning-Dreams." *Studies in Philology* 45 (1948):50–59.

14. Xerxes and Alexander: Dreams of America in Claramonte's *El nuevo rey Gallinato*

Frederick A. de Armas

The Spanish Golden Age shared with classical antiquity and Renaissance Europe a deep concern with oneiric phenomena. The basic division established by Homer and echoed by Virgil, between dreams as insubstantial visions emerging from a "gate of ivory" and dreams as prophecies or revelations from the gods emerging from a "gate of horn," was preserved and refined by Renaissance theorists who, following Artemidorus and Macrobius, transformed this simple division into more complex classifications.[1] The literature of the Spanish Golden Age includes abundant examples of oneiric phenomena, from fictional dream visions utilized to question the dominant ideology to the description of dreams in dramatic works by characters who often wonder if their vision carries a prophetic message.[2] This essay analyzes one of the *comedias* of the period in order to show how the opposition between the two gates is central to the dramatic conflict and how the dream can both support and bring into question ideological contexts.

Andrés de Claramonte's *El nuevo rey Gallinato* was published among a selection of his works by María del Carmen Hernández Valcárcel "in order to show how a mediocre play was able to succeed due to its exotic setting" (Claramonte 1983,115), a judgment that does little to dispel the notion that Claramonte was an ignorant actor/producer whose *comedias* were "built from bits and pieces lifted from the works of others" (Williamsen 1982, 41). Indeed, a recent review of a book by Alfredo Rodríguez López Vázquez, a critic who "has been on a crusade, whose objective it is to add to Andrés de Claramonte's canon some of the most famous Golden Age plays of doubtful authorship" (Ruano de la Haza 1987, 471), uses *El nuevo rey Gallinato* as an example of a work so tasteless[3] that it could not possibly have been written by the same dramatist who composed the canonical *El burlador de Sevilla* (p. 472). If Claramonte is considered as a second- or third-rate playwright, and *El nuevo rey Gallinato* is viewed as one of his least successful *comedias*, why choose this particular play as focus for this study of oneiric phenomena in Golden Age Spanish drama?

　　El nuevo rey Gallinato, although not a rousing *comedia*, is a work that cannot be perceived as tasteless or as a patchwork product. It is an innovative dramatic text that may have helped to trigger the small but significant corpus of seventeenth-century *comedias* dealing with America. Ever since Menéndez Pelayo explained that Lope was the first Golden Age playwright to use this theme (Menéndez Pelayo 1949, 312), critics have listed *El nuevo mundo descubierto por Colón* as the first *comedia nueva* on the New World.[4] Morley and Bruerton posit a date of composition between 1598 and 1603 (Morley and Bruerton 1968, 370), dates that have been corroborated by J. Lemartinel and Charles Minguet in their edition of the play (Lope de Vega Cárpio 1980, xv). *El nuevo rey Gallinato* also belongs to this period. Pointing to a performance in Salamanca on April 29, 1604, Charles Ganelin adds: "In fact, a passing reference to King Philip III and Queen Margarita (married on 18 April, 1599) and to the Court in Madrid (which did not move to Valladolid until January, 1601), suggests that the play was written between April 1599 and January 1601" (Ganelin 1989, 15–16). Consequently, *El nuevo rey Gallinato* not only deserves to be included among the few American plays writ- ten during the Golden Age,[5] but may displace Lope's *El nuevo mundo* as the first *comedia nueva* dealing with the New World.

　　Tzvetan Todorov, who has delved into the "problematics of the exterior and remote other" (Todorov 1984, 3) in his study of the dis- covery and conquest of America, has shown how the European move- ment "to assimilate the other, to do away with an exterior alterity" almost succeeded at a time when Europe found an interior other: "We no longer believe in wild men in the forests, but we have discovered the beast in man. . . . The instauration of the unconscious can be con- sidered as the culminating point of this discovery of the other in one- self" (pp. 247, 249). And this unconscious, as Jung affirms, is most easily accessible through oneiric phenomena since "dreams are the most common and most normal expression of the unconscious psy- che" (Jung 1978, 287).

　　El nuevo rey Gallinato not only deals with the encounter with the remote other, but incorporates oneiric phenomena that conjoin the exterior discovery with an exploration of the inner recesses of the human psyche. There is also a kind of dream-like quality to the *come-*

dia itself, something that should not come as a surprise to the student of Jung, since he discovered "a definite structure . . . not unlike that of drama" (Jung 1978, 294) in the "average" dream. This link between dream and drama was particularly lively during the Spanish Golden Age. Looking at Ortega y Gasset's notion of the "double being" of both the actor and the dreamer, and at Antonin Artaud's vision of theater as a "total operation in which man must resume his place between dreams and events," Jackson A. Cope has demonstrated that both authors developed their "dramaturgical theory" which links dream and theater "in their response to Renaissance drama" (Cope 1973, 7–11). Cope thus discovers during the Renaissance a theater guided by "a deeply subjective dream world in which the psyche overflows to inundate 'form' with its own power, its chaotic anti-form" (p. 11). This critic agrees with Northrop Frye's assessment that Shakespeare's dramas "follow the contours of the myth beneath' (Cope 1973, 12; Frye 1965, 61). Cope's book culminates with a discussion of the dramatic masterpiece of the Spanish Golden Age, Calderón's *La vida es sueño*, which, together with Plato's *Republic*, shows how "In dreams begin responsibility—and its opposite" (Cope 1973, 250). *El nuevo rey Gallinato*, like other Renaissance dramatic texts, will follow the contours of myths and dreams—both being related concepts in Joseph Campbell's theories: "Dream is the personalized myth, myth the depersonalized dream" (Campbell 1956, 19). These *comedias* will thus inundate form with a deeper structure (which Cope refers to as anti-form), the structure of mythic and oneiric phenomena. The freedom granted by these new structures will be reflected in both the desire for liberty within a character and a new form of responsibility that may emerge from the character's confrontation with mythic/oneiric phenomena.

The "statement of place," the first stage of the dream-drama in Jung's scheme, provides the spectators of Claramonte's *comedia* with the sensation that they have entered a realm different from that of everyday life. This sensation may well reflect Cope's concept of anti-form. Musical instruments associated with paganism[6] accompany a song that evokes an alien mythology. The song also describes the wealth and beauty of an Indian princess, Tipolda, who travels to the sea in order to meet her spiritual father, the Sun. The spectator has come face to face with the "remote other" but it appears in such a fantastic manner that the vision comes closer to an interior other, an image of wish-fulfillment in its beauty and opulence. Consequently, the remote other is not accurately represented in historical terms, but takes on the shape of a delightful dream. Among the devices used to eschew historical representation in favor of a more generalized vision is the blending of Americanisms with words that derive from different "others." For example, the American term *xabas* is set to rhyme with *aljabas*, a term of Arabic origin (Claramonte 1983, 180–81). Both are conjoined since they have a similar meaning, bag or container. The Indians' Sun worship also fails to bring specificity to the remote other, since such a ritual is a common feature of many mythologies and, as Morínigo explains, it was the form of worship which the popular imagination related to any form of barbarism (Morínigo 1946, 130).

But perhaps the most striking device used to transform the remote other into an interior other, a dream-like drama lacking the specificity of historical discourse, is the actual statement of place, the information given as to the location of the drama. The *comedia* depicts two kingdoms, Chile and "Cambox," separated by a river (Claramonte 1983, 225). Although the former is obviously an American location, the latter, according to Hernández Valcárcel, is an "imaginary kingdom" (p. 178). In reality, this is the kingdom of Cambodia, which was often labeled as "Camboxa" during the epoch (Tadman 1957, cx, n. 16). This confusion of place, the juxtaposition of an American and an Asian realm, is typical of dreams where remote places are often brought together.

It is to this exotic and dreamlike land that the Spaniards in the play will travel. In separate *relaciones* [reports] the reader/spectator is given information as to the background of the two principal travelers. Their destiny is revealed through astrological references. The first, a woman named María, tells that she was born in Zamora under a malefic horoscope (Claramonte 1983, 186). The second traveler was also born there, but was told that the stars promised him supreme happiness:

> En mis principios primeros
> dijo un astrólogo falso
> que una suprema ventura
> me prometían los astros

[in my early youth / a false astrologer said / that the stars promised me / the highest fortune] (p. 201).

El nuevo rey Gallinato chronicles the fulfillment of these astrological predictions and thus exemplifies the principle of synchronicity, "the parallelism of time and meaning between psychic and psychophysical events" as described by Jung (Jung 1978, 531). This acausal principle, although found in waking state events, is more common in dreams. María's horoscope provides sufficient clues as to the specific nature of her malefic planetary aspect. She explains that the contrary aspects stem from the largest star or planet. In the Ptolemaic system the largest planet, Saturn, was also considered the most malefic. Further proof that Saturn is threatening her is provided in her description of an event that occurred the night she was born: lightning destroyed the clock tower (Claramonte 1983, 186). This event clearly points to the destructive effects of Saturn in his role as Chronos, god of time.

María soon experiences the negative influence of the most malefic of Ptolemaic planets. Wishing to wed Rodrigo Gallinato, she is faced with the parents' opposition based on the poverty of both families. This situation is consonant with a malefic saturnine influence since, as Renaissance philosopher Marsilio Ficino explains, "The astrologers say that Venus and Saturn are enemies of each other" (69). Consequently, the affairs of the planet Venus (love and marriage) are often frustrated by its enemy, Saturn. The synchronicity of events is made even clearer here by reference to poverty, since this is also one of Saturn's qualities.[7] Jerónimo Cortés explains that Saturn "Denota lloros, sospiros, carceles, destruyciones, peregrinaciones y muertes" [denotes tears, sighs, incarceration, destruction, pilgrimages and death] (Hurtado Torres 1984, 33). María's tears and laments are the result of her saturnine horoscope. Although her sadness vanishes briefly as she plans to elope with Rodrigo Gallinato, another disaster evinces once again the relationship between a psychic event, Saturn's influence, and a psychophysical occurrence, her loss of Gallinato. María's hardships now include *peregrinaciones*, since she is forced to marry a friend of Gallinato and together they sail for the New World. In the midst of a saturnine journey, another astral disaster takes place: María is shipwrecked off the coast of Cambox. Her fall into the ocean signals her entrance into the unconscious realm. Dreams of floods and drowning are related by Jung and Edinger to the alchemical *solutio*, a stage where the negative aspects of the ego seem to dissolve in order to bring about a rebirth (Jung 1963, 357; Edinger 1985, 52–3, 58, 68). Off the coast of the New World, María's near-drowning opens the way for her entrance into the American "dream."

While María is involved in the synchronistic disasters of Chronos/Saturn, Rodrigo Gallinato awaits the promise of success embodied in his horoscope. Successive failures lead him to rail against the "astrólogo falso" (Claramonte 1983, 201) who elaborated the prediction of happiness. His dearest wish since early childhood has been to succeed in a martial enterprise:

Fuy ficionado a las armas
desde mis primeros años
y tuve los pensamientos
de Jerjes y de Alejandro

[I was inclined towards the martial arts since my childhood and
my thoughts were like those of Xerxes and Alexander] (p. 202).

In his laments Gallinato is unaware that he will soon succeed.
When the auspicious time arrives, the stars move him swiftly into
place: the admiral of the fleet departing for Peru befriends Gallinato
and invites him to sail to the New World. Once he arrives in Peru,
Gallinato is sent along with a small force to Cambox since the Indians from this Asian/American region have asked for Spanish assistance against Chile. Having arrived in Cambox, the Spanish soldiers
want to return to Peru since their captain, don Juan de Velasco, has
died during the ocean voyage. Accepting the call to adventure, Gallinato harangues the forces and inspires them to land. As a child, Gallinato had thoughts of being like Xerxes and Alexander. Now he can
hope to actualize his fantasies in this fantastic land.

Gallinato's entrance into the American dream/fantasy allows
him to perceive more clearly his own unconscious processes. He hears
voices within his self. They are represented on stage as Faith and
Idolatry, one urging him to fight, the other to return to Spain.
Caught in this debate, he falls asleep. In a dream, Fortune tells him
that he can be a new Alexander (p. 248). Even Alexander appears to
him, further corroborating this possibility. America is thus becoming
the land of wish fulfillment for Gallinato since one of the two heroes
he had chosen as a child to represent martial triumph considers him
as his successor. At the same time, the spectator is left to wonder why
Xerxes is omitted from the dream. There are at least two reasons for
the oneiric selectivity. The first is that Alexander represents the successful conqueror, while Xerxes's image is ambivalent since he failed
in his conquest of Greece. The second has to do with the opposition
between prophetic and fantastic visions, dreams emerging from gates
of ivory or of horn. Alexander often had oracular or prophetic
dreams, so his presence in Gallinato's vision lends it authority. Xerxes,
on the other hand, has been used as the foremost example in antiquity of the danger of following a dream's counsel.

The discussion of Xerxes's problematic dreams appears in the
seventh book of Herodotus's *Histories*. After reversing his decision
and calling off the invasion of Greece, Xerxes went to sleep and
dreamt that: "the figure of a man, tall and of noble aspect, stood by

his bed. 'Lord of Persia,' the phantom said, 'have you changed your mind and decided not to lead an army against Greece in spite of your proclamation to your subjects that troops should be raised? You are wrong to change; and there is one here who will not forgive you for doing so'" (Herodotus 1954, 421). Paying no attention to the dream, Xerxes reasserts that there will be no war with Greece. But the following night the phantom appears to him again as he sleeps and warns him that if he does not undertake the war "just as in a moment you rose to greatness and power, so in a moment will you be brought low again." Disturbed by the recurring vision, Xerxes calls on Artabanus, the chief opponent of war with Greece, and relates what has transpired. Artabanus responds: "but dreams do not come from God . . . nearly always these drifting phantoms are the shadows of what we have been thinking during the day" (Herodotus 1954, 423). Artabanus is here defining the dream in terms of one of Macrobius's five types of oneiric phenomena, the nightmare, "caused by mental or physical distress, or anxiety about the future" (Macrobius 1952, 88). This type has no prophetic content. Such dreams are very different from what Macrobius labels the "oracular" and "prophetic"[8] in which "a parent, or a pious or revered man, or a priest, or even a god clearly reveals what will or will not transpire and what action to take or to avoid" (Macrobius 1952, 90).[9] The presence of a figure of authority in Xerxes's dream prompts Artabanus to add cautiously that "perhaps there is, indeed, something divine in it" (Herodotus 1954, 423).

How then can the two types of dreams be separated? Artabanus suggests that if Xerxes's dream is more than just a fantasy, that if it is indeed of divine origin, then the god or supernatural messenger should also appear to him. In order to decide if the king's dream was caused by distress or anxiety or whether it was prophetic, Artabanus changes places with the king. Wearing Xerxes's clothes and sleeping in his bed, Artabanus dreams of the same enigmatic figure that had appeared to the king. This phantom threatens Artabanus in the dream saying: "You will not escape unpunished, either now or hereafter, for seeking to turn aside the course of destiny" (Herodotus 1954, 423–4). Artabanus then accepts the dreams he and the king had experienced as oracular and expects them to be prophetic, signifying the triumph of Persia over Greece. He thus urges Xerxes to go to war. Instead of the expected triumph, however, disaster ensues at the naval battle of Salamis. This outcome brings into question the vision's reliability[10] and tends to place it in the realm of the nightmare. But, the dream had been oracular in that a noble person appeared delivering a message. It was also tested through recurrence and through a second dreamer. Consequently, it should be an oracular dream and not a nightmare. If the criteria are considered valid, why did the phantasm or god send Xerxes into disaster?

These questions seem to have no bearing on Gallinato, since the dream discussed above includes only one of the two martial figures he revered in his youth, one whose dreams were oracular (Lewis 1976, 111). There is, however, a second dream in *El nuevo rey Gallinato*, one that contrasts with Gallinato's oracular and prophetic vision. Polipolo, king of Chile, relates his dream as follows:

> Anoche empecé a dormir
> y llegándose a mi cama
> mi nombre empezó a decir;
> dije en sueños: "¿Quién me llama?"
> "Quién te viene a destruir,
> dijo, Ongol me llamo y sólo
> soy yo dios en cuanto mira
> el sol de un polo a otro polo;
> Guacol contra ti se aíra,
> huye, triste Polipolo;
> porque a Tipolda pediste
> te ha de destruir feroz"

> [Last night, as I fell asleep, he came to my bed and called out my name. I said in my sleep: "Who is calling me?" "He who comes to destroy you," he said. "My name is Ongol and I am god when the sun shines from pole to pole. Guacol is angry at you. Flee, miserable Polipolo! Since you asked for Tipolda's hand, the fierce god will destroy you"] (Claramonte 1983, 218–19).

Polipolo's dream is presided over by a being that commands as much authority as the figures in Gallinato's dream. For here we have a god named Ongol, the deity revered by the inhabitants of Cambox. Ongol shows himself to his enemy, telling him to flee, since Guacol, king of Cambox, is angry and wishes to destroy him. Like Xerxes, Polipolo "tests" his dream. He finds proof of its reliability in that some of his soldiers claim to have seen Ongol descending from the heavens and threatening them with thunderbolts (p. 218). Polipolo's response to this "reliable" oracular dream is to ready his own army to attack Cambox before he is attacked. Although Polipolo believes in the oracular nature of his dream and reacts accordingly to its contents, the audience knows the contents are false. Guacol is not angry with

Polipolo for having asked for his daughter in marriage. The Cambodians are not readying to attack Chile. The test of reliability is also false, since the audience is aware that the soldiers encountered not Ongol, but Spaniards wielding firearms. Polipolo engages in war because of false information received in a dream. This response proves as disastrous as Xerxes's decision to wage war on the Greeks based on his oneiric experiences. Xerxes's absence from Gallinato's dream connotes his presence in the other dream described in the play, the one that seems unreliable.

Most critics who have studied Xerxes's dreams in Herodotus see in them the workings of history or fate. Henry Wood, for example, explains that: "The appearance of the dream-vision . . . is a symbol of the situation itself, revealed as an internal necessity of historical dynamics" (Wood 1972, 152); while Stewart Flory asserts: "Xerxes . . . is a prisoner of fate" (Flory 1987, 76). It seems, then, that the dreams in Herodotus are "oracular" in that they are divine instruments that help to bring about the fated outcome. Xerxes is forced by oracular dreams to wage war, even though such an enterprise will end in failure.[11] The Persian king's struggle with fate creates a tragic dimension, foregrounded by Aeschylus in his drama *The Persians*. Polipolo also follows his dream into a tragic war,[12] although there are differences. In Herodotus, the phantom never actually lies to Xerxes, never really promises him success. He only commands him to fight. In *El nuevo rey Gallinato*, Ongol lies to Polipolo, inventing a Cambodian menace. Rather than urging Polipolo to battle, the deity tells him to flee, knowing full well that the Chileans are a warlike group and that threats of war can only incite them to fight. While Xerxes obeys the dream, Polipolo seems to be going against the oracular vision. The Chilean king's bravery will make his failure particularly tragic.

As in Herodotus's *Histories*, the initial battles in the *comedia* are won by those who had the dream. Xerxes and Polipolo easily overwhelm their foes. In *El nuevo rey Gallinato* the reversal comes as María intervenes in the battle. This is the *peripeteia* or third phase of the dream-drama that according to Jung follows the second phase or development of plot. In this third stage, "something decisive happens or something changes completely" (Jung 1978, 295). The unfortunate María, having survived the shipwreck and the other disasters inflicted by a malefic Saturn, emerges from the waters at the moment when Princess Tipolda searches for her sun god. María is thus taken as a solar deity by the Cambodians (Claramonte 1983, 184). Their splendid treatment of her and her developing friendship with Tipolda lead María to support the Cambodians in battle against Chile. As she saves the Cambodians from defeat and charges against Polipolo's armies, the Spanish woman becomes an image of death. The enemy king describes her this way: "La muerte a espantarme viene / . . . Yo la vi / con flechas, con arco y pieles" [Death comes to terrify me . . . I saw her with bow and arrow, dressed in skins] (p. 238).

Having experienced drowning, a symbolic entrance into the unconscious realm (the dream of America), María in her *peripeteia* sheds her accidental aspects and assumes a more essential nature. As a being who encompasses the destiny of Saturn, María becomes identified with this astrological god. Although the Cambodians thought of her as the sun god, she has turned out to be a black sun, the planet that actually stands in opposition to the luminary due to its cold nature, alien to physical growth and life.[13] Saturn is not only the god of time, but also the god of death: Albertus Magnus shows him carrying a sickle (Albertus Magnus 1973, 65) and the planet is often seen as the "cause of hasty death" (Heneinger [c. 1585] 1979, 162). Through her journey into the unconscious, María has actualized her worst fears and transcended them through acceptance. She has become the deathlike Saturn she once dreaded. Explaining the positive power of the seventh Ptolemaic planet, Jungian analyst Liz Greene states: "Human beings do not earn free will except through self-discovery, and they do not attempt self-discovery until things become so painful that they have no other choice" (Greene 1976, 11). María's pain has led her to discover that death is an aspect of her own self. Freed of her fear and anxieties she can now use this destructive and redemptive power to save those who helped her when she was in need, the Cambodians.

But the Cambodians know that one "deity" is not enough to save them from the bellicose Chileans. Their embassy to Peru having proved successful, they are now aided by Gallinato and his troops, whom they refer as "dioses u hombres" [gods or men] who "traéis vuestra descendencia / y vuestro orígen del cielo" [are descended and originate in the heavens] (Claramonte 1983, 222). Polipolo, who once confronted María in battle and labeled her as death, now faces Gallinato, exclaiming "Rendido estoy, por el Sol" [I am defeated by the Sun] (p. 263). If María is the *sol niger* (Saturn, planet of death), then Gallinato is the opposing astrological body, the sun. The Spanish hero has become that which he always dreamed of being, a new Alexander, a solar hero who triumphs against a mighty host—two hundred Spaniards are enough to defeat thousands of valiant Chilean troops. In this wish-fulfillment dream, a poor soldier not only achieves a great conquest but is also offered the crown of Cambodia and the hand of the Princess Tipolda. Gallinato's fate is more exalted than that of the ideal knight in the chivalric romances. While a figure such as Amadís can gain a kingdom and marry a princess, he does so as a man of royal lineage,[14] whereas Gallinato is a poor soldier. Marcos Morínigo has argued that one of the reasons for the scarcity of plays dealing with America during the Golden Age is the "insuficiente prestigio heróico de la conquista" [insufficient heroic prestige of the conquest] (Morínigo 1946, 18). In this early play Claramonte has avoided such pitfalls by creating a fantastic hero whose astonishing conquest and successes reveal the American venture as a wish-fulfillment dream. Like Alexander, Gallinato has become master of more than one continent, having conquered Chile (America) and Cambodia (Asia). His oracular dream has proven to be prophetic.

Indeed, dreams tend to come true in the New World, since America as a remote other has been transformed in this *comedia* into an interior other, a land of dreams where characters often wonder if what they are seeing is a vision. María, coming face to face with Gallinato, asks: "¿Es sueño, fantasma o sombra?" [Are you a dream, a ghost or a shadow?] (Claramonte 1983, 254). In this land, unconscious structures and fears surface. In clear synchronicity, María's key astrological aspect materializes. She becomes an icon of the deity that persecutes her. As the planet of death and disaster, she is far removed from the realm of Venus. She can frighten an army into flight, but when she attempts to rekindle Gallinato's love, he teaches her duty, a saturnine trait, telling her to search for her husband, Oña.

Although the Spaniards' dreams and desires or fears come true in the New World, the original inhabitants of the land are caught in a dream that is leading them to oblivion, to the deepest recesses of the unconscious. Polipolo's dream of conquest, his reaction to an oracular vision, leads him to experience disaster at the hands of a less powerful nation, imitating Xerxes's fate at the hands of the Greeks. But while Xerxes's oracular dreams simply ordered him to fulfill his destiny, Polipolo's vision provides him with erroneous information. It may be that pagan gods, at the hands of a Christian writer, are shown as mendacious. After all, in Dante's *La Divina commedia*, Virgil talks about having lived "nel tempo de li dei falsi e bugiardi" [in the time of the false and lying gods] (Dante Aligheri 1972, I.72). Even the Greek philosophers objected to the lies of their own gods.[15] The parallels between Polipolo and Xerxes, although based on the lies of the gods or divine emissaries, seem to point to the necessity of lying in the fulfillment of destiny. Just as Xerxes must attack Greece and be defeated, the Chilean king must attack Cambodia so that this Asian kingdom can request Spanish assistance, thus opening the way for the conquest, and for the fulfillment of the Spanish dream in America. Such a triumph leads to the colonization, assimilation, and subjection of the remote other.[16] Perhaps the mendacious nature of Polipolo's dream shows not the inferiority of the pagan gods, but the duplicitous nature of the Spaniards who conquer with lies. After all, Oña disguises himself as a pagan god and uses his firearm to mimic the thunderbolt in order to manipulate the natives. The Spaniards are not gods, but humans who utilize a more complex technology and are adept at false communication. They are not the chivalric heroes they think they are, but a conquering people who desire the riches of the remote other, their *codicia* [greed] being noticed even by Princess Tipolda (Claramonte 1983, 277).

According to Jung, dreams often characterize the life of a hero and dramatize his alchemical transformation into a greater man (Jung 1978, 293). In spite of Gallinato's heroic and magnanimous deeds, the metal that is sought in this *comedia* is more often physical gold. The philosopher's stone emerges from the integration of all aspects into a greater whole, but the *lysis* or solution (Jung 1978, 244) of the dream/drama of *El nuevo rey Gallinato* has not fulfilled its compensating function since aspects "which in conscious life are too little valued" (Jung 1978, 244) remain marginalized. In spite of marrying Tipolda, Gallinato sees the remote other's culture as inferior. His is not a marriage of equality, but of colonization: Tipolda must convert to Christianity while the Indians must accept King Philip of Spain as their overlord, and must become the "subject producer of objects" (Todorov 1984, 176). This contrasts with the expected conclusion of an alchemical drama where marriage is viewed as a *coniunctio*, or bringing together of opposites, to create what Jungian analyst Edward Edinger defines as a wholeness based on "transpersonal love" devoid of "personal desirousness" (Edinger 1985, 223). Although Gallinato protests that he is conquering and marrying for God and country, he is in reality guilty of personal desirousness, and thus fails to achieve wholeness through marriage. One key element in the final *coniunctio* is the image of a wedding between heaven and earth. In *El nuevo rey Gallinato*, Tipolda is "parienta del Sol" [a relative of the Sun] (Claramonte 1983, 278), and thus represents the heavenly aspects of the marriage. But Gallinato subverts the *coniunctio* by considering her as a lesser creature to be colonized. Thus the wedding, instead of representing the alchemical *coincidentia oppositorum* as in other dramas such as Calderón's *La vida es sueño* (de Armas 1992, "King's Son"), portrays a failed experiment and the consequences of colonization.

By insisting on closure through the acceptance of the dominant ideology and the consequent rejection of the worth of the remote other, the ending of the *comedia* subverts the oneiric experience of the New World. However, this experience can be recaptured by foregrounding Polipolo's dream. Its content clashes with the ideological conclusion of the drama, not only revealing the lies of the conquerors, but also showing the tragic failure of an ancient culture that, like the Persian empire, was considered by Europeans as a barbarian other that must be colonized.[17] While Alexander's dream of glory is represented in Gallinato's wish-fulfillment dream, Xerxes's tragic destiny as gleaned through Polipolo's vision lends the defeated peoples a tragic mantle that transcends disaster. Having lost the golden sun to the Spaniards, they must accept María's *sol niger* as their future god'.[18] Claramonte's *El nuevo rey Gallinato* is a compelling adaptation of the chivalric spirit and of the epic and tragic clashes between the Greeks and the Barbarians to the landscape of a New World. But in this American dream the success of the solar hero who rises from poor soldier to king serves to eclipse the "other" until a time when, as Todorov envisions, the world learns to "experience difference in equality" (Todorov 1984, 249).

Notes

1. Macrobius divided dreams into five types: the enigmatic dream, the prophetic vision, the oracular dream, the nightmare and the apparition. While the first three corresponded to the "Gate of Horn," the last two had no prophetic significance (Macrobius 1952, 87–88). For a survey of dream classifications see Lewis and Palley. For an overview of Renaissance writings on dreams see Schreier Rupprecht.

2. Miguel Avilés has studied and edited three Golden Age dream-visions: Juan Maldonado's *Sueño* (1532), the anonymous *Sueño de la ciudad en ruinas* (1588) and Melchor de Fonseca y Almeida's *Sueño político* showing how they reflect a "counter-ideology" (Avilés 1981, 48). As for the drama of the Golden Age, the best known example of a prophetic dream occurs in Lope de Vega's *El caballero de Olmedo* discussed by Hall, McCrary, and Palley among others. The dreams in Calderón's *La vida es sueño* are both prophetic and political (de Armas 1986).

3. "But the reader's reluctance to accept Professor Rodríguez's thesis has as much to do with the status of Claramonte as a second-rate or third-rate dramatist (a dramatist who could write in *El nuevo rey Gallinato* the lines "Sal, sal sol hermoso / sal divino Sol" [Come out, come out, beautiful Sun, / come out divine Sun], a veritable nightmare for an actor with a lisp, can

hardly be considered a serious contender for the authorship of *El burlador*). . . . (Ruano de la Haza 1987,472).

4. It was preceded in the sixteenth century by the *Auto de las cortes de la muerte* by Michael the Carvajal and Luis Hurtado. Scene nineteen shows a group of American Indians who come to the tribunal of death to complain of their treatment at the hands of the Spaniards. For a discussion of the *auto* see Morínigo 1946, 42–7; Ruiz Ramón 1988, 72–82; and Shannon 1989, 1–4.

5. The three major dramatists of the Golden Age wrote a total of seven *comedias* on the subject, three by Lope de Vega (*El nuevo mundo, Arauco domado* and *El Brasil Restituído*), three by Tirso de Molina (the *Pizarro* trilogy), and one by Calderón (*La aurora en Copacabana*). Ruiz de Alarcón, in spite of his Mexican upbringing, wrote only one play concerning the New World (*Las hazañas del Marqués de Cañete*). Eight other plays by lesser known dramatists complete the list of sixteen *comedias* on American themes written during the late sixteenth and seventeenth centuries. *El nuevo rey Gallinato* must be added to this list.

6. "Salen los indios con guirnalda, sonajas y panderetes" [The indians emerge with garlands, timbrels and tambourines] (Claramonte 1983, 178). Covarrubias writes: "Los egypcios usavan destas sonajas en las fiestas y sacrificios que hazán a la diosa Isis" [The Egyptians used these timbrels in the feasts and sacrifices dedicated to the goddess Isis] (Covarrubias 1943, 944).

7. Jerónimo Cortés attributes to the planet "carestías en los mantenimientos" (Hurtado Torres 1984, 33). For a description of Saturn's qualities and how they are reflected in Calderón's *comedias* see de Armas 1987, 1981. On Saturn in Claramonte see de Armas 1990.

8. "We call a dream a prophetic vision if it actually comes true" (Macrobius 1952, 90).

9. Artabanus's explanation also corresponds to the "moral cause" listed by Ciruelo in his threefold classification of dreams where images appear "por la mucha atención que de día ponen en las cosas en que se ocupan" [for the continued attention given to things that occupy a person during the day] (Ciruelo 1979, 65). But Ciruelo adds that the dreamer should pay attention even to these dreams since "algunas vezes en sueños aciertan mejor en ver lo que deuen de hazer" [sometimes in dreams they are better able to perceive how they should act] (p. 65). This type of dream is very different from the "causa theologal" where dreams are "reuelacion de dios, o de algun angel bueno, o malo" [revelation from a god, a good angel or a bad one] (p. 65).

10. Macrobius states that oracular, prophetic, and enigmatic dreams are "reliable" (Macrobius 1952, 90).

11. Some argue that Xerxes could have gone against the fated war and that his failure shows him as a weak king: "Paradoxically, the central incident shows the King weakly struggling against the fate of Empire; it was 'in him' to postpone disaster, and he did not" (Myers 1953, 217–18).

12. Although Xerxes's dreams never provided him with false information, Polipolo's vision is mendacious. The god Ongol would have known the

bellicose nature of the Chileans and should have expected Polipolo's warlike response. It could be argued then that Ongol provided Polipolo with false information in order to have him engage in a disastrous war. And yet, such an explanation does not hold up since Ongol would have known that his Cambodians were weaker than Polipolo's Chileans. In order to win, the Cambodians have to call on the Spaniards and are eventually colonized by them. Ongol, then, brings about his people's downfall. Rather than seeing the vision as one of a specific deity, it should be viewed very much like Xerxes's dreams as the imposition of transnational fate.

13. The relationship between Saturn and the sun goes as far back as Babylonian astrology, according to Raymond Klibansky *et al.* (Klibansky, Panofsky, and Saxl 1972, 136). A. Bouché-Leclerq comments: "Peut-etre les Chaldéens se représentaient-ils Saturne comme un soleil, vieilli, refroidi, ralenti" [Perhaps the Chaldeans conceived of Saturn as an old, cold, and slow sun] (Bouché-Leclerq [1899] 1979, 93).

14. "The protagonist of a romance of chivalry is always male and invariably of royal blood" (Eisenberg 1982, 56).

15. One of the aims of censorship in Plato's *Republic* is to eliminate any passages in literary texts where gods "mislead us by lies" (Plato 1974, 53). In this context, Socrates states: "We praise many things in Homer, but we will not approve of the dream which Zeus sent to Agamemnon" (p. 53). In Book Two of the *Iliad*, Zeus promises success to Agamemnon if he attacks Troy immediately. This dream, much like Polipolo's vision, tells an untruth.

16. When Gallinato marries Princess Tipolda he is allowed by Guacan to transform the customs of the court and introduce Spanish structures (Claramonte 1983, 281).

17. Todorov has shown how the Indians were incapable of telling lies and thus were unable to comprehend the Spaniard's duplicitous speech (Todorov 1984, 89–91). Todorov also discusses the colonialist ideology where the goal "is still the submission of these lands to the crown of Spain" (p. 174).

18. "He [Saturn] is also a symbol of the psychic process, natural to all human beings, by which an individual may utilise the experiences of pain, restriction, and discipline as a means for greater consciousness and fulfillment" (Greene 1976, 10).

References

Albertus Magnus. *The Book of Secrets of Albertus Magnus of the Virtues of Herbs, Stones and Certain Beasts.* Edited by Michael R. Best and Frank H. Brightman. Oxford: Oxford University Press, 1973.

Avilés, Miguel. *Sueños ficticios y lucha ideológica en el Siglo de Oro.* Madrid: Editora Nacional, 1981.

Bouché-Leclerq, A. *L'astrologie grecque*. 1899. Reprint. Chicago: Bolchazy-Carducci, 1979.

Campbell, Joseph. *Hero with a Thousand Faces*. New York: Meridian Books, 1956.

Ciruelo, Pedro. *Reprouacion de las supersticiones y hechizerias*. Edited by Alva V. Ebersole. Valencia: Albatros-Hispanófila, 1979.

Claramonte, Andrés de. *Comedias*. Edited by María del Carmen Hernández Valcárcel. Murcia: Academia Alfonso X el Sabio, 1983.

Cope, Jackson I. *The Theater and the Dream. From Metaphor to Form in Renaissance Drama*. Baltimore: Johns Hopkins University Press, 1973.

Covarrubias, Sebastián de. *Tesoro de la lengua castellana o española*. Edited by Martín de Riquer. Barcelona: Horta, 1943.

Dante Alighieri, *La Divina commedia*. Edited and annotated by C. H. Grandgent and Charles S. Singleton. Cambridge: Harvard University Press, 1972.

de Armas, Frederick A. "Claramonte's New World: Representing the Other in *El nuevo rey Gallinato*." In *Acta of the XVIII F.I.L.L.M Congress*. Novi Sad, Yugoslavia (in press).

———. "Icons of Saturn: Astrologer-Kings in Calderón's *Comedias*." *Forum for Modern Language Studies* 23 (1987): 117–30.

———. "The King's Son and the Morning Dew: Alchemy in Calderón's *La vida es sueño*." *Hispanic Review* (in press).

———. "Saturn and the Enchantress: Lope's *La desdichada Estefanía* and Claramonte's *La infelice Dorotea*." *Romance Languages Annual* 1 (1990): 1417–23.

———. "The Saturn Factor: Examples of Astrological Imagery in Lope de Vega's Works." In *Studies in Honor of Everett W. Hesse*, edited by William C. McCrary and José A. Madrigal. Lincoln, Nebraska: Society of Spanish and Spanish-American Studies, 1981.

————. *The Return of Astraea. An Astral-Imperial Myth in Calderón.* Lexington: University Press of Kentucky, 1986.

Edinger, Edward F. *Anatomy of the Psyche.* La Salle, Illinois: Open Court, 1985.

Eisenberg, Daniel. *Romances of Chivalry in the Spanish Golden Age.* Newark, Delaware: Juan de la Cuesta, 1982.

Flory, Stewart. *The Archaic Smile of Herodotus.* Detroit: Wayne State University Press, 1987.

Frye, Northrop. *A Natural Perspective: The Development of Shakesperean Comedy and Romance.* Princeton: Princeton University Press, 1965.

Ganelin, Charles, ed. Andrés de Claramonte, *La infelice Dorotea.* London: Tamesis, 1989.

Greene, Liz. *Saturn. A New Look at an Old Devil.* York Beach, Maine: Samuel Weiser, 1976.

Hall, H. Gaston. "Observation and Symbolism in Lope's *El caballero de Olmedo.*" *Modern Language Review* 80 (1985): 62–79.

Herodotus. *The Histories.* Translated by Aubrey de Sélincourt. Baltimore: Penguin Books, 1954.

Hurtado Torres, Antonio. *La astrología en la literatura del Siglo de Oro.* Alicante Instituto de Estudios Alicantinos, 1984.

Jung, C. G. "On the Nature of Dreams." In *The Structure and Dynamics of the Psyche.* Corr. 2nd ed., translated by R. F. C. Hull. Princeton: Princeton University Press, 1978, 281–97.

————. *Mysterium Coniunctionis*. Translated by R. F. C. Hull. Princeton: Princeton University Press, 1963.

Heneinger, S. K., ed. *The Kalender of Sheepehards (c. 1585)*. Delmar, New York: Scholar's Facsimilies, 1979.

Klibansky, Raymond, Edwin Panofsky, and Fritz Saxl. *Saturn and Melancholy*. London: Thomas Nelson, 1972.

Lewis, Naphtali. *The Interpretation of Dreams and Portents*. Toronto: Samuel Stevens Hakkerst and Co., 1976.

Lope de Vega Cárpio, Félix. *El nuevo mundo descubierto Dor Colón*. Edited by J. Lemartinel and Charles Minguet. Lille: Presses Universitaires de Lille, 1980.

Macrobius. *Commentary on the Dream of Scipio*. Edited and translated by William Harris Stahl. New York: Columbia University Press, 1952.

McCrary, William C. *The Goldfinch and the Hawk. A Study of Lope de Vega's Tragedy "El Caballero de Olmedo."* Vol. 62, University of North Carolina Studies in the Romance Languages and Literatures, Chapel Hill: University of North Carolina Press, 1966.

Menéndez Pelayo, Marcelino. *Obras completas. Estudios sobre el teatro de Lope de Vega*. Vol. 33. Edited by Enrique Sánchez Reyes. Santander: Aldus, 1949.

Morely, S. Griswold and Courtney Bruerton. *Cronología de las comedias de Lope de Vega*. Madrid: Gredos, 1968.

Morínigo, Marcos A. *América en el teatro de Lope de Vega*. Buenos Aires: Instituto de Filologia, 1946.

Myers, John L. *Herodotus. Father of History*. Oxford: Clarendon Press, 1953.

Palley, Julian. *The Ambiguous Mirror. Dreams in Spanish Literature*. Chapel Hill: Hispanófila, 1983.

Plato, *The Republic*. Translated by G. M. A. Grube. Indianapolis: Hackett Publishing Company, 1974.

Ruano de la Haza, José. Review of Alfredo Rodríguez López Vázquez's *Andrés de Claramonte y "El Burlador de Sevilla"* and *El Burlador de Sevilla. Atribuído tradicionalmente a Tirso de Molina*. In *Modern Language Review* 85 (1990): 471–73.

Ruiz Ramón, Francisco. *Celebración y catarsis (Leer el teatro español)*. Murcia: Universidad de Murcia, 1988.

Rupprecht, Carol Schreier. "Our Acknowledged Ancestors: Dream Theorists of Antiquity, the Middle Ages, and the Renaissance." *Psychiatric Journal of the University of Ottawa* 15 (1990): 117–22.

Shannon, Robert M. *Visions of the New World in the Drama of Lope de Vega*. New York: Peter Lang, 1989.

Tadman, B. J. *"Juan Juarez Gallinato*: An Edition of *El nuevo rey Gallinato y bentura por desgracia* by Claramonte from the Unpublished Ms. 15.319 in the Biblioteca Nacional with a Study of the Historical and Literary Background of the Theme." Master's thesis, University of London, May, 1957.

Todorov, Tzvetan. *The Conquest of America*. [1982] Translated by Richard Howard. New York: Harper and Row, 1984.

Williamsen, Vern. *The Minor Dramatists of Seventeenth-Century Spain*. Boston: Twayne, 1982.

Wood, Henry. *The Histories of Herodotus. An Analysis of the Formal Structure*. The Hague: Mouton, 1972.

15. Variations of the Prophetic Dream in Modern Russian Literature

C. Nicholas Lee

Russian literature came of age in the era of romanticism at the beginning of the nineteenth century, and thus reflected the romantic interest in a variety of paranormal perceptual phenomena, among which the dream played a prominent part. The most eloquent spokesman for the dream as the theater of heightened perceptions was Fyodor Tyutchev (1803–1873), who developed his own oneiric metaphysics, where the dream served as a bridge between the ordered surface of waking life and the chaos of nocturnal existence.

The dream is explicitly prophetic in *The Vision* (1829):

> There is an hour at night full of an awesome wonder
> When universal silence o'er the cosmos lies
> And when life's chariot rolls, wakening no thunder,
> Into the sanctuary of the skies.
>
> The dark of chaos comes, land, sky and water merging;
> Sleep Atlas-like treads earth, its weight like lead;
> The gods with dreams prophetic fire the virgin
> Soul of the Muse; all else is dead.[1]

The mythological and pantheistic, the individual and the cosmos, chaos and sleep, juxtaposed in a variety of configurations, inform a cycle of poems where dreams open the way to poetic inspiration and mystical transport in a loose thematic framework "partly romantic, partly classical, and uniquely Tjutčevian."[2] The romantic component derives from Tyutchev's interest in Schelling's notions of *Urgrund*, the source of all; the sometimes frightening and sometimes benevolent

Abgrund, to which all returns; and the *Ungrund*, in which all distinctions disappear (Pratt 1983, 104).

The persona in Tyutchev's metaphysical poetry almost always yields passively to external manifestations of nature in a state of *samozabven'je*, a liberation from self-consciousness that leads to Schellingian awareness of a universe in which what appears to be chaotic is really a part of the sublime order of nature (Pratt 1983, 105). This *samozabven'je* is typically associated with a dreamlike state in the persona, in nature, or in both. This romantic vision has a pantheistic component in the way it breaks down the barrier erected by the conscious intervention of reason between the individual and the cosmos: "man experiences a sense of unreality like that of dreams or visions, a sense of being lost in his own self, and the final revelation that he has returned to his original source—the essence of his own soul" (Pratt 1983, 70–71).

The classicism of Tyutchev's imagery and style in the dream poems reinforces his romantic intuition that reason is an alien element in a fundamentally chaotic universe.[3] Its thematic corollary has been linked with the myth of creation from chaos as retold in Ovid's *Metamorphoses*. It can be safely assumed that the poet, thoroughly trained in the Latin classics, was familiar with Ovid's version of the legend, and possibly a Latin translation of Hesiod's account (Pratt 1983, 28). In Tyutchev's "night-chaos"[4] lyrics the chaos that gives birth to creation in the ancient legends becomes a source of poetic inspiration as the elemental natural force designated *stixija*, "the irrational side of man's existence, his subconscious and his passions . . . that part of the human psyche which has a voice . . . and speaks to us in dreams" (Pratt 1983, 29).

Some of Tyutchev's chaos poems dramatize a dynamic interchange between *stixija* in nature and the passive individual human soul, both alike in a state of *samozabven'je* engendered by sleep and dreams. A poem of the 1830s beginning with the words "How sweetly slumbers the dark-green garden" sketches a scene where "[a] curtain has been lowered over the world of day; movement has weakened, labor has fallen asleep," yet "[o]ver the sleeping city, as in the tops of the forest, a miraculous nightly hum has awakened." The invisible noise humming over the sleeping city in the slumbering garden is not simply impossible to explain, but even inaccessible to the waking consciousness: "Is it that a bodiless, audible but invisible world of mortal thoughts freed by sleep now hovers in the night chaos?" (Pratt 1983, 113). In "What are you howling about, night wind?" (1836), Schelling's *Abgrund* lurks in the "sleeping storms" hovering over a uni-

verse the poetic persona fears to arouse, terrified at "How avidly the
world of the night soul hearkens to its favorite tale!" (Pratt 1983, 115)

The slumber of nature draws the persona after it in a dream
vision evoked in a poem of 1828:

> As round this earthly globe the oceans pour,
> All earthly life is wrapped in dreams of wonder;
> Then night comes on and with its waves of thunder
> That ocean *[stixija]* beats upon its shore.

> For thus it speaks: it forces us, demanding. . .
> Now quivers by the pier our magic barque;
> The tide comes up and bears us from the landing
> And deep into the welt'ring dark.

> The vault of heaven with stellar glory rounded,
> Mysterious, peers downward from the height—
> As we sail on by blazing gulfs surrounded
> Across the wide abyss of night.[5]

There is a dual paradox in the relationship between "us," carried
along by the tide in the magic barque, and the mysterious nocturnal
forces carrying us into "welt'ring darkness," which has been linked
with sexual procreation as well as spiritual regeneration. The journey
takes place in a universe that exists independently of "our" consciousness of it, on the one hand. On the other hand, however, these external phenomena, emblematic of a nature totally independent of
humanity, evoke an internal experience: "The opening simile establishes the two aspects, with the ocean, in reality a force outside man,
equated with dreams, which Tjutcvev recognizes as products of the
inner workings of man's soul" (Pratt 1983, 31–35).

In sharp contrast to the other chaos poems, where "dreams . . .
simply exist as amorphous irrational phenomena of unknowable content" (Pratt 1983, 41), stands "A Dream at Sea" (1836), where the
persona makes a conscious use of his imagination totally uncharacteristic of the other chaos poems:

> Both the sea and the storm rocked our bark; I was sleepy and given
> over to every caprice of the waves. Two infinities were within me, and
> they played with me at will. Around me the cliffs resounded like cym-
> bals, the winds called out and the waves sang. I lay deafened by the
> chaos of sounds, but above the chaos of sounds skimmed my dream.
> Painfully vivid, magically mute, it wafted lightly over the thundering
> darkness. In the waves of a fever it unfolded its world—the earth shone
> green, the ether brightened—labyrinthine gardens, palaces, columns,

and myriads of silent crowds swarmed around. I came to know many supernatural characters, saw magical creatures, mysterious birds; I strode like God along the summits of creation, and under me glowed the motionless world. But through all the realms, like the wail of a magician, I heard the roar of the sea's abyss, and into the silent realm of visions and dreams burst the foam of the roaring waves. (Pratt 1983, 114)

These lines display several features that distinguish them from Tyutchev's other chaos lyrics: the persona is a specific "I" mentioned eleven times in the poem; the allusion to a fever suggests a prosaically physiological possible motivation for his visions; the dream is specific, and "represents the rational. Everything is clear and bright; things are identified and classified" (Pratt 1983, 41). The persona assumes lordship in a universe where he has formerly been nothing more than a passive, undifferentiated observer: he has "become Prometheus" (Gregg 1965, 98), "actually takes on the role of God within his dream" (Pratt 1983, 42). The poem apparently turns Tyutchev's oneiric metaphysics on its head: the persona "not only exhibits a total lack of *samozabven'je*, but he also tries to make nature into the dream of man, opposing the reality hinted at in the other chaos poems and finally articulated in one of Tjutcvev's last poems—that man exists only as a dream of nature" (Pratt 1983, 42). One exegesis explains the discrepancy between this and the rest of Tyutchev's chaos poems by relating the argument of "A Dream at Sea" to the notion of a chain of being that reaches from inert matter to the conscious soul in Schelling's *Naturphilosophie* (Ralph Matlaw, whose views are summarized in Gregg 1965, 96–97). Another sees the intuition of "two infinities" in the poem as a synthesis of Schelling and Pascal (Gregg 1965, 99). A third considers the dream as an instance of hubris punished by the intervention of the storm into the dream of the persona. The fourth reaches the conclusion that "the image of the poet as creator acts as a foil for the mystic personae who lurk behind the scenes in [*A Vision* and 'As round this earthly globe']."[6] In the hubris interpretation the persona ignores Schelling's statement, in *On Human Freedom*, that "[i]n man is the deepest abyss and the highest heaven, or two centers," and the concomitant association of "the deepest abyss with surrender to self-will, and the highest heaven with surrender to—and merging with—the universal will" (Pratt 1983, 44).

These brief remarks make it abundantly clear that dreams and dream visions in Tyutchev's poetry are freighted with heavy but generally nonspecific philosophical significance, which reflects the ambiance of German romanticism in which he moved during the twenty-two years (1822–44) he spent in the West pursuing a diplomatic career. With the arguable exception of "A Dream at Sea," the dominant, if not the exclusive, motif in the chaos poems is "the anti-rational aspect of *samozabven'je*, . . . often through dream or sleep imagery" (Pratt 1983, 72). In a specifically Russian cultural context, Alexander Sergeevich Pushkin (1799–1837), Russia's greatest poet, uses a prophetic dream as a medium for the anti-rational aspect of folk superstition in *Eugene Onegin* (1825–33, first complete edition 1833), the verse narrative that began the great tradition of the novel, which reached its full maturity in the 1860s.

The heroine of *Eugene Onegin* is Tatyana Larina, a young girl who lives in a world of patriarchal tradition on her estate in the country. Like Onegin, the progenitor of the superfluous men who populated virtually all the great Russian novels of the nineteenth century, "Tanya (profoundly Russian being, herself not knowing how or why)"[7] has a significance that extends beyond the specific work of literature in which she appears: she is the first truly national heroine in Russian literature, ancestress of many pure women in nineteenth-century fiction whose moral courage exposes the shallowness of the superfluous men they love. Socially she belongs to the lower ranks of the gentry, but she is typical of her station in being closer to the peasants on her estate than to the urbanized nobility represented by Onegin. Her artless country simplicity, which serves as a counterfoil for his jaded city sophistication, includes an unquestioning belief in all the superstitions she shares with the serf girls who are her closest companions:

> Tatyana shared with full conviction
> the simple faith of olden days
> in dreams and cards and their prediction
> and portents of the lunar phase.
> Omens dismayed her with their presage;
> each object held a secret message
> for her instruction, and her breast
> was by forebodings much oppressed. (117, V)

Tatyana's prophetic dream highlights the complexities of her personality, illustrating the inner consistency between what she is both before and after she falls in love with Onegin: pure, passionate, indifferent to the ways of the world, wise in the ways of the heart. The nightmare is motivated both by her essential nature and her immediate circumstances. The poet Lensky, her sister Olga's fiancé, introduces her to Onegin, a neighboring landowner who has left the worldly pleasures of St. Petersburg after inheriting his deceased uncle's estate. Susceptible both to the matchmaking instincts of the neighbors and the romantic notions of the contemporary novels that comprise much of her reading, Tatyana decides Onegin is the man fate has destined for her, though Pushkin implies her destiny was pre-determined: "she fell in love—the hour was fated . . . so fires of spring will bring to birth a seedling fallen in the earth" (68, VII).

Obedient to both the inner promptings of her heart and the conventions of sentimental fiction, Tatyana declares her love for One-gin in a letter, only to receive a gentle rejection accompanied by a con-descending lecture on the perils of yielding to youthful impetuosity. Crushed, she withdraws into herself, drawing some consolation from participation in the rituals of Russian country life. These include the tradition of telling fortunes during the period between Christmas and New Year's: "The Larins kept the old tradition: maid-servants from the whole estate would on those evenings guess the fate of the two girls. . . ." (116, IV).[8]

On the night before her name-day party, "Prepared for prophecy and fable, she did what nurse advised she do and in the bath-house had a table that night, in secret, set for two; then sudden fear attacked Tatyana . . ." (119, X), she goes to bed, and has a gruesome, obliquely prophetic nightmare. Walking across a snowy plain, she reaches a stream that stops her until an enormous bear reaches his paw out to help her across and then pursues her on the other side. When she falls, he lifts her in his arms and deposits her in the entrance hall of the dilapidated cottage belonging to his "cousin" (Russian *kum*, a word corresponding to "gossip" in medieval and Renaissance English litera-ture), where through a chink she sees the terrifying fauna of Russian popular demonology: "a group of monsters round a table" (122–23, XVI–XVII).[9]

Tatyana recognizes Onegin presiding over this company and cracks the door open. The draft extinguishes the candle, he walks to the door, opens it, and she is exposed to the company, who all claim her until he tells them in a "voice of thunder" (124, XX), "She's *mine!*" He has set her down on a bench and is laying his head on her shoul-der when Olga and Lensky suddenly appear. The enraged Onegin picks up a carving-knife, "—and in the tangle Lensky's thrown down. The murk is thick and growing thicker; then, heart-shaking, a scream rings out . . . the cabin's quaking . . . Tanya comes to in utter fright . . ." (125, XXI).

Next morning her sister Olga asks Tatyana what she dreamt about, expecting a predictable answer amenable to a conventional interpretation. Tatyana says nothing as she pores through her well-worn copy of Martin Zadeka's divination book, "But her trepidation Martin Zadeka fails to mend; the horrid nightmare must portend a hideous deal of tribulation" (126, XXIV).

Tatyana's dream does indeed prophesy events too complex for the straightforward exegesis of a popular guide to divination. At her name-day party she sees Onegin again for the first time since the painful meeting when he responded to her letter. He, annoyed at Lensky for persuading him to waste his time with a bunch of country bumpkins and infuriated at Tatyana's ill-concealed agitation, takes his revenge by flirting with Olga, who is to marry the poet in two weeks but responds with thoughtless coquetry to Onegin's attentions. Outraged, Lensky challenges his best friend to a duel in which the challenger loses his life. Onegin flees abroad, Olga soon finds another husband, and Tatyana remains alone on the family estate, faithful to the man she continues to love even after realizing his essential shallowness. After having rejected all local suitors, she is persuaded to go to Moscow in search of a husband. When Onegin returns after six years of wandering, she has married a general of his acquaintance and become a poised, gracious woman of the world. Now seized by the same passion she had confessed in her letter to him years before, Onegin pours out his passion in several unanswered notes to her, the first of them quoted verbatim. After months of languishing in the torments of unrequited love, he ignores her refusal to see him in private, goes to her house, and surprises her alone: "she holds a letter up, and leaning cheek upon hand she softly cries in a still stream that never dies" (214, XL). Their story reaches its ironic denouement when she confesses she still loves him but banishes him nonetheless, determined to honor her vow of fidelity to her husband.

The prophetic dream here uses the simple vocabulary of folk tradition to foreshadow the complex fate of an anti-Onegin, a girl who never loses her honesty and integrity even after moving to the city and attaining a high social position: in the final scene with him, "Who in the princess for that second would not have recognised again our hapless Tatyana? . . . The simple maiden, whose heart on dreams was wont to thrive, in her once more has come alive" (215, XL). The folkloric dream landscape, fraught with perils from the elements and wild beasts, represents Tatyana's fears of her feelings and her future, while her submissive surrender to forces beyond her control is rewarded by gentleness from both the bear and his human hypostasis as Onegin.

Tatyana is also a passive spectator at the violent denouement of her prophetic dream: Onegin seizes the carving knife "quick as quick," and Lensky is thrown down in a "tangle" (125, XXI) over which the girl has no control. She cannot alter fate, but in yielding to it she can save herself.

The particulars of Tatyana's nightmare hold keys to her character. The fears bared in her dream are those of the defenseless peasant heroine of Russian fairy tales protected in the daunting vicissitudes of her fate by magical powers: "Yet—fear itself she found presented a hidden beauty in the end: our disposition being invented by nature, contradiction's friend" (118, VII). Portents disclose the mysteries of fate, which hold the promise of good as well as evil: "Tatyana looks with pulses racing at sunken wax inside a bowl: beyond a doubt, its wondrous tracing foretells for her some wondrous role . . ." (882, VIII).

Tatyana runs through a landscape as "profoundly Russian" as her character. It is a bear, the Russian national animal, "hairy, tumbled, enormous" (120, XII), who helps her cross the stream on an unsteady wooden bridge, something she could never have done by herself and would never even have attempted had fear not spurred her on. On the other side "ahead of her a pinewood slumbers in the full beauty of its frown" (121, XIII). The bear pursues her not to harm her, but to carry her to a forest cottage like those where wise, virtuous maidens in Russian fairy tales overcome forces that seek to destroy them: "there's a small window shining in it, and from within come noise and cheer; the bear explains: 'my cousin's here—come in and warm yourself a minute!' " (122, XV).

Once she notices Onegin is "host" to the "group of monsters" in the room, "Tanya's no longer quite so frightened," but the man who made her endure a humiliating lecture about love in waking life once more exposes all the terrifying sexual vulnerabilities of an innocent but passionate adolescent girl. When she cracks the door to eavesdrop and the draft blows out the candles, the only light comes from Onegin, who rises "with eyes aflame" (123, XVIII). He opens the door, she tries to escape, but fails to overcome the immobility that frustrates attempts at flight in dreams, "and to the vision of those mortal monsters the maiden stood revealed" (124, XIX). They all "bellow out 'she's mine, she's mine,' " until Onegin claims her and she yields to him submissively as to his "cousin" the bear. When Olga and her fiancé enter in a "blaze of sudden brightness," Onegin, "eyes rolling, arms uplifted, furious, damns the intruders," and attacks Lensky, "while Tanya lies, and almost swoons, and almost dies" (124, XX). A

Freudian explanation of this denouement suggests Tatyana wished for the death of her sister and her sister's intended so as to have everything connected with Onegin all to herself. In a more straightforward folkloric interpretation, Onegin and mutual attraction between him and Tatyana belong in an uncanny realm of frightening darkness hostile to the brightness associated with Olga and Lensky. A third reading is implicit in Tatyana's parting words to Onegin, where she consciously accepts her responsibility along with his in their failure to attain a "bliss" that "was so near, so altogether attainable" (218, XVLII) when they first knew each other.

The imaginative trappings of Tatyana's prophetic dream refract the irrational chaos Tyutchev saw at the heart of life through the prism of the Russian folk imagination. In the fiction of Lev Nikolaevich Tolstoy (1828–1910) the prophetic dream, however irrational in its essential nature, generally serves a rational purpose, as an oblique illustration of the continuum between the individual psychic life and the universal laws of existence.

For Tolstoy's male characters in particular, bold, schematic visions in prophetic dreams provide intuitive solutions to metaphysical problems that baffle the rational mind in waking life. *War and Peace* (published serially from 1863–69, first published as a book in 1869) contains three striking scenes where such dreams come to prominent male characters after they relinquish conscious control over their thoughts. All three dream epiphanies have some connection with the Battle of Borodino, the single engagement that most fully symbolizes Russia's agony and triumph in the struggle with Napoleon's invading armies during the Great War of the Fatherland in 1812.

In the first of the *War and Peace* dream episodes Pierre Bezukhov, the fictional emanation of Tolstoy's visionary side, falls asleep in his carriage in the courtyard of an inn in Mozhaysk, after having spent time with brave Russian soldiers in the Borodino position where the French attack was most furious and Russian losses particularly great. The sound of artillery fire briefly wakens him, producing reactions first of fright and horror, then of peace, and finally of admiration for *them*, the humble foot soldiers at Borodino whose solidarity, courage, and faith have made a deep impression on him. His dream visions include flashbacks to the evening when he challenged his wife's lover to a duel during a dinner at the Moscow English Club, where he also sees an older man named Bazdeev, his sponsor during his brief involvement with Freemasonry: " 'Yes, that is he! It is my benefactor. But he died!' thought Pierre. 'Yes, he died and I did not know he was alive. How sorry I am that he died, and how glad I am that he is alive again.' "[10] Bazdeev serves as a bridge between the soldiers and his society friends "(in his dream the category to which these men belonged was as clearly defined in his mind as the category of those he termed *they*)" (p. 941). The dream is constructed on a counterpoint between the shouting of his worldly friends, the booming from the battlefield, and the words of Bazdeev, "talking of goodness and the possibility of being what *they* were" (p. 941).

They, however, pay no attention. Pierre gets up to address them, feels his legs cold and bare, wakens for a few moments to discover his cloak has slipped off him, then embarks on a new dream episode in the same vein as what he has just seen: "Afterwards when he recalled these thoughts Pierre was convinced that someone outside himself had spoken them, though the impressions of that day had evoked them. He had never, it seemed to him, been able to think and express his thoughts like that when awake" (p. 941). These thoughts find expression in a brief collection of aphorisms about freedom and necessity as well as the fear of death and victory over it, expressed with an eloquence uncharacteristic of Pierre in his waking state. Shortly the sound of a human voice ends his oneiric epiphany:

> "The hardest thing [Pierre went on thinking, or hearing in his dream] is to be able in your soul to unite the meaning of all. To unite all?" he asked himself. "No, not to unite. Thoughts cannot be united, but to *harness* all these thoughts together is what we need! Yes, one *must harness* them, *must harness* them!" he repeated to himself with inward rapture, feeling that these words and they alone expressed what he wanted to say, and solved the question that tormented him. (p. 941)

The word "harness" comes from his groom, waking him up so that he can harness the horses and they can drive away in Pierre's carriage. He resists the claims of the waking world unsuccessfully, but vigorously:

> "No, I don't want that, I don't want to see and understand that. I want to understand what was revealing itself to me in my dream. One second more and I should have understood it all! But what am I to do? Harness, but how can I harness everything?" and Pierre felt with horror that the meaning of all he had seen and thought in the dream had been destroyed. (p. 942)

Pierre has another prophetic dream in the village of Shamshevo. It immediately follows the death of Platon Karataev, the stoically philosophical Christian peasant who befriended Pierre in prison and was shot because he was too weak to walk with the prisoners of war the French were evacuating from Moscow. In this instance Tolstoy explicitly outlines the contours of the dream for his readers: "Again real events mingled with dreams and again someone, he or another, gave expression to his thoughts, and even the same thoughts that had been expressed in his dream at Mozhaysk" (p. 1181).

Once more the person elucidating Pierre's thoughts is a mature man of wise and benevolent disposition, like Bazdeev in the earlier dream, whose moral and intellectual authority Pierre has voluntarily accepted in his conscious life. These figures act as surrogates to his biological father, an almost total stranger whose one gift, wealth, has been a source of tribulation as well as privilege for Pierre. The father figure in this prophetic dream is "a long-forgotten, kindly old man who had given him geography lessons in Switzerland" (p. 1181). He uses a globe to symbolize the coinherence of every human life. The globe is "alive—a vibrating ball without fixed dimensions," completely covered by drops that change shape and size like raindrops on a windowpane. The teacher explains that God is in the center of the globe and the drops represent individual human destinies: " 'each drop tries to expand so as to reflect Him to the greatest extent. And it grows, merges, disappears from the surface, sinks to the depths, and again emerges. There now, Karataev has spread out and disappeared. Do you understand, my child?' said the teacher" (pp. 1181–82). In Shamshevo, as earlier in Mozhaysk, Pierre has no sooner registered the dream in his consciousness than an external stimulus rouses him from sleep: " 'Do you understand, damn you?' shouted a voice, and Pierre woke up" (p. 1182).

Here as elsewhere in his novels, Tolstoy's dramatic instinct dictates that a brief, striking dream vision be interrupted by external events and set aside until the dreamer has the leisure to contemplate its deeper significance. This technique enriches the narrative texture of a long fictional work by providing for changes of pace and mood. It also imparts human interest to a historical narrative by prompting fictional characters to ponder the meaning of mass social phenomena in the context of their individual destinies. The prophetic dream at Shamshevo absolves Pierre from any feelings of guilt for having refused to admit even to himself what happened at Karataev. In life Karataev expanded so as to reflect God to the greatest extent by living out his simple peasant faith with everyone who shared his captivity, thus bringing Pierre back from a state of spiritual prostration to a new, deeper appreciation of life's joys, sorrows, possibilities, and limitations. Reassured in his prophetic dream that physical annihilation means absorption into the divine center of eternity, Pierre is prepared to continue witnessing to the truth of Karataev's faith by embodying it in his own life.

Pierre's dreams are way stations on a long, torturous journey to wholeness during which his intuitive indecisiveness proves a hindrance as much as a help. But a prophetic dream also visits Prince Andrew Bolkonsky, the personification of Tolstoy's active, skeptical side, at the most decisive moment of his life. Prince Andrew's dream prepares him for his own death in a way that can be both compared and contrasted with the dream at Shamshevo that reconciles Pierre to death in general and Karataev's death in particular. With his fondness for paradox Tolstoy presents Prince Andrew's prophetic dream as "an awakening from life" (p. 1091). The dreams of both central male characters in *War and Peace* have certain structural features in common. Each features a dominant visual symbol and contains a crowd that engages in discourse sometimes trifling and sometimes weighty. This discourse provides a stimulus for the aphoristic formulation of the dreamer's thoughts and intuitions. The dominant image in Prince Andrew's dream is a double door, comparable to the globe in Pierre's Shamshevo vision. Prince Andrew also confronts an abstract *it*, comparable to the concrete but undifferentiated *they* of Pierre's Mozhaysk dream. With the same helpless terror Tatyana experienced in her prophetic dream, Prince Andrew tries and fails to keep *it* from coming through the door:

> *It* entered, and it was death, and Prince Andrew died.
>
> But at the instant he died, Prince Andrew remembered that he was asleep, and at the very instant he died, having made an effort, he awoke.
>
> "Yes, it was death! I died—and woke up. Yes, death is an awakening!" (p. 1090)

Here Tolstoy further extends the function of the prophetic dream as a medium of revelation. It not only consoles a credulously intuitive man like Pierre when he wonders about the deaths of others, it also prepares a stubborn doubter like Prince Andrew not simply to face, but even to welcome, his own death. It enables him to forgive those who caused him pain in life by shifting his focus to a dimension of experience beyond earthly existence.

It is a mark of Tolstoy's uninterrupted growth as a writer and thinker that the next time prophetic dreams play a significant role in one of his novels, they help characterize a woman of much greater psychological ambiguity than the men who find keys to the truth in the dream visions of *War and Peace*. The dreams of the key male characters in the historical novel clarify moral problems that resist rational, conscious solution. In *Anna Karenina* (1873–77), however, the title character's recurrent nightmare dramatizes her failure to come to grips with the vital issue of conjugal fidelity in her waking life. Tatyana's nocturnal vision holds the promise of beauty redeeming fear and courage overcoming pain; Pierre's and Prince Andrew's dreams reveal profound truths about community and immortality; but Anna's nightmare portends doom instead of providing reassurance, and obscures rather than clarifies the mysteries of her fate.

Anna's prophetic dream, based on an apparently trifling episode, functions as a foreshadowing device that provides an interesting contrast to Tatyana's nightmare. By her participation in her dream, Tatyana influences its outcome, whereas Anna's absence from her recurrent nightmare suggests that the moral law determines her fate despite her conscious abdication of responsibility for the consequences of her actions.[11] When Anna gets off the train at the railway station in Moscow, where she has come to intervene in a marital crisis involving her brother, a watchman, "either tipsy or too much muffled up because of the severe cold," is run over by a train, and handsome young Count Vronsky, who is meeting his mother at the station, gives the dead man's wife 200 roubles.[12] Her first meeting with Vronsky is portentous not only because of this incident, but also because she knows a great deal about Vronsky beforehand from his mother, who has made the journey from St. Petersburg with her. It is perhaps for this reason that Anna immediately pays exceptionally close attention to Vronsky. Tolstoy makes it clear that he senses her interest instantly and performs his act of conspicuous generosity at least in part to make a favorable impression on her. Less clear is the reason why she is so upset by the accident, telling her brother, "It is a bad omen" (p. 60).

In Moscow Anna reacts with almost unseemly pleasure to Vronsky's attentions when they meet again at a ball, a setting of sensual intoxication Tolstoy always represents as a threat to women's virtue. The ball scene has a double portent for them both again, dashing the hopes of her brother's sister Kitty for marriage to Vronsky and thereby bringing him closer to Anna in ways that both disquiet and enrapture her. She succeeds in repairing the breach between her brother and his wife, and boards the train for St. Petersburg convinced she will never see Vronsky again. Sitting in the carriage waiting for the train to start, she is in the state of physical relaxation and suspended psychological animation that typically serves as a transition to Tolstoy's dream scenes. Body and mind interact in a cause-and-effect relationship that makes the dreams in Tolstoy's fiction into projections of character as much as revelations from external sources.[13]

She is still turning impressions of the ball over in her mind as she alternately reads a novel, becomes distracted by identifying herself with characters in it, brushes off qualms of conscience, then loses a clear awareness of where she is and lazily subsides into a state somewhere between waking and dreaming: "she was afraid of giving way to these delirious thoughts. Something seemed to draw her to them, but she had the power to give way to them or to resist" (pp. 92–93). She absentmindedly notices several figures muffled up to avoid the severe cold, like the watchman killed by the train on her arrival in Moscow: a guard passing through the carriage "closely wrapped up and covered with snow on one side" (p. 91) and a "lean peasant in [a] long nankin coat with a button missing" (p. 93) who comes into the compartment to stoke the fire. As she oscillates between sleeping and waking, her vision and her interpretation of it both become distorted:

> The peasant in the long coat started gnawing at something on the wall; the old woman began stretching her legs the whole length of the carriage, which she filled with a black cloud; then something squeaked and clattered in a dreadful manner, as if some one was being torn to pieces; then a blinding red light appeared, and at last everything was hidden by a wall. Anna felt as if she had fallen through the floor. But all this did not seem dreadful, but amusing. (p. 93)

When the train stops at a station, she shakes off her drowsiness and gets out, briefly noticing a railway worker who stoops on the platform and strikes the carriage wheels with a hammer. Then she sees another man walking toward her. It is Vronsky, and he makes an oblique avowal of love, while "the wind, as if it had mastered all obstacles, scattered the snow from the carriage roofs, and set a loose sheet of iron clattering; and in front the deep whistle of the engine howled mournfully and dismally" (p. 94). Anna irresolutely rebuffs Vronsky and returns to her carriage, "going over in her imagination what had just taken place. Though she could remember neither his or her own words, she instinctively felt that that momentary conversation had drawn them terribly near to one another . . ." (p. 95).

Pushkin makes a clear distinction between Tatyana asleep and awake, but Anna draws closer to Vronsky in a sort of waking spiritual and perceptual dream although, or perhaps because, she assures herself she is in control of her feelings. The drowsily distorted visions in the carriage should have been dissipated by breathing frosty winter air, but instead she meets the raging snowstorm, a standard Russian metaphor for elemental forces of fate or passion beyond human control. The contrast between the symbolic function of winter images in Pushkin and Tolstoy is striking. The snow that frightens Tatyana in her dream intoxicates Anna in a fully conscious state. Tatyana is timid but fundamentally strong; Anna is bold but basically weak.

Nearly a year later, when Anna has consummated her adulterous relationship with Vronsky, she suppresses her anxieties when awake, but her conscience punishes her in dreams ordinarily associated with wish-fulfillment, where she does not have to abandon her cherished son in order to join her lover:[14]

> But in her dreams when she had no control over her thoughts, her position appeared to her in all its shocking nakedness. One dream she had almost every night. She dreamt that both at once were her husbands, and lavished their caresses on her. Alexey Alexandrovich wept, kissing her hands, saying: 'How beautiful it is now!' and Alexey Vronsky was there too, and he also was her husband. And she was surprised that formerly this had seemed impossible to her, and laughingly explained to them how much simpler it really was, and that they were both now contented and happy. But this dream weighed on her like a nightmare, and she woke from it filled with horror. (p. 136)

A few months later, when everyone expects her to die of puerperal fever during her confinement with the daughter she bears Vronsky, Anna makes the two Alexeys in her life act out her dream as she persuades each take the other's hand (p. 376). As a result of this coerced reconciliation Karenin ceases condemning Anna and tries to make the baby part of the family, but Anna refuses to renounce her dream of adulterous love and soon goes abroad with Vronsky and their child.

Just before a tryst during the period after Anna has conceived but before she has left her husband, Vronsky dozes off into a dream that jumbles images of Anna and a peasant who has played an important part as a beater in a recent bear hunt. He wakens in a state of agitation:

> "What has happened? What horrors I dreamt! Yes, yes, the peasant, the beater—I think he was small and dirty with a tangled beard—was stooping down and doing something or other, and suddenly began to say strange words in French. That is all there was in that dream," he thought. "But why did it seem so terrible?" He vividly recalled the peasant and the incomprehensible words that the man had uttered, and a shudder of terror ran down his back. (p. 324)

During his rendezvous with Anna, she tells him she will die because she has had a dream, and "Vronsky immediately remembered the peasant of his dream" (p. 329). A long time before she had dreamed of running into the bedroom to fetch or locate something—"you know how it happens in dreams"—and finding something standing in the corner: "And that something turned round, and I saw it was a peasant with a rough beard, small and dreadful. I wanted to run away, but he stooped over a sack and was fumbling about in it . . ." (p. 329).

The same sort of peasant speaks French in the nightmares of both Vronsky and Anna. For different reasons, however, they both fail to find any connection between the peasant's words and the fatal accident they witnessed at their first meeting. Whether Vronsky finds the words literally incomprehensible or understands them well enough to realize they are "strange," he does not repeat them, unable or unwilling to attach any specific significance to them. As Anna describes her nightmare she quotes the peasant's words, but does not even try to make sense of them. Obsessed with the fear of death in childbirth, she focuses instead on what is said by Korney, her husband's manservant:

> "He [the peasant] fumbles about and mumbles French words, so quickly, so quickly, and with a burr, you know: *'Il faut le battre, le fer, le broyer, le pétrir. . . .'* And in my horror I tried to wake, but I woke still in a dream and began asking myself what it could mean and Korney says to me: 'You will die in childbed, in childbed, ma'am. . . .' Then I woke." (p. 329)

The sense of doom in the bond of passion between the lovers is further reinforced by their participation in the same nightmare. "Her face was full of horror. And Vronsky, remembering his dream, felt the same horror filling his soul" (p. 329). He tells her that her premonition of death is nonsense, "but he felt that there was no conviction in his voice" (p. 329). Part of what makes their shared fate so burdensome is that it is private, unmitigated by the consolations of the folk traditions that take some of the terror from Tatyana's prophetic nightmare.

For both lovers the moral, social, psychological, and emotional strains of their liaison deprive them of sleep. Less high strung than Anna, Vronsky normally has no trouble sleeping, but when she nearly dies in childbirth, lack of sleep deprives him of his usual *sang froid*. After three sleepless nights at her bedside and the humiliation of the reconciliation she has forced him to make with Karenin, he attempts suicide because his turbulent emotions keep him awake (pp. 378–80).

Insomnia becomes a chronic affliction for Anna, even as she rhapsodizes to her brother's wife about the joys of life on Vronsky's country estate, in an ironic variation on the metaphor in Prince Andrew's dream from *War and Peace:* "Something magical has happened to me: like a dream where one feels frightened and creepy, and suddenly wakes up with the knowledge that no such terrors exist. I have wakened up!" (p. 556). In actual fact, despite the idyllic circumstances, Anna's mental torments make it impossible for her to sleep without opium or morphia and a candle beside her bed. On the morning of her suicide Anna has her prophetic dream for the last time. The peasant's words in this version are now downright "senseless," as incomprehensible to her in her utter desolation as everything else in her life:

> a terrible nightmare, which had come to her several times even before her union with Vronsky, repeated itself and woke her. An old man with a tangled beard was leaning over some iron and doing something, while muttering senseless words in French; and as always in that nightmare (this was what made it terrible) she felt this peasant was paying no attention to her but was doing something dreadful to her with the iron. And she awoke in a cold perspiration. (p. 680)

As she boards the train that is to take her to Vronsky she glances out the window, where "A grimy, misshapen peasant in a cap from under which his touzled hair stuck out, passed that window, stooping over the carriage wheels. 'There is something familiar about that misshapen peasant,' she thought. And remembering her dream she went to the opposite door, trembling with fright" (p. 692). She finally fulfills the prophecy of her recurrent nightmare when she finds Vronsky is not at the station to meet her: "Suddenly remembering the man who had been run over the day she first met Vronsky, she realized what she had to do" (p. 694). In the last seconds of her life, narrated by the omniscient author, the horror aroused by the peasant in the recurring nightmare alternates with the flickering light of the candle that gutters more fitfully as the shadows in her life grow more impenetrable:

> A little peasant muttering something was working at the rails. The candle, by the light of which she had been reading that book filled with anxieties, deceptions, grief, and evil, flared up with a brighter light than before, lit up for her all that had before been dark, flickered, began to grow dim, and went out for ever. (p. 695)

The recurrent nightmare serves not only as a foreshadowing of the doom that awaits those who flout the moral law, but also as a *leitmotif* that exposes a passivity in Anna's nature diametrically opposed to Tatyana's firmness. Although the helpless adolescent yields to forces beyond her control, she has the strength of character to refuse a liaison with the man she loves even though, or more accurately because, she is married to a man whom she does not love but to whom she has vowed fidelity. In the same predicament, where Tatyana stays firm, Anna yields.

Because Anna either cannot or will not discern its relevance in her own life, the nightmare that starts out as a warning gradually becomes a companion and finally the tempter that leads her to her death. In each of its occurrences it acquires more associations and more complex aesthetic shadings. With the one exception of the dream involving both Alexeys, the agency of fate is always a peasant, and always grotesque in some way or other: muffled, covered with snow, lean, with hair tangled or tousled, speaking either quite unintelligibly, or absurdly and inappropriately, mumbling French phrases both nonsensical and menacing in their reference to beating, pounding, and kneading the iron that produces the rails for the trains that create and destroy the happiness of the adulterous lovers.

The prophetic nightmare visits both Anna and Vronsky, and at the end Tolstoy even makes it retroactive, to the time before her sexual relationship with Vronsky, although the beginning chapters of the novel itself allude only to presentiments rather than dreams. The early images of snow and storm, with the concomitant excitement of braving natural forces with destructive potentials, disappear once the moral law has been transgressed, to be displaced by the prophetic dream, accompanied by lengthening shadows each time it is retold, replaced by dim chiaroscuro only in the last moments of Anna's life.

The importance of prophetic dreams in some of the greatest works of Russian literature reflects constants deeply imbedded in the national culture. The sense of impenetrability between the worlds of spirit and matter is the distinctive contribution to world literature made by the nineteenth-century Russian realism that Solzhenitsyn has consciously revived in the twentieth century. The masterpieces of Russian realism overcome the dichotomy established in nineteenth-century cultural history between the holy Russia defended by the Slavophiles and the brave new rational world of tangible achievement preached by their opponents in the Westernizing camp. In evoking the sense of harmonious coexistence between soul and body so strong in Russian temperament, the literary device of the prophetic dream has particular potency and resonance.

The intuition that the spirit-matter continuum is active in everyone not only makes Russian literature both exotic and accessible to Western readers, but also gives it a characteristically Russian dimension of collective egalitarianism. The passion for idealistic German metaphysics expressed in Tyutchev's chaos poems was shared by everyone in the Russian intelligentsia in the early decades of the nine-

teenth century. The ambiguities of their own inner life absorb Tolstoy's intellectuals as much as the complexities of other people's ideas
do. The seed of the great lady lies dormant in the soul of Tatyana
while she is still a country girl, and the presentiments adolescent
Tatyana finds in dreams preoccupy Anna in the world of high society.
Gazing into the night sky, Tyutchev, Tatyana, Pierre, Prince Andrew,
and Anna all see the same signs and simply call them by different
names. All of them, unsophisticated girls, worldly men, poets and
prosaists, authors and the characters they create, share a conviction
that the key to the riddles of life and death, for individuals and
nations, lies in realms inaccessible to reason, and that dreams provide
entry into those realms.

Notes

1. Trans. Irina Zheleznova, *Russian Nineteenth-Century Verse*, ed. Irina
Zheleznova (Moscow: Raduga, 1983), p. 180.

2. Sarah Pratt, *The Semantics of Chaos*, Slavistische Beiträge (München:
Otto Sagner Verlag, 1983), p. 30.

3. Pratt notes that "one finds that the same basic notion of creativity
acts as the foundation for both poems [*A Vision* and 'As round this earthly
globe,' to be discussed below—CNL]. This is a notion that combines a
romantic insistence on the irrational origins of the creative process and a
nearly classical portrayal of the creative forces of nature as objective phenomena totally independent of the subjective view of the poet" (Pratt 1983, 35).

4. Richard Gregg, *Fyodor Tiutchev: The Evolution of a Poet* (New York:
Columbia University Press, 1965), p. 102. Pratt refers to them simply as
"chaos poems," and so shall I in further discussion.

5. Trans. Alan Myers, *An Age Ago: A Selection of Nineteenth-Century
Russian Poetry* (New York: Farrar-Straus-Giroux, 1988), p. 105.

6. The last two readings are both Pratt's. The former is expressed in
Semantics declaring that the poem "acts as a foil for the poems discussed
above because it seems to portray chaos as the destroyer of inspiration rather
than as the source of creativity" (Pratt 1983, 39). The latter appears in *Russian Metaphysical Romanticism* (Stanford: Stanford University Press 1984, p.
115). The Tyutchev material in the earlier publication reappears almost, but
not quite, verbatim in the later, longer publication, which discusses other
Romantic poets as well. Since so little time separates the treatment of the
same materials in monographs published in the United States and Germany,
I cannot say which reflects the author's final conclusion. The latter interpretation is less "Procrustean" (Gregg 1965, 97) than the former, admitting the
possibility that the dream can have something more than the undifferentiat-

ed symbolic significance to which it would be restricted if these poems were purely Schellingian and not "uniquely Tjutčevian."

7. *Eugene Onegin*, trans. Charles Johnson (New York: Viking, 1978), p. 116, ch. 5, st. IV. When not otherwise noted, all quotations are from this chapter. For each citation stanza numbers will be added after page numbers for the benefit of readers using other translations.

8. Suzanne Massie, in *Land of the Firebird: The Beauty of Old Russia* (New York: Simon & Schuster, 1980), pp. 361–62, recounts some of these rituals, as recorded in the Russian Folk Encyclopedia of 1845: ". . . it was the tradition to tell fortunes every day in a whole variety of ways. Several mirrors were placed to reflect one into another, and a candle was placed before them: one's fate might appear in the mirror. A shadow of a burning paper would be thrown on the wall or a large candle melted into a bowl of water, and the figure made gave a clue as to who would be the future beloved. In the villages, maidens and boys would make a circle, and in front of each maiden a little pile of grain was placed. A hungry rooster would be brought in and the one whose grain was pecked first would be married within the year. Girls [including Tatyana—CNL] went out into the courtyard or street and asked the first passerby his name; that was a clue to the name of the beloved."

9. Pushkin names nearly a dozen, including a skeleton, a dwarf, and various unnatural combinations of incompatible animals, insects, and birds in a single body. None of them has any independent existence in Russian folklore. Vladimir Nabokov even notes, "To judge by the corrections in the drafts . . . and fair copy . . . Pushkin had considerable trouble in choosing his animals" (Nabokov 1975).

10. *War and Peace*, trans. Louise and Aylmer Maude (New York: Simon & Schuster, 1942), p. 940. Subsequent references will only include page number.

11. *Anna Karenina* reflects Tolstoy's transition from the glorification of the irrational in *War and Peace* to the rigorous rational morality he preached from the time of his spiritual crisis in 1880 to his death thirty years later. In the words of D. S. Mirsky, "In Tolstoy's final conception the moral law, which acts through the medium of conscience, is a law in the strict scientific sense, in the same sense as gravitation or any other law." *A History of Russian Literature from Its Beginnings to 1900*, ed. Francis J. Whitfield (New York: Vintage Russian Library, 1958), p. 308.

12. *Anna Karenina*, trans. Louise and Aylmer Maude (New York: Norton, 1968), p. 59. Subsequent references will only include page number.

13. See my "Dreams and Daydreams in the Early Fiction of L. N. Tolstoj," *American Contributions to the Seventh International Congress of Slavists, Warsaw, August 21–27, 1973, Volume II: Literature and Folklore*, ed. Victor Terras, pp. 373–92.

14. The component of traditional family morality in *Anna Karenina* is obviously stronger than in contemporary novels that extol free love, such as Nikolai Gavrilovich Chernyshevsky's immensely popular *What is to be Done?* (1863). Nonetheless, despite the fact that *Anna Karenina* has the Biblical

epigraph "Vengeance is mine, I will repay," R. F. Christian astutely observes that Tolstoy is interested not in "absolute categories of justice (the same punishment for the same offense), but individual people and their own sense of what is right and wrong. Anna has a conscience and suffers for it. [Her adulterous society friend] Betsy has no conscience, and she neither feels that adultery is wrong nor experiences unhappiness because of it. It is not for men to judge between them, for men did not implant that conscience. God has the right, so the epigraph may be taken to imply."

References

Gregg, Richard. *Fyodor Tiutchev: The Evolution of a Poet.* New York: Columbia University Press, 1965.

Lee, C. Nicholas. "Dreams and Daydreams in the Early Fiction of L. N. Tolstoj." *American Contributions to the Seventh International Congress of Slavists, Warsaw, August 21–27, 1973,* Vol. II: Literature and Folklore, edited by Victor Terras. 373–92.

Massie, Suzanne. *Land of the Firebird: The Beauty of Old Russia.* New York: Simon & Schuster, 1980.

Mirsky, D. S. *A History of Russian Literature from Its Beginnings to 1900.* Edited by Francis J. Whitfield. New York: Vintage Russian Library, 1958.

Pratt, Sarah. *Russian Metaphysical Romanticism.* Stanford: Stanford University Press, 1984.

———. *The Semantics of Chaos.* Slavistisch Beiträge. München: Otto Sagner Verlag, 1983.

Pushkin, Alexander Seergeevich. *Eugene Onegin.* Translated by Charles Johnston. New York: Viking, 1978.

———. *Eugene Onegin: A Novel in Verse,* translated from the Russian with a Commentary by Vladimir Nabokov. Princeton: Princeton University Press, 1975. Rev. ed., Vol. II.

R. F. Christian. *Tolstoy: A Critical Introduction* (Cambridge University Press, 1969), p. 174.

Tolstoy, L. N. *Anna Karenina*. Translated by Louise and Aylmer Maude. New York: Simon & Schuster, 1942.

Tyutchev, Fyodor. "A Dream at Sea." In Pratt 1983.

————. "As round this earthly globe." In *An Age Ago: A Selection of Nineteenth-Century Russian Poetry*, translated and edited by Alan Myers. New York: Farrar-Straus-Giroux, 1988.

————. "The Vision." In *Russian Nineteenth-Century Verse*. Translated and edited by Irina Zheleznova. Moscow: Raduga, 1983.

CONTRIBUTORS

John Brennan, since 1985 a Foreign Service officer with the U.S. Department of State, has served as Consul in Osaka and Kobe, Japan, as well as in Beijing, and has now taken up a two-year post in Chengdu, western China. He is a graduate of Columbia and a doctoral candidate in Comparative Literature at Washington University, St. Louis. His article on dreams, divination, and statecraft in ancient Chinese poetry and prose commentary is drawn in part from his dissertation in progress.

Kelly Bulkley is a lecturer in the social sciences division of the University of Chicago with the Ph.D. in Religion, Ethics, and Human Sciences at the Divinity School of the university, who also holds degrees from Stanford (B.A.) and Harvard (M.T.S.). An officer on the Board of Directors of the Association for the Study of Dreams, he was host of the 1990 A.S.D. Conference in Chicago, Ill. His research focuses on dreams, religious meaning, interpretation, and modern culture. He has published numerous articles and book reviews for periodicals of dream-focused associations.

Frederick A. de Armas is Distinguished Professor of Spanish and Comparative Literature and Fellow of the Institute for the Arts and Humanistic Studies at Pennsylvania State University. He received his Ph.D. in Comparative Literature from the University of North Carolina and has taught at Louisiana State University and the University of Missouri. He has published extensively in the field of Golden Age Spanish literature, having written seven books and over sixty articles, including many on dreams. His latest book, *The Return of Astraea: An Astral-Imperial Myth in Calderón* (University Press of Kentucky, 1986) deals with mythical, occult, and oneiric aspects of Calderón's theater.

Ken Frieden holds the Ph.D. in Comparative Literature from Yale University. He is currently Assistant Professor in the Department of Near Eastern and Judaic Languages and Literatures and in the Comparative Literature Program at Emory University. His most recent book is *Freud's Dream of Interpretation* (State University Press of New York, 1990). He also authored *Genius and Monologue* (Cornell, 1985).

Harriet Goldberg, Professor of Spanish at Villanova University, is an his-pano-medievalist whose publications range widely. She has written on dreams, literary portraiture, chromatic theory in literature, antifeminism, antisemitism, and folkloric topics such as fables, sermonic exempla, riddles, and proverbs. Her work has appeared in journals such as *Hispania* and *Romance Quarterly*; her critical edition and study of Fray Martin de Cordo-ba's *Jardin de nobles donzellas* was published in 1974 by the University of North Carolina Press.

Norman N. Holland is Marston-Milbauer Professor of English at the Uni-versity of Florida and founder of the Institute for Psychological Study of the Arts there. A graduate of the Boston Psychoanalytic Institute, he is perhaps best known from his (recently reissued) classic using psychoanalytic theory to read literary texts, *The Dynamics of Literary Response*. This was followed by publication of several more books including *Poems in Persons* (1973), *The Brain of Robert Frost* (1988), and the new comprehensive reference book for the field, *Holland's Guide to Psychoanalytic Psychology and Literature-and-Psy-chology* (Oxford University Press, 1990).

C. Nicholas Lee, Professor of Russian for twenty-five years at the University of Colorado, holds the Ph.D. from Harvard University and has had scholar-ships and fellowships at Georgetown University, Ludwig-Maximilians Uni-versität, Munich, The University of Paris, and Moscow State University. He has authored one book and many articles on topics primarily concerned with Russian prose of the nineteenth and twentieth centuries, specifically Mark Aldanov, Leo Tolstoy, and Alexander Solzhenitsyn. He has also taught at Bucknell.

Suzi Naiburg holds the Ph.D. from the University of Chicago and is cur-rently completing a book-length study entitled *The Appalling Other in Henry James*. She is a research associate in the Women's Studies Program at Har-vard University and a candidate in the Massachusetts Institute for Psycho-analysis. Formerly the Executive Director of the C.G. Jung Society of New Mexico, she has presented papers or led seminars for the Modern Language Association, the International Conference on Literature and Psychoanalysis, the C.G. Jung Institute of San Francisco, the C.G. Jung Foundation of New York, and the Association for the Study of Dreams.

Laurence M. Porter is Professor of French and Comparative Literature at Michigan State University; he studied at Harvard and at the Sorbonne. He is the author of *The Literary Dream in French Romanticism; The Renaissance of the Lyric in French Romanticism; The Crisis of French Symbolism*; and *"The Interpretation of Dreams": Freud's Theories Revisited*. He serves on the editorial boards of *Comparative Forum, Degre Second, Nineteenth-Century French Stud-ies*, and *Studies in Twentieth-Century Literature*. He also served as Andrew W. Mellon Distinguished Visiting Professor of Comparative Literature at the University of Pittsburgh.

Carol Schreier Rupprecht, editor, is Professor of Comparative Literature at Hamilton College in Clinton, N.Y., and former President of the internation-al Association for the Study of Dreams. She holds the Ph.D. in Comparative

Literature from Yale. She has written and lectured widely on dreams including presentations in Ireland, Israel, Japan, The Netherlands, and The People's Republic of China. Co-editor with Estella Lauter of *Feminist Archetypal Theory: Interdisciplinary Re-visions of Jungian Thought* (University of Tennessee Press, 1985), she is completing a book, *Oneiros in the Renaissance: Dream Theory and Dream Poetry in Sixteenth-Century Italy and England.*

Bert O. States, Professor of Dramatic Art at the University of California, Santa Barbara, has written on drama, literature, and dreams for over twenty-five years. Several essays on the dream have appeared in *Dreamworks* and *Hudson Review.* His most recent book is *The Rhetoric of Dreams* (Cornell, 1988) and he has just completed a book-length manuscript, *Dreaming and Storytelling.* He is also the author of *Irony and Drama: A Poetics* (Cornell, 1971), *The Shape of Paradox: An Essay on "Waiting for Godot"* (California, 1977), and *Great Reckonings in Little Rooms: On the Phenomenology of Theater* (California, 1985). His critical approach is chiefly structuralist and/or phenomenological.

Kay Stockholder, Professor of English at the University of British Columbia, Vancouver, since 1962, is the author of *Dream Works: Lovers and Families in Shakespeare's Plays* (Toronto, 1987). Educated at Hunter College and Columbia with the Ph.D. from the University of Washington in Seattle, she is a specialist in Shakespeare and in Elizabethan and Jacobean drama, with many journal publications bringing together historical and psychological approaches. Recent activities include presentations at the first Institute for Psychological Study of the Arts Conference, the Shakespeare Association of America, the Association for the Study of Dreams, and the European/American Conference on Literature and Psychology.

Joseph Westlund, Professor of English at Northeastern University, Boston, Mass., is the author of *Shakespeare's Reparative Comedies: A Psychoanalytic View of the Middle Plays* (Chicago, 1984) as well as many articles on literature and psychology. He has presented frequently at the Center for the Psychoanalytic Study of the Arts in Buffalo, N.Y., and was a participant in the first conference of the Institute for Psychological Study of the Arts in Gainesville, Fla.

Jane White-Lewis, M.A., holds a diploma from the Jung Institute of New York with a thesis on nightmares. She is a Jungian analyst in private practice in Guilford, Conn. and New York City. A member of the Board of Directors and Vice President of the Association for the Study of Dreams, she served as Program Chair for the sixth annual A.S.D. Conference in Chicago. She has also contributed articles and book reviews to the association's *Newsletter* and to the Jungian journal *Quadrant*, made conference presentations in London and in several states, and lectured for the Connecticut Association for Jungian Psychology.

INDEX

311